PHOTOSHOP CS3

for Windows and Macintosh
Visual QuickStart Guide

Elaine Weinmann
Peter Lourekas

Peachpit Press

Visual QuickStart Guide

Photoshop CS3 for Windows and Macintosh

Elaine Weinmann and Peter Lourekas

Peachpit Press

1249 Eighth Street
Berkeley, CA 94710

510/524-2178
510/524-2221 (fax)

Find us on the Web at www.peachpit.com

Visual QuickStart Guide is a trademark of Peachpit Press, a division of Pearson Education

Cover design: Peachpit Press
Interior design: Elaine Weinmann
Production: Elaine Weinmann and Peter Lourekas
Illustrations: Elaine Weinmann and Peter Lourekas, except as noted

Colophon

This book was created with Adobe InDesign CS2 on two Power Macintosh G5s. The primary fonts used were ITC Stone Serif, ITC Officina Sans, Myriad, and ITC New Baskerville from Adobe Systems Inc.

Notice of Rights

Notice of Liability

ISBN-13: 978-0-321-47379-0

ISBN-10: 0-321-47379-5

9 8 7 6 5 4 3

Printed and bound in the United States of America

How this book came about

Sometime in the mid-'80s, a smart guy in Berkeley, California, by the name of Ted Nace got a brainstorm. He decided to start up a computer book publishing company, which he called Peachpit Press (how he came up with the name is another story). The books he published were innovative and user-friendly and offered a fresh approach to learning computer graphics.

I (Elaine) found myself teaching a course in QuarkXPress not long thereafter, and I yearned for a book that would offer steps, like a recipe book, for learning various techniques. If nothing else, I thought, it would make my job easier. Then I got a brainstorm of my own. "What the heck, I have nothing to lose," I said to Peter, and made a cold call to Ted. I hadn't written anything longer than a shopping list before, but I had an art background, teaching, and practical experience under my belt, and Ted, bless him, let me take the plunge.

Ted supported innovation, not just in the content of the books that he published, but also in their production. He figured since many of his authors were experienced desktop publishers, why not let them typeset and illustrate their own books? Although the rabbit logo was already on the cover of Peachpit's Visual QuickStart Guide series, the tips, numbered steps, and many other design features that you see in our books were my innovations, fine-tuned with Ted's feedback. The first book I wrote and book packaged was *QuarkXPress 3.1: Visual QuickStart Guide*. I invited my husband, Peter, to come on board for the second book, *Photoshop 2.5: Visual QuickStart Guide,* and our 24/7 partnership continues today.

What started as a serendipitous idea turned into a career. We write, rewrite, design, typeset, illustrate, and test all of our books, and when we're done sweating over all the nitpicky details and are ready to up the prescription on our reading glasses, we hand the electronic files off to the production folks at Peachpit Press for a final "preflight" check.

In 1996, Ted Nace handed the baton to his hand-picked successor, Nancy Aldrich-Ruenzel, who took the baton and ran with it...

Acknowledgments

Under Nancy Aldrich-Ruenzel's energetic leadership, Peachpit Press continues to be a thriving and dynamic publishing house. We're grateful to her for encouraging us to redo this book in full color, and for her unwavering confidence in us.

Victor Gavenda, our technical editor at Peachpit, carefully tests the book in Windows and, as of this edition, wears a second hat as our editor-editor (are we lucky, or what?).

Production Editor Lisa Brazieal does an expert job of spearheading the prepress production and sends the files off to Courier Printing.

Peachpit Press is also blessed to have Nancy Davis, editor-in-chief; Gary-Paul Prince, PTG tradeshow and conventions manager; and Keasley Jones, business manager, on staff; and a host of other terrific folks.

Melinda Patelli, director, Image Resource Center, and Elaine Soares, photo researcher at Pearson Education, the parent company of Peachpit Press, procured the stock images used throughout the book and responded quickly to all our requests.

In our "virtual" book packaging department, Rebecca Pepper did a thorough and thoughtful job of copy editing, Steve Rath generated a superb index, and Leona Benten did the under-the-wire proofreading.

For creating a great product that's a pleasure to use and write about, and for helping beta testers like ourselves untangle the mysteries of Photoshop by way of the online forum, hats off to John Nack, Photoshop product manager; Vishal Khandpur, Adobe Photoshop prerelease program associate; and other members of the Photoshop CS3 beta team.

Most important, our heartfelt thanks to Alicia and Simona for putting up with preoccupied parents and having to beg for computer time.

Elaine Weinmann and Peter Lourekas

Introduction

We're in full color!

After years of readers clamoring for color pictures, our publisher decided to take the plunge into full color with this edition. Full color not only made it possible to show off Photoshop in all its glory, it also enabled us to illustrate the instructional steps and concepts more precisely. With all new pictures, fully updated text, and a brand new layout, this book is a complete remodel!

You can download the images!

Another thing we've heard numerous requests for is photo files. With the images that we've made available for you to download (see the directory on the following page), you can follow along with our text even more closely.

You do it your way

You're not restricted to using the downloadable photos that accompany the text. For any given set of instructions, you can substitute a photo of your own or choose a different photo from the assortment we offer. If you're a beginning Photoshop user, you can start by reading and following our instructions from A to Z (or let your instructor guide you through the text), then repeat any of the tasks using different photos or variables (dialog box, palette settings, presets, etc.) until they become second nature. Experienced users looking to upgrade their skill set may prefer to just spot-read the chapters of interest.

We do it our way

To reflect the innovations in Photoshop and in the rapidly changing field of digital photography, we tossed out instructions for defunct or out-moded techniques to make room for new ones. We speak our minds if we think a tool isn't useful or a feature just plain doesn't work well—and if we think a new or improved feature warrants applause, you'll hear that, too.

Take the easy road

With each upgrade, Photoshop becomes more feature-laden. There are multiple ways to accomplish a given task or edit, which can be confusing—especially for first-time users. To make your life easier, we direct you to the most efficient route (or two) so you can accomplish your goal with as little time and effort as possible. Case in point: If you can get to a command via a context menu, palette menu, or the menu bar, we encourage you to use the context menu because it's the most convenient method—and maybe list the palette menu as an alternate choice for a rainy day—but skip the trek to the menu bar.

Make your edits temporary

Whether you're a newcomer to Photoshop or a longtime user, you'll enjoy its ever-increasing flexibility. You can edit (and delete) such image elements as layers, type, masks, layer comps, brush presets, and color swatches. You can reverse one or a series of editing steps via the History palette. And you can apply such editable and removable features as layer effects, Smart Filters, type warp, fill layers, and adjustment layers. Because Photoshop gives you so many ways to edit a document without making permanent changes, you can relax and enjoy the process.

Why we wrote (and keep rewriting!) this book

Our objective is to write instructions that are succinct, easy to follow, amply illustrated, and methodically tested—like a good cookbook. We want you to learn the essentials in Photoshop without having to wade through gobbledygook. Equally important, we like to explain not just how features work, but also why and in what context they're most useful, and—here's the fun part—to show you how to use Photoshop as a creative tool. Whether your goal is to create beautiful, compelling, imaginative, or simply the most professional-looking images possible, we hope the skills you learn in this book will be of service. We hope you enjoy using this book as much as we enjoyed creating it.

Elaine Weinmann and Peter Lourekas

Downloadable images*

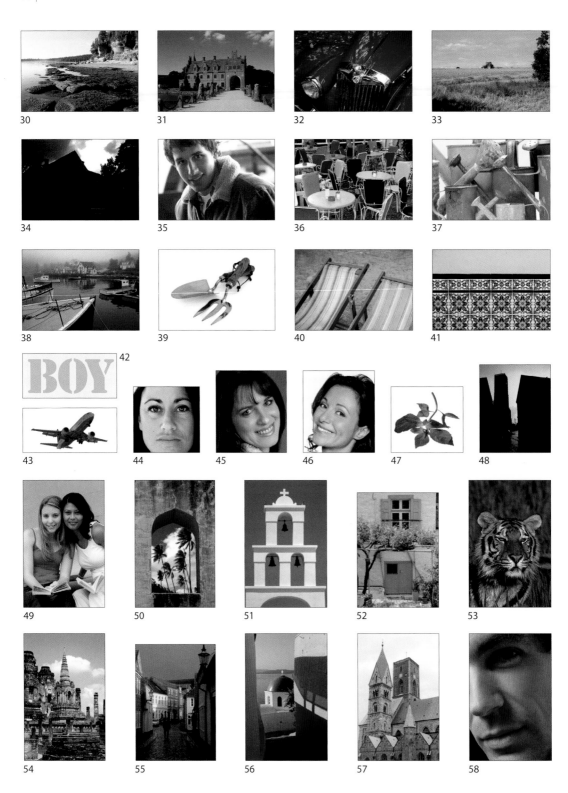

30

31

32

33

34

35

36

37

38

39

40

41

42

43

44

45

46

47

48

49

50

51

52

53

54

55

56

57

58

BOY

Chapters at a glance

TABLE OF CONTENTS

★ signifies a feature is NEW (is Photoshop CS3 only)

Contents

Welcome to Photoshop! Using this chapter, you'll launch Photoshop and become acquainted with the Photoshop interface—menus, tools, palettes, and lingo. You can read this chapter with or without glancing at (or fiddling with) the program features onscreen. Later, you can use it as a reference guide as you work. (Once you're up and running in Photoshop, don't forget to reread the "Working Smart" tips at the end of this chapter.)

To launch Photoshop in Windows:

Do one of the following:

In Windows 2000 or XP, click the Start button on the taskbar, choose All Programs, then click Adobe Photoshop CS3.

Open the C:\Program Files\Adobe\Adobe Photoshop CS3 folder in My Computer, then double-click Photoshop.exe.

Double-click a Photoshop file icon. **Ps**

To launch Photoshop in the Mac OS:

Do one of the following:

Click the Photoshop icon **Ps** in the Dock. (If you don't have a Photoshop icon there yet, open the Adobe Photoshop CS3 folder in the Applications folder, then drag the Adobe Photoshop CS3 application icon into the Dock.)

Open the Adobe Photoshop CS3 folder in the Applications folder, then double-click the Adobe Photoshop CS3 application icon. **Ps**

Double-click any Photoshop file icon (thumbnail).

NOT SEEING ENOUGH ONSCREEN?

If you want to open a file quickly to make the screen more "alive" as you read through this chapter, navigate to the **Samples** folder inside the Photoshop application folder, then double-click any image file that has a ".tif" extension, such as "Ducky.tif." (Don't worry…you'll soon learn everything you need to know about importing photos and creating documents.)

NEW STUFF

Where you see this symbol ★, it signifies a feature that is **new** to **Photoshop CS3.**

PHOTOSHOP INTERFACE

1

The Photoshop screen in the Mac OS

Press any **menu bar** heading to access dialog boxes and commands. Many of the same commands can be chosen quickly from a context menu (see page 25) or palette menu, or via a palette button.

Use the **Options bar** to choose settings for the current tool.

Click the **Go to Bridge** button to go to Bridge, a separate application that you'll use to open and sort files (it ships with Photoshop).

The **title bar** shows a tiny thumbnail of the image, the document title, file format, zoom level, current layer (or the Background), document color mode, and bit depth, and sometimes a color proofing device, too!

Tools palette

The 4 **screen modes** control the onscreen environment behind the image.

From the **status bar** menu, choose which information you want the bar to display. Efficiency is the percentage of time Photoshop is processing edits as opposed to writing to the scratch disk. Note: If Version Cue is enabled in Photoshop > Preferences > File Handling, these options are listed on a Show submenu. (To reset the timer, hold down Alt/Option and choose Timing.)

In the Standard version of Photoshop, there are 20 movable **palettes**, most of which are used for image editing. A few palettes, such as Info and Histogram, provide information only.

The Photoshop screen in Windows

*Press any **menu bar** heading to access dialog boxes and commands. Many of the same commands can be chosen quickly via a context menu (see page 25) or palette menu, or via a palette button.*

*Use the **Options bar** to choose settings for the current tool.*

*The **title bar** lists the document title, file format, zoom level, current layer (or the Background), document color mode, and bit depth.*

*Click the **Go to Bridge** button to go to Bridge, a separate application that you'll use to open and sort files (it ships with Photoshop).*

Tools palette

*The 4 **screen modes** control the onscreen environment behind the image.*

*From the **status bar** menu, choose what information you want the bar to display. Efficiency is the percentage of time Photoshop is processing edits as opposed to writing to the scratch disk. Note: If Version Cue is enabled in Photoshop > Preferences > File Handling, these options are listed on a Show submenu. (To reset the timer, hold down Alt/Option and choose Timing.)*

*In the Standard version of Photoshop, there are 20 movable **palettes**, most of which are used for image editing. A few palettes, such as Info and Histogram, provide information only.*

The menus

Photoshop

About Photoshop...
About Plug-In ▶
Preferences ▶

Services ▶

Hide Photoshop ^⌘H
Hide Others ⌥⌘H
Show All

Quit Photoshop ⌘Q

File

New...	⌘N
Open...	⌘O
Browse...	⌥⌘O
Open As Smart Object...	
Open Recent	▶
Device Central...	
Close	⌘W
Close All	⌥⌘W
Close and Go To Bridge...	⇧⌘W
Save	⌘S
Save As...	⇧⌘S
Check In...	
Save for Web & Devices...	⌥⇧⌘S
Revert	F12
Place...	
Import	▶
Export	▶
Automate	▶
Scripts	▶
File Info...	⌥⇧⌘I
Page Setup...	⇧⌘P
Print...	⌘P
Print One Copy	⌥⇧⌘P

Edit

Undo Copy Pixels	⌘Z
Step Forward	⇧⌘Z
Step Backward	⌥⌘Z
Fade...	⇧⌘F
Cut	⌘X
Copy	⌘C
Copy Merged	⇧⌘C
Paste	⌘V
Paste Into	⇧⌘V
Clear	
Check Spelling...	
Find and Replace Text...	
Fill...	⇧F5
Stroke...	
Free Transform	⌘T
Transform	▶
Auto-Align Layers...	
Auto-Blend Layers	
Define Brush Preset...	
Define Pattern...	
Define Custom Shape...	
Purge	▶
Adobe PDF Presets...	
Preset Manager...	
Color Settings...	⇧⌘K
Assign Profile...	
Convert to Profile...	
Keyboard Shortcuts...	⌥⇧⌘K
Menus...	⌥⇧⌘M

Image

Mode	▶
Adjustments	▶
Duplicate...	
Apply Image...	
Calculations...	
Image Size...	⌥⌘I
Canvas Size...	⌥⌘C
Pixel Aspect Ratio	▶
Rotate Canvas	▶
Crop	
Trim...	
Reveal All	
Variables	▶
Apply Data Set...	
Trap...	

WHAT'S DIFFERENT IN WINDOWS?

➤ **About Photoshop** and **About Plug-in** are on the Help menu.

➤ **Preferences** is on the Edit menu.

➤ **Exit Photoshop** is on the File menu.

➤ There is no Photoshop menu. The Services, Hide Photoshop, Hide Others, and Show All commands are Mac only.

➤ File > **Open As** is Windows only.

➤ Window > Arrange > Arrange Icons is Windows only; Window > Arrange > Minimize and Window > Arrange > Minimize and Bring All to Front are Mac only.

SET PREFERENCES WHEN READY

Many computer how-to books tell you how to set **document** and **application preferences** (default settings) early in the game. We prefer to get you working with the editing features of a program first, but may ask you to set a preference or two in the course of executing a specific task. If you want to get an overall view of the preferences at any time, see Chapter 25.

➤ To open the **Preferences** dialog box in Photoshop, press **Ctrl-K/Cmd-K** or choose Edit (Photoshop, in the Mac OS) > Preferences > General or one of the other choices on the menu. When the Preferences dialog box opens, click one of the 10 pane names on the left side or click Prev or Next.

Layer

New	▶
Duplicate Layer...	
Delete	▶
Layer Properties...	
Layer Style	▶
Smart Filter	▶
New Fill Layer	▶
New Adjustment Layer	▶
Change Layer Content	▶
Layer Content Options...	
Layer Mask	▶
Vector Mask	▶
Create Clipping Mask	⌥⌘G
Smart Objects	▶
Type	▶
Rasterize	▶
New Layer Based Slice	
Group Layers	⌘G
Ungroup Layers	⇧⌘G
Hide Layers	
Arrange	▶
Align	▶
Distribute	▶
Lock All Layers in Group...	
Link Layers	
Select Linked Layers	
Merge Down	⌘E
Merge Visible	⇧⌘E
Flatten Image	
Matting	▶

Select

All	⌘A
Deselect	⌘D
Reselect	⇧⌘D
Inverse	⇧⌘I
All Layers	⌥⌘A
Deselect Layers	
Similar Layers	
Color Range...	
Refine Edge...	⌥⌘R
Modify	▶
Grow	
Similar	
Transform Selection	
Load Selection...	
Save Selection...	

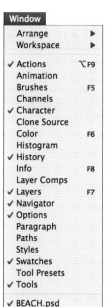

Window

Arrange	▶
Workspace	▶
✓ Actions	⌥F9
Animation	
Brushes	F5
Channels	
✓ Character	
Clone Source	
Color	F6
Histogram	
✓ History	
Info	F8
Layer Comps	
✓ Layers	F7
✓ Navigator	
✓ Options	
Paragraph	
Paths	
Styles	
✓ Swatches	
Tool Presets	
✓ Tools	
✓ BEACH.psd	

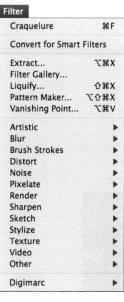

Filter

Craquelure	⌘F
Convert for Smart Filters	
Extract...	⌥⌘X
Filter Gallery...	
Liquify...	⇧⌘X
Pattern Maker...	⌥⇧⌘X
Vanishing Point...	⌥⌘V
Artistic	▶
Blur	▶
Brush Strokes	▶
Distort	▶
Noise	▶
Pixelate	▶
Render	▶
Sharpen	▶
Sketch	▶
Stylize	▶
Texture	▶
Video	▶
Other	▶
Digimarc	▶

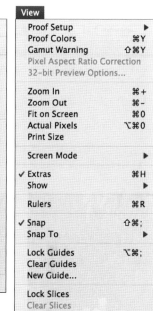

View

Proof Setup	▶
Proof Colors	⌘Y
Gamut Warning	⇧⌘Y
Pixel Aspect Ratio Correction	
32-bit Preview Options...	
Zoom In	⌘+
Zoom Out	⌘−
Fit on Screen	⌘0
Actual Pixels	⌥⌘0
Print Size	
Screen Mode	▶
✓ Extras	⌘H
Show	▶
Rulers	⌘R
✓ Snap	⇧⌘;
Snap To	▶
Lock Guides	⌥⌘;
Clear Guides	
New Guide...	
Lock Slices	
Clear Slices	

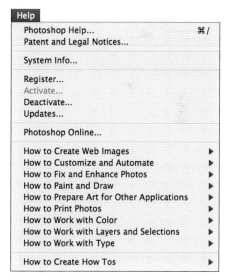

Help

Photoshop Help...	⌘/
Patent and Legal Notices...	
System Info...	
Register...	
Activate...	
Deactivate...	
Updates...	
Photoshop Online...	
How to Create Web Images	▶
How to Customize and Automate	▶
How to Fix and Enhance Photos	▶
How to Paint and Draw	▶
How to Prepare Art for Other Applications	▶
How to Print Photos	▶
How to Work with Color	▶
How to Work with Layers and Selections	▶
How to Work with Type	▶
How to Create How Tos	▶

WHICH VERSION OF PHOTOSHOP?

This book covers the **Standard** version of Photoshop — not the Extended version — so it doesn't contain information about such extended features as the Analysis menu and the Measurement Log palette.

The Tools palette

Using the Tools palette

The Tools palette, illustrated on pages 7–9, contains 60 tools and a handful of buttons. Believe it or not, by the end of this book, you'll be intimately—or at least marginally—familiar with most of them! To show the Tools palette if it's hidden, choose Window > **Tools.**

To **choose a tool,** do one of the following:

➤ If the desired tool is visible on the Tools palette, click the **icon.**

➤ To cycle through related tools in the same slot, **Alt-click/Option-click** the visible one.

➤ Click the tiny arrowhead next to a tool icon to choose a related tool from a **menu.**

➤ For fast access with your cursor anywhere (except if you're creating type), press the designated **letter shortcut.** The shortcuts are shown in the screen captures on the next three pages and in tool tips onscreen.**A** With Use Shift Key for Tool Switch unchecked in Preferences > General, simply press the designated letter to cycle through related tools in the same slot (for example, press "L" to cycle through the three Lasso tools). With the Use Shift Key for Tool Switch option checked, you have to press Shift plus the designated letter. (See, you've already learned your first Preference!)

To learn about the function of a tool as you're using it, look at the bottom of the **Info** palette (see page 17). (If no tool information is listed, choose Palette Options from the Info palette menu, then check Show Tool Hints.) Tool tips and brief descriptions (hints) are also available for tools in some dialog boxes, such as Refine Edge and Print.

Before you start to use a tool you've selected, you need to choose settings for it from the **Options** bar at the top of your screen. For example, for the Brush tool, you'll choose a brush tip, blending mode, opacity percentage, and other settings. If the Options bar is hidden, choose Window > Options. (Read more about the Options bar on page 9.)

Options bar settings remain in effect for each tool until you change them, reset that tool, or reset all tools. To reset the default settings for a tool, right-click/Control-click the tool thumbnail on the Options bar and choose **Reset Tool** from the context menu.**B** To reset all tools, choose **Reset All Tools** from the same menu.

In Preferences > Cursors, you can specify whether **tool pointers** look like their Tools palette icon or a crosshair or, for some tools, a circle the size of—or half the size of—the current brush diameter, with or without a crosshair (see page 388).

TOOL TIPS ARE EVERYWHERE!

If **Show Tool Tips** is checked in Photoshop > Preferences > **Interface** and you rest the pointer on a tool icon without clicking the mouse button, the tool name and shortcut will pop up onscreen.**A** You can use the same method to learn the function or name of palette, Options bar, and dialog box features. Some dialog boxes also have hints—descriptive information that changes depending on the location of the pointer in the dialog box.

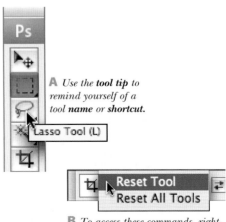

A *Use the **tool tip** to remind yourself of a tool **name** or **shortcut.***

B *To access these commands, right-click/Control-click the thumbnail for the current **tool** on the Options bar.*

Tools on the Tools palette

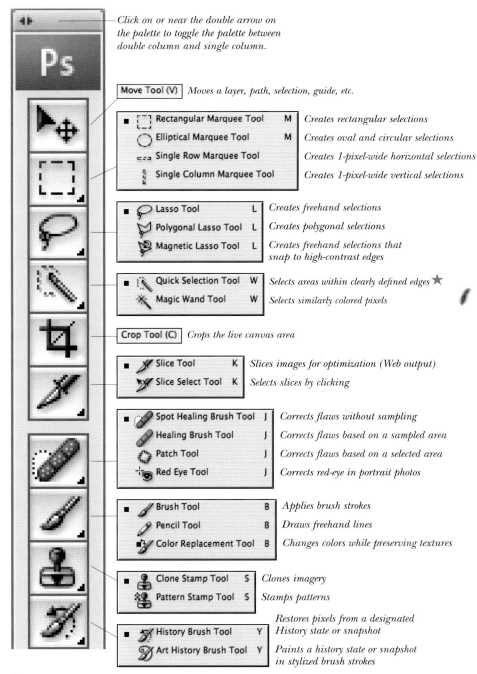

Click on or near the double arrow on the palette to toggle the palette between double column and single column.

Move Tool (V) — *Moves a layer, path, selection, guide, etc.*

■ Rectangular Marquee Tool — M — *Creates rectangular selections*
Elliptical Marquee Tool — M — *Creates oval and circular selections*
Single Row Marquee Tool — *Creates 1-pixel-wide horizontal selections*
Single Column Marquee Tool — *Creates 1-pixel-wide vertical selections*

■ Lasso Tool — L — *Creates freehand selections*
Polygonal Lasso Tool — L — *Creates polygonal selections*
Magnetic Lasso Tool — L — *Creates freehand selections that snap to high-contrast edges*

■ Quick Selection Tool — W — *Selects areas within clearly defined edges* ★
Magic Wand Tool — W — *Selects similarly colored pixels*

Crop Tool (C) — *Crops the live canvas area*

■ Slice Tool — K — *Slices images for optimization (Web output)*
Slice Select Tool — K — *Selects slices by clicking*

■ Spot Healing Brush Tool — J — *Corrects flaws without sampling*
Healing Brush Tool — J — *Corrects flaws based on a sampled area*
Patch Tool — J — *Corrects flaws based on a selected area*
Red Eye Tool — J — *Corrects red-eye in portrait photos*

■ Brush Tool — B — *Applies brush strokes*
Pencil Tool — B — *Draws freehand lines*
Color Replacement Tool — B — *Changes colors while preserving textures*

■ Clone Stamp Tool — S — *Clones imagery*
Pattern Stamp Tool — S — *Stamps patterns*

■ History Brush Tool — Y — *Restores pixels from a designated History state or snapshot*
Art History Brush Tool — Y — *Paints a history state or snapshot in stylized brush strokes*

A *The upper part of the* **Tools** *palette*

Continued on the following page

Eraser Tool	E	*Erases any imagery*
Background Eraser Tool	E	*Erases a sampled color to transparency*
Magic Eraser Tool	E	*Erases similarly colored pixels by clicking*

| Gradient Tool | G | *Creates soft color blends* |
| Paint Bucket Tool | G | *Fills similarly colored areas by clicking* |

Blur Tool	R	*Blurs edges*
Sharpen Tool	R	*Sharpens edges*
Smudge Tool	R	*Smudges colors*

Dodge Tool	O	*Lightens pixels*
Burn Tool	O	*Darkens pixels*
Sponge Tool	O	*Saturates or desaturates pixels*

Pen Tool	P	*Draws curved and straight-edged shapes/paths*
Freeform Pen Tool	P	*Draws freehand shapes/paths*
Add Anchor Point Tool		*Adds anchor points to a path*
Delete Anchor Point Tool		*Deletes anchor points from a path*
Convert Point Tool		*Converts corner anchor points into curve points, and vice versa*

Horizontal Type Tool	T	*Creates editable type on its own layer*
Vertical Type Tool	T	*Creates vertically oriented editable type*
Horizontal Type Mask Tool	T	*Creates horizontal type-shaped selections*
Vertical Type Mask Tool	T	*Creates vertical type-shaped selections*

| Path Selection Tool | A | *Selects whole vector paths* |
| Direct Selection Tool | A | *Selects path segments and points* |

Rectangle Tool	U	*Creates rectangular shape layers/paths*
Rounded Rectangle Tool	U	*Creates rounded-corner shape layers/paths*
Ellipse Tool	U	*Creates oval shape layers/paths*
Polygon Tool	U	*Creates polygonal shape layers/paths*
Line Tool	U	*Creates straight-line shape layers/paths*
Custom Shape Tool	U	*Creates predefined custom shape layers/paths*

| Notes Tool | N | *Creates Acrobat-compatible annotations* |
| Audio Annotation Tool | N | *Creates audio annotations* |

A *The midsection of the **Tools palette***

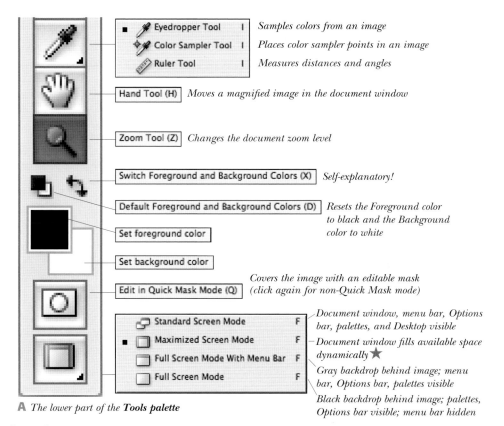

Eyedropper Tool	I	*Samples colors from an image*
Color Sampler Tool	I	*Places color sampler points in an image*
Ruler Tool	I	*Measures distances and angles*

Hand Tool (H) *Moves a magnified image in the document window*

Zoom Tool (Z) *Changes the document zoom level*

Switch Foreground and Background Colors (X) *Self-explanatory!*

Default Foreground and Background Colors (D) *Resets the Foreground color to black and the Background color to white*

Set foreground color

Set background color

Edit in Quick Mask Mode (Q) *Covers the image with an editable mask (click again for non-Quick Mask mode)*

Standard Screen Mode	F	*Document window, menu bar, Options bar, palettes, and Desktop visible*
Maximized Screen Mode	F	*Document window fills available space dynamically* ★
Full Screen Mode With Menu Bar	F	*Gray backdrop behind image; menu bar, Options bar, palettes visible*
Full Screen Mode	F	*Black backdrop behind image; palettes, Options bar visible; menu bar hidden*

A *The lower part of the **Tools palette***

The Options bar

You'll use the Options bar to choose settings every time you switch tools—and sometimes even while using the same tool.**B** (If the bar is hidden, choose Window > Options.) Options bar features change dynamically depending on which tool is selected, but your choices remain in effect for each tool until you change them. You can drag the bar anywhere onscreen by its left edge.

*Click the icon or arrowhead to open a **preset picker** (pop-up palette).*

Opacity: 52%

C *A **scrubby slider***

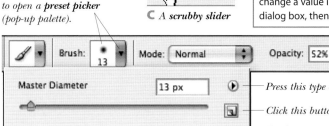

Master Diameter   13 px   ▶ ———— *Press this type of arrowhead to open a **menu**.*

———— *Click this button to create a **new preset**.*

*To **close** a preset picker or any other pop-up palette, click anywhere outside it or click the arrowhead on the Options bar.*

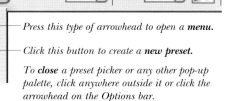

B *Part of the **Options bar**, with the Brush tool chosen*

The palettes

Using the palettes ★

Most edits made in Photoshop require the use of one palette or another. Version CS3 introduces a clever new system for storing and accessing palettes so they're easily expandable and collapsible and don't intrude on the document window when you're not using them. As expected, with enhanced flexibility, you also get greater complexity.

By default, some of the most commonly used palettes are grouped into vertical **docks** (dark gray areas) on the far right side **A** of your screen —except the Tools palette, which is on the left side. Each dock can hold as many or as few palettes or palette groups as you like. We'll show you how to reconfigure the docks to suit your working style.

Show/hide a palette: To show a palette, choose the palette name from the Window menu. The palette will display either in its default group and dock or in its last location. To bring a palette to the front of its group, click the tab (palette name). A few palettes can also be shown/hidden via keyboard shortcuts, which are listed on the Window menu.

Show/hide a palette (icon): Click the icon **B** or palette name. If Auto-Collapse Icon Palettes is checked in Preferences > Interface and you open a palette from an icon, it collapses back to the icon when you click away from it. With this preference unchecked, the palette stays expanded. To collapse it, click the collapse/expand button ⏵⏵ on the palette bar, palette tab, or palette icon.

Expand/collapse a palette (non-icon) **or group vertically:** Double-click the palette tab; or click the light gray bar (above the palette tabs); or click the palette or group minimize/maximize button. ▬

Use a palette menu: Click the ⬛≡ icon to open a menu for whichever palette is in the front of that particular group.

Close a palette or group: To close (but not collapse) a palette, click the close button ✕ on its tab, as in ⎹ Layers ✕⎸. To close a palette group, click the ✕ on the gray bar. To close a group that's an icon, expand the dock first by clicking the collapse/expand button.⏵⏵ (To reopen a palette, use the Window menu.)

Collapse/expand a whole dock into icons with names: Click the collapse/expand button ⏵⏵ or the dark gray bar at the top of the dock.**C** To further collapse the dock to just icons (no names), drag

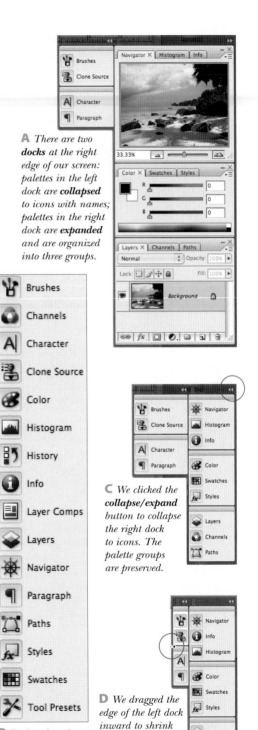

A *There are two* **docks** *at the right edge of our screen: palettes in the left dock are* **collapsed** *to icons with names; palettes in the right dock are* **expanded** *and are organized into three groups.*

B *Each* **palette** *has a unique* **icon.** *Try to memorize the ones you use most often.*

C *We clicked the* **collapse/expand** *button to collapse the right dock to icons. The palette groups are preserved.*

D *We dragged the edge of the left dock inward to shrink that dock to just* **icons** *(no names).*

the vertical edge of the dock inward horizontally (**D**, previous page); to expand it, do the reverse.

Widen/narrow a dock and palettes (non-icon): Position the mouse over the vertical edge of the dock (✦✥ cursor), then drag sideways.

Lengthen or shorten a palette, group, or dock: Position the mouse over the dark gray line at the bottom of the palette or dock (↕ cursor), then drag upward or downward. Other palettes/groups in the same group or dock will scale accordingly.

Move a palette to a different slot, same group: Drag the palette tab (name) horizontally.

Move a palette to a different group: Drag the palette tab over the bar of the desired group, and release when the blue drop zone border appears.**A**

Move a palette group upward/downward in a dock: Drag the gray bar, and release when the blue drop zone line appears in the desired location.**B**

Create a new dock: Drag a palette tab or gray bar sideways over the vertical edge of the dock,**C** and release when the blue vertical drop zone bar appears. Note: Depending on the current workspace settings, when you open a hidden palette from the Window menu, it may appear in a new dock.

Make a palette or group freestanding: Drag the palette tab, icon, or group bar out of the dock. To move a freestanding group, drag the group bar.

Reconfigure a dock (icon): Use similar methods as for an expanded group. Drag the group bar over the edge of a dock to create a new dock; drag it between groups to restack it; or drag it over another gray bar to combine it with that group. The blue drop zone will indicate the new location for the palette or group.

➤ To reset the palettes to their default locations and show/hide state, choose Default Workspace from the Workspace menu on the Options bar. To reset just the palette locations, choose Window > Workspace > Reset Palette Locations.

➤ To create custom workspaces that remember palette locations and which palettes are showing or hidden, see pages 89–90.

➤ For any tool that uses a brush, you can click the Toggle Palette button 🗎 on the Options bar to show/hide the Brushes palette. For the Type tool, this button opens the Character palette.

➤ To learn more about showing/hiding palettes, see page 86.

A *A blue drop zone border appears as we drag a palette into a **different group**.*

B *A blue horizontal drop zone bar appears as we **move** a palette group upward in the same dock.*

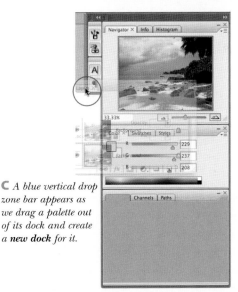

C *A blue vertical drop zone bar appears as we drag a palette out of its dock and create a **new dock** for it.*

The palettes illustrated

Brushes palette

You'll use the Brushes palette to choose and customize brush tips for many tools, such as the Brush, Pencil, Clone Stamp, Pattern Stamp, History Brush, Art History Brush, Eraser, Blur, Sharpen, Smudge, Dodge, Burn, and Sponge. You can also use it to choose options for a graphics tablet and stylus. Click an options set on the left side of the palette to display options on the right. The preview at the bottom of the palette represents the current brush tip and settings.

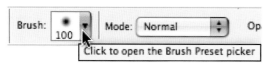

Click to open the Brush Preset picker

THE GAME PLAN

The palettes are illustrated in alphabetical order beginning on this page, except for the Tools palette, which is illustrated on pages 7–9, and the Options bar, which is illustrated on page 9. The Actions and Animations palettes aren't illustrated.

PICKER OR PALETTE?

You can choose brush tips for the painting and editing tools from either the **Brushes palette** or the **Brush Preset picker,** a pop-up palette that opens from the Options bar (shown at left). To close the Brush Preset picker, click outside it or click the Brush arrowhead again. Commands to load, append, and save brushes and brush libraries are available on the Brushes palette menu and the Brush Preset picker menu.

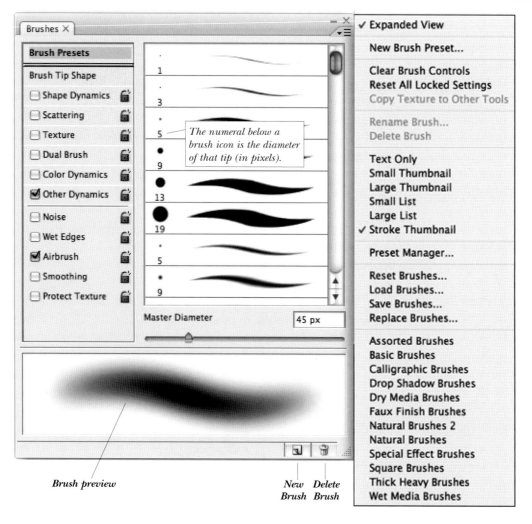

Brush preview

New Brush   Delete Brush

Channels palette

The Channels palette lists the color channels that make up an image. To display one of the channels by itself in the document window, click the channel name or use the keystroke listed on the palette. To redisplay the composite channel, such as RGB or CMYK, click the topmost channel on the palette, or press Ctrl-~/Cmd-~ (tilde).

You can also use this palette to save and load alpha channels (saved selections), and to create and store spot color channels, which commercial printers use to produce individual color plates for premixed inks.

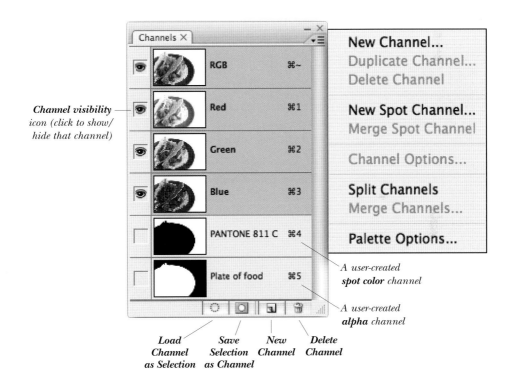

Channel visibility icon (click to show/ hide that channel)

A user-created **spot color** *channel*

A user-created **alpha** *channel*

Load Channel as Selection *Save Selection as Channel* *New Channel* *Delete Channel*

Character palette

You can choose attributes for any of the type tools via the Character palette, illustrated below, or from the Options bar. Open this palette from the Window menu, or by clicking the 🗐 button on the Options bar when a type tool is selected.

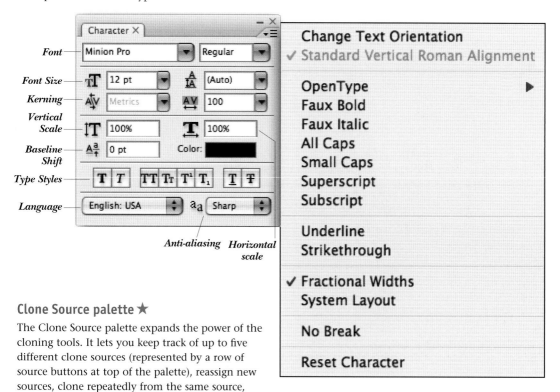

Clone Source palette ★

The Clone Source palette expands the power of the cloning tools. It lets you keep track of up to five different clone sources (represented by a row of source buttons at top of the palette), reassign new sources, clone repeatedly from the same source, and scale, rotate, or reposition source pixels before or as you clone them.

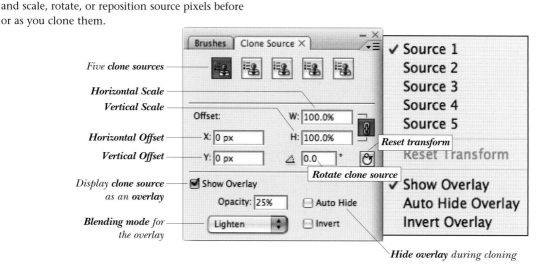

Color palette

The Color palette is but one of the vehicles for mixing colors in Photoshop. Choose a color model for the sliders or color bar from the palette menu, then mix a color using the sliders or quick-select a color by clicking the color bar. To open the Color Picker or Color Libraries dialog box, from which you can also choose colors, click once on the Foreground or Background color square if it's already selected (has a black border), or double-click the square if it's not selected. Colors are applied via painting and editing tools and via some commands, such as Canvas Size.

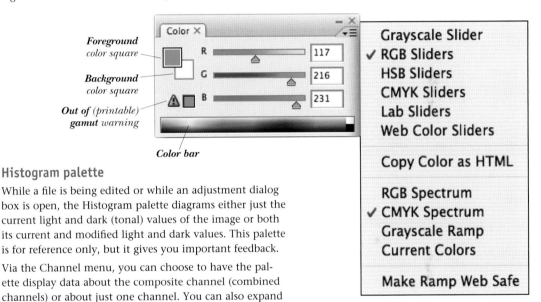

Foreground color square

Background color square

Out of (printable) gamut warning

Color bar

Histogram palette

While a file is being edited or while an adjustment dialog box is open, the Histogram palette diagrams either just the current light and dark (tonal) values of the image or both its current and modified light and dark values. This palette is for reference only, but it gives you important feedback.

Via the Channel menu, you can choose to have the palette display data about the composite channel (combined channels) or about just one channel. You can also expand the palette to display histograms for all the channels.

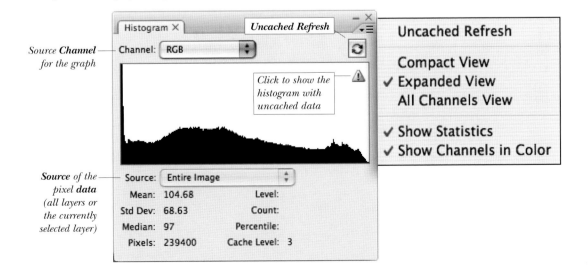

Source Channel for the graph

Click to show the histogram with uncached data

Source of the pixel data (all layers or the currently selected layer)

History palette

Using the History palette, you can reverse your editing steps in the current work session. Each brush stroke, filter application, or other image-editing command is listed as a separate state on the palette, with the bottommost state being the most recent. If you click a prior state, the document reverts to that stage of the editing process. In linear mode, the default mode for the palette, if you click an earlier state and resume image editing from that state (or delete that state), all subsequent (dimmed) states are discarded.

The New Snapshot command creates a state that stays on the palette until you close the image, regardless of the number of subsequent edits.

When you drag with the History Brush tool, the areas under your strokes are restored to the currently designated source state. The Art History Brush does the same thing, but in stylized strokes.

Source for the *History Brush*

User-created snapshot *of a state*

History State *slider*   New Document *from Current State*   New Snapshot   Delete Current State

Info palette

The Info palette displays a color breakdown of the pixel under the pointer at its current location in the document window. While any color adjustment dialog box is open, the palette displays before and after color readouts. The Info palette also lists the current location of the pointer on the x/y axis.

Other information may display on the palette, depending on which tool is being used, such as the distance between points when you move a selection, draw a shape, or use the Ruler tool; the dimensions of a selection or crop marquee; or the width (W), height (H), angle (A), and horizontal skew (H) or vertical skew (V) of a layer, selection, or vector object as you transform it. The palette will also show readouts for up to four color samplers that you've placed in your document.

Press one of the tiny arrowheads to choose a color model for that readout (it can differ from the current document color mode). Or to do this via a dialog box, choose Palette Options from the palette menu, then in the Info Palette Options dialog box (shown below), change the mode for the First Color Readout and Second Color Readout. In the same dialog box, you can also change the Ruler Units for the palette (Mouse Coordinates); check which Status Information you want displayed in the lower part of the palette; and check Show Tool Hints to display interactive information about the current tool or edit.

➤ To choose a different unit of measurement for the Info palette and for the rulers in the document window, click the arrowhead on the Info palette for the X/Y readout.

Color breakdown *for the pixel currently under the pointer*

Click the arrowhead to choose a different ***color model*** *for that readout.*

Width *and* ***height*** *of the current* ***selection***

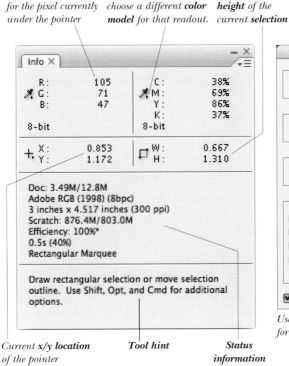

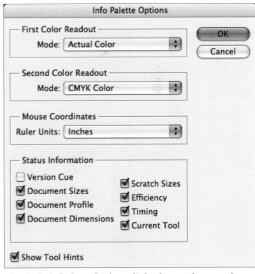

Use the ***Info Palette Options*** *dialog box to choose preferences for the Info palette.*

Current ***x/y location*** *of the pointer*

Tool hint

Status information

Layer Comps palette

When you create a layer comp (short for "composition"), it includes, collectively, the characteristics of the currently selected layer: visibility (which layers are showing or hidden), the position of imagery, and appearance (applied layer styles, including the layer blending mode). Creating layer comps is useful for deciding between several document versions or for presenting design variations to a client. For example, say you create several variations of a book cover. You make each version into a layer comp, say, with or without lettering, or with the lettering or background image in two different colors. When presenting the design to your client, instead of opening and closing separate files, you simply display each version sequentially within the same file by clicking the Apply Layer Comp icon on and off for each one on the Layer Comps palette.

Layer comps save with the document in which they're created. Whereas histories affect all editing done to an image but can't be saved, layer comps can be saved but let you display only layer options and settings.

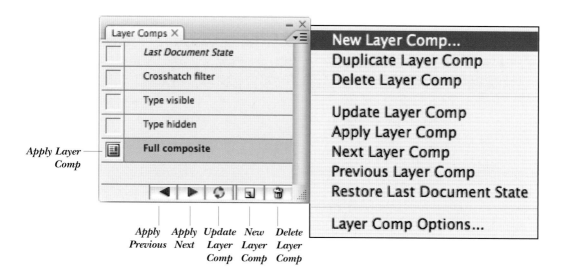

Apply Layer Comp

Apply Previous · *Apply Next* · *Update Layer Comp* · *New Layer Comp* · *Delete Layer Comp*

Layers palette

Every new image contains either a solid-color Background or a transparent layer, on top of which you can add layers of many types. Using the Layers palette, you can create, show/hide, duplicate, group, link, merge, flatten, delete, and restack layers; change the layer blending mode, opacity, and fill opacity; attach masks; and apply layer effects.

Only the currently selected layer can be edited. To select a layer, click the thumbnail or click next to (but not on) the layer name. The palette looks complex, but you'll soon be using it all the time!

These are the type of layers that you can create, or that Photoshop creates automatically:

➤ **Image** layers.

➤ **Fill** and **adjustment** layers, to apply temporary color or tonal adjustments to underlying layers.

➤ **Editable type** layers, which are created automatically when you use the Horizontal Type or Vertical Type tool.

➤ **Smart Object** layers, which are created automatically when you bring an Illustrator vector file, another Photoshop file, or a Raw (digital camera) file into a Photoshop document via File > Place. Double-click a Smart Object layer, and the object reopens in its original application for editing; save and close it, and the object updates in Photoshop. Apply a filter to a Smart Object layer, and it becomes a Smart Filter, ★ which, like an adjustment layer, is editable and removable.

➤ **Shape** layers, which contain vector shapes.

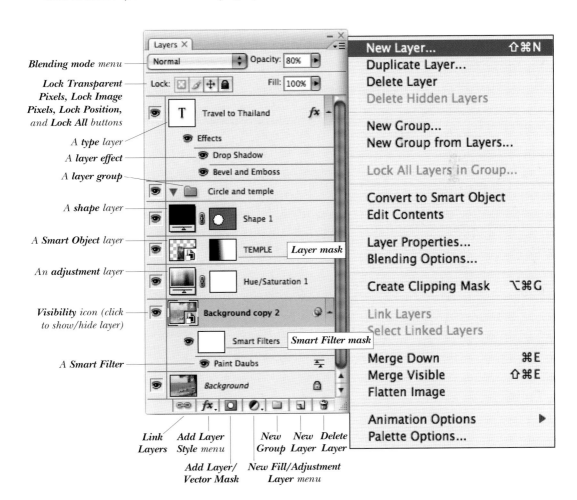

Navigator palette

You can use the Navigator palette to move a magnified image in the document window or change the document zoom level—or if you prefer, you can accomplish the same tasks using tools and keyboard shortcuts.

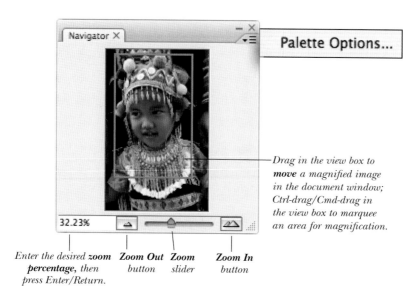

Palette Options...

Drag in the view box to *move* a magnified image in the document window; Ctrl-drag/Cmd-drag in the view box to marquee an area for magnification.

Enter the desired **zoom percentage,** then press Enter/Return.

Zoom Out button

Zoom slider

Zoom In button

Paragraph palette

After creating paragraph type, you can use the Paragraph palette to apply attributes such as horizontal alignment, indentation, space before, space after, and auto hyphenation. Additional type formatting features are accesssed via the palette menu.

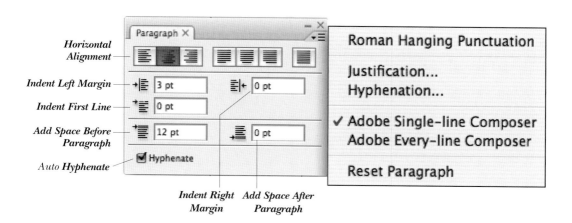

Horizontal Alignment

Indent Left Margin

Indent First Line

Add Space Before Paragraph

Auto Hyphenate

Indent Right Margin   *Add Space After Paragraph*

Roman Hanging Punctuation

Justification...
Hyphenation...

✓ Adobe Single-line Composer
Adobe Every-line Composer

Reset Paragraph

Paths palette

In addition to the bitmap image that serves as the foundation of your Photoshop document, you can also draw vector shapes, called paths, which consist of curved and straight-line segments connected by anchor points. You can use the Paths palette to save, activate, duplicate, apply a fill or stroke to, and delete paths, and to load paths as selections.

You can draw a path directly with a shape tool or the Pen tool, or you can create a selection and then convert the selection into a path. Conversely, to create a precisely drawn selection, you can draw a path and then convert it into a selection. Once a path is drawn, you can apply a color to its fill or stroke and you can reshape it by using the Pen tool or any of its relatives: the Add Anchor Point, Delete Anchor Point, and Convert Point tools.

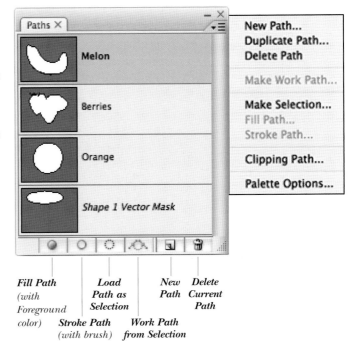

Fill Path (with Foreground color) *Load Path as Selection* *New Path* *Delete Current Path*
Stroke Path (with brush) *Work Path from Selection*

Styles palette

You can conveniently store a collection of layer settings—such as layer effects, opacity, blending mode, and fill opacity—as a style on the Styles palette. Once stored, styles can be applied to any layer with a click of the mouse. Custom style libraries can be loaded, appended, and saved via commands on the palette menu.

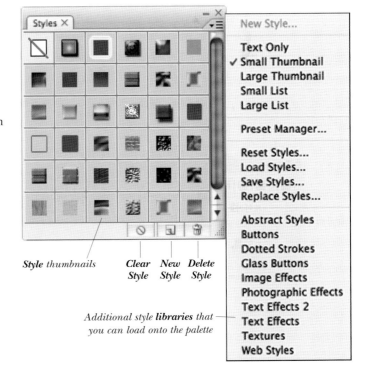

Style thumbnails *Clear Style* *New Style* *Delete Style*

*Additional style **libraries** that you can load onto the palette*

Swatches palette

The Swatches palette is used for storing and choosing colors. Custom swatch libraries (such as PANTONE) can be saved, loaded, and appended via commands on the palette menu.

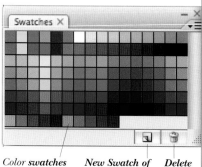

*Color swatches   New Swatch of   Delete
            Foreground Color   Swatch*

*Predefined swatch
libraries (sets)
that you can load
onto the palette*

New Swatch...

✓ Small Thumbnail
Large Thumbnail
Small List
Large List

Preset Manager...

Reset Swatches...
Load Swatches...
Save Swatches...
Save Swatches for Exchange...
Replace Swatches...

ANPA Colors
DIC Color Guide
FOCOLTONE Colors
HKS E Process
HKS E
HKS K Process
HKS K
HKS N Process
HKS N
HKS Z Process
HKS Z
Mac OS
PANTONE Color Bridge
PANTONE Color BridgeEuro
PANTONE metallic coated
PANTONE pastel coated
PANTONE pastel uncoated
PANTONE process coated
PANTONE process uncoated
PANTONE solid coated
PANTONE solid matte
PANTONE solid to process EURO
PANTONE solid to process
PANTONE solid uncoated
Photo Filter Colors
TOYO 94 COLOR FINDER
TOYO COLOR FINDER
TRUMATCH Colors
VisiBone
VisiBone2
Web Hues
Web Safe Colors
Web Spectrum
Windows

Tool Presets palette

You can save and reuse tool settings just as you can any other type of preset. Say, for example, you frequently resize and crop images to a particular set of dimensions using the Crop tool. If you save a preset for the tool with those width, height, and resolution parameters, the next time you use the tool, instead of having to type in the numbers, all you have to do is click your Crop tool preset on either the Tool Presets palette or the Tool Preset picker (both shown below).

Using the Tool Presets palette, you can save, store, load, sort, rename, reset, and delete tool presets; the presets are available for all Photoshop files. To have the palette list the presets for the current tool only, check Current Tool Only, or uncheck this option to display the presets for all tools.

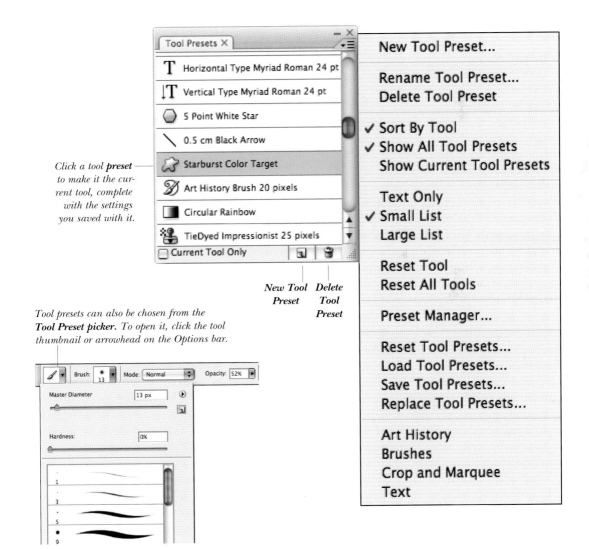

*Click a tool **preset** to make it the current tool, complete with the settings you saved with it.*

New Tool Preset Delete Tool Preset

Tool presets can also be chosen from the **Tool Preset picker.** *To open it, click the tool thumbnail or arrowhead on the Options bar.*

Mini-glossary

Adjustment and fill layers

Unlike a standard layer, an adjustment or fill layer doesn't alter image pixels until you merge it with the underlying layer. They're useful for trying out color and tonal adjustments, plus you can edit them at any time.

Blending mode

Menu options that control the color interaction between layers.

Brightness, hue, saturation

Brightness is the relative lightness of a color; the hue is the wavelength of light that gives a color its name (such as "red" or "blue"); and saturation is the purity of a color (how much gray it contains).

Histogram

A histogram is a graph of the current light and dark tonal values in an image. Learning how to read a histogram as you apply adjustment commands can help you judge their impact; the histogram updates as you edit your document.

Layer effect

To any layer, you can apply and choose settings for an assortment of editable and removable effects, such as Drop Shadow, Outer Glow, or Gradient Overlay.

Optimization

Optimization, the preparation of an image for Web output, involves choosing file format, color, and size parameters. If you divide an image into slices, you can then apply different optimization settings to each slice.

Pixels

Pixels, short for "picture elements," are the building blocks that make up a digital image—the tiny individual dots that a digital camera uses to capture a scene or that a computer uses to display an image onscreen. When working in Photoshop and for Web output, you'll need to be aware of the pixel dimensions, or total number of pixels, of an image. For print output, you'll need to be aware of the resolution of your image—the number of pixels per unit of measure (usually per inch, or "pixels per inch").

Preset

A preset is a swatch, brush, gradient, pattern, shape, contour, or style, or a collection of tool settings that you save and store for easy access.

Raw, Camera Raw

Digital cameras capture photos as raw image data; the Camera Raw dialog box in Photoshop lets you apply corrections to your Raw files before you convert and open them.

Selection

A selection is an area of an image that you isolate using a variety of methods; the unselected area is protected from editing. You can create a selection by using a selection tool (e.g., Lasso) or command (e.g., Color Range), by converting a path into a selection, or by loading an alpha channel as a selection. Selections are identified by a "marching ants" marquee. Areas of an image can also be protected by using a layer mask or Quick Mask, in which black or a color designates the protected pixels.

Smart Object, Smart Filter

A Smart Object layer is created manually when you convert one or more layers in an image into a Smart Object; or automatically when you place an Illustrator file, another Photoshop file, or a Camera Raw file into a Photoshop document. If you double-click a Smart Object layer to edit its contents in the original application, then save and close it, the object will update in the Photoshop file (that's the "smart" part). Apply a filter to a Smart Object and it becomes a Smart Filter. ★ Smart Filters can be modified, hidden, or removed at any time, and you can apply multiple Smart Filters to the same Smart Object.

Style

A style is an effect or combination of effects, plus Layers palette settings such as visibility, opacity, and blending mode, that you can save to, store in, and apply via the Styles palette.

Vector

In addition to pixel imagery, Photoshop gives you the tools to create mathematically defined vector paths, shapes, and editable type. Vector objects print at the printer resolution (crisp and sharp), not at the file resolution.

Working smart

Add these techniques to your repertoire gradually as you become familiar with them, and you'll soon become a Photoshop wizard!

Undo

▶ To undo the last modification, choose Edit > **Undo** (Ctrl-Z/Cmd-Z). (Not every command or edit can be undone.)

▶ To undo multiple edits, click a prior state on the **History** palette, or use the **History Brush** tool to restore selective areas. Click the **New Snapshot** button at the bottom of the History palette periodically; then you can click a snapshot thumbnail at any time to revert to that version of your document.

Save time

▶ Use **Bridge** to search for, sort, open, move, copy, place, rename, and delete files, and to activate Automate commands for Photoshop.

▶ Create and save theme-oriented **workspaces,** complete with color-coded menu labels. Collapse the palettes you use least frequently to **icons** to preserve screen space.★

▶ Memorize the **keyboard shortcuts** for frequently used commands and tools. To learn the shortcuts for tools, use the tool tips onscreen or refer to pages 7–9 in this book. We list shortcuts in most of our instructions.

▶ Use **scrubby sliders** to change values quickly: Drag slightly to the left or right on the name or icon for an option that has a value field (such as "Opacity" on the Layers palette). With the pointer in a field, you can also change the value by pressing the up or down **arrow** key.

Stay flexible using layers

▶ Put image components (such as imagery and type) on separate **layers.** Merge layer pairs together periodically to conserve memory, and discard any layers you don't need.

▶ Use **adjustment layers** and **fill layers** to try out tonal and color adjustments or apply color tints without permanently altering the underlying layer.

▶ Apply editable and removable **layer effects.**

Continued on the following page

A *The context menu for editable type*

B *The context menu for a selection*

C *The context menu for the color bar on the Color palette*

➤ Place Camera Raw images or vector objects from Illustrator into Photoshop as **Smart Objects** for easy editing and updating.

➤ Apply filters as **Smart Filters** to Smart Object layers. Like adjustment layers, Smart Filters are editable and removable.

➤ Use **layer comps** to show off variations of a document to your clients without having to open and close separate files.

Save and reuse

➤ Save each collection of layer effects and Layers palette settings as a **style** in the Styles palette for use in any Photoshop file.

➤ Create and save **presets** for brushes, swatches, gradients, type, patterns, shapes, contours, styles—and tools—for use in any Photoshop file.

➤ Save custom color swatches, shapes, brushes, etc. in **libraries** for safekeeping and easy access.

➤ Save a selection to an **alpha** (grayscale) **channel**, then load it as a selection when needed.

Save memory

➤ Choose the Edit > **Purge** submenu commands periodically to regain RAM used for the Clipboard, the Undo command, the History palette, or All (of the above).

➤ Work with your document in RGB Color mode in order to access all the Photoshop commands. To proof the document onscreen (simulate CMYK Color mode), choose View > Proof Setup > Working CMYK. When you're done editing the file, save a copy of it in the proper color mode and minimum resolution and dimensions for your target output device. Remember that vector layers, such as editable type and shapes, output at the printer resolution, not at the file resolution.

USE THE AVAILABLE INFO

➤ Are you unsure what an icon means or a palette or dialog box option does? Rest the pointer on it, and a helpful **tool tip** will pop up onscreen.

➤ Some dialog boxes have a **Description** field that contains information about whichever option your pointer is currently over.

➤ Keep an eye on the **Info** palette for color breakdowns, document data (e.g., dimensions, size, resolution, profile), and tool hints (tips about the currently selected tool).

➤ Use the **Histogram** palette to monitor changes to the tonal ranges in an image as you apply color and tonal adjustments.

Before you start image editing, you need to learn about the Photoshop color basics: channels, document color modes, calibration, color settings, printer profiles—and the important steps of incorporating color management into image editing and output.

Displays, modes, and channels

Onscreen, your Photoshop image is a **bitmap**—a geometric arrangement (mapping) of dots on a rectangular grid. Each dot, or pixel, represents a different color or shade. Drag with a painting tool, such as the Brush, across an area of a layer, and pixels below your pointer will be recolored. With your document at a high zoom level, you can see, and even edit, individual pixels.**A** Bitmap programs like Photoshop are best suited for producing painterly, photographic, or photorealistic images that contain subtle gradations of color, known as continuous tones. The images you edit in Photoshop can originate from a digital camera or scanned photo, from a file you've saved in another application, or from scratch using painting tools and editing commands, such as filters.

To display color images, a computer display projects **red**, **green**, and **blue** (RGB) **light**. Combined in their purest form, these additive primaries produce white light. Send your Photoshop file for commercial, four-color process printing, and your print shop will render the image by using **cyan** (C), **magenta** (M), **yellow** (Y), and **black** (K) inks. Since computer displays use the RGB model, they can only simulate the CMYK inks that are used in commercial printing.

The successful translation of a digital image to a printed one isn't as simple as you might think. To begin with, the same document can look surprisingly different on different displays due to such variables as ambient lighting, display temperature, and even the room color. Plus, many colors that you see in the natural world or that can be displayed onscreen can't be printed (have no ink equivalents), and some colors that can be printed can't be displayed onscreen. Luckily, the color management techniques that we

Continued on the following page

A In this close-up of part the image shown above, you can see individual pixels.

COLOR MANAGEMENT

2

IN THIS CHAPTER

outline in this chapter will help to smooth out the kinks in the color workflow from digital to print.

➤ In Photoshop, you can choose colors using the grayscale, RGB (red-green-blue), HSB (hue-saturation-brightness), CMYK (cyan-magenta-yellow-black), or Lab (lightness, a-component, and b-component) color model, or you can choose colors from a color matching system, such as PANTONE. If you choose a color in Photoshop that isn't within the gamut of printable colors, an exclamation point will appear on the Color palette.**A** Exclamation points will also display on the Info palette if the color currently under the pointer is outside the printable gamut.**B** If you follow our steps for color management, though, you won't have to worry about converting individual colors.

Channels

In Photoshop, images are composed of semitransparent overlays of colored light, called **channels.** For example, images in RGB Color mode have three channels: Red, Green, and Blue. To illustrate, open a color image, then click Red, Green, or Blue on the Channels palette to display only that channel. Click the topmost channel name on the Channels palette to restore the composite display. Only the currently highlighted channel(s) can be edited. Although you can make color adjustments to individual channels, usually you'll be editing all of the channels at once while viewing the multichannel, composite image.

In addition to the core channels discussed above, you can also add two other types of channels. You can save a selection as a mask in a grayscale (alpha) channel, and you can add channels for individual spot colors.**C**

The more channels a document contains, the larger its file storage size. A document in RGB Color mode, which has three channels (Red, Green, and Blue), will be three times larger than the same document in Grayscale mode, which has only one channel. In CMYK Color mode, a document has four channels (Cyan, Magenta, Yellow, and Black) and is even larger.

Document color modes

A document can be converted to, displayed in, and edited in these color modes: **Bitmap, Grayscale, Duotone, Indexed Color, RGB Color, CMYK Color, Lab Color,** or **Multichannel.** You'll use RGB and CMYK most often. To convert a document to a different mode, make a choice from the Image >

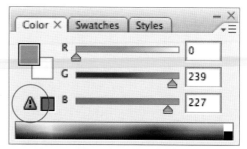

A *Out-of-gamut* indicator on the **Color** palette

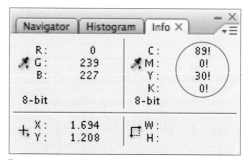

B *Out-of-gamut* indicators on the **Info** palette

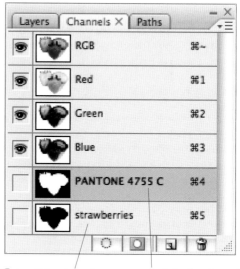

C *An **alpha** channel*   *A **spot color** channel*

Mode submenu. **A** (To access a mode that's dimmed on the menu, you must first convert your file to a different mode as an intermediate step. For example, to be converted to Indexed Color mode, a file must be in RGB Color or Grayscale mode.)

Some mode conversions can cause noticeable color shifts. For example, if you convert a file from RGB Color mode to CMYK Color mode, printable colors will be substituted for the luminous RGB colors. The fewer times a file is converted, the better, as each conversion changes the color more.

Some conversions also flatten layers, such as a conversion to Indexed Color, Multichannel, or Bitmap mode. In other cases, you can click Don't Flatten in an alert dialog box to preserve layers.

The availability of some commands and tool options in Photoshop varies depending on the current document color mode.

Digital cameras and medium- to low-end scanners produce RGB images. For faster editing and in order to access all the filters in Photoshop, keep your files in RGB Color mode. You'll need to convert your files (or copies of your files) to CMYK Color mode only for commercial printing. You can use View > **Proof Setup B** in conjunction with View > **Proof Colors** (Ctrl-Y/Cmd-Y) to preview ("soft-proof") your RGB document in a simulation of CMYK Color mode without performing an actual mode change. Most desktop color inkjet printers, especially those that use six or more ink colors, can process RGB Color files directly from Photoshop.

Images that are saved by high-end scanners in CMYK Color mode should be kept in that mode to preserve their color data. Photoshop CS3 can handle large scans, even those saved with a higher pixel depth of 16 bits or 32 bits per channel—although only limited edits can be made to 32-bit files.

The following is a brief summary of the color modes that you can convert a document to in Photoshop:

In **Bitmap** mode, pixels are only 100% black or 100% white, and no layers, filters, or adjustment commands are available. (To convert a file to this mode, put it into Grayscale mode first.)

In **Grayscale** mode, pixels are black, white, or up to 254 shades of gray (a total of 256). If you convert a file from one of the color modes to Grayscale mode and then save and close it, the luminosity (light and dark) values will remain intact, but the color information will be deleted permanently.

Continued on the following page

DEFAULT CHANNELS PER IMAGE MODE

One	Three	Four
Bitmap	RGB	CMYK
Grayscale	Lab	
Duotone	Multichannel	Multichannel
Indexed Color		

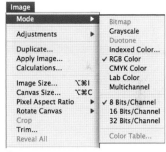

A *The* **Mode** *submenu*

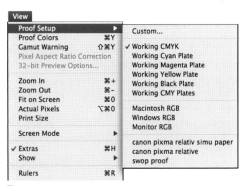

B *The* **Proof Setup** *submenu*

To produce a **duotone**, two or more extra printing plates are added to a grayscale image to enhance its richness and tonal depth. This requires special preparatory steps in Photoshop and expertise on the part of your commercial printer.

Files in **Indexed Color** mode have a single channel and a color table that holds a maximum of 256 colors or shades (8-bit color). The relatively small file sizes of Indexed Color files once made this mode useful for Web output, but it's been surpassed by better methods, such as the Save for Web & Devices dialog box.

RGB Color **A** is the most versatile mode of all and the one you'll use most often. It's the mode in which digital cameras save your photos, the only mode in which all the Photoshop tool options and filters are accessible, and the mode of choice for online output and for export to video and multimedia applications.

In Photoshop, although you can display and edit your files in **CMYK Color** mode, **B** we recommend editing them in RGB Color mode, then converting a copy of the files to CMYK Color mode only when required for color separation or for export to a page layout application.

Lab Color **C** is a three-channel mode that was developed for the purpose of achieving consistency among various devices, such as printers and displays. Lab color files are device-independent, meaning their color definitions stay the same regardless of how a particular output device defines color. The channels represent lightness (the image details), the colors green to red, and the colors blue to yellow; the lightness and color values can be edited independently of one another. Although Photoshop uses Lab Color to produce better conversions between RGB and CMYK color mode, there's rarely a need for users to convert files to Lab Color mode.

Multichannel images contain multiple 256-level grayscale channels. Some Photoshop pros assemble individual channels from several images into one final composite image in this mode. If you convert an image from RGB Color to Multichannel mode, its Red, Green, and Blue channels will be converted to Cyan, Magenta, and Yellow; this may lighten the image and reduce the contrast.

With this foundation in color basics, you're ready to take the plunge into color management.

A *The number of* **channels** *varies with the document color mode. This image is in* **RGB Color** *mode.*

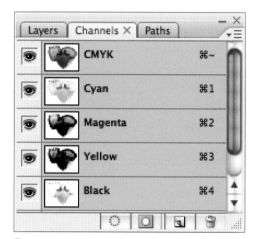

B *CMYK Color* mode

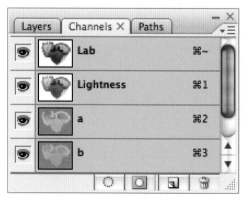

C *Lab Color* mode

Color management basics

Problems with color can creep up on you when various hardware devices and software packages you use treat color differently. If you were to compare how an image looks in an assortment of imaging programs and Web browsers, the colors might look completely different in each case and may not match the picture you originally shot with your digital camera or digitized via a scanner. Print the image, and you'll probably find that your results are different yet again. In some cases, you might find these differences to be slight and unobjectionable, but in other cases, such color changes can wreak havoc with your design and turn a project into a disaster!

A color management system can solve most of these problems by acting as a color interpreter. Such a system knows how each device and program interprets color and will adjust colors where necessary to keep them as consistent as possible as you shift your file among various programs or devices. The applications in the Adobe Creative Suite 3 use standardized ICC (International Color Consortium) profiles to tell your color management system how specific devices use color.

A particular device can capture and reproduce only a limited range (gamut) of colors. This is known as the **color space** of that device. The mathematical description of the color space of each device is called the **color profile.** An input device, such as a camera, attaches its own profile to the files it produces; the color management system uses that profile to define the colors in your document. Photoshop uses the document profile to display and edit document colors; or if the document doesn't have a profile, Photoshop uses the current working space (a color space you choose for Photoshop) instead.

Color management is especially important if you're going to use the same image for multiple purposes, such as for online and print output. Be sure to consult with your prepress service provider or commercial printer (if you're using one) about color management to ensure that your color management workflows work smoothly with theirs.

A straightforward approach to color management

The "meat" of this chapter consists of instructions for choosing color management options, which you should follow before you do any image editing in Photoshop. Our instructions are centered around using **Adobe RGB** as the color space for your image editing work to create color consistency throughout your workflow. We'll show you how to set the color space of your digital camera to Adobe RGB, calibrate your display, specify Adobe RGB as the color space in Photoshop, acquire the proper profiles for your printer and paper type, and use those profiles to soft-proof your picture.

In the Print chapter, we'll show you how color management comes into play when outputting files from a color inkjet printer (a device that expects files to be in RGB color). In this case, the most important step is to choose the correct output profile for your printer. We'll also show you how to choose the appropriate output profiles when outputting to the Web or to a commercial press.

Establishing Adobe RGB as the color space for a digital camera

Most high-end, advanced amateur digital cameras and digital SLR cameras have an onscreen menu that lets you customize how the camera processes digital images. Although we'll use the Canon EOS Digital Rebel/EOS 300D as our representative model for setting a camera to the Adobe RGB color space (see the next page), you'll follow a similar procedure to set the color space for your camera.

If you shoot in JPEG format, you should choose Adobe RGB as the color space for your camera, regardless of which model you have. If you shoot Raw files, these steps are optional; you'll assign the Adobe RGB color space when you convert your photos via the Camera Raw plug-in.

Continued on the following page

To set a camera's color space to Adobe RGB:

1. On the back of the camera, click the **Menu** button to access the menu on the LCD screen, then if necessary, press the **Jump** button to select the **Shooting Menu** tab.**A**

2. Press the down arrow to select the **Parameters** category (some cameras call this category Optimize).**B** Press the **Set** button to move to the submenu on the right (on some cameras, you need to press an arrow key instead).

3. Press the up/down arrow to select **Adobe RGB** (on some cameras you have to choose a Color Mode category first to get to Adobe RGB).**C–D**

4. Press the **Set** button, then press the **Menu** button to exit the Menu screen.

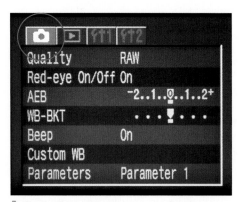

A *On the Canon Menu screen, we select the* ***Shooting Menu*** *tab.*

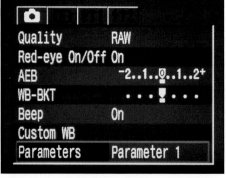

B *We select the* ***Parameters*** *category next, then press* ***Set*** *to get to the submenu.*

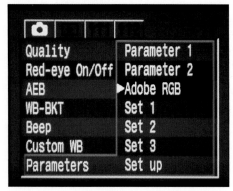

C *We choose* ***Adobe RGB*** *from the submenu.*

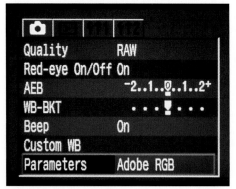

D ***Adobe RGB*** *is now the parameter (color space) for our camera.*

Calibrating your display

Display types

There are two basic types of computer displays: CRT (cathode ray tube, as in a traditional TV set) and LCD (liquid crystal display, or flat panel). The display performance of a **CRT** fluctuates due to its analog technology and the fact that its display phosphors (which produce the glowing dots onscreen) fade over time. Also, it must be calibrated at least once a month using its built-in brightness and contrast controls. A CRT display, can be calibrated reliably for only about 3 years.

An **LCD** display uses a grid of fixed-sized liquid crystals that filter color coming from a back light source. Although you can adjust only the brightness on an LCD (not the contrast), the LCD digital technology offers more reliable color conisistency than a CRT without the characteristic flickering of a CRT. The newest LCD models provide good viewing angles, display accurate color, and use a daylight temperature of 6500K for the white point (see below). They're produced under tighter manufacturing standards than CRTs. Plus, in most cases the color profile that's provided with an LCD display (and that is installed in your system automatically) describes the display characteristics accurately.

Three important settings

Calibrating a display involves adjusting three basic characteristics. You'll set the **brightness** (white level) to a consistent working standard; set the **contrast** (dark level) to the maximum value; and finally, make sure that a **neutral gray** (gray level) is displayed using equal values of R, G, and B. To adjust these three characteristics, calibration programs evaluate the display's white point, black point, and gamma:

➤ The **white point** data enables the display to project a pure white that matches an industry-standard color temperature. Photographers usually use a D65/6500K temperature setting for the white point.

➤ The **black point** is the darkest black a display can project. All other dark shades will be lighter than darkest black to ensure the proper display of shadow details.

➤ The **gamma** is the onscreen brightness of the midtones, exactly midway between pure black and pure white. This setting affects how the rest of the midtone shades are distributed, not the lightest or darkest shades. Photography experts recommend using a gamma of 2.2 in Windows and the Macintosh.

You can use a software calibration program or calibration hardware to produce a display profile with the proper white point, black point, and gamma data settings. The Adobe color management system, in turn, will use this data to display colors in your Photoshop document.

In the next section, we'll step Mac users through basic display calibration procedures using the Displays utility in the Mac operating system. Windows users will need to purchase a hardware calibration device, as Adobe has discontinued shipping the Adobe Gamma utility.

Pssst! How the pros do it

To achieve precise calibration, industry professionals use hardware gadgets such as colorimeters and spectrophotometers. Instead of relying on subjective "eyeball" judgements, the colorimeters and step-by-step wizard tutorials that are included with these devices let you calibrate your display more accurately.

The good news is that these hardware gadgets are more affordable than they used to be. A "starter" hardware version will run you somewhere between $250 and $350; higher-end devices are more costly. Among the moderately priced calibrators, our informal reading of hardware reviews and other industry publications yielded ColorVision's Spyder2Pro Studio and GretagMacbeth's Eye-One Display 2 as the current favorites (we use Spyder2Pro).

➤ For an in-depth, step-by-step guide to using the Spyder2Pro colorimeter, see *Print Like a Pro: A Digital Photographer's Guide* by Jon Canfield (Peachpit Press, 2006).

Continued on the following page

The first step toward achieving color consistency is to **calibrate** your **display** (monitor) by adjusting the contrast, brightness, gamma, color balance, and white point. In the Mac OS, you'll use the operating system's display calibration utility in System Preferences > Displays.

The Displays utility generates an ICC profile, which the Mac operating system installs and refers to in order to display colors accurately onscreen. You need only calibrate your display and save the settings as an ICC profile once; thereafter, the profile will be available to all applications and color management systems.

To calibrate your display in the Mac OS:

1. If you have a CRT display, let it warm up for 30 minutes to allow the display to stabilize. For a CRT or LCD, make the desktop pattern light gray and establish a level of room lighting that you can count on remaining constant.

2. Choose Apple > **System Preferences**, click **Displays**, click the **Color** tab, then click **Calibrate**. The Display Calibrator Assistant appears onscreen. **A**

   Check **Expert Mode** to access the advanced options. (Beginners, don't worry, you can handle this!)

   Note: Some options discussed in the following steps may not apply to LCD (flat-panel) displays.

3. Click **Continue** to advance to the next options panel.

4. CRTs only: For **Display Adjustment**, leave the contrast at the maximum setting, but adjust the brightness until the light gray oval is barely visible and the background looks like solid black. **B** Click Continue.

5. For both CRT and LCD displays, in the **Determine your display's native response** screen, a gray square represents a combined grayscale reading of your display. To adjust the luminance, move the slider until the solid gray apple shape matches the surrounding, stripey box (try squinting). You'll march through a series of five screens in which you adjust the brightness of the gray shape (the left square) and remove any hint of color (the right square). Click Continue.

A *This screen in the **Display Calibrator Assistant** is the starting point for calibrating your display in the Mac OS.*

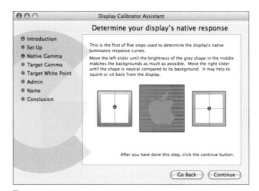

B *The first step in calibrating a **CRT** display is to set the **contrast** and **brightness** to the proper values.*

6. For **Select a target gamma**, move the slider to 2.2,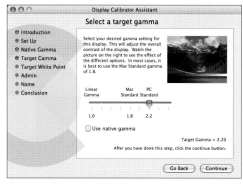 the standard gamma used in the image-editing industry and for Apple Cinema displays. Click Continue.

7. For **Select a target white point**, move the slider to a target white point based on the kind of work you'll be doing.**B** Photographers use D65, and you should, too. Click Continue.

8. In the Administrator options screen, check **Allow other users to use this calibration** to share your new profile with the other users of your machine. Click Continue.

9. Finally, name the profile, click Continue, then click Done. It will be saved in Users/[user name]/Library/ColorSync/Profiles (or if you checked "Allow other users..." it will be stored in Library/ColorSync/Profiles/Displays) and can be accessed via the RGB menu in the Working Spaces area of the Color Settings dialog box (we'll explore that dialog box in the next section).

A *For a CRT or LCD display, choose a **gamma** setting.*

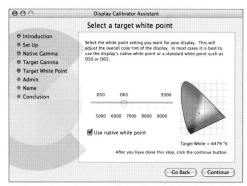

B *Choose the **target white point** that's appropriate for the type of work you do.*

CALIBRATE, THEN RECALIBRATE

If, after calibrating your display, you adjust the display's brightness and contrast settings or change the room lighting (for example, by opening or closing your window shades), remember to **recalibrate** it!

FINDING THE CALIBRATION UTILITY

In the Mac OS, choose Apple > System Preferences, click **Displays,** then in the Displays panel, click the **Color** tab.

Choosing a color space for Photoshop

Continuing with our color management steps, you'll use the Color Settings dialog box to set the color space for Photoshop. Note: These are generic instructions. If you want to get up and running quickly in the Adobe RGB color space without wading through all these options, follow the instructions in the sidebar on the next page.

To choose predefined color management settings:

1. Choose Edit > **Color Settings** (Ctrl-Shift-K/Cmd-Shift-K). The Color Settings dialog box opens (**A**, next page).

2. Choose a preset from the **Settings** menu (we'll summarize the four basic presets):

   Monitor Color sets the RGB working space to your display profile. This is a good choice for video output, but not for print output.

   North America General Purpose 2 meets the requirements for screen and print output in the U.S. and Canada. All profile warnings are off.

   North America Prepress 2 manages color to conform with common press conditions in the U.S. The default RGB color space assigned to this setting is Adobe RGB. When CMYK documents are opened, their values are preserved.

   North America Web/Internet is designed for online output. All RGB images are converted to the sRGB color space.

3. The **Working Spaces** control how RGB and CMYK colors will be treated in a document that lacks an embedded profile. You can either leave these settings as is or choose other options (the RGB options are discussed below). For the CMYK setting, you should ask your output service provider which working space to choose. You can also specify a dot gain value or gamma setting for Gray (grayscale) images.

   Choose one of these RGB color spaces:

   Monitor RGB [current monitor name] sets the RGB working space to your display profile, which is useful if you know that other applications you'll be using for your project don't support color management. Keep in mind, however, that if you share files that use your monitor profile (as the color space) with

---

> **DOCUMENT-SPECIFIC COLOR**
>
> Photoshop supports **document-specific color,** meaning that each document keeps its own color profile. The profile controls how colors in the file are previewed onscreen, edited, and converted on output. For documents that lack an embedded profile, Photoshop generates previews using the current working space.

another user, their monitor profile will be substituted for the RGB working space. This may undermine the color consistency that you're aiming for.

ColorSync RGB (Mac OS only) matches the Photoshop RGB space to the space specified in the Apple ColorSync Utility. This can be the profile you created using System Preferences > Displays when you calibrated your display. If you share this configuration with another user, it will utilize the ColorSync space specified in that user's system.

Adobe RGB (1998) contains a wide range of colors and is useful when converting RGB images to CMYK images. As you may have guessed by now, this is our preferred choice for print output, but it isn't a good choice for online output.

Apple RGB is useful if you need to work with older desktop publishing files for output to Mac displays, as it reflects the characteristics of older standard Apple 13-inch monitors.

ColorMatch RGB contains a smaller range of colors than Adobe RGB (1998), but because it matches the color space of Radius Pressview displays, it's useful for print work.

ProPhoto RGB contains a very wide range of colors and is useful for output to high-end dye sublimation and inkjet printers.

sRGB IEC61966-2.1 is a good choice for Web output, as it reflects the settings on the average computer display. Many hardware and software manufacturers are using this as the default space for scanners, low-end printers, and software. Note that for prepress work, Adobe RGB and ColorMatch RGB are the preferred choices.

4. Click OK.

FAST TRACK TO ADOBE RGB (1998)

If you use Photoshop primarily to produce images for print output on a commercial or color inkjet printer — and you've followed our instructions for color management so far — you can make one simple choice in the Color Settings dialog and be done with it! Choose Edit > **Color Settings,** then choose **Settings: North America Prepress 2** (foreign readers, choose an equivalent for your output device and geographic location). This preset changes the RGB working space to **Adobe RGB (1998)** and sets the color management policies to the safe choice of **Preserve Embedded Profiles** (so each file you open in Photoshop keeps its own profile).

Note: The Adobe RGB color space includes more colors in the CMYK print range than the sRGB color space, which is designed for online output, does. For some reason, Adobe feels compelled to keep sRGB as the default RGB working space (as listed in Edit > Color Settings), but it can spell disaster for print output.

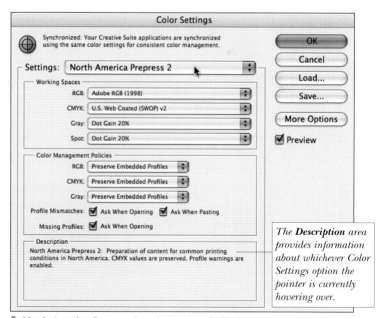

A *North America Prepress 2 is chosen from the* **Settings** *menu in the* **Color Settings** *dialog box.*

Synchronizing color settings

If the color settings in another Adobe Creative Suite program (e.g., Illustrator or InDesign) don't match the current settings in Photoshop, an alert will display in the Color Settings dialog box.**A** If you don't own the complete Adobe Creative Suite, you'll have to start up the errant application and fix its color settings by hand. If you're fortunate enough to have the whole suite, you can use the Suite Color Settings dialog box in Bridge to **synchronize** the **color settings** of all of the programs in the suite.

Before synchronizing the color settings via Bridge, make sure you've chosen the proper settings in Photoshop.

To synchronize color settings using Bridge:

1. In Bridge, choose Edit > **Creative Suite Color Settings** (Ctrl-Shift-K/Cmd-Shift-K). The Suite Color Settings dialog box opens.**B**

2. Click the settings preset you chose in Photoshop, then click **Apply.** Bridge will change (synchronize) the color settings of the other Adobe Creative Suite applications to match the selected preset.

MATCHING SETTINGS

The presets in the **Suite Color Settings** dialog box will be same as on the **Settings** menu in the **Color Settings** dialog box (see page 36) if Show Expanded List of Color Settings Files is unchecked in the former and fewer options are displaying (you don't click More Options) in the latter.

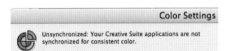

A *This alert in the* **Color Setttings** *dialog box in Photoshop tells us that the color settings in our Creative Suite applications* **aren't synchronized** *(don't match).*

B *Use the* **Suite Color Settings** *dialog box to* **synchronize** *the color settings of all the applications in the Adobe Creative Suite.*

Customizing your color policies

The current **color management policies** govern whether Photoshop honors or overrides the document settings if the color profile in a file you open or import doesn't match the current color settings in Photoshop. If you chose the North America Prepress 2 setting in the Color Settings dialog box, as per the sidebar on page 37, the Ask When Opening policy (the safest one, in our opinion) is already chosen for you, and you can skip these instructions.

To customize your color management policies:

1. Choose Edit > **Color Settings** (Ctrl-Shift-K/ Cmd-Shift-K). The Color Settings dialog box opens.**A**

2. From the **Color Management Policies** menus, choose an option for files that you open or import into Photoshop:

   Off to prevent Photoshop from color-managing the files.

   Preserve Embedded Profiles if you expect to work with both color-managed and noncolor-managed documents. Each file will keep its own profile.

Convert to Working... to have all documents that you open/import into Photoshop adopt the current color working space. This is usually the best choice for Web output.

3. Do any of the following optional steps:

   For **Profile Mismatches**, if you check **Ask When Opening**, Photoshop will display an alert if the color profile in a file you're opening doesn't match the current working space. Via the alert, you'll have the option to override the current color management policy for each file.

   Check **Ask When Pasting** to have Photoshop display an alert if it encounters a color profile mismatch when you paste color imagery into a document. The alert lets you override your color management policy when pasting.

   For files with **Missing Profiles**, check **Ask When Opening** to have Photoshop display an alert with an option to assign a profile.

4. Click OK.

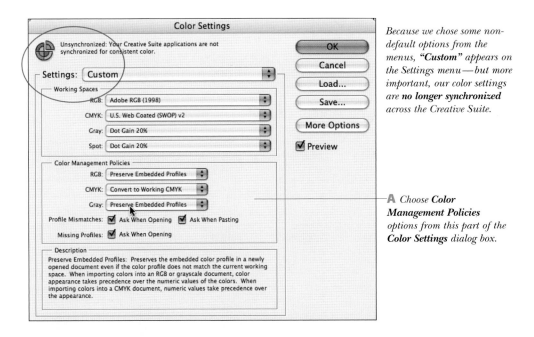

*Because we chose some non-default options from the menus, "Custom" appears on the Settings menu—but more important, our color settings are **no longer synchronized** across the Creative Suite.*

A *Choose **Color Management Policies** options from this part of the **Color Settings** dialog box.*

Saving custom color settings

For desktop color printing, we recommended choosing the North American Prepress 2 color setting; for commercial printing, let the pros supply the proper color settings. Ask your print shop to send you a .csf file with all the correct Working Spaces and Color Management Policies settings for their particular press. Then all you need to do is install that custom color settings file in the proper location, as per the instructions below, and you'll be able to access it via the Settings menu in the Color Settings dialog box.

To save custom color settings as defaults for the Creative Suite:

1. In Windows, put the file in Program Files\Common Files\Adobe\Color\Settings.

   In the Mac OS, put the file in User/[user name]/Library/Application Support/Adobe/Color/Settings.

2. To access the newly saved settings file, relaunch Photoshop, open the Color Settings dialog box, then choose the .csf file name from the Settings menu.

If your print shop gives you a list of settings to choose in the Color Settings dialog box—but not a .csf file—you can **save** that collection of **settings** as a **.csf** file, as per these instructions.

To save custom color settings:

1. Choose Edit > **Color Settings** (Ctrl-Shift-K/Cmd-Shift-K). The Color Settings dialog box opens.

2. Enter the required settings by choosing and checking the appropriate options.

3. Click **Save** and enter a file name (it's a good idea to include the type of printer in the name), keeping the .csf extension and default location (the Settings folder). Click Save.

4. Click OK to exit the Color Settings dialog box.

Acquiring printer profiles

Thus far, we've helped you set your camera to the Adobe RGB color space, calibrate your display, and specify Adobe RGB as the color space for Photoshop. Next we'll show you how to **acquire** the proper **printer profile(s)** so you can incorporate color management into your specific printing scenario.

To download a printer profile:

Most printer manufacturers have a website from which you can download either an ICC profile for a specific printer/paper combination or a printer driver that contains a collection of specific ICC printer/paper profiles. Be sure to choose a profile that matches the particular printer/paper combination you'll be using.

1. On the following page, we step you through the websites for two manufacturers of widely used printers: **Epson** (Epson.com) **A–C** and **Canon** (Canon.com).**D–F**

   You can also download an ICC profile for a specific printer/paper combo from the website for a paper manufacturer, such as illford.com or crane.com/museo.

   Note: The profiles for the newest printer models probably aren't available yet on these sites.

2. After visiting the website, follow the installation instructions for whichever file you downloaded. In our section on proofing colors, we'll show you how to use it.

PROFILES FOR THE PIXMA IP 6600 INKJET

The names of the Canon ICC profiles tend to be cryptic and abbreviated, as shown below. We've decoded a partial list of the profiles that install with the Canon PIXMA iP 6600 driver. Choose the profile that matches your paper choice; for a high- or top-quality image, choose a profile with a quality setting of 1.

PR1 Photo Paper Pro, custom quality setting 1

SP1 Photo Paper Plus Glossy, custom quality setting 1

MP2 Matte Finish paper, custom quality setting 2

FINDING A PROFILE FOR AN EPSON INKJET PRINTER

A *On the Epson home page, choose* **Drivers & Support** > **Printers.**

B *Click* **Ink Jet** *under* **Printers,** *then choose your printer model from the list of printers.*

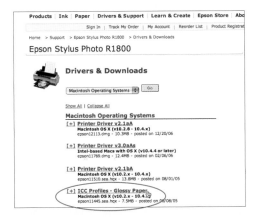

C *Click the* **Drivers & Downloads** *option for your system, click the* **ICC** *profile that matches your printer/ paper combo, and follow the instructions.*

FINDING A PROFILE FOR A CANON INKJET PRINTER

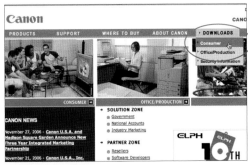

D *On the Canon home page, choose* **Downloads** > **Consumer.**

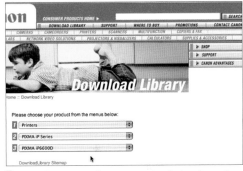

E *From the menus, choose a category (printer), product type (printer series), and printer model.*

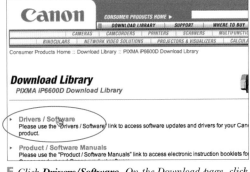

F *Click* **Drivers/Software.** *On the Download page, click the appropriate printer driver for your system. The driver will install the profiles automatically.*

Changing color profiles

When a file's profile doesn't match the current working space (Adobe RGB, in our case) or is missing a color profile altogether, you can use the **Assign Profile** command to assign the proper profile. You may notice visible color shifts if the color data of the file is reinterpreted to match the new profile, but rest assured, the color data in the actual image is preserved. Do keep Preview checked, though, so you can see what you're getting into.

To change or delete a file's color profile:

1. Choose Edit > **Assign Profile**. The Assign Profile dialog box opens.**A** Check Preview. If the file contains layers, an alert may appear, warning you that the appearance of the layers may change; click OK.

2. Click one of the following:

   To delete the color profile, click **Don't Color Manage This Document**.

   To assign your current working space to the file, click **Working** [document color mode and the name of the working space you're using]. If you followed our instructions for color management, you've already specified Adobe RGB as the Working RGB space, but you can click this option for any photo or scan that wasn't captured using the Adobe RGB color space.

   To assign a different profile, click **Profile**, then choose a profile that differs from your working space.

3. Click OK.

The **Convert to Profile** command lets you preview a conversion to an assortment of output profiles and intents, then converts the color data to the chosen profile. Note! This command performs a mode conversion and changes the color data in your file.

To convert a file's color profile:

1. Choose Edit > **Convert to Profile**. The Convert to Profile dialog box opens.**B** Check Preview.

2. From the **Destination Space: Profile** menu, choose a profile to convert the file to (it doesn't have to be the current working space).

3. Under Conversion Options, choose an **Intent** (see the sidebar on page 44).

WHERE THE CURRENT PROFILE IS LISTED

► If you choose **Document Profile** from the status bar menu at the bottom of the application/document window, the current profile will appear on the status bar.

► In the Save As dialog box, if you save a file in a format that supports embedded profiles, such as Photoshop (PSD) or Photoshop PDF, you can check **ICC Profile...** (Windows)/**Embed Color Profile...** (Mac) to embed the profile with the file—if one has been assigned. In the Print dialog box, the profile appears in the print area next to "Document."

A Use the **Assign Profile** dialog box to either delete a *color profile* or assign a new one.

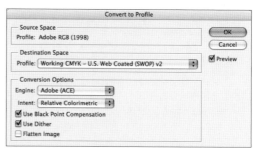

B Use the **Convert to Profile** dialog box to **convert** your document to a different color profile. In this case, we're switching from the Adobe RGB profile to our working CMYK profile for a standard web press that uses coated paper.

---

4. Leave the default Engine as **Adobe (ACE)** and keep the **Use Black Point Compensation** and **Use Dither** options checked.

5. *Optional:* Check **Flatten Image** to merge all layers and adjustment layers.

6. Click OK.

Proofing colors onscreen

In this final step in color management, you'll create a **custom proof setting** for your specific **inkjet** printer and paper, which you'll use to view a soft proof (simulation) of your print output. Although the screen proof isn't perfectly accurate, it does give you a rough idea of how your colors will look without costing you a penny.

To proof an inkjet print onscreen:

1. From the View > **Proof Setup** submenu, choose **Custom**. The Customize Proof Condition dialog box opens.**A**

2. You'll choose custom proofing settings for your output device. Check Preview, then from the **Device to Simulate** menu, choose the color profile for your inkjet printer and paper (this is the profile you either downloaded from a website or installed with your printer driver file).

3. Uncheck **Preserve RGB Numbers,** if available. Photoshop will simulate how the colors will look when converted to the output profile. This option is available only when the color mode of the output profile that you chose from the Device to Simulate menu matches that of the current file (e.g., if your image is in RGB Color mode and will be output on an RGB printer).

4. Choose a **Rendering Intent** to control how colors will change as the image is shifted from one profile to another (see the sidebar on the next page). We recommend choosing either Perceptual or Relative Colorimetric, but you can evaluate each one via the preview.

Check **Black Point Compensation** to allow adjustments to be made for differences in black points among different color spaces. With this option chosen, the full dynamic range of the image color space is mapped to the full dynamic range of the output device (printer) color space. With this option off, blacks in the image may display or print as grays. We recommend checking this option when outputting to an inkjet printer.

5. *Optional:* For **Display Options (On-Screen),** check Simulate Paper Color to preview the white of the printing paper as defined in the printer profile; or for printing on uncoated paper, check Simulate Black Ink to preview the full range of black values that the printer can produce.

6. Click **Save** to save your custom proof setup. Enter a name, keep the .psf extension, and keep the location as the default Proofing folder. Saved proof setups are listed on the Customize Proof Condition menu and at the bottom of the View > Proof Setup submenu.

7. Click OK. View > **Proof Colors** will be checked automatically to let you see the soft proof. Also, the Device to Simulate profile will be listed in the document title bar.

Remember, the Proof Setup options control only how Photoshop simulates colors onscreen. Colors in the actual file aren't converted to the chosen profile until you convert the document color mode (e.g., from RGB to CMYK) or send your file to an inkjet printer.

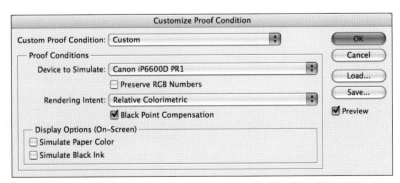

A *To create a soft proof of our document, in the* **Customize Proof Condition** *dialog box, we've chosen the profile for our Canon Pixma inkjet printer as the* **Device to Simulate.**

Via one of the four presets on the **Proof Setup** submenu, you can soft-proof the colors in your RGB file onscreen to simulate what they'll look like when printed using CMYK inks or when viewed online on a Windows or Mac display.

To proof colors for commercial printing or online output:

1. From the View > **Proof Setup** submenu, choose the preset for the output display type that you want Photoshop to simulate:

   Working CMYK to simulate colors for whichever commercial press is currently chosen on the CMYK menu under Working Spaces in Edit > Color Settings.

   Macintosh RGB or **Windows RGB** to simulate colors for online output using the Mac gamma (1.8) or Windows gamma (2.2) as the proofing space.

   Monitor RGB to soft-proof colors using the custom display profile for your monitor.

2. View > **Proof Colors** will be checked automatically. Uncheck it to turn off soft-proofing at any time (Ctrl-Y/Cmd-Y).

Moving on

Congratulations! You completed the first part of the color management workflow. You set your camera to the Adobe RGB color space, calibrated your display, specified Adobe RGB as the color space for Photoshop, acquired the profile for your inkjet printer model, assigned the Adobe RGB profile to any files that didn't use that color space at the outset, and created a soft-proof setting for your particular inkjet printer and paper using those profiles.

What's left? You'll need to focus on color management again when you prepare your file for printing. In the Print chapter, we'll show you how to let Photoshop handle color conversions for an inkjet printer using the same printer profiles you used for the soft proof. The benefit of using a color management workflow is that it keeps colors more consistent from camera to display to printout. Now you can use Photoshop features to enhance images from your camera or scanner, knowing that the colors in your printout will more closely match what you're viewing onscreen. In the next chapter, you'll learn about digital cameras and creating Photoshop documents.

THE RENDERING INTENTS

➤ **Perceptual** changes colors in a way that seems natural to the human eye, while attempting to preserve the appearance of the overall image. It's a good choice for continuous-tone images.

➤ **Saturation** changes colors with the intent of preserving vivid colors, but compromises color fidelity in order to do so. It's a good choice for charts and business graphics.

➤ **Absolute Colorimetric** maintains color accuracy only for colors that fall within the destination color gamut (i.e., color range of your printer) but sacrifices the accuracy of out-of-gamut colors.

➤ **Relative Colorimetric,** the default intent for all the Adobe predefined settings in the Color Settings dialog box, compares the white, or highlight, of your document's color space to the white of the destination color space (the white of the paper, for a printer), shifting colors where needed. This is the best Intent choice for documents in which most of the colors fall within the color range of your printer (the destination gamut), because it preserves most of the original colors.

Note: Consult your printer manual when choosing a rendering intent. For example, some inkjet printers favor Perceptual over Relative Colorimetric.

We start this chapter off with a few basic pointers on buying a digital camera and shooting digital photos. Then you'll learn how to download your digital photos, calculate an appropriate resolution for a file, learn about scanning software, create a new document, create document presets, use the Place command, save and copy your files, and close up shop.

Although Photoshop lets you create, open, edit, and save your files in over a dozen different formats, **A–B** on a day-to-day basis you'll probably use only a handful of those formats, such as TIFF, GIF, JPEG, EPS, Photoshop PDF, and PSD (the native Photoshop file format). The Large Document format, or PSB (nicknamed "Photoshop Big"), is just for huge files; see the sidebar on page 55.

Because Photoshop reads so many different file formats, you can use the program to open images from many sources, such as digital cameras, scanners, drawing applications, and video captures. You can edit a single image, create a montage of imagery from multiple files, or create images entirely within Photoshop by using brushes, filters, and other commands. In the next chapter, you'll learn how to open existing files.

Using digital cameras

Digital cameras are fast becoming the primary source of imagery for Photoshop users. Pictures that are digitized by a camera can be upoaded directly to a computer, thus eliminating the need for scanning.

Continued on the following page

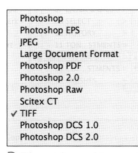

A *Files can be saved in any of these* ***formats*** *in* ***Windows.***

B *Files can be saved in any of these* ***formats*** *in the* ***Mac OS.***

Buying a digital camera

If you're shopping for a digital camera, the first step is to figure out which model suits your output requirements and budget. Camera manufacturers usually list the resolution of a model as width and height dimensions in pixels (such as 3000 pixels x 2000 pixels). If you multiply the two values, you'll arrive at a number in the millions. That number is the camera's **megapixel value**, which is the number of pixels the camera captures. If your camera captures enough pixels, you'll be able to print high-quality closeups and enlargements of your photos, so the megapixel value is one of the key factors to consider when deciding which model to buy.

Compact, inexpensive "point-and-shoot" cameras offer few or no manual controls and have a resolution of 3 to 5 megapixels. They capture enough detail to produce decent quality 4" x 6" prints (not larger) and acceptable Web output.

Advanced amateur camera models have a resolution of 5 to 8 megapixels. You can get high-quality 8" x 10" prints from these cameras, and they offer more manual controls.

Professional camera models (such as digital SLRs) have a resolution of 8 to 11 megapixels or higher and can produce high-quality 11" x 14" prints or larger—but they're costly. The digital light sensors in such cameras are superior to the sensors in the lesser cameras and thus can capture higher-quality and more precise pixel data.

The very high megapixel cameras aren't for everyone—and not just because of their high price tag. Images with a high megapixel count have larger file sizes and longer upload times from camera to computer, and require a larger hard drive for storage. (See our comparison of megapixels and print size on page 52.) Unless you often print large photos (11" x 14" or larger) or tend to crop your pictures, a 6- to 8-megapixel camera will be more appropriate for your needs.

Aside from the megapixel count, look for a camera with a large digital sensor chip (a larger chip makes for greater detail and less visual "noise"), and make sure the camera can accommodate a wide variety of lenses.

To learn more about digital cameras, we recommend the *Digital Photography Field Guide* by Baron & Peck (Peachpit Press) and *Complete*

Digital Photography by Ben Long (Charles River Media). You could also do a Google search for "digital camera field guide."

Shooting digital photographs

You've purchased or borrowed a camera—now you need to know how to use it. To get the best-quality photographs, choose your camera settings wisely. Here are some basic guidelines:

➤ Medium and high-end digital cameras let you choose an **ISO** setting, which controls the sensitivity of the camera's digital sensor to light (comparable to film speed in film photography). High ISO settings tend to produce digital noise in low-light areas, so try to choose the minimum ISO setting that still lets you get the desired exposure.

➤ Decide whether to have your camera capture the photos in the **JPEG** format or as unprocessed **Raw** files.*

➤ Choose a **color space** for your camera: sRGB for onscreen or Web output; Adobe RGB for print output.

➤ For JPEGs, choose a **white balance** setting that's appropriate for the lighting conditions in which you're shooting photos; the camera will process the image data based on this setting. For Raw files, ignore the white balance setting, as the images won't be processed inside the camera.

➤ If your camera has a **histogram** display (read our discussion of histograms on pages 178–179), use the histogram to interpret the correctness of your **exposure** before snapping the shutter. Don't deliberately over- or underexpose your photos. If you overexpose them, too much detail will be lost from the highlight areas; if you underexpose them (stop down too much), too much detail will be lost from the shadows. Remember, Photoshop can process and adjust only the details that your camera captures.

Regardless of whether you shoot JPEG or Raw photos, exposure deficiencies, color casts, and other imaging problems can be corrected via the Camera Raw dialog box, then further corrected via adjustment commands in Photoshop.

Each camera model produces its own version of a Raw file. We'll refer to such files collectively as "Raw files."

Downloading photos

When you use a digital camera, your photos are stored in a removable memory card—most likely a CompactFlash (CF) or Secure Digital (SD) card. To download images from your camera to a computer, you'll need to use a USB or Firewire cable, depending on which connection your camera supports. (Of the two, Firewire is faster.) If you want to be able to shoot, store, and download photos without having to tether your camera to a computer, you can remove the memory card and insert it into a card reader device, then download from the card reader to your computer via a USB cable.

When you download images from a camera, your system's default application for acquiring images launches automatically. In Windows XP, the default application is the Scanner and Camera Wizard; in Windows Vista, it's the Importing Pictures and Video Wizard; and in the Mac OS, the default application is either iPhoto or Image Capture. Image Capture can download Raw photos, and by the time you read this, maybe iPhoto can, too.

Not to be outdone, Adobe now includes the **Photo Downloader** application with Bridge.

To download photos via a card reader and the Photo Downloader: ★

1. Take the card out of your camera and insert it into the appropriate slot in the card reader.

2. Plug the card reader into your computer. If the default system application for acquiring photos launches, exit/quit that application.

3. Launch Bridge, then do the following:

   In Windows, click **Adobe Bridge CS3 Photo Downloader** in the Autoplay window.

   In the Mac OS, choose File > **Get Photos from Camera.**

   The Photo Downloader dialog box opens.**A** If an alert dialog box appears and you want to make Photo Downloader the default capture application, click Yes; otherwise, click No (see also page 392).

4. From the **Get Photos from** menu in the Source area, select your card reader.

5. In the **Import Settings** area, do the following:

   To change the save location, click **Browse/Choose**, then navigate to the desired folder. Click OK/Choose again to select that folder and return to the Downloader dialog box.

A *The **Photo Downloader, Standard** dialog*

To create a new subfolder (within the folder you just selected): choose a naming convention from the **Create Subfolder(s)** menu; or choose Custom Name and enter your own folder name (or choose None for no new subfolder).

Optional: To assign your digital images recognizable names and shorter sequential numbers instead of the long default number, choose Custom Name from the Rename Files menu, then enter a name and a starting number. A sample of your entries will display in the Example field.

Note: In some camera models, each Raw photo is paired with a .thm file that contains nonessential image data that you don't need to download; this .thm file will be hidden in Bridge. If you use the Rename option, each downloaded .thm file will take up a number in the number sequence, producing gaps in the sequence. If this bothers you, choose Do Not Rename Files from the Rename Files menu and use the Batch Rename command in Bridge to rename your files instead.

Continued on the following page

Check **Open Adobe Bridge** to have the photos display in Bridge when the download is completed.

We highly recommend that you check **Save Copies to** and click **Browse/Choose** to send copies of your photos to a designated folder.

6. If you want to download only some of the photos from your memory card, click **Advanced Dialog** to switch to the larger Advanced dialog box.**A** Below the thumbnail window, click **UnCheck All**, then check the box below each photo you want to download. Or click, then Shift-click a sequence of photos, then check the box for one of them; a check mark will appear below each selected photo.

Optional: In the Apply Metadata area, enter Author and Copyright info to be added to the metadata of all downloaded photos (this metadata info will display in Bridge).

➤ To redisplay the Standard dialog box at any time, click Standard Dialog.

7. Click **Get Photos** to start the download process. When the downloading is finished, the Photo Downloader dialog box is dismissed automatically. If you checked the Open Adobe Bridge option, your photos will now display in a new window in Bridge. Don't worry about viewing your image thumbnails or opening files just yet. You'll learn how to do that in the next chapter.

8. Now that you're done with Photo Downloader, you should insert a blank CD ROM disk and burn the copies of your photo files to the CD as a permanent backup copy. (In the Mac OS, you can do this via drag-and-drop right in the Finder.) See your system Help files to learn how to copy files to a CD.

A *This **Advanced** dialog of the **Photo Downloader** contains many of the same options as the Standard dialog, plus metadata features and the option to select which photos will be downloaded.*

16 Bits/Channel mode

In Photoshop, you have a choice of working with your files in 8, 16, or 32 Bits/Channel mode (Image > Mode submenu). There are many advantages to working with your files in 16 Bits/Channel versus 8 Bits/Channel mode, and few advantages to working with 32-bits/channel files—at least not yet.

The wider the dynamic color range of the input device, the finer the subtleties of color and shade it can capture. Most advanced amateur and professional digital SLR cameras capture a minimum of 12 bits of accurate data per channel. Like cameras, scanners range widely in quality. Whereas consumer-level scanners can capture 10 bits of accurate data per channel, high-end professional scanners can capture up to 16 bits of accurate data per channel.

You can't get good-quality output unless you capture a wide tonal range at the outset. Shadow areas in particular are notoriously hard to capture well. Start off with a high-resolution scan or a photo from a digital camera that can capture 12 to 16 bits per channel, and you've got a head start, because the file will contain an abundance of pixels in all levels of the tonal spectrum.

You also can't get good-quality output unless the full tonal range is preserved as you edit your file. The extra pixels in 16-bit images help mitigate the reduction in image quality that editing and resampling commands in Photoshop can cause to your file.**A–B** The tonal adjustment commands in particular, such as Levels and Curves, remove pixel data and change the distribution of pixels across the tonal spectrum. In 8-bit images, such changes will be visible on high-end print output, whereas

16-bit images won't show signs of pixel loss even after destructive edits because they contain an ample number of pixels in all parts of the tonal spectrum.

To summarize, here are basic facts about 16-bit files that you need to know:

➤ Photoshop can open 16-bit files in CMYK or RGB mode.

➤ 16-bit files can be saved in the following widely-used formats: Photoshop (.psd), Large Document (.psb), PDF (.pdf), PNG (.png), TIFF (.tif), and JPEG2000.

➤ With only a few restrictions, 16-bit images can be successfully edited and adjusted in Photoshop. Most of the filters on the Blur, Noise, Render, Sharpen, and Other submenus on the Filter menu are available, as well as the Distort > Lens Correction filter, but filters on the other submenus are not. The Art History brush isn't available (no great loss, as this tool just adds distortion).

➤ For print output, your output service provider may request that you convert your 16-bit images to 8-bit (choose Image > Mode > 8 Bits/Channel).

And finally, if system or storage limitations prevent you from working with 16-bit images, we recommend this two-stage approach: Perform your initial tonal corrections (such as Levels and Curves adjustments) on the 16-bit image, then convert it to 8-bit for further editing.

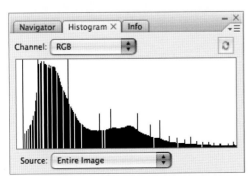

A *As a result of a Levels command adjustment, this* **8-bit** *image exhibits signs of tonal degradation (spikes and gaps)…*

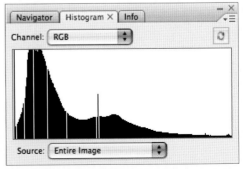

B *…whereas after the same Levels adjustment in this* **16-bit** *version of the same image, smooth tonal transitions are preserved.*

Calculating the file resolution

Resolution for print

Digital cameras preserve either all the pixels they capture (in Raw files) or a portion of the pixels they capture (in small, medium, or large JPEGs). Using scanner software, you can set the input resolution to control the number of pixels the device captures.

High-resolution images contain more pixels, and thus finer detail, but also have larger file sizes, take longer to render onscreen, require more processing time for edits, and take longer to print. Low-resolution images, on the other hand, look coarse and jagged and lack detail when printed. Luckily, there are methods for changing the resolution value of a digital file, because you don't want it to be larger or smaller than you need for your intended output device. Your file should have the proper resolution to obtain the desired output quality—but not much higher.

➤ When opening Raw digital photos, you'll set the output resolution in the **Camera Raw** dialog box (see page 233).

➤ For JPEG photos, you'll set the image resolution in the **Image Size** dialog box (see page 92) after opening the file in Photoshop.

➤ When scanning, you'll set the image resolution via the **scanning software.**

The print resolution for digitized images (from camera or scanner) is calculated in **pixels per inch** (ppi). **A–C** For high-end print output, before selecting a resolution for a file, ask your commercial printer what resolution and halftone screen frequency they're going to use for their printer or imagesetter. Usually, for a grayscale image, the proper resolution will be in the neighborhood of one-and-a-half times the halftone screen frequency (lines per inch) of the output device, or twice the halftone screen frequency for a color image. We caution you that these are just general guidelines; each print shop has specific requirements for their particular output devices.

For output to an inkjet (desktop) printer, choose a resolution of 240 to 300 ppi.

Resolution for the Web

When creating an image for Web output, you need to estimate how large your user's browser window is likely to be, then calculate how much of that window you want your image to cover. Most

A *72 ppi*

B *150 ppi*

C *300 ppi*

viewers have their browser window open to around 800 x 600 pixels. Subtract the space taken up by the menu bar, scroll bars, and other controls in the browser interface, and you're left with a "live area" of approximately 740 x 460 pixels at most. For most viewers, the browser window doesn't fill the entire screen, so you can count on your image filling only around **660 x 420** pixels.

➤ To quickly create a 660 x 420-pixel document with a resolution of 72 ppi, in File > New, choose Preset: Web, and choose the desired pixel size for your document (see page 54).★

The resolution of your Photoshop files can be customized for a particular output device. For a scan, you'll choose the resolution at the outset using the scanning software. For a digital photo, you can change the resolution using the File > Image Size command after opening it in Photoshop (see page 92).

To calculate the resolution for print output:

1. Create a new document (File > New), enter Width and Height dimensions for the print output, choose Resolution: 72 pixels/inch, choose Color Mode: RGB Color, then click OK. (Stay tuned: You'll adjust the resolution in step 5.)

2. Choose Image > **Image Size.** The Image Size dialog box opens.

3. Click **Auto** on the right side of the dialog box. The Auto Resolution dialog box opens.**A**

4. Enter the **Screen** frequency of your output device, that is, the lpi, or lines per inch, setting to be used by your desktop or commercial printer.

5. Click **Quality: Good** (1½ x screen frequency) or **Best** (2 x screen frequency).

6. Click OK.

7. Jot down the value you see in the Document Size: **Resolution** field. You can enter that value in three possible locations: in the Camera Raw dialog box when converting a Raw digital photo, when using the Image Size command, or when scanning your photo. (Note: If you're going to scale the image in Photoshop, multiply the resolution by that scale factor to arrive at the proper resolution for scanning. For example, to shrink the image by half, multiply the resolution value by .5.)

8. Now that you've gotten the information you need, click Cancel.

A *Using the **Auto Resolution** dialog box, you can calculate the appropriate resolution for a file based on your chosen print output parameters.*

File storage sizes				
Size (In Inches)	PPI (Resolution)	Black/White 1-Bit	Grayscale 8-Bit	RGB Color 24-Bit
2 x 3	150	17 KB	132 KB	436 KB
	300	67 KB	528 KB	1.66 MB
4 x 5	150	56 KB	440 KB	1.39 MB
	300	221 KB	1.72 MB	5.44 MB
8 x 10	150	220 KB	1.72 MB	5.44 MB
	300	879 KB	6.87 MB	21.64 MB

File storage sizes are for a one-layer TIFF file with no alpha channels.

Potential number of gray levels at various output resolutions and screen frequencies (print output)					
Output Resolution (dpi)	Screen Frequency (lpi)				
	60	85	100	133	150
300	26	13			
600	101	51	37	21	
1270	*	224	162	92	72
2540		*	*	*	*

Note: Ask your commercial printer what screen frequency (lpi) and resolution (dpi) to specify for imagesetting. Some imagesetters can achieve resolutions above 2540 dpi. Note that the number of gray levels decreases as the screen frequency (lpi) increases.

*PostScript Level 2 printers output a maximum of 256 gray levels; PostScript Level 3 printers can output more than 256 levels.

Megapixels, resolution, and print sizes					
Image Resolution	Megapixels (rounded off)				
	2	3	6	8	11
150 ppi	8 x 10 in.	11 x 14 in.	14 x 20 in.	16 x 20 in.	18 x 24 in.
300 ppi	4 x 6 in.	5 x 7 in.	7 x 10 in.	8 x 10 in.	10 x 14 in.

Note: The print sizes listed above are approximations. For a more detailed listing of print sizes, search the Web for "translate megapixels to print size."

Using a scanner

Using a scanning device and scanning software, slides, flat artwork (e.g., drawings), and printed photographs can be digitized (translated into numbers) so they can be read, displayed, edited, and printed by a computer. You can scan images directly into Photoshop, or you or your output service provider can use third-party scanning software and save the scan in one of the file formats that Photoshop can read.

Garbage in, garbage out

You can't get a high-quality scan without a high-quality original. This is especially important for print output. Some scanners will increase the contrast and compress the tonal range of an image, so an important first step is to start off with a photograph that has a wide tonal range.

Choose the right scanner for the job

The quality of the scanning device itself also has a major impact on image quality. If you're going to dramatically transform your document in Photoshop (say, by applying Artistic or Distort filters or by performing drastic color adjustments), you can get away with using an inexpensive desktop scanner and choosing the scan settings yourself. Another option that nets more accurate color and crisper details is to scan a transparency on a slide scanner. Both types of scanners produce RGB files.

For professional-quality print output, take the time (and money) to have an output service provider scan your artwork on either a high-resolution CCD scanner (such as a Scitex Smart scanner) or a drum scanner. These devices capture a wider dynamic range of color and shade and can optically distinguish subtle differences in luminosity, even in shadow areas. High-end scanners produce RGB or CMYK scans and larger file sizes than desktop scanners.

Choose the right settings

Whichever device you decide to use, a third important requirement for producing a good-quality scan is to choose the proper settings. If you use an output service provider, they'll choose those settings for you, but if you're going to scan the photo yourself, take the time to set your scanning parameters carefully!

Choosing settings for a desktop scanner

You can scan directly into Photoshop or you can use third-party scanning software. Your software will have its own version of most of the options listed below (feature names vary from one product to another). The quality and file storage size of a resulting scan will vary according to several factors under your control, such as the mode, resolution, scale, and crop size.

If you access your scanner from Photoshop, choose File > Import > [your scanner model] in Photoshop. Otherwise, launch your scanning software.

Preview: Place your artwork in the scanner, then click Preview, PreScan, or an equivalent button.

Scan mode: Choose Black-and-White Line Art (no grays), Grayscale, or Color (choose millions of colors, if available). The file size of an image scanned in Color will be approximately three times larger than scanned in Grayscale.

Resolution: Choose a resolution value that will allow you to obtain the desired quality output from your printer. For grayscale printing on a printer with a 133-line screen, enter 200 ppi as your scan resolution; for color printing, enter 300 ppi; or for line art, enter a high scanning resolution (600 ppi or higher). It's always best to scan an image at or above the size and resolution needed for your output device. To determine the resolution needed for a scan, follow the instructions on page 51.

Cropping: If you're going to use only part of the original image, you can reduce the area to be scanned by moving the handles of the bounding box in the preview area. Cropping can significantly reduce the file size of your scanned image.

Scale: You can enlarge the dimensions of an image by raising the scale percentage above 100%, but doing so may cause it to look blurry, because the software uses interpolation (mathematical guesswork) to fill in the missing information.

Scan: Click Scan, and choose a location in which to save your new file. In the next chapter, you'll learn how to open files via Bridge.

Creating new, blank documents

In these instructions, you'll create a new, blank document. Into this document, you can drag and drop or copy and paste imagery from other files, and of course you can edit it by using all the image-editing features that Photoshop has to offer, such as brushes, effects, filters, etc.

To create a new, blank document:

1. Choose File > **New** (Ctrl-N/Cmd-N). The New dialog box opens.**A**

2. Enter a name in the **Name** field.

3. Do either of the following:

   To choose a preset size, choose from the **Preset** menu.★ The presets are listed in three categories: the Default Photoshop Size; paper sizes for commercial and desktop printers; and screen sizes for Web, film, and video output. Next, choose a specific size for that preset category from the **Size** menu.

   To create a custom size, choose a unit of measure from the menu next to the Width field; the same unit will be chosen automatically for the Height. Or hold down Shift while choosing a unit to change the value for that dimension only. Next, enter **Width** and **Height** values (or use the scrubby sliders).

4. Enter the **Resolution** required for your target output device—whether it's an imagesetter or the Web (see pages 50–51). You can use the scrubby slider here, too.

5. Choose a document **Color Mode,** then from the adjacent menu, choose **8 bit** or **16 bit** as the color depth. You can also convert the image to a different color mode later (see "Document color modes" on page 28).

6. Note the **Image Size** listed in the lower right side of the dialog box. If you need to reduce that storage size, you can choose smaller dimensions, a lower resolution, or a lower bit depth.

7. For the Background of the image, choose **Background Contents: White** or **Background Color**; or choose **Transparent** if you want the bottommost tier of the document to be a layer. (To choose a Background color, see pages 185–191. To learn about layers, see Chapter 7.)

8. *Optional:* When you click the Advanced arrowhead, the Color Profile menu becomes available. You can assign a color profile here, or you can do it later via Edit > Assign Profile. The list of profiles will vary depending on which Color

Continued on the following page

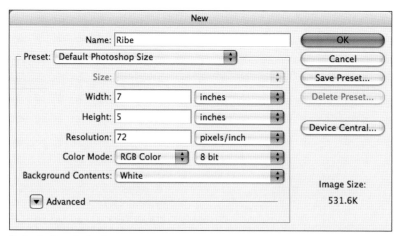

A *In the New dialog box, enter a Name; choose a Preset size or enter Width, Height, and Resolution values; and choose Color Mode and Background Contents options.*

Mode you've chosen. To learn more about color profiles, see pages 31 and 36.

For Web or print output, leave the **Pixel Aspect Ratio** on the default setting of Square Pixels; or for video output, choose one of the other options. For more information about these options, see Photoshop Help.

9. Click OK. A new, blank document window will appear onscreen. **A–B** To save this new file, see page 58.

➤ To force the New dialog box settings to match those of another open document, with the New dialog box open, from the bottom of the Preset menu, choose the name of the document that has the desired dimensions.

➤ If the current contents of the Clipboard originated from Photoshop or Illustrator, the New dialog box will automatically display those dimensions. Choosing Clipboard from the Preset pop-up in the New dialog box accomplishes the same thing. If you want to prevent the Clipboard dimensions from displaying, hold down Alt/Option as you choose File > New; the last-used file dimensions will display instead.

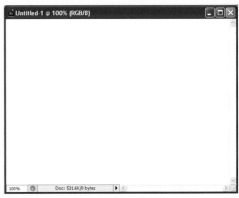

A *A **new document window** in Windows*

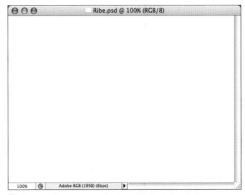

B *A **new document window** in the Mac OS*

PHOTOSHOP BIG

In Photoshop, you can create and save files as large as 300,000 x 300,000 pixels — over 2 gigabytes (GB) — and they can contain up to 56 user-created channels. These gonzo files can be saved in the **Large Document (.psb)** format, which is designed specifically to handle large documents. Files in this format can be opened and edited only in Photoshop versions CS through CS3.

So what are we supposed to do with these files? Well, as Victor, our technical editor, points out, 30,000 x 30,000 pixels is the largest file size that can be printed. So if you have the space to store and work with PSB files, great, but you'll have to lower the resolution drastically in order to output them (duplicate the file first, of course).

If you tend to use the same document size, color mode, or other settings repeatedly in the New dialog box, take the time to **create a document preset** (or presets) for those settings. Thereafter, you'll be able to access your settings via the Preset menu, which will save you startup time when you create new files.

To create a document preset:

1. Choose File > **New** or press Ctrl-N/Cmd-N. The New dialog box opens.

2. Choose settings, such as width, height, resolution, color mode, bit depth, background contents, color profile, and pixel aspect ratio. For any setting that you don't want to include in the preset, simply don't choose a value; you'll exclude it from the preset in step 5.

3. Click **Save Preset.** The New Document Preset dialog box opens.**A**

4. Enter a **Preset Name.**

5. For **Include in Saved Settings,** uncheck any New dialog box settings that you don't want to include in the preset.

6. Click OK. Your new preset will appear on the Preset menu in the New dialog box.

➤ To delete a user-created preset, choose it from the Preset menu, click Delete Preset, then click Yes (this can't be undone).

CHOOSE YOUR DEFAULTS

In Preferences > Units & Rulers, for **New Document Presets Resolutions,** you can enter **Print Resolution** and **Screen Resolution** values. One or the other value will appear in the Resolution field in the File > New dialog box when you choose a preset from the Preset menu. ★ The Print Resolution value (default 300 ppi) is used for the paper and photo presets; the Screen Resolution value (default 72 ppi) is used for the Web, Mobile & Devices, and Film & Video presets.

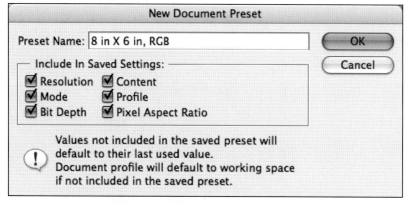

A Use the **New Document Preset** dialog box to control which of the current settings in the New dialog box will be saved in your new document preset.

Using the Place command

When you **place vector art** into a Photoshop document, it arrives as vector art on a new **Smart Object** layer, but is rendered in the resolution of the Photoshop image when you output the file. The higher the resolution of the Photoshop image, the sharper the rendering.

To place a PDF or Adobe Illustrator file in a Photoshop image:

1. Open a Photoshop document.

2. Do either of the following:

   In Bridge, locate and click a file, then choose File > Place > **In Photoshop.**

   In Photoshop, choose File > **Place**, locate and click a file, then click Place.

3. The Place PDF or Open as Smart Object ★ dialog box opens.**A** Don't worry about which dialog opens; they contain mostly the same options. Choose a Thumbnail Size; for a multi-page PDF file, also choose a page; and choose a Crop To option (we recommend Bounding Box to exclude any white areas outside the artwork). Click OK.

4. First, a bounding box will appear in the Photoshop document, then the art will render inside it.

5. Do any of these optional steps (use the Undo command to undo any of them):

   To **scale** the placed art, drag a handle on the bounding box. Shift-drag a corner handle to scale it proportionally.**B**

   To **move** the placed art, drag inside the bounding box.

   To **rotate** the placed art, position the pointer outside the bounding box (curved pointer), then drag. You can move the center point to rotate the art around a different point.

6. To accept the placed art, press Enter/Return or double-click inside the bounding box. The placed art will appear on a new Smart Object layer (see pages 302–304).**C**

➤ To delete the placed art before accepting it, press Esc.

➤ To open any Illustrator vector or PDF file as a Smart Object in its own Photoshop file, choose File > Open as Smart Object (in Photoshop). ★ The same Open as Smart Object dialog box opens.

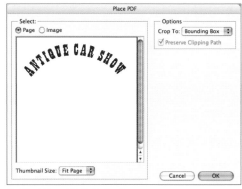

A *The **Place PDF** dialog box*

B *Move the **placed object** to the desired location (scale it, if desired), then press Enter/Return to accept it.*

C *When we accepted the object, it became an embedded **Smart Object**. If we edit the type size, style, or color in the embedded file, it will update in our Photoshop file (see page 349).*

Saving files

If you're not sure which format to use when **saving** a **file** for the first time, we strongly recommend the native Photoshop format, PSD. For one thing, PSD files are more compact than TIFF files (see also the sidebar on the following page).

To save an unsaved document:

1. If the document window contains any imagery, you can choose File > **Save** (Ctrl-S/Cmd-S); if it's completely blank, choose File > **Save As.** The Save As dialog box opens.

2. Type a name in the **File name** field A/Save As field (A, next page).

3. Choose a **location** for the file.

   In Windows, if you need to navigate to a different folder or drive, use the **Save In** menu at the top of the dialog box.

   In the Mac OS, click a drive or folder in the **Sidebar** panel on the left side. To locate a recently used folder, use the menu below the Save As field.

4. Choose a file format from the **Format** menu. Only the native Photoshop (PSD), Large Document (PSB), TIFF, and Photoshop PDF formats support layers, which you'll learn about in Chapter 7.

5. If you're not familiar with the features listed in the **Save** area, you can leave the settings as is. The As a Copy option is discussed on page 60.

6. If the file contains an embedded color profile and the format you're saving to supports profiles, in the **Color** area, you can check **ICC Profile/Embed Color Profile:** [profile name] (see page 42).

7. Click Save.

➤ In the Mac OS, to have Photoshop append a three-character extension (e.g., .tif, .psd) to the file name automatically when saving a file for the first time, in Preferences > File Handling, choose Append File Extension: Always or Ask When Saving. Extensions are required when exporting Macintosh files to the Windows platform or when posting files to a Web server.

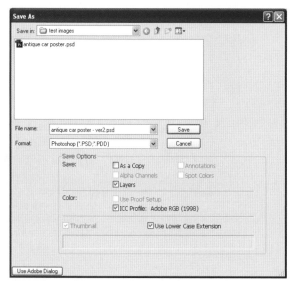

A *The **Save As** dialog box in **Windows***

SAVING A FLATTENED VERSION

If you choose **Maximize PSD and PSB File Compatibility: Always** in Photoshop Preferences > File Handling, whenever you save a file that contains layers in the PSD or PSB format, a flattened version is saved with it—it's updated with each Save. This is helpful when exporting Photoshop images to applications that don't read layers. Or if you'd rather decide on a file-by-file basis whether to save an extra flattened version with your file, choose **Ask** from the menu instead. In this case, each time you use the Save As command, an alert dialog box will appear, giving you the option to include the extra image.

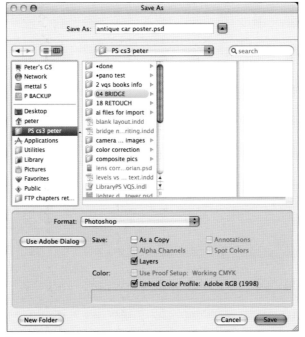

A *The Save As dialog box in the Mac OS*

After saving a file for the first time, each subsequent use of the **Save** command saves over (overwrites) the last version.

To save a previously saved file:

Choose File > **Save** (Ctrl-S/Cmd-S).

The simple **Revert** command restores your document to the last-saved version.

Note: We know you can't learn everything at once, but keep in mind for the future that the History palette, which we discuss in Chapter 10, serves as a full-service multiple undo feature. Revert does show up as a state on the History palette, so you can undo a Revert by clicking an earlier history state.

To revert to the last saved version:

Choose File > **Revert**.

CHOOSING THE RIGHT FORMAT

Photoshop (PSD), Large Document (PSB), TIFF, and **Photoshop PDF** are the only formats that preserve the following Photoshop features:

➤ Multiple layers and layer transparency

➤ Shape layers

➤ Smart Objects

➤ Adjustment layers

➤ Editable type layers

➤ Layer effects

➤ Alpha channels

➤ Grids and guides

In addition to the above-mentioned formats, the PICT, JPEG, and Photoshop EPS formats also preserve ICC color management profiles.

To prepare your document for printing from another application, or to export it to an application that doesn't read Photoshop layers, read about the **EPS, PDF,** and **TIFF** formats on pages 413–416.

For Web output, read about the **GIF** and **JPEG** formats on pages 417–422.

The **Save As** command lets you save a copy of your file under a new name or in a different format. Save it under a new name to create a design, color mode, or adjustment variation. For example, you could save a copy of a file in CMYK Color mode while keeping the original in RGB Color mode.

Another important use of this command is to prepare your Photoshop file for Web output or for export to another application. For applications that can't read Photoshop layers (most can't), you'll need to save a flattened (nonlayered) copy of your file in a format that's appropriate for the target output device.

To save a new version of a file:

1. Choose File > **Save As** (Ctrl-Shift-S/Cmd-Shift-S). The Save As dialog box opens.**A–B**

2. Change the name in the **File name/Save As** field.

3. Choose a **location** in which to save the new version by using the Save In menu in Windows or the Sidebar panel and columns in the Mac OS.

4. *Optional:* Choose a different file format from the Format menu. Only formats that are available for the current document color mode and bit depth will appear on the list.

   Beware! If the format you've chosen doesn't support multiple layers, the Layers option will become dimmed, a yellow alert icon will display, and the new version will be flattened.

5. Check any available options in the **Save** area, as desired. Check **As a Copy** to have the copy remain closed and the original stay open; or leave this option unchecked to have the original close and the copy stay open.

6. In the **Color** area, check ICC **Profile/Embed Color Profile:** [profile name], if available (see page 42).

7. Click Save. For the TIFF format, follow the instructions on page 413; for EPS, see pages 414–415; for PDF, see page 416; for GIF, see page 419; or for JPEG, see page 421. For other formats, see Photoshop Help.

➤ If you don't change the file name in the Save As dialog box and you click Save, an alert dialog box will appear. Click Yes/Replace to save over the original file or click No/Cancel to get back to the Save As dialog box.

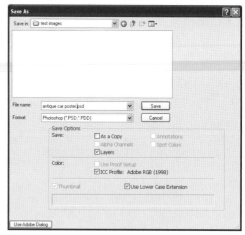

A *The **Save As** dialog box in **Windows***

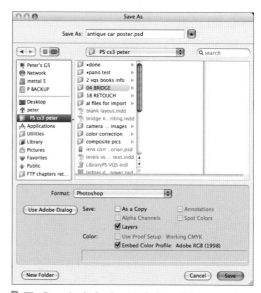

B *The **Save As** dialog box in the **Mac OS***

A DESIGNER'S FRIEND

Another way to create document variations — but within the same file — is by using the **Layer Comps** palette; see pages 380–382.

Using the **status bar** and menu at the bottom of the document window, you can get information about a file that's already open in Photoshop, find out how Photoshop is currently using memory, or learn the name of the current tool.

To use the status bar:

From the Show submenu on the status bar menu at the bottom of the application/document window, choose one of the following:

(For Version Cue, see your network administrator or Photoshop Help.)

Document Sizes to list the approximate file storage size of a flattened version of the file if it were saved in the PSD format (the value on the left) and the storage size of the file with layers (the value on the right).**A**

Document Profile to list the embedded color profile (the words "Untagged [RGB or CMYK]" appear if the file hasn't been assigned a profile).

Document Dimensions to list the image dimensions (width, height, and resolution).

Scratch Sizes to list the amount of RAM Photoshop is using for all currently open files (the value on the left) and the amount of RAM currently available to Photoshop (the value on the right). If the first value is greater than the second, it means Photoshop is currently utilizing virtual memory on the scratch disk.

Efficiency to list the percentage of processing time that's currently being devoted to actual program operations in RAM. A percentage below 100 indicates the scratch disk is being used.

Current Tool to list the name of the currently chosen tool.

➤ Press and hold on the status bar to display a thumbnail-size preview of the image relative to the current paper size, including custom printing marks, if any.

➤ If you don't see the status bar, make the document window wider, and it should appear.

To see data about a specific file, use the **Metadata** panel in **Bridge.**

To find out the storage size (and other data) about a file:

1. In Bridge, select an image thumbnail.

2. In the **Metadata** panel, under **File Properties**, look for the **File Size** value.**B**

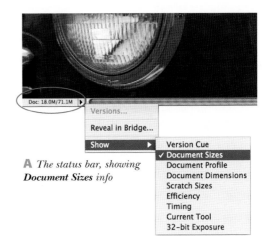

A *The status bar, showing* **Document Sizes** *info*

Show ▶
— Version Cue
✓ Document Sizes
— Document Profile
— Document Dimensions
— Scratch Sizes
— Efficiency
— Timing
— Current Tool
— 32–bit Exposure

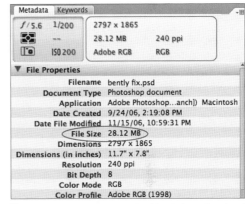

B *To learn the storage size of a file, click its thumbnail in Bridge, then in the* **Metadata** *panel,* **File Properties** *category, look for the* **File Size** *listing.*

GETTING INFO FAST

Regardless of which info option is chosen on the status bar menu, you can always Alt-press/Option-press the **status bar** to display information about the current image, such as its dimensions, number of channels, color mode, bit depth, and resolution.

Ending a work session

To close a document:

Do either of the following:

Click the **Close** button in the upper right corner of the document window (Win) **A**/upper left corner of the document window (Mac).**B**

Choose File > **Close** (Ctrl-W/Cmd-W).

If you attempt to close a file that was modified since it was last saved, a warning prompt will appear.**C** Click No/Don't Save to close the file without saving it; or click Yes/Save to save the file before closing; or click Cancel to cancel the close operation.

➤ In the Mac OS, a little dot will appear in the red close button of a document window if the file has been edited since it was last saved.

➤ In Photoshop, to close a file and launch or go to Bridge, choose File > **Close and Go to Bridge** (Ctrl-Shift-W/Cmd-Shift-W).

To exit/quit Photoshop:

1. In Windows, choose File > **Exit** (Ctrl-Q) or click the application window Close button.

In the Mac OS, choose Photoshop > **Quit Photoshop** (Cmd-Q).

2. All open Photoshop files will close. If any changes were made to any open file since it was last saved, a prompt will appear. Click No (N)/Don't Save (D) to close the file without saving it; or click Yes (Y)/Save(S) to save it before exiting/quitting; or click Cancel to cancel the exit/quit.

A *In **Windows**, click the **Close** (X) button.*

B *In the **Mac OS**, click the **Close** (red) button.*

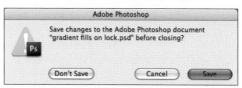

C *If you try to close a file that contains unsaved changes, this prompt will appear. A similar prompt appears if you exit/quit Photoshop and any open files contain unsaved changes.*

The Bridge application ships with Photoshop and is aptly named because it serves as a conduit among all the programs in the Adobe Creative Suite. In Chapter 2, you learned how to use Bridge to synchronize the color settings for the whole Creative Suite. With its large thumbnail previews of files from Adobe Creative Suite applications, Bridge is also the best vehicle for opening files— plus it offers many other useful features.A In Bridge you can you display, arrange, rate, and sort thumbnails; organize thumbnails into collapsible stacks;★ rate or reject images; assign keywords to files; use a loupe to examine details on any image thumbnail; and view data (metadata) about any image, such as the shooting conditions a camera recorded into a digital photo. ★ You don't need to learn everything in this chapter at once. Master the basics in the first half of the chapter, then explore other features at your leisure.

Launching Bridge

To launch Bridge:

Do one of the following:

In Photoshop, near the middle of the Options bar, click the **Go to Bridge** button 📷 (Ctrl-Alt-O/Cmd-Option-O).

Double-click the **Bridge** application icon Br in Program Files\Adobe\Adobe Bridge CS3 in Windows; Applications/Adobe Bridge CS3 in the Mac OS.

In the Mac OS, click the **Bridge** icon Br on the **Dock**. The Bridge window opens.

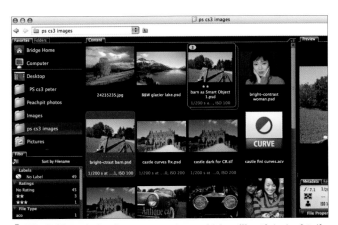

A *The **Bridge** window has many sections, which we'll explain in detail.*

The Bridge window

Panels and panes

The Bridge window contains three panes: a large pane in the center and a vertical pane on either side (**A**, next page). Each pane contains one or more panels, which are accessed via tabs: **Favorites**, **Folders**, **Filter**, **Content**, **Preview**, **Metadata**, and **Keywords**. Panels in the side panes let you manage files, filter the display of thumbnails, and display image data; the large central panel—the one you'll use most—displays image thumbnails. You can hide/show or resize any of the panels or move any panel into another pane.

We'll explore some of the panels in depth later in this chapter, but for now, here's a brief summary:

The **Favorites** panel displays a list of folders that you've designated as favorites, for quick access. Via check boxes in the Favorite Items area of Bridge Preferences > General, you can control which folders appear in the top part of the panel. To add a folder to the user-created list of folders in the lower part of the panel, drag the folder from the Content panel (the center pane) or from the Finder into the Favorites panel, and release the mouse when the plus sign pointer displays; or click the folder and choose File > Add to Favorites. To remove a Favorites folder from the list, click it, then choose File > Remove from Favorites.

The **Folders** panel contains a scroll window with a hierarchical listing of all the top-level and nested folders on your hard drive.

The **Filter** panel ★ is dynamic, meaning the categories listed (such as File Type, Keywords, Date Created, and Date Modified) change depending on what data is available for files in the current folder. For example, if you haven't applied ratings to any files in the current folder, you won't see a Ratings category. Should you apply a rating to a thumbnail, the Ratings category will magically appear. Click an arrowhead to expand/collapse a category. Click a listing within a category, and only thumbnails that match the listing will display in the Content panel; click again to uncheck the listing and display the files that were filtered out. This is a new, fast way to sort and display images.

In the center pane of the Bridge window, the **Content** panel displays image thumbnails and/or thumbnails for nested folders within the currently selected folder. The file name and other file data are listed below each thumbnail.

The **Preview** panel displays a larger preview of the currently selected image (or folder) thumbnail. If you select a video file, the Preview will display a controller for playing the video. You can also preview two or more selected thumbnails in this panel for quick comparison, and magnify areas of a thumbnail with a loupe. ★

The **Metadata** panel lists information about the currently selected thumbnail: a quick summary in the "placard" at the top ★ (**B**, next page) and detailed listings in categories below. The File Properties category, for example, lists the file name, format, date created, date modified, etc. To expand or collapse a category, click the arrowhead.

You can use the IPTC Core category in the Metadata panel to attach creator, description, copyright, and other information to the currently selected file. (IPTC is an information standard for transferring and publishing text and images.) Click the field next to a listing, enter or modify the file description information, press Tab to cycle through and edit other data, then click the green Apply button ✓ in the lower right corner.

If a digital photo is selected, the Camera Data (EXIF) category displays the camera settings that were used to capture the photo. If the photo was edited in Camera Raw, those settings will be listed in a category called Camera Raw (like the Filter panel, this panel is also dynamic). To learn more about the Metadata panel, see Bridge Help.

Use the **Keywords** panel to assign descriptive keywords to images, such as an event, name, location, or other criteria. You can find image thumbnails via a keyword search, or display files based on keywords using the Filter panel.

Side pane   *Center* pane   *Side* pane

A *You can use* **Bridge** *to locate, view, and organize image thumbnails and, of course, open your files into Photoshop. The Default workspace is shown here.*

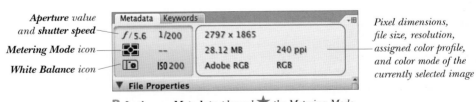

Aperture value and **shutter speed**
Metering Mode icon
White Balance icon

Pixel dimensions, file size, resolution, assigned color profile, and color mode of the currently selected image

B *In the new* **Metadata** *placard,* ★ *the Metering Mode and White Balance icons represent the settings used to shoot the currently selected photo. The settings are listed below, in the Camera Data and Camera Raw categories.*

Opening files from Bridge

You can **open** as many files in Photoshop as currently available RAM and scratch disk space allow. (Note: To open a Raw, JPEG, or TIFF digital photo into Camera Raw, see Chapter 15.)

To open files from Bridge:

1. In the **Folders** panel, navigate to the file you want to open. Scroll upward or downward, expand/collapse any folder by clicking the arrowhead, or open and display the contents of a folder by clicking its thumbnail. You can also choose from a list of Favorites or Recent Folders on the Look In menu at the top of the Bridge window, or click a folder that you've placed in the **Favorites** panel.

   ► To display the contents of a folder, double-click the folder thumbnail in the Content panel.

   ► To move up a level in the current folder hierarchy, click the Go Up button ⬆ at the top of the Bridge window.

2. In the Content panel, click an image thumbnail (a file format that Photoshop can open). The thumbnail will now have a colored border, a preview will appear in the Preview panel, and data about the file will be listed in the Metadata panel. (To select multiple images, Ctrl-click/Cmd-click nonconsecutive thumbnails; **A** or

click the first thumbnail in a series of consecutive thumbnails, then Shift-click the last.)

   ► If an image has a number in the upper left corner, it's part of a stack (grouping of thumbnails). You can click the top image thumbnail in a stack to open just that image. To select other images in a stack, see page 74.

3. Double-click any thumbnail (it can be one of the thumbnails you selected) or press Ctrl-O/Cmd-O. Photoshop will launch, if it isn't already running, and the image(s) will appear onscreen. See also "Dealing with the ifs" on page 82.

   ► By default, the Bridge window stays open after you use it to open a file. To minimize/close the Bridge window as you open a file, hold down Alt/Option as you double-click a thumbnail.

   ► If a file has been opened and modified already in Camera Raw, you'll see this icon ⬙ in the top right corner of its thumbnail.

What lies ahead in this chapter

There's so much more to Bridge than simply clicking a thumbnail or two and opening a file! Starting on the next page, you can learn how to customize your Bridge window. Or to help you keep your sanity when faced with the ever-increasing number of digital images you'll be working with, turn to pages 72–73, where we show you how to label, sort, and filter out your image thumbnails.

A *Ctrl-click/Cmd-click to select multiple file **thumbnails**.*

> **JUMPING BETWEEN DOCUMENTS**
>
> In Photoshop, if multiple documents are open, you can do any of the following to switch among them:
>
> ► Click in a **document window.**
>
> ► Choose a file name from the bottom of the **Window** menu.
>
> ► Cycle among the open documents by pressing **Ctrl-Tab/Control-Tab.**
>
> To reopen a file that was recently opened and then closed, in Photoshop, choose that file name from the File > Open Recent submenu.

Choosing a workspace for Bridge

To reconfigure the Bridge window automatically, you can choose from 6 **predefined workspaces.**

To choose a predefined workspace for Bridge ★

From any one of the 3 **workspace** menus in the lower right corner of the Bridge window, **A** choose **Default, Light Table, File Navigator, Metadata Focus, Horizontal Filmstrip,** or **Vertical Filmstrip;** or use one of the shortcuts listed in the sidebar at left. The workspaces are illustrated in **B–C**, this page and **A–B**, next page.

A *Choose a predefined workspace from one of the* ***workspace*** *menus.*

B *In the **Light Table** workspace, the Content panel takes up the whole Bridge window so you can see a large number of images in a folder at once.*

C *In the **File Navigator** workspace, you have access to the Folders panel for opening folders. You can drag images onto folder names to move or copy them.*

Illustrations continue on the following page

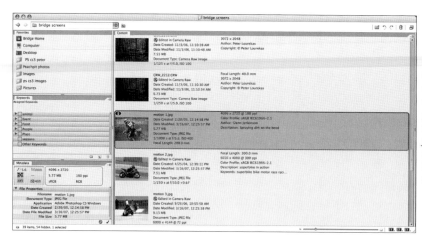

A *In the* **Metadata Focus** *workspace, you have access to the* **Metadata** *panel to view and edit the embedded metadata for the currently selected image, and access to the* **Keyword** *panel to assign and remove keywords.*

B *In the* **Horizontal** *or* **Vertical** *(shown)* **Filmstrip** *workspace, you can use the arrow keys to cycle through thumbnails in the current folder; see a large preview of the current image; and access a loupe (click the large preview) to examine small details.*

Examining thumbnails ★

To compare two thumbnails in the Preview panel: ★

1. In Bridge, to display a large Preview panel, choose **Horizontal Filmstrip** or **Vertical Filmstrip** from one of the workspace menus.

2. In the **Content** panel, click a thumbnail, then Shift-click the prior or next thumbnail or Ctrl-click/Cmd-click any other thumbnail.

3. Large versions of the two selected thumbnails will display in the **Preview** panel.

➤ Ctrl-click/Cmd-click to add more thumbnails to the panel. Ctrl-click/Cmd-click a selected thumbnail in the Content panel to deselect it and remove it from the Preview panel.

To examine picture details using a loupe: ★

1. Click a thumbnail in the **Preview** panel or in a **Flimstrip** layout. The loupe will display. **B**

2. Click an area to view it close up in the **loupe**. By default, pixels display in the loupe at 100% view (the zoom level is listed below the preview). Press + to zoom in on the loupe display or - to zoom out. Click another area or drag the loupe to examine another area of the image.

3. *Optional:* If you're previewing two thumbnails, click the other preview thumbnail to display a second loupe. If you Ctrl-drag/Cmd-drag either loupe, they'll move simultaneously, enabling you to compare a similar area in both images.

4. Click on the loupe to remove it.

Customizing the Bridge window

To change the backdrop and thumbnail data in the Bridge window: ★

1. Choose Edit (Bridge, in the Mac OS) > **Preferences** (Ctrl-K/Cmd-K). The Preferences dialog box opens.

2. On the left side, click **General**, and in the Appearance area,**A** do any of the following:

   Move the **User Interface Brightness** slider to set the gray value for the side panes.

   Move the **Image Backdrop** slider to set a separate backdrop value for the center pane and the Preview panel.**B** (When we work in Bridge, we use black for our center pane and dark gray for the side panes, but for printing reasons, we used lighters colors for the figures in this book.)

   Choose an **Accent Color** for the border around the currently selected folder, thumbnail, or stack, and for categories in the Metadata panel.

3. Click **Thumbnails** to switch to that pane. From the **Detail: Show** menus, choose to display up to four additional lines of metadata (image info) below the image thumbnails. Use this option to list information that's important to you. Also decide whether to **Show Tooltips.**

4. Click OK.

➤ To toggle the display of metadata on or off in the Content panel, press Ctrl-T/Cmd-T.

➤ To learn more about the Bridge Preferences, see pages 392–393 and Bridge > Help.

A *Using the **Appearance** options in Bridge Preferences > General, you can customize the **colors** in the Bridge interface.*

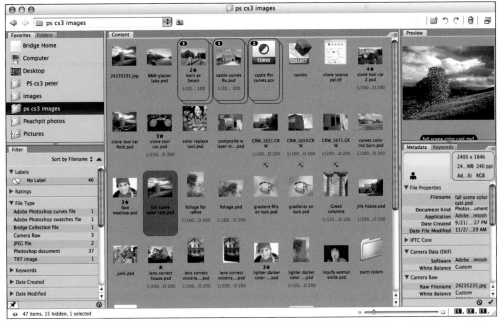

B *We chose the **Appearance** settings shown in the previous figure to change the center pane to dark gray and the panes on the sides to medium gray.*

To further customize the Bridge workspace, you can resize, move, or hide any of the **panels.** If you save your layout as a user-created workspace, as per the instructions on the next page, you'll be able to access it again quickly at any time.

To customize the layout of Bridge:

Do any of the following:

To make a panel **taller/shorter,** drag the horizontal bar upward/downward;**A** other panels in the same group will scale accordingly.

To make a whole pane **wider** or **narrower,** drag the vertical bar sideways;**B** the center pane will resize accordingly.

To display only the Content pane in a compact window, click the Compact Mode button ⬚ in the upper right corner of the Bridge window; click it again to restore the full window.

To **minimize/collapse** any panel (except Content) to a tab only, double-click its tab.

Drag any panel tab (name) into another panel **group** (release the mouse when the blue "drop zone" frame appears around the desired group).

Drag a panel tab above/below another panel (release the mouse when a horizontal blue drop zone line appears in the desired location).

To have the center pane fill the entire window, click the **Show/Hide Panels** button ◀▶ in the lower left corner of the Bridge window or press Tab; repeat to redisplay the side panes.

To change the **size** of the **thumbnails,** move the thumbnail slider (below the Content panel);**C** or click the Smaller Thumbnail Size button ⬚ or Larger Thumbnail Size button.⬚

To display image thumbnails and folders in the Content panel, check **Show Folders** on the View menu. To display image thumbnails but not folders, choose the command again (to remove the check mark).

A *Moving the horizontal bar upward shortens the Favorites/Folder panels and lengthens the Filter panel.*

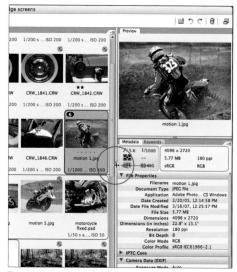

B *Moving the vertical bar for the right pane to the left widens the Preview and Metadata panels.*

C *Moving the thumbnail slider resizes the* **thumbnails** *in the center pane.*

If you **save** your customized **workspaces** in Bridge, you won't have to spend time setting up your workspace each time you relaunch the application.

To save a Bridge workspace: ★

1. Choose a size and location of the overall Bridge window, a size (and groupings) for the panels, and a thumbnail size for the Content panel.

2. From any of the 3 **workspace** menus in the lower right corner of the Bridge window, choose **Save Workspace**. The Save Workspace dialog box opens.

3. Enter a Name for the workspace, choose a Keyboard Shortcut (or choose None), check Save Window Location as Part of Workspace and/or check Save Sort Order as Part of Workspace (both are optional), then click Save. (To learn about sorting thumbnails, see page 73.)

To access saved workspaces: ★

To choose any predefined or saved workspace, choose the workspace name from one of the **workspace** menus. The workspace you choose will become the default for that button. Click the button to redisplay that particular workspace.

Any changes you make to the current workspace, such as resizing a panel, will be saved to the button you assigned that workspace to. (Click a different workspace button, then click the button for the modified workspace, and you'll see what we mean.) To redisplay a workspace without your changes, choose it from the workspace menu instead of clicking the button.

Moving and copying files

You can move files to a different folder by dragging them or by using a command.

To move or copy files to other folders:
Method 1 (by dragging)

1. Click the **Folders** panel tab. Display the desired subfolder (expand any folders, if necessary).

2. Select one or more thumbnails in the **Content** panel, then drag them over a folder name in the Folders panel to move them, or hold down Alt/Option and drag them over a folder name to copy them.

Method 2 (context menu) ★

1. Select one or more thumbnails in the **Content** panel.

2. Right-click/Ctrl-click in the Bridge window, then from the **Move To** or **Copy To** submenu on the context menu, do either of the following: Choose a folder name from the Recent Folders submenu; or click Choose Folder to open the navigation dialog box, locate a folder, then click OK/Choose.

THE REAL THING

To locate an "actual" file in Explorer/Finder, click a thumbnail in Bridge, then choose File > **Reveal in Explorer/Reveal in Finder.** The folder that the file resides in will open in a window in Explorer/Finder and the file icon will be selected.

Filtering the display of thumbnails

If you **assign thumbnails** a star rating and/or color label, you'll be able to display them based on the presence or absence of that rating or label and find them easily via the Filter panel and Find command.

To label and rate thumbnails:

1. Select one or more thumbnails in the **Content** panel (Ctrl-click/Cmd-click nonconsecutive thumbnails, or click, then Shift-click consecutive thumbnails).

2. Do any of the following:

   Right-click/Control–click one of the thumbnails and from the **Label** submenu on the context menu, choose a category. (To change the categories, see page 393.)

   From the **Label** menu, choose a star **Rating** and/or a **Label** category.**A–B** Each category is represented by a different color behind the stars.

   Click a thumbnail, then click any one of the 5 **dots** below the thumbnail. Stars will appear.**C**

   Use any of the keyboard **shortcuts** listed on the Label menu.

➤ To remove a star, click the star to its left. To remove all the stars from a thumbnail, click to the left of the first star.**D**

➤ If tool tips get in the way of your adding or removing stars, go to Preferences > General for Bridge and uncheck Show Tooltips.

OK, so not every photo you take is perfect. You can apply a rating of **Reject** to the image thumbnails that you want to hide from the Content panel but aren't quite ready to delete from your hard drive.

To reject files: ★

1. Select one or more image thumbnails.

2. Choose Label > **Reject** (Alt-Del/Option-Delete). The thumbnails will be rated and hidden.

To redisplay all rejected thumbnails: ★

Choose View > **Show Reject Files.** All thumbnails that have a Reject rating will redisplay and the word "Reject" will be listed above each file name.**E**

➤ In the Ratings category in the Filter panel, check (click) Reject to display only the files in the current folder that have a Reject rating.

➤ To remove a Reject rating from a selected thumbnail or thumbnails, choose Label > No Rating (Ctrl-0/Cmd-0).

A *From the **Label** menu, choose a star rating or label category. (Note: Depending on your version of Bridge, the label menu will list either the categories shown at left or color names.)*

Red
Yellow
Green
Blue
Purple

B *This thumbnail has an **Approved** (green) rating.*

C *On this selected thumbnail, we clicked the third dot to assign a **3-star** rating.*

D *Then we clicked to the left of the stars to **remove** all the stars.*

E *This poor thumbnail has a **Reject** rating.*

The sorting order you choose from the new **Filter** panel ★ affects the order in which thumbnails display in the Content panel. Criteria you check in the main part of the Filter panel, which lists data specific to files in the current folder, control which thumbnails display. By choosing a sorting order and by checking the desired filter criteria, you'll be able to locate the files you need more quickly and efficiently. The sorting order of thumbnails is also important for batch and automate operations, as these commands process files based on the current sequence of thumbnails.

The current **sorting order** applies to all folders and thumbnails that are displayed in Bridge, not to one specific folder.

To choose a sorting method: ★

1. From the menu at the top of the **Filter** panel, ⬍ choose a **sorting** order (such as By Date Created or By Document Type).**A** Thumbnails will rearrange themselves in the Content panel.

2. Click the arrowhead to toggle the sort between **Ascending Order** ▲ and **Descending Order.** ▼

By checking specific **criteria** in the **Filter** panel, such as label, star rating, file type, date created, date modified, orientation, etc., you can control which thumbnails display in any given folder. To display, a thumbnail must match all checked criteria.

To display thumbnails based on category: ★

1. Open a folder of images in Bridge.

2. If the Filter panel isn't showing, choose the **Default** workspace from any **workspace** menu.

3. Check (click) a listing within a category to display thumbnails that match that criterion.**B** To display thumbnails that match additional criteria, check other listings in the **same** category. To narrow the selection of thumbnails that display, check a listing in a **different** category.

4. To remove a check mark from the Filter panel, click the listing again. Hidden thumbnails will redisplay.

➤ To apply the current check marks as you display other folders, click the Keep Filter When Browsing 🔖 button at the bottom of the Filter panel.

➤ To remove all check marks from the Filter panel for the current folder, click the Clear Filter ⊘ button at the bottom of the panel (Ctrl-Alt-A/Cmd-Option-A).

A *Choose a sorting method from the* **Sort By** *menu in the* **Filter** *panel. This command changes the order in which thumbnails display in Bridge, not the order of the actual files on your hard drive.*

B *Because we've checked the* **2-star** *option under* **Ratings** *in the Filter panel, only thumbnails matching that criterion (that have two stars) will display in the Content panel.*

Grouping thumbnails into stacks

Before getting into stacks, start with the simple technique of **dragging thumbnails** to change their location in the Content panel.

To rearrange thumbnails manually:

Drag a thumbnail (or select, then drag multiple thumbnails) to a new location. It will remain where you place it unless you change the sorting order or perform a stacking operation. The Sort order (listed at the top of the Filter panel) switches to "Sort Manually."

Like sorting papers into manila folders on your desk, by grouping thumbnails into **stacks**, you'll be able to organize them and reduce the number of thumbnails that display at a given time.

To group thumbnails into a stack: ★

1. Shift-click a sequence of thumbnails or Ctrl-click/Cmd-click individual thumbnails.**A** The image you click first will become the "stack thumbnail" (will be on top of the stack).

2. Choose Stacks > **Group as Stack** (Ctrl-G/Cmd-G) or right-click/Control-click and choose Stack > **Group as Stack.B** The stack will look like two playing cards in a pile, and instead of all the individual thumbnails, you'll see just the stack thumbnail on top. The number in the upper left corner indicates the current number of thumbnails in the stack.

To select thumbnails in a stack: ★

To **select and display** all the thumbnails in a stack, click the stack number. Click the number again to collapse the stack. The stack is still selected.

To **select** all the thumbnails in a stack but keep the stack **collapsed**, click the stack border (bottom "card") or Alt-click/Option-click the stack thumbnail.

To rearrange thumbnails in a stack: ★

To **rearrange** a thumbnail in an expanded stack, click it to deselect the other selected thumbnails, then drag it to a new location (as shown by the colored drop zone line).**C**

To move a whole stack: ★

1. Alt-click/Option-click a stack that's in its collapsed state, to select it.

2. Drag the image thumbnail (not the border).

A *Select several thumbnails to be grouped into a stack.*

B *A* **stack** *is created. The number in the upper left corner indicates how many thumbnails the stack contains.*

C *Drag a thumbnail to rearrange it within a stack.*

➤ If you drag the top thumbnail of an unselected stack, you'll move just that thumbnail, not the whole stack.

To add a thumbnail to a stack: ★

Click a thumbnail, then drag it into a stack.

➤ We use stacks to group thumbnails for merging into a panorama (Photomerge command).

To remove thumbnails from a stack: ★

1. Click the stack number to expand the stack.
2. Click a thumbnail (to deselect the other thumbnails), then drag it out of the stack.**A**

To ungroup a whole stack: ★

1. Click the stack number to expand and select all the thumbnails in the stack.
2. Choose Stacks > **Ungroup from Stack** (Control-Shift-G/Cmd-Shift-G) or right-click/Control-click and choose Stack > **Ungroup from Stack.** The stack number and border will disappear.

Managing files

To create a new folder:

1. Via the Folders panel or via the Look In menu at the top of the Bridge window, navigate to the folder that you want to place the new folder in.
2. Click the **New Folder** button 🖿 at the top of the window, type a name in the highlighted field, then press Enter/Return.

To delete files:

1. Click a thumbnail (or Ctrl-click/Cmd-click multiple thumbnails or Shift-click a series of thumbnails), then press Ctrl-Backspace/Cmd-Delete.
2. Click OK. Beware! You can also delete a whole folder full of files. To retrieve a deleted file or folder, double-click the Recycle Bin/Trash icon for the operating system, then drag the item into the Content panel in Bridge.

To rename a file:

1. Click a thumbnail, then click the file name; text to the left of the period will become highlighted.
2. Type a new name **B** (don't try to delete the extension), then press Enter/Return or click outside the name field.

motion 3.jpg   motion 4.jpg   motion 5.jpg

plane 1.jpg   motorcycle fixed.psd   CRW_1845.CRW
1/50 s at f/4.0, ISO 50   1/200 s at f/4.0, ISO 200

A *Drag a thumbnail out of a stack.*

CRW_1846.CRW

B *Change the file name.*

When you download digital photos from your camera to your computer, they keep the sequential numerical labels (e.g., "CRW-0016") that were assigned to them by your camera. To help you identify your photos, you can give them more recognizable names (e.g., "Dancer" or "Dog") via the **Batch Rename** command in a few quick steps.

To batch-rename files:

1. In Bridge, click then Shift-click a series of consecutive thumbnails, or Ctrl-click/Cmd-click nonconsecutive thumbnails, or press Ctrl-A/ Cmd-A to select all the thumbnails in the current window.

2. Choose Tools > **Batch Rename** (Ctrl-Shift-R/ Cmd-Shift-R). The Batch Rename dialog box opens.**A**

3. For the **Destination Folder,** choose:

   Rename in Same Folder to rename the files and leave them in their current location.

   Move to Other Folder to rename the files and move them to a new location.

   Copy to Other Folder to leave the original files unchanged and rename the copies in the new location—this is a quick and easy way to

duplicate your photos. We recommend using this option, especially if you didn't duplicate your files when you downloaded them.

For the Move or Copy option, click **Browse,** choose or create a new folder location, then click OK/Choose.

4. For **New Filenames,** do either of the following:

   Choose an option from one of the menus in the left-hand column. Text lets you enter text for the new file names (probably the best choice); Current Filename lets you modify the original name; and Sequence Number and Sequence Letter let you include a number or letter that increments from file name to file name (enter a starting number or letter).

   Click the ⊕ button to add another row of criteria fields; click the ⊖ button to remove a row of fields.

   The current and new names will be listed in the **Preview** area at the bottom of the dialog box.

5. For **Options:** Compatibility, check any other operating system that you want your renamed files to be compatible with.

6. Click **Rename.**

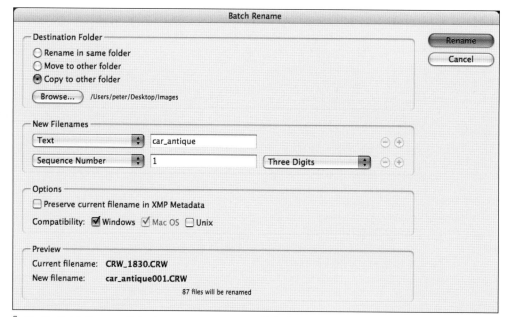

A *Via the **Batch Rename** dialog box, you can rename multiple thumbnails at once.*

Searching for files

To find files via Bridge:

1. In Bridge, choose Edit > **Find** (Ctrl-F/Cmd-F). The Find dialog box opens.**A**

2. From the **Look In** menu, choose a folder to search through. To select a folder that's not on the list, choose Look In > Browse, locate the desired folder, then click OK/Choose.

3. From the menus in the **Criteria** area, choose search criteria (e.g., file name, date created, label, rating, camera settings, etc.), choose a parameter from the adjoining menu, and enter data in the field. To include additional criteria in the search, click the ⊕, then choose/enter more search criteria.

4. From the **Match** menu, choose "If any criteria are met" to find files based on one or more criteria, or choose "If all criteria are met" to narrow the selection to files that meet all the chosen criteria.

5. Check **Include All Subfolders** to search all subfolders within the folder you chose in step 2.

6. *Optional:* Check Include Non-indexed Files to search through files that Bridge hasn't yet indexed (any folder Bridge has yet to display). This will make the search run more slowly.

7. Do either of the following:

   To copy the search results and send them to a **temporary** folder called Search Results, click **Find.** The files will display in the Content panel and the **Search Results** folder will appear on the Recent Folders list, which you can access from the Look In menu at the top of the Bridge window. Each time you perform a search and click Find, another generic Search Results listing appears on the menu, with no hint as to its content. This quickly becomes confusing.

   To save a copy of the search results to a **permanent** file group, click **Save as Collection.** ★ In the Save Collection dialog box, enter a Name, choose a location (the current folder is okay), then click Save; the files will display in the Content panel. Navigate to the folder you chose for the collection; a **Collect** thumbnail bearing the name you entered will display in the Content panel. Double-click the thumbnail to rerun the search and view the search results.

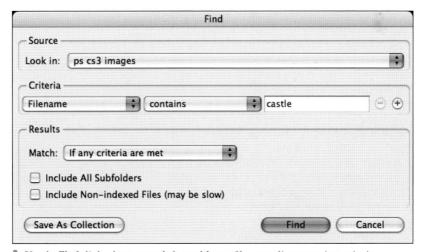

A *Use the **Find** dialog box to search for and locate files according to various criteria.*

Exporting the Bridge cache

Each time a folder is displayed in the Content panel in Bridge, the program automatically creates a cache file containing information about the files in that folder, such as the data for displaying ratings, labels, and high-quality thumbnails. Having the cache helps speed up the display of thumbnails when you choose that folder again. If you want to include this display information with files you copy to a removable disk or to a shared folder on a network, you'll need to copy the cache files—but before you can do so, you have to **build** the **cache files** and export them to the current folder.

To export the cache to the current folder: ★

1. Choose Edit (Bridge, in the Mac OS) > Preferences > Advanced. In the Cache area, check **Automatically Export Caches to Folder When Possible**, then click OK.

2. Choose Tools > Cache > **Build Cache for Subfolders**, then click OK when the alert dialog box appears.

3. Two hidden cache files—named .BridgeCache (metadata cache) and .BridgeCacheT (thumbnail cache)—will be placed into the currently displayed folder.

   If you use the File > Move To (or Copy To) command in Bridge to move (or copy) selected thumbnails, the folder cache you just created will also move or copy, thanks to the export option that you turned on in Preferences > Advanced.

   ➤ To display the cache files in the Content panel, choose View > Show Hidden Files.

If you suspect a folder cache may be causing a display problem, **purging** it may resolve the issue. Doing so will also cause Bridge to regenerate the high-quality thumbnails, so be patient while this occurs.

To rebuild the cache files:

To rebuild the cache files in the current folder, choose Tools > Cache > **Purge Cache for Folder** "[current folder name]". ★ Two new (hidden) cache files will be generated.

ALAS, POOR OPEN COMMAND

With Bridge now taking center stage, the Open command is relegated to this puny little sidebar! To use the Open command in Photoshop, choose File > **Open** (Ctrl-O/Cmd-O). To locate the file you want to open, choose All Formats/All Readable Documents at the top of the dialog box, or choose a format from the Files of Type/Format menu; click the desired file name; then click Open.

Another way to open a file is by double-clicking its **file icon** in Windows Explorer/Finder; this will also launch Photoshop if it's not already running.

Assigning keywords to files

Keywords (identifying text) are used by search utilities to locate files and by file management programs to organize them. In Bridge, you can **create keywords** and **assign** them to your files. You can also locate files in Bridge by using the Find command with Keywords as a search criterion or by checking the desired keywords under the Keywords category in the Filter panel.

To create and assign keywords to files:
Method 1 (via the Keywords panel) ★

1. In the **Keywords** panel, you can create keywords in sets (categories). Select an existing set or create a new one by clicking the **New Keyword Set** button,🗀 then typing a set name.

2. To create a new keyword, click a set name, then click the **New Keyword** button.🔳 Enter one keyword, or enter a series of keywords separated by commas.**A**

3. To **assign** a keyword to an image, click an image thumbnail (or select multiple thumbnails), then click the box to the left of a keyword to make a check mark appear.**B**

➤ To rename a keyword or set, click the word or set, choose Rename from the Keywords panel menu, then type a name.

➤ To remove a keyword or set, click the word or set, click the Delete Keyword button,🗑 then click Yes in the alert dialog box.

➤ You can drag any keyword into a different set.

   Note: If you import a file that has keywords assigned to it already, those keywords will be listed separately (with check boxes) in the Other Keywords set in the Keywords panel, as separate listings under Keywords in the Filter panel, and in the File Info dialog box.

Method 2 (via File Info)

1. Select one or more thumbnails.

2. Choose File > **File Info** (Ctrl-Alt-Shift-I/Cmd-Option-Shift-I). The File Info dialog box will open, giving you access to the file's metadata.

3. In the categories column at the left, click **Description.**

4. In the **Keywords** field, enter the desired keywords, separated by commas.

5. Click OK.

A *We created a **new set** called "Food," kept the set selected, then via the **New Keyword** button, added four new keywords to that set.*

B *Click a thumbnail, then check the **keywords** that you want to assign to that image.*

Opening PDF and Illustrator files

When you open **Adobe Illustrator** or **PDF** files in Photoshop, they're rasterized automatically, meaning they're converted from their native vector format into the Photoshop pixel format. For a PDF, you can open one or more PDF pages or extract raster images from the file. Follow these instructions to open a PDF or Adobe Illustrator (AI) file as a new rasterized document. Follow the instructions on page 57 to place a PDF or Illustrator file as a Smart Object into an existing Photoshop file.

Note: When opened in Photoshop CS3, Adobe Illustrator files that are saved with the Create PDF Compatible file option open in the Photoshop PDF format, not EPS.

To open a PDF or Adobe Illustrator file as a new document:

1. In Bridge, locate and click the PDF or AI file you want to open, then choose File > Open With > **Adobe Photoshop CS3** or right-click/Ctrl-click the image thumbnail and choose Open With > Adobe Photoshop CS3 from the context menu. The Import PDF dialog box opens.

2. For **Select**, do the following:

   Click **Pages** to view the whole PDF pages **A** or click **Images** to view just the images in the PDF file.**B** If you clicked Images, click the image (or select multiple images) you want to open, then click OK—you're done. If you clicked Pages, follow the remaining steps.

   Note: If the PDF you're opening contains multiple pages, click the thumbnail for the desired page, or Shift-click or Cmd-click to select multiple pages. Each selected page is going to open as a separate Photoshop file.

   ➤ From the Thumbnail Size menu, choose a size for the thumbnails.

3. Under **Page Options**, do the following:

   Optional: Type a **Name** for the new document.

   Choose a **Crop To** option. We suggest choosing Bounding Box (the default) to exclude any white areas outside the artwork.

   Check **Anti-aliased** to reduce jaggies and soften the edge transitions.

4. For **Image Size**, do the following:

   For a whole PDF page, you can enter the desired maximum **Width** and **Height** for the Photoshop document (or documents, for

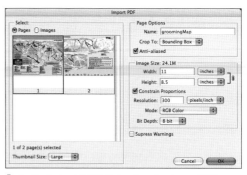

A *In the **Import PDF** dialog box, to open a PDF as a whole page, click **Pages**, click a page, then choose options for the new Photoshop file.*

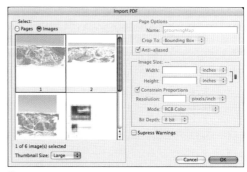

B *Or to open just an image from a PDF file, click **Images**, click an image, then click OK.*

ILLUSTRATOR FILES INTO PHOTOSHOP

You can get Adobe Illustrator files into Photoshop via any of the following methods:

Open command	Opens the file as a new document; converts paths into pixels
Place command *(To place type, see page 349.)*	Opens the file as a Smart Object layer in an existing Photoshop document
Drag path from Illustrator into a Photoshop document	Appears as a new Smart Object layer
Copy object in Illustrator, **Paste** into a Photoshop document	Via Paste dialog box, choose to paste as a Smart Object, pixels, path, or shape layer; the latter two options preserve the shapes as vector objects

multiple pages) or you can leave those dimensions as is. You can also check **Constrain Proportions** to preserve the aspect ratio of the original PDF to prevent distortion.★

Enter the **Resolution** required for your final output device. Entering the correct final resolution now, before the image is rasterized, yields a better rendering.

From the **Mode** menu, choose a document color mode. If the document contains a profile, that profile will also be listed. Adobe RGB is the color space in our color management workflow, so we recommend choosing RGB.

Choose a **Bit Depth.**

We recommend leaving Suppress Warnings unchecked to allow an alert to display if a color profile conflict arises.

5. Click OK.

➤ If you didn't check PDF Compatible when you saved your file in Illustrator, the thumbnail in the Import PDF dialog box will display only a repeating text message. Reopen the Illustrator file in Illustrator, choose File > Save As, rename or replace the file, then click Save. In the Illustrator Options dialog box, check Create PDF Compatible File, then click OK. Now go ahead and open the file in Photoshop.

➤ To create a solid Background for an imported PDF in Photoshop, create a new layer, fill it with white, then choose Layer > New > Background from Layer.

For these instructions, you need to set a preference to allow the **Paste** dialog box to display when you paste an Adobe Illustrator file. In Illustrator, in Preferences > File Handling & Clipboard, check Copy As: PDF and AICB, and click Preserve Appearance and Overprints.

To paste Illustrator art into Photoshop:

1. Edit > **Copy** an object in Illustrator, then, in a Photoshop document, choose Edit > **Paste.** The Paste dialog box opens.

2. Click **Paste As: Smart Object** (to keep the vector object editable) or **Pixels** (to rasterize the object). To learn about Smart Object layers, see pages 302–304.

THE CASE OF THE IMPORTED EPS ★

EPS files are imported into Photoshop in a slightly different manner than AI or PDF files.

➤ If you open an EPS file into Photoshop via Photoshop File > **Open** or via Bridge File > **Open With,** the Rasterize Generic EPS Format dialog box displays.**A** Choose image Width, Height, Resolution, and Mode options, then click OK.

➤ If you use the File > **Place** command in either Photoshop or Bridge, the EPS file will open directly into Photoshop; no import dialog box will display. The file will appear in a bounding box at first (for scaling, rotating, and moving), and will become a Smart Object layer when you press Enter/Return.

➤ If you use the File > **Open as Smart Object** command in Photoshop, the Rasterize Generic EPS Format dialog box will display. Click OK, and the file will become a Smart Object layer.

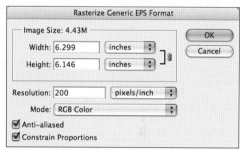

A *The **Rasterize Generic EPS Format** dialog box displays if you use the Open or Open As Smart Object command to open an EPS file in Photoshop.*

AUTO SCALE

If **Resize Image During Paste/Place** is checked in Photoshop Preferences > General and you paste or place a pixel or vector image into Photoshop, the image is scaled to fit the current canvas area automatically.

CMYK COLORS FROM ILLUSTRATOR

To import an Illustrator file that contains CMYK colors, use File > Place to add it to a Photoshop document as a Smart Object (see page 57). This way, the file can stay in RGB Color mode for your work in Photoshop, the CMYK colors in the Smart Object are preserved, and you can convert the whole file to CMYK Color mode for output.

Dealing with the "ifs"

➤ If you open a file in Photoshop that's using a **missing font** (the font isn't available or installed), an alert dialog box will appear **A** and an alert triangle will appear in the thumbnail for the offending layer on the Layers palette.**B** If you then try to edit the layer, yet another alert dialog box will appear.**C** You have two choices: Click OK to have Photoshop change the font to a generic one; or click Cancel, close the Photoshop document, install the required font, then reopen the document.

➤ If the **Embedded Profile Mismatch** alert dialog box appears, it means the file's color profile doesn't match the current working space. See page 39.

➤ If the file you want to open simply won't open, it may be because the required **plug-in module** for that format (e.g., Scitex CT or PICT Resource) isn't in the Photoshop Plug-Ins folder. Install the correct plug-in, then try opening the file again.

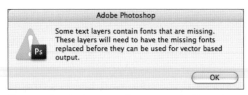

A *This alert dialog box will appear if the **file** you're opening is using a **missing font**.*

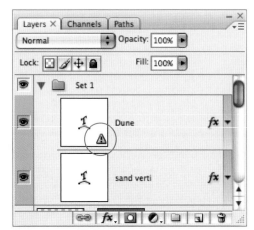

B *This is the **missing fonts** alert icon for an editable type layer on the **Layers** palette.*

C *This alert dialog box will appear if you try to edit an **editable type layer** that's using a **missing font**.*

Now that you've learned how to create a document, you're ready to customize your workspace. In this chapter, you'll learn how to change the zoom level of an image; move a magnified image in its window; switch screen modes; hide/show the palettes; hide/show and assign color labels to menu and palette menu commands; and create and save custom workspaces.

Changing zoom levels

In this section you'll learn how to change the zoom level for an image, move an image in its window, and switch screen modes.

You can display an entire image in the document window or magnify part of an image to work on a small detail. The zoom level is listed as a percentage in three locations: on the title bar of the document window, in the lower left corner of the application/document window, and in the lower left corner of the **Navigator** palette. (The zoom level doesn't affect the output size.)

To change the zoom level using the Navigator palette:

See the illustration below.**A**

*If the image is magnified, you can drag the view box on the thumbnail to **move** the image in the window. Or Ctrl-drag/Cmd-drag across part of the thumbnail (as shown below) to marquee that area for **magnification**.*

*Type the desired **zoom percentage,** then press Enter/Return). To zoom to a percentage and keep the field highlighted, press Shift-Enter/Shift-Return.*

*Move the **Zoom slider**.*

*Click the **Zoom Out** button to zoom out.*

*Click the **Zoom In** button to zoom in.*

A *You can use the **Navigator** palette to change the **zoom level** of an image or **move** a magnified image in the document window.*

WORKSPACES

5

To change the zoom level using the Zoom tool:

1. Choose the **Zoom** tool (Z). 🔍

2. *Optional:* On the Options bar, you can check Resize Windows to Fit to allow the document window to resize as you zoom in or out. The document window will resize only up to the first palette dock on the right side of your screen. ★

3. Do any of the following:

   To **zoom in**, click in the document window, **A** or drag a marquee across an area to magnify that area.

   To **zoom out**, Alt-click/Option-click in the document window. **B**

   To set the zoom level to 100%, click **Actual Pixels** on the Options bar.

   To display the entire image at the largest possible size that can fit on your application window/screen, click **Fit Screen** on the Options bar.

   Click **Print Size** on the Options bar to display the image at its print size (this is only an approximation of the actual print size).

➤ You can also change the zoom level by double-clicking the zoom percentage field in the lower left corner of the application/document window, typing the desired zoom percentage, then pressing Enter/Return.

SHORTCUTS FOR ZOOMING IN/OUT

	Windows	Mac OS
Zoom in incrementally*	Ctrl- + (plus)	Cmd- + (plus)
Zoom out incrementally*	Ctrl- – (minus)	Cmd- – (minus)
Zoom in**	Ctrl-Spacebar click or drag	Cmd-Spacebar click or drag
Zoom out**	Alt-Spacebar click or drag	Option-Spacebar click or drag
Actual pixels/ 100% view	Ctrl-Alt-0 (zero)	Cmd-Option-0 (zero)
Fit on Screen	Ctrl-0	Cmd-0

If Zoom Resizes Windows is checked in Preferences > General, the document window resizes, too. Add Alt/ Option to the shortcut to produce the opposite effect from the current preference setting (to allow the document window to resize or prevent it from resizing).

** *Also works when a dialog box with a Preview is open.*

A *Click in the document window with the Zoom tool to zoom in (plus sign pointer).*

B *Alt-click/Option-click in the document window with the Zoom tool to zoom out (minus sign pointer).*

If the zoom level is above 100%, you may need to **move the image in the document window** to bring the area you want to edit into view.

To move a magnified image in its window:

Do any of the following:

Click outside, or drag, the view box on the **Navigator palette.A**

Choose the **Hand** tool (H) 🖐 or press Spacebar, then drag in the document window.**B**

Click the up or down scroll arrow in the lower right corner of the **document window.** Or to move the image more quickly, drag the horizontal or vertical scroll bar.

If you have **multiple documents** open (say, in a tiling formation), you can save time by **scrolling** or **zooming** all of them at once.

To scroll or zoom in multiple windows:

1. Open two or more documents and put them into Standard screen mode (see "Changing screen modes" below).

2. Do either of the following:

   Hold down Shift while scrolling with the **Hand** tool or while zooming with the **Zoom** tool (or via a keyboard shortcut) to scroll/zoom all open Photoshop document windows.

   Check **Scroll All Windows** on the Options bar before using the **Hand** tool, or check **Zoom All Windows** on the Options bar before using the **Zoom** tool.

➤ If two or more document windows are open, you can choose Window > Arrange > Match Zoom to force all the windows to match the zoom level of the currently active image; or Match Location to synchronize the position of all the images in their windows; or Match Zoom & Location to perform both functions.

Changing screen modes

The **screen modes** change which Photoshop interface features are showing or hidden. Our hands down favorite is the new Maximized screen mode.

To change screen modes:

From the **Screen Mode** menu at the bottom of the Tools palette,**C** ★ choose a screen mode, or press **F** to cycle through the options:

Continued on the following page

A *Click outside, or drag, the view box on the* **Navigator** *palette to move a magnified image...*

B *...or move an image in the document window with the* **Hand** *tool.*

CUSTOMIZE THE BACKGROUND ★

To change the color around or behind the image (from the default gray) for the current screen mode, right-click/Ctrl-click that area and choose **Gray, Black,** or **Custom** (the last chosen custom color) from the context menu, or choose **Select Custom Color** and choose a color from the picker.

C *Choose from the* **Screen Mode** *menu at the bottom of the Tools palette (or press* **F** *to cycle through the modes).*

Standard Screen Mode to display the document window, menu bar, Options bar, and palettes, with the Desktop visible behind everything. This is the default screen mode.

Maximized Screen Mode ★ to display the image on a gray (default color) background (obscuring the Desktop) and expand the document window to fill the space between the Tools palette on the left, the Options bar, and palettes on the right. This mode is dynamic, meaning that if you make a palette dock wider or narrower, the document window will resize accordingly and the image will recenter itself on the background.

Full Screen Mode with Menu Bar to display the image on a gray (default color) background (obscuring the Desktop), with the document window, menu bar, Options bar, and palettes visible, but no dynamic adjustments.

Full Screen Mode to display the image on a gray (default color) background, with the palettes and Options bar visible, but not the document window controls or menu bar (or the Dock, in Mac), and no dynamic readjustment.

➤ In the latter two modes, you can use the Hand tool to reposition the image on the background.

Hiding/showing palettes

If you really want to maximize your screen space, **hide** the currently **open palettes**, then make them reappear only when you need to use them. If you hide the palettes when in Maximized screen mode, the document window will resize automatically to the maximum screen width; redisplay the palettes, and the window will resize again as needed. ★

To hide/show the palettes:

Do any of the following:

Press **Tab** to hide/show the Tools palette and any open palettes or freestanding palettes.

Press **Shift-Tab** to hide/show just the palettes, leaving the Tools palette open.

To make hidden, docked palettes reappear: ★

With the palettes hidden as per the instructions above, move the pointer to the very edge of your monitor. The palette docks (not freestanding palettes) will redisplay temporarily. **A–B** Move the pointer away from the palettes, and they'll disappear again.

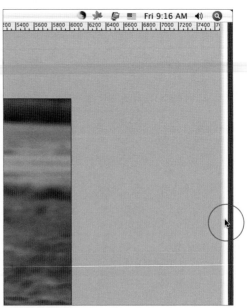

A *When palettes are hidden, position the pointer at the very edge of the monitor...*

B *...and the palette docks will **reappear temporarily**. Move the pointer away from the palettes, and they'll disappear again. Easy come, easy go. (To learn more about palettes and docks, see pages 10–11.)*

Customizing menus

The sheer number of commands in Photoshop can be daunting, but there are ways to make the interface more user-friendly. Using the Keyboard Shortcuts and Menus dialog box, you can assign **color labels** to menu bar and palette menu commands to make them easier to locate, as well as to **hide** any commands you don't use.

Just to get a taste of how the labels look and how they might be useful, from the Workspace menu on the Options bar or from the Window > Workspace submenu, choose one of the predefined workspaces, such as Color and Tonal Correction **A** or Painting and Retouching **B** (click Yes/OK when the alert dialog box appears), then take a few minutes to browse through the menu bar and a few palette menus. On pages 89–90, you'll learn how to save your menu labels and screen layout (palette locations) as a workspace.

To assign color labels to, or hide/show, menu commands:

1. To open the **Keyboard Shortcuts and Menus** dialog box, (**A**, next page) do either of the following:

   Choose Edit > **Menus** (Ctrl-Alt-Shift-M/ Cmd-Option-Shift-M).

   Choose Window > Workspace > **Keyboard Shortcuts and Menus**, then click the Menus tab.

2. If you've already created a custom menu set that you want to edit, choose it from the **Set** menu (see step 5, below).

3. From the **Menu For** menu, choose Application Menus or Palette Menus.

4. Expand any menu header or palette name by clicking the arrowhead, then:

   To **hide** a command, click the visibility (eye) icon; click again to redisplay it.

   To assign a **color label** to a command, click in the Color column and choose a color from the menu. To remove a color label, choose None.

5. To create a **new menu set** based on all the current settings, click the button, enter or change the name (keep the default location, which is the Menu Customization folder), then click Save. User-created sets are listed on the Set menu.

Continued on the following page

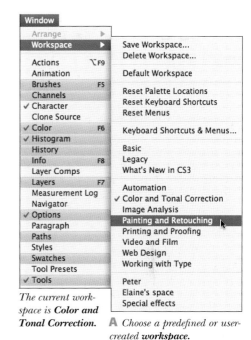

*The current workspace is **Color and Tonal Correction.*** **A** *Choose a predefined or user-created **workspace.***

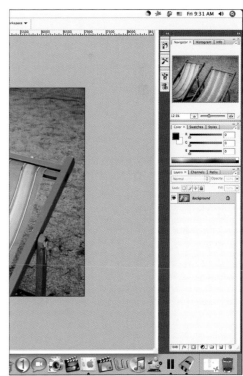

B *The right side of the screen with the **Painting and Retouching** workspace chosen*

To save your edits to the **current set**, click the 💾 button.

(To delete the current set, click the 🗑 button, then click Yes in the alert dialog box.)

6. Click OK. Note: The Show Menu Colors option in Preferences > Interface determines whether color labels are displayed or not.

To make all menu commands visible and remove all color labels:

Choose Window > Workspace > **Reset Menus.**

Note: If you made changes in the Keyboard Shortcuts and Menus dialog box but didn't save them, choosing the Reset Menus command will cause an alert dialog box to appear. Click Save, accept the current name, click Save again, then click Replace in the next alert dialog box.

ASSIGNING CUSTOM SHORTCUTS

To assign custom shortcuts, in the Keyboard Shortcuts and Menus dialog box, click the **Keyboard Shortcuts** tab, choose Application Menus, Palette Menus, or Tools from the **Shortcuts For** menu, then enter or change the shortcut for any of the commands listed.

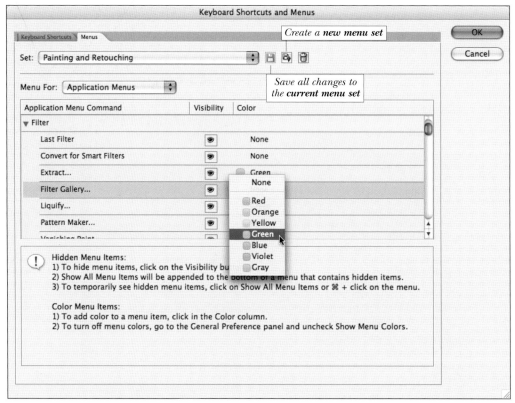

A *Use the* **Menus** *pane of the* **Keyboard Shortcuts and Menus** *dialog box to* **hide/show** *or assign a* **color tint** *to menu and palette menu commands.*

Saving workspaces

Our goal in writing this chapter is to teach you not only how to customize your working environment in Photoshop, but also how to save yourself setup time when you begin a new work session. A first step in this direction is to check Remember Palette Locations in Preferences (Ctrl-K/Cmd-K) > Interface. This way, all the palettes that are open when you exit/quit Photoshop will reappear in the same location when you relaunch the program.

To save yourself even more time, set up and **save workspaces** for different kinds of tasks, **A** as per the instructions below. Workspace settings can include palette locations, custom keyboard shortcuts, and menu visibility and color labels settings (menu sets).

Your custom workspaces should reflect your normal work habits. For example, to set up a text-intensive workspace, you would open the Character and Paragraph palettes and assign color labels to commands that you normally use when creating text. Or to create a painting workspace, you would open the Brushes, Color, and Swatches palettes, assign color labels to the brush preset commands, and maybe hide some unrelated commands.

To create a custom workspace:

1. Do any or all of the following:

Open and **position** all the **palettes** where you want them, in the desired palette groups and docks.

Collapse the palettes you use occasionally to **icons** and **close** the ones you rarely use.

Resize any of the palettes, resize any of the pickers that open from the Options bar, or change the height and/or width of any of the palette docks.

Choose a thumbnail, swatch size, or other **palette options** from any of the palette menus, or from any of the preset menus that open from the Options bar.

Use the **Keyboard Shortcuts and Menus** dialog box to assign custom keyboard shortcuts, color labels, and visibility settings. For shortcuts, see the sidebar on the previous page; for menu visibility and color label settings, see the previous two pages.

2. From the Workspace menu on the Options bar, choose Save Workspace; ★ or choose

Continued on the following page

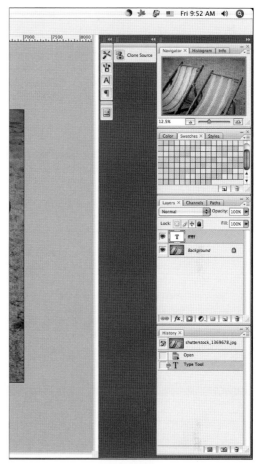

A *The palette setup in **Elaine's image-editing workspace***

Window > Workspace > **Save Workspace.** The Save Workspace dialog box opens. 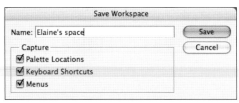 A

3. Enter a descriptive **Name** (include your name, if you like) for the new workspace.

4. In the **Capture** area, check which interface features you want saved in the workspace.

5. Click Save. Your workspace will be listed on, and can be chosen from, the upper portion of the Workspace menu on the Options bar **B** (or for a slower trek, on the lower portion of the Window > Workspace submenu).

   Note: To edit a workspace, choose the workspace you want to edit, make the desired changes to the interface, then save the workspace under the same name (click Replace when the alert dialog box appears).

➤ On a computer with dual displays, you can distribute individual palettes (not the palette docks) between the displays and save that arrangement as part of a workspace.

At any time, you can go back to square one and restore the **factory-default** palette locations, shortcuts, menu visibility, and labels.

To restore the default workspace:

Do either of the following:

From the Workspace menu on the Options bar, choose **Default Workspace.** ★

To reset one category of features at a time, choose Window > Workspace > **Reset Palette Locations, Reset Keyboard Shortcuts**, or **Reset Menus.**

To delete a custom workspace:

1. From the Workspace menu, choose **Delete Workspace.** ★ The Delete Workspace dialog box opens. **C**

2. Choose the name of the custom (user-created) workspace you want to get rid of, or choose All to delete all the custom workspaces.

3. Click Delete, then click Yes in the alert dialog box.

A *In the **Save Workspace** dialog box, enter a name for your workspace and check which features of the Photoshop interface you want to save in it.*

B *Choose a predefined or user-created workspace from the **Workspace** menu on the Options bar.*

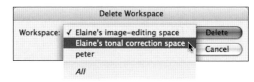

C *In the **Delete Workspace** dialog box, choose a user-created workspace or choose All.*

Before applying adjustment or image-editing commands, you need to make sure your document is the proper size and orientation and is cropped to your liking. In this chapter, you'll learn how to change the resolution and/or dimensions of an image; change its canvas size; and crop, flip, rotate, and straighten it.

Changing resolution and dimensions

In this section, you'll encounter three terms:

➤ The number of pixels a file contains is its **pixel count**, or pixel dimensions (as in 3000 x 2000 pixels).

➤ The **resolution** ("res," for short) of a file is measured in pixels per inch (as in 250 or 300 ppi). The higher the resolution, the finer the detail.

➤ The process of changing the pixel count of a file is called **resampling**.

Some input devices (such as digital cameras that capture 6 megapixels or more, and high-end scanners), produce files with a higher pixel count than is needed for most standard printing devices. In Photoshop, you can take advantage of a high pixel count to increase the print size or print resolution for your output device. You can keep the pixel count constant as you increase the print size (and thereby lower the resolution) or increase the resolution (and thereby lower the print size). In either case, the image quality isn't diminished because no resampling has occurred.

You will need to resample a file if it contains too few or too many pixels to meet the resolution requirement of your target output device. If you resample a file as you increase its resolution, pixels will be added to the file and its storage size will increase accordingly. Resample a file as you decrease its resolution (downsample it), and pixels will be deleted. The only way to get those pixels back is by clicking a prior state on the History palette before closing the file. Even more important, resampling makes an image less sharp. This can be a problem for print output (not Web output), depending on the output resolution and how drastically the file is resampled, although it can be remedied somewhat by applying a sharpening filter afterward (see pages 264–268).

We'll show you how to resize three common types of files for print output—low res/large dimensions, high res/small dimensions, and medium res/small dimensions—and how to resize a file for Web output.

PIXEL BASICS

By default, photographs from a digital SLR camera have a low resolution (72 to 180 ppi) and very large width and height dimensions. They contain a sufficient number of pixels for high-quality output (prints as large as 8" x 10"), provided you increase the resolution to the proper value. You can do this via the **Image Size** command in Photoshop.

To change the resolution of a digital photo (low res/large dimensions) for print output:

1. Choose Image > **Image Size** (Ctrl-Alt-I/Cmd-Option-I). The Image Size dialog box opens. **A**

2. Because you need to increase the image resolution, uncheck **Resample Image.** When you lower the Width and Height (step 4), the resolution will increase automatically.

3. In the **Document Size** area, choose a unit of measure from the menu next to the Width field (we chose inches); the same unit will be chosen automatically for the Height.

4. Enter the **Width** or **Height** for the desired printout size; the Resolution value increases.

5. If the resolution falls between 240 and 300 pixels/inch ("ppi," for short), you've achieved your goal—just click OK. **B** The pixel dimensions didn't change, so resharpening won't be necessary (**A–B**, next page).

   If the resolution is higher than 300 ppi, check **Resample Image,** then enter a **Resolution** of 300. Also, from the menu at the bottom of the dialog box, choose a resampling method. The **Bicubic (best for smooth gradients), Bicubic Smoother (best for enlargement),** and **Bicubic Sharper (best for reduction)** options cause the least reduction in image quality. Because you resampled the image, the pixel dimensions changed. You'll need to resharpen the image after clicking OK (see pages 264–268).

6. *Optional:* Check or uncheck **Scale Styles** to control whether any applied layer styles in the image will be scaled to fit the new size (see Chapter 20).

7. Click OK.

➤ To restore the settings that were in place when you opened the Image Size dialog box, Alt-click/Option-click Reset.

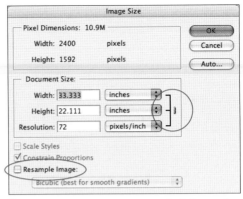

A *In the **Image Size** dialog box, **uncheck Resample Image.** The **Width, Height** and **Resolution** are now interdependent (as shown by the link icon).*

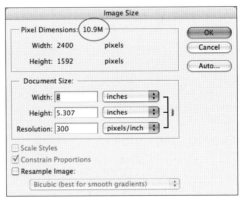

B *When we changed the **Width** value to 8, the **Height** value readjusted automatically and the **Resolution** value increased to 300, but the **Pixel Dimensions** stayed the same.*

JPEGS FROM BRIDGE TO CAMERA RAW

From the new version of Bridge (2.0), you can open JPEG files into Photoshop by way of the **Camera Raw** dialog box. ★ By default, Camera Raw assigns a resolution of **240 ppi** to all files it opens into Photoshop. To achieve that 240 ppi resolution, Camera Raw preserves the pixel count but adjusts the Width and Height (Document Size). To raise the resolution of a JPEG file (say, to 300 ppi) or to reduce its Document Size dimensions, follow the instructions on this page.

A *The original photo has dimensions of **33" x 22"** (much too large for our printer) and a resolution of **72** ppi.*

B *Via the **Image Size** dialog box, we reduced the photo size to 8" x 5"; the resolution increased automatically to 300 ppi. The pixel count didn't change, so the image size and quality were preserved.*

In many cases, scanned images have a high resolution and small size dimensions, and contain enough pixels for large printouts.

To resize a scanned image (high res/small dimensions) for print output:

1. Choose Image > **Image Size** (Ctrl-Alt-I/Cmd-Option-I). The Image Size dialog box opens.

2. Make sure **Resample Image** is unchecked.

3. Increase the **Width** or **Height** to the size needed for your printout. The Resolution will decrease.

   If the Resolution falls between 240 and 300 ppi, you're done; click OK. No resampling occurred, so no resharpening is necessary.

   If the Resolution is still higher than 300 ppi, check **Resample Image,** **C** then lower the **Resolution** to 300. From the menu at the bottom of the dialog box, choose **Bicubic Smoother (best for enlargement)** as the interpolation method. You've just resampled the image, so you'll need to resharpen it after clicking OK (see pages 264–268).

4. *Optional:* Check or uncheck **Scale Styles** to control whether layer effects in the image will be scaled to fit the new size (see Chapter 20).

5. Click OK.

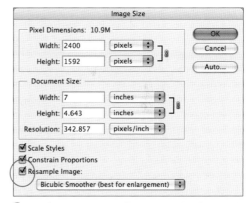

C *Our first attempt at reallocating pixels left us with too high a resolution, so we check **Resample Image**, then **lower** just the **Resolution** (not the Width and Height).*

Small files (resolution of 180 to 200 ppi) don't contain enough pixels to be enlarged without resampling, so they must be **resampled** to achieve the dimensions needed for **print output.**

To resize a scanned image (medium res/ small dimensions) for print output:

1. Choose Image > **Image Size** (Ctrl-Alt-I/Cmd-Option-I). The Image Size dialog box opens.

2. Check both **Resample Image** and **Constrain Proportions.**

3. Enter the desired **Width** for your printout. The Height value will change proportionately and the file storage size and pixel dimensions will increase.

4. Click OK. Since the image was resampled, you should use a sharpening filter to resharpen it (see pages 264–268).

For **Web output,** your files must have a lower pixel count than for print output, because the monitors they'll be viewed on are low-resolution devices. In this case, more than likely you'll need to **downsample** your files (discard image pixels) to achieve the desired output size.

To change the pixel dimensions of an image for Web output:

1. Using File > Save As, copy your file, then choose Image > **Image Size** (Ctrl-Alt-I/Cmd-Option-I). The Image Size dialog box opens.**A**

2. Make sure **Resample Image** is checked.

3. From the menu at the bottom of the dialog box, choose the **Bicubic Sharper (best for reduction)** resampling method, which will degrade the image the least.

4. To preserve the width-to-height ratio of the image, check **Constrain Proportions.**

5. Set the **Resolution** to 72 ppi.

6. In the **Pixel Dimensions** area, choose pixels from the menu (the default unit), then enter the exact Width and/or Height dimensions needed.**B**

7. Click OK.

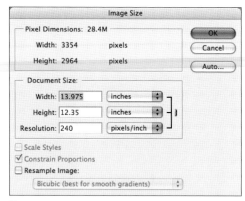

A *These are the initial* **Image Size** *values of a typical digital photo. To prepare this photo for Web output, we need to lower the pixel count.*

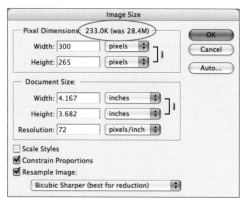

B *We* ***checked Resample Image,*** *changed the* ***Resolution*** *to 72, and set the* ***Width*** *(in the Pixel Dimensions area) to 300. The* ***file size*** *(listed at the top) is now smaller because we lowered the pixel count. The image is now appropriately sized for viewing online.*

COPYCAT

In some dialog boxes that have **Width** and **Height** fields, if you choose a unit of measure from the menu for the Width, the same unit will be chosen automatically for the Height, and vice versa. If you want to prevent this from happening, hold down **Shift** as you choose a unit; the unit will change just for that dimension.

COMPARING PIXEL COUNTS, RESOLUTION, AND IMAGE SIZE

The four images below will help you grasp the concept of **resolution** and how it affects **image size.** The first two figures compare the same image at two different resolutions; the latter two compare the print sizes for those resolutions.

The moral here: Don't judge the size of an image or its output quality based solely on its onscreen size. Instead, compare two factors: the current zoom level of the image in the document window and the image resolution.

A *This image has a resolution of 300 ppi (as listed in the status bar when Document Dimensions is chosen).*

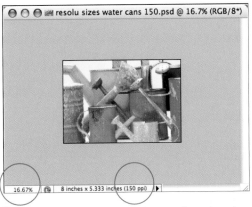

B *This is the same image with the same dimensions, but here the resolution is 150 ppi—half the original. When viewed at the same zoom level (16.7%) the low-resolution image displays at only half the size because it contains fewer pixels (has a lower pixel count).*

C *For this 300 ppi image, we chose View > **Print Size**, which zoomed the image to an onscreen approximation of the printout size (that is, the Document Dimensions, as listed on the status bar). Note the zoom level is 24%.*

D *We also chose View > **Print Size** for this low-res (150 ppi) version of the image; the zoom level here is **48%.** Although this image and the image shown at left will print at the same size, the print quality will be different because this image has a lower pixel count. Moral: Don't use Print Size view to evaluate print quality.*

Changing the canvas size

Using the **Canvas Size** command, you can enlarge or shrink the live, editable image area. You can add pixels to one, two, three, or all four sides of the image.

Note: You can also enlarge or reduce the canvas area by dragging a marquee with the Crop tool (see page 99) or reduce the canvas area by using the Crop command (see page 100).

To change the canvas size:

1. Choose Image > **Canvas Size** (Ctrl-Alt-C/ Cmd-Option-C). The Canvas Size dialog box opens.

2. *Optional:* Choose a different unit of measure from the Width menu; the same unit will be chosen automatically for the Height. Or to choose different units, hold down Shift as you choose each one.

3. Do either of the following:

    Enter new **Width** and/or **Height** values. The dimensions are independent of one another; changing one won't affect the other.**A–B**

    Check **Relative**, then in the **Width** and **Height** fields enter the amount by which you want to increase or decrease each dimension. To decrease either dimension, enter a negative value.

4. *Optional:* To reposition the image on its new canvas, click one of the Anchor arrows. The white (Win)/gray (Mac) square represents the existing image area.

5. From the **Canvas Extension Color** menu, choose a color for the added pixels. Or to choose a custom color, choose Other or click the color square next to the menu, then click a color in the Color Picker (see page 186) or in the document window. If the image doesn't have a Background (take a look on the Layers palette), this menu won't be available.

6. Click OK.**C** Any added canvas area will automatically be filled with the color you chose in the previous step, unless the image contains layers but not a Background, in which case the added canvas area will be transparent.

A *The original image*

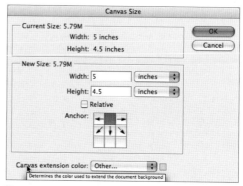

B *Compare the **Current Size** to the **New Size** as you change the Width and Height values. In this case, we clicked the top **Anchor** square and increased the Height to add pixels to the bottom of the image.*

C *After adding pixels to the bottom of the **canvas** area, we created editable type on its own layer.*

Cropping images

You can crop an image by using the Crop tool, the Crop command, or the Trim command. First, the **Crop tool.**

To crop an image using a marquee:

1. Choose the **Crop** tool (C). ⌐
2. Drag a marquee over the part of the image you want to keep. **A**
3. On the Options bar, do the following:

   If you're cropping a layer (not the Background), you can either click **Cropped Area: Delete** to delete the cropped-out areas or click **Hide** to have those areas save with the file but extend beyond the visible canvas area. (You can use the Move tool later to move hidden pixels back into view.)

   Check **Shield** to darken the area outside the crop marquee with a cropping shield (to help you see what will remain after cropping). You can change the shield color by clicking the Color swatch, or change the Opacity percentage of the shield.

   For the **Perspective** option, see Photoshop Help. We prefer to use the Lens Correction filter to correct perspective problems (see pages 262–263).

4. Do any of these optional steps:

   To **resize** the marquee, drag any handle (double-arrow pointer). Shift-drag a corner handle to preserve the proportions of the marquee; Alt-drag/Option-drag a handle to resize the marquee from its center.

   To **reposition** the marquee, drag inside it.

   To **rotate** the marquee, position the cursor just outside it (curved arrow pointer), then drag in a circular direction. (This is a quick way to both crop and straighten a photo.) To change the axis point around which the marquee rotates, drag the circle away from the center of the marquee before rotating. The image orientation will change after the next step.

5. Do one of the following:

   Press Enter/Return. **B**

   Double-click inside the marquee.

   Right-click/Control-click the image and choose Crop.

➤ To cancel a crop marquee, press Esc, or right-click/Control-click and choose Cancel.

A *With the **Crop** tool, drag a marquee over the area you want to keep; the crop shield will appear.*

B *The image is **cropped**.*

Next, we'll show you how you can crop away unwanted portions of an image with the **Crop** tool and wind up with a standard photo size.

To crop an image to a specific size:

1. Open an image, and choose the **Crop** tool (C). 🔲

2. Do either of the following:

   On the Options bar, enter **Width** and **Height** values for the final image. (You can click the Swap Width and Height button ⇄ to switch the current values.)

   To crop using the Width, Height, and Resolution values from another open image, click in that other image, click **Front Image** on the Options bar, then click back in the image to be cropped.

3. Enter the current image **Resolution** to prevent Photoshop from changing it when cropping. It's okay to lower the image resolution (resample it downward), but don't raise it.

   If you clicked **Front Image** and the front image has a different resolution than the image you're cropping, the cropped image will be resampled to that resolution. Remember to apply a sharpening filter afterward; see pages 264–268.

   ► To empty the Width, Height, and Resolution fields at any time, click Clear.

4. Drag a crop marquee on the image.**A** You can drag inside the marquee to reposition it.

5. To accept the crop, double-click inside the marquee; or right-click/Control-click and choose Crop; or press Enter/Return.**B**

   ► To crop an image to fit inside a smaller one, see page 147.

A *We entered a Width of 6″ and a Height of 4″ on the Options bar for the* **Crop** *tool, then dragged a marquee. (The marquee will always keep our chosen 4-to-6 ratio.)*

B *The image is* **cropped** *to a standard photo size of 4 x 6 inches (scaled down for this illustration).*

When you **crop** with a **marquee** that's larger than the image, you effectively increase the canvas size. Unlike the Canvas Size command, this technique gives you manual control over how much and where the canvas area is added. Another use for this technique is to reveal imagery that extends beyond the live canvas area.

To enlarge the canvas area using the Crop tool:

1. Choose a Background color (see Chapter 12).

2. To reveal more of the work canvas (gray area) around the image, either enlarge the document window by dragging the lower right corner or press F for Maximized screen mode.

3. Choose the **Crop** tool (C). 🔲

4. Drag a crop marquee within the image.

5. Drag any of the handles of the marquee into the work canvas (outside the live canvas area). **A** You can drag any center handle to add more canvas area to just that edge of the image.

6. Do one of the following: **B**

   Double-click inside the marquee.

   Press Enter/Return.

   Right-click/Control-click the image and choose Crop.

   If the image has a Background (Layers palette), the added canvas area will fill with the current Background color. If the image doesn't have a Background, the added canvas area will fill with transparent pixels.

   Furthermore, pixels on any layer that were formerly hidden outside the live canvas area may now fall within it, and thus will now be visible.

A *Drag any of the crop marquee handles **outside** the canvas area, into the work canvas. We're dragging the bottom center handle downward to add more canvas area to the bottom of the image.*

B *When we accepted the crop, the added canvas pixels filled automatically with white, our chosen Background color.*

OVERRIDING THE SNAP

Normally, if you resize a crop marquee near the edge of the canvas area and View > Snap To > **Document Bounds** is on, the crop edges will snap to the edge of the canvas area. To override this snap function (let's say you want to crop slightly inside or outside the edge of the image), turn the Snap To > Document Bounds feature off; or start dragging a marquee handle, then hold down **Ctrl-Shift/Cmd-Shift** as you drag the handle near the edge of the canvas area.

The **Crop** command is simple and straightforward, but unlike the Crop tool, you can't use it to change the image resolution.

To crop an image using the Crop command:

1. Choose the **Rectangular Marquee** tool (M or Shift-M).⬚

2. Do either of the following:

   Draw a **marquee** over the part of the image you want to keep.**A**

   To constrain the proportions of the marquee to a width-to-height ratio or size (such as a standard size for a photo print), on the Options bar, choose **Style: Fixed Ratio** or **Fixed Size**, enter the desired **Width** and **Height** ratio or values, then drag in the document window.

3. *Optional:* To scale the marquee, right-click/ Control-click and choose Transform Selection, Shift-drag a corner handle, then double-click inside the marquee to accept the change.

4. Choose Image > **Crop**, then deselect (Ctrl-D/ Cmd-D).**B**

The **Trim** command trims away any excess transparent or solid-color areas from around an entire image—be it a frame, border, or solid-color background. (You'll still wind up with a rectangular image.)

To crop an image closely using the Trim command:

1. Choose Image > **Trim**. The Trim dialog box opens.

2. Click a **Based On** option:

   Transparent Pixels trims away transparency from the edges of the image. If the image doesn't contain transparent pixels, this option won't be available.

   Top Left Pixel Color removes any border areas that match the color of the left uppermost pixel in the image.

   Bottom Right Pixel Color removes any border areas that match the color of the right bottommost pixel in the image.

3. Check which areas of the image you want the command to **Trim Away: Top, Bottom, Left,** and/or **Right.**

4. Click OK.

A *With the* **Rectangular Marquee** *tool, draw a marquee over the part of the image you want to keep.*

B *After choosing Image >* **Crop**

Follow these instructions if you want to **preserve** the existing **width** to **height ratio** of an image as you **crop** it.

To crop an image according to its existing aspect ratio:

1. With an image open, choose the **Crop** tool (C).

2. Drag a **marquee** diagonally across the entire image, from one corner to the opposite corner.

3. Shift-drag a **corner** handle on the crop marquee to resize the marquee proportionately to the desired crop size.

4. *Optional:* Drag within the marquee to reposition it over the portion of the image you want to keep.**A**

5. Double-click inside the marquee; or right-click/ Control-click and choose Crop; or press Enter/ Return.**B**

Flipping and rotating images

You can **flip** all the layers in an image to create a mirror image, or flip one layer at a time. (To learn about layers, see the next chapter.)

To flip an image or a layer:

Do either of the following:

To flip all the layers, choose Image > Rotate Canvas > **Flip Canvas Horizontal** or **Flip Canvas Vertical.C–D**

To flip one layer at a time, choose Edit > Transform > **Flip Horizontal** or **Flip Vertical.** You can use this command to "unflip" a type layer (to make it readable again) after flipping a whole image.

A *We dragged a marquee across the entire image with the **Crop** tool, Shift-dragged a handle, then moved the marquee over the area we want to keep.*

B *We accepted the crop. The original width to height ratio was preserved.*

C *The original image*

D *We chose **Flip Canvas > Horizontal.***

The **Rotate Canvas** commands rotate all the layers in an image. (To rotate just one layer at a time, use a rotate command on the Edit > Transform submenu instead.)

To rotate an image by an exact amount:

Do either of the following:

Choose Image > Rotate Canvas > **180°, 90° CW** (clockwise), or **90° CCW** (counterclockwise).

Choose Image > Rotate Canvas > **Arbitrary.** The Rotate Canvas dialog box opens. Enter an **Angle** value, click **°CW** (clockwise) or **°CCW** (counterclockwise), then click OK.

You didn't use a tripod for that unforgettable moment? Did a sloppy job of scanning? You can use the **Ruler** tool to straighten it out.

To straighten a crooked image:

1. Choose the **Ruler** tool (formerly the Measure tool; it's grouped with the Eyedropper tool).

2. Drag along a feature of the image that you want to orient horizontally or vertically, noting the angle (A: value) on the Options bar.

3. Choose Image > Rotate Canvas > **Arbitrary.** The angle you dragged will appear in the Angle field.

4. Click OK. You can crop the image to remove any background color areas that resulted from the rotation.

A COMMAND THAT CROPS AND STRAIGHTENS

The File > Automate > **Crop and Straighten Photos** command is an action (automated script) that searches for straight edges and rectangular areas in an image, copies a rectangular section that it finds into a new document window, and rotates the image, if necessary, to square it off. You can scan multiple images at a time and let the command sort them into individual documents, or you can use this command to unrotate a document that you've already rotated.

If you think the Crop and Straighten Photos command sounds too good to be true, you're partially correct. For one thing, it's not as smart as you are, so it can be fooled. For example, it may mistake a shadow that the scanner detected around the actual photo for the edge of the image. Also, your images may end up being slightly off square. To help the command do its job properly, don't overlap pictures in the scanner or let them hang off the side.

A *We dragged the **Ruler** tool from left to right along the crooked railing.*

B *We used the Rotate Canvas > **Arbitrary** command to rotate the image along the angle we drew with the Ruler tool.*

C *We used the **Crop** tool to remove the white areas. Now the image looks level.*

The beauty of assigning various parts of a document to layers is that you can edit them individually—maybe some text on one layer, a silhouetted shape on another, and an overall background image behind. An image can contain only one Background (note the uppercase "B"), which is always fully opaque, but you can add as many layers as you like. Unlike the Background, a layer can contain partially or fully transparent areas. By default, transparent areas on a layer are represented by a checkerboard pattern.**A–B**

Creating layers

If you choose Background Contents: White or Background Color as you create a new document (File > New), the bottommost tier of the image will be the Background. If you choose Background Contents: Transparent instead, the first tier will be a layer, and the document won't contain a Background.

Layers are controlled via the **Layers** palette (Window > Layers). The Background, if present, is always listed at the bottom. This palette is so indispensable for image editing, it's the star player in two other chapters and plays an important supporting role in many others. In this chapter you'll learn basic techniques, such as how to create, duplicate, select, restack, group, hide/show, move, merge, and flatten image layers. In other chapters, you'll learn about adjustment, editable type, Smart Object, and shape layers; layer masks; layer opacity and blending mode controls—and more!

A *This image contains two image layers: an editable type layer (warped) and imagery on the Background.*

WANT A SNEAK PREVIEW?

Open image #5 of the downloadable images and show the Layers palette. Click a layer name, then click the **visibility** (eye) icon on/off for that layer; repeat for any other layers.

7

LAYER BASICS

B *The **Layers** palette for the image shown at left*

When you paste a selection, create type with the Horizontal or Vertical Type tool, or create a shape, a new layer is created automatically for you. In this section, you'll learn how to **create new**, **blank image layers** yourself. You may add as many layers to a file as available memory and storage allow.

To create a layer:

1. Do either of the following:

   To create a layer with Opacity and Fill percentages of **100%** and **Normal** mode, click the **New Layer** button ▣ at the bottom of the Layers palette and skip the remaining steps.

   To choose **options** for the new layer as you create it, Alt-click/Option-click the **New Layer** button ▣ at the bottom of the Layers palette; or press Ctrl-Shift-N/Cmd-Shift-N. The New Layer dialog box opens.**A** Follow the remaining steps.

2. Do any of the following optional steps:

   Change the layer **Name.**

   Skip the Use Previous Layer to Create Clipping Mask option for now until you get used to creating and using layers (see page 174).

   Choose a nonprinting **Color** for the area on the Layers palette behind the visibility icon.👁 You can use the color labels to identify layers by category (type layers, adjustment layers, etc.).

   (For now, skip the blending Mode and Opacity options.)

3. Click OK. The new layer will appear directly above the previously selected layer.

   Note: Layers make your Photoshop files considerably larger,**B** so when you're completely done editing your image, consider using a merge or flatten command to shrink it back down. See pages 114–116 in this chapter.

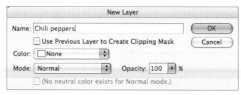

A *Use the New Layer dialog box to name and choose options for a layer.*

B *After adding layers to your file, from the status bar menu, choose **Document Sizes**. The first value is the image size as if the layers were flattened; the second value is the approximate size of the image with layers and channels. This document contains three image layers, which explains why the second value is almost triple the first.*

PRESERVING OR FLATTENING LAYERS

When using File > Save As, provided the Layers box is checked, the following file formats will save a document with layers intact: **Photoshop PDF, Photoshop, Large Document Format,** and **TIFF.**

   File formats that don't preserve layers flatten them automatically and convert any transparency in the bottommost layer to opaque white.

   Also, when switching document color modes (e.g., from RGB to CMYK), be sure to click **Don't Flatten** or **Don't Merge** if you want to preserve layers!

Another way to create a layer is by **copying** or **cutting imagery** from an existing layer or the Background and putting it on its own layer.

To turn selected pixels into a layer:

1. On the Layers palette, click a layer or the Background, then create a selection in the document window.**A**

2. Do either of the following:

   To place a copy of the selected pixels on a new layer and leave the **original** layer intact, right-click/Control-click in the document window and choose **Layer Via Copy** (Ctrl-J/Cmd-J).**B**

   To place the selected pixels on a new layer and **remove** them from the original layer, right-click/Control-click in the document window and choose **Layer Via Cut** (Ctrl-Shift-J/Cmd-Shift-J).

   Either way, a new layer appears on the palette.

Follow these instructions to **duplicate** a **layer** or **layer group** or to turn a copy of the Background into a layer. (To learn about layer groups, see pages 108–110.)

To duplicate a layer or layer group:

Do any of the following:

Click a layer or layer group, then press **Ctrl-J/Cmd-J.**

Drag a layer, layer group, or the Background over the **New Layer** button 🔲 at the bottom of the Layers palette. The duplicate will appear above the original.

Right-click/Control-click a layer, layer group, or the Background and choose **Duplicate Layer** or **Duplicate Group**, change the name in the "As" field for the duplicate, if desired, then click OK.**C**

➤ To rename any layer, double-click the layer name on the palette, type the new name, then press Enter/Return.

➤ When you duplicate a layer, any layer mask and/or effects on that layer will be duplicated, too. If you duplicate a Smart Object layer, any Smart Filters on that layer will also be duplicated.

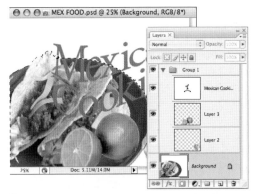

A *An area of the Background is selected (the plate).*

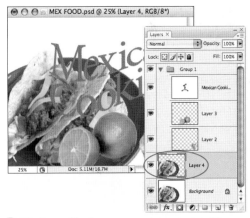

B *The **Layer Via Copy** command put a copy of the selection onto a new layer.*

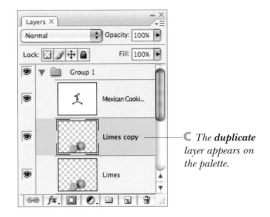

C *The **duplicate** layer appears on the palette.*

There are many things you can do to a layer that you can't do to the Background. For example, you can't move the Background upward in the layer stack; change its blending mode, opacity percentage, or fill percentage; attach a mask to it; or embellish it with layer effects. You can, however, **convert** the **Background** into a **layer**, at which time it will adopt all the normal layer functions.

To convert the Background into a layer:

Do either of the following:

Alt-double-click/Option-double-click the Background on the Layers palette to turn it into a layer without choosing options.

Double-click the Background on the Layers palette.**A** The New Layer dialog box opens.**B** Type a new Name, choose a Color for the area behind the visibility icon 👁 on the palette, if desired, choose a Mode, choose an Opacity percentage, then click OK.**C**

If you need to create a Background for a file that doesn't have one, you can **convert** any existing **layer** into the **Background**.

To convert a layer into the Background:

1. Click a layer.

2. Choose Layer > New > **Background from Layer.** The new Background will appear at the bottom of the stack on the Layers palette.

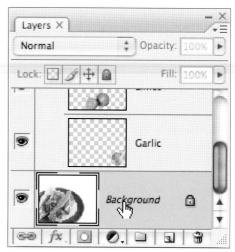

A *Double-click the **Background**.*

B *Enter a Name and choose options for the layer-to-be.*

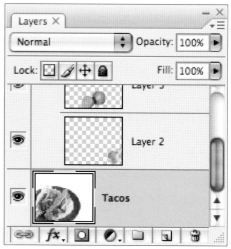

C *The former Background is now a fully functional layer*.

Selecting layers

Get in the habit of remembering to **select** the **layer(s)** you want to work on before making changes to your document. This signals to Photoshop which part of your document you want to edit. The currently selected layer or layer group has a blue highlight,**A** and the name of that layer or layer group is listed in the title bar of the document window. (To create layer groups, see pages 108–109.)

To select layers via the Layers palette:

Do one of the following:

To select a **layer** or **layer group**, click either the layer thumbnail or the area to the right of the layer or group name.

To select **multiple layers**, click a layer, then Shift-click the last in a series of consecutively listed layers, or Ctrl-click/Cmd-click individual layers (Ctrl-click/Cmd-click to deselect individual layers).

To select **all** the layers in your document (but not the Background), choose Select > All Layers (Ctrl-Alt-A/Cmd-Option-A).

To select **all layers** of a **similar kind**, such as all image layers, shape layers, or adjustment layers, right-click/Control-click one of the layers in the desired category and choose Select Similar Layers.

To select a layer or layer group with the Move tool:

1. Choose the **Move** tool (V).

2. Do either of the following:

   Right-click/Control-click in the document window and choose a **layer** or **layer group** name on the context menu.**B** (Ctrl-right-click/Cmd-Control-click with any other tool selected.) Only layers containing nontransparent pixels under the pointer will be listed on the context menu.

   Check **Auto-Select** on the Move tool Options bar, choose Group or Layer, ★ then click any visible pixels in the document window.

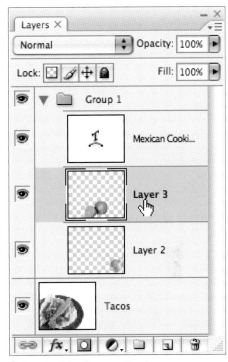

A *Simply click a layer to **select** it.*

B *On the context menu, choose the layer you want to select.*

Restacking layers

To restack layers:

Drag a layer or group name upward or downward on the palette, and release the mouse when a dark horizontal line appears in the desired location.**A–B**

➤ To move the Background upward on the list, you must convert it into a layer first (see page 106). You can't stack any layers below the Background.

➤ You can also restack a selected layer by choosing a command on the Layer > Arrange submenu.

Working with layer groups

Layer groups are to layers what folders are to files: they allow you to collect, label, and organize. By using layer groups, you can shorten the list of names on the palette, which makes for less scrolling up and down.**C** Groups can be nested inside other groups, up to five levels deep.

In addition to being handy for tidying up, by putting layers in a group, you can move, rotate, scale, duplicate, restack, lock/unlock, and hide/show them simultaneously.

Any adjustment layer, blending mode (except for Pass Through), or opacity percentage that you apply to a group will affect just the layers within that group. A layer mask, when applied to a layer group, will affect all the layers in that group.

To create a layer group:

Method 1

1. Do either of the following:

   To create a group without choosing settings for it, click the layer above which you want the group to appear, then click the **New Group** button 🗀 at the bottom of the Layers palette.

   To choose settings for the group as you create it, **Alt-click/Option-click** the New Group button or choose **New Group** from the palette menu, change the Name, Color, blending Mode, or Opacity setting for the new group, if desired; then click OK.

2. On the Layers palette, drag layers into the new layer group. Release the mouse when the dark drop zone rectangle appears.

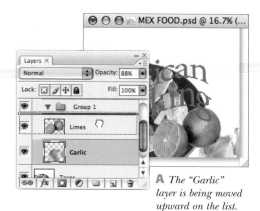

A *The "Garlic" layer is being moved upward on the list.*

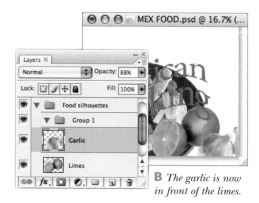

B *The garlic is now in front of the limes.*

C *The "Limes" and "Garlic" layers are in a group.*

Method 2

1. Click a layer, then Shift-click or Ctrl-click/Cmd-click two or more layers.

2. Do either of the following:

   Press **Ctrl-G/Cmd-G.**

   From the palette menu, choose **New Group from Layers.** The selected layers will be nested in the new group.

➤ Click the arrow to expand/collapse any group list.

➤ To group layers into a Smart Object, see page 302.

To rename a layer or layer group:

1. Double-click a layer or layer group name on the Layers palette.

2. Type a new name.**A**

3. Press Enter/Return or click away from the name.

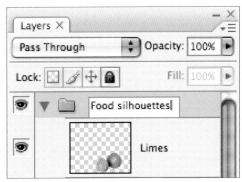

A *A **layer group** is being **renamed**.*

MOVING LAYERS OUT OF A GROUP

➤ To move a layer **out of a group,** drag the layer above or below any layer outside the group.

➤ To move a layer **to another group,** drag it over the group name or icon.

➤ If you end up with an **empty** group folder that you want to delete, expand it to make sure it's truly empty, then drag it onto the Delete Layer button.

USING THE CONTEXT MENU

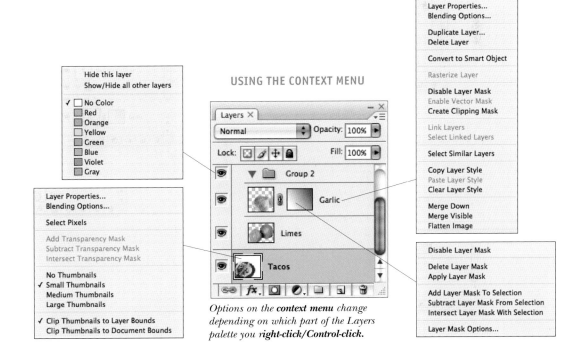

*Options on the **context menu** change depending on which part of the Layers palette you **right-click/Control-click**.*

You can **delete** a **layer group** and its layers or merely **disband** the group and keep the layers.

To delete or disband a layer group:

Do one of the following:

On the Layers palette, click a group. Click the **Delete Layer** button, 🗑 then click **Group Only** or **Group and Contents;** or to bypass the prompt and delete the group and its contents, Alt-click/Option-click the Delete Layer button.

Right-click/Control-click a group and choose **Delete Group** from the context menu, then click **Group Only** or **Group and Contents.**

To disband a layer group without deleting the layers it contains, click the group, then press **Ctrl-Shift-G/Cmd-Shift-G.** The group icon disappears.

Deleting individual layers

To delete a layer:

Do either of the following:

On the Layers palette, click a layer. Click the **Delete Layer** button, 🗑 then click Yes; or to bypass the prompt, Alt-click/Option-click the Delete Layer button.

Right-click/Control-click the layer you want to delete, choose **Delete Layer** from the context menu, then click Yes.

➤ Change your mind? Choose Edit > Undo or click the prior state on the History palette.

Hiding/showing layers

By **hiding layers** you're not currently working on, you remove them as a visual distraction. Only visible layers will print. (Note: When we write "layers" in the following instructions, we're referring collectively to layers and the Background.)

To hide or show layers:

Do one of the following:

To hide a **layer** or **layer group,** click the visibility icon 👁 on the Layers palette.**A–B** Click there again to redisplay the layer or layer group.

To hide or show **multiple layers,** drag upward or downward in the visibility column.

To hide or show **all layers** except the **one** you click on, Alt-click/Option-click a visibility icon or right-click/Control-click in the visibility column and choose Show/Hide all other layers.

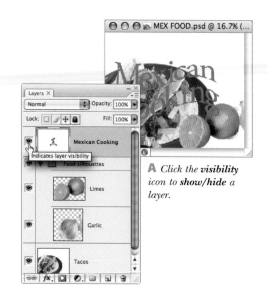

A *Click the **visibility** icon to **show/hide** a layer.*

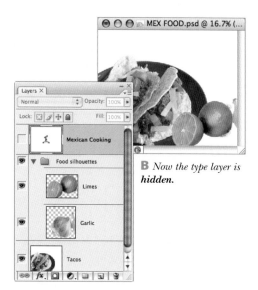

B *Now the type layer is **hidden.***

Moving layer content

Follow these instructions to **move** a **layer or group** of layers by dragging. (To move linked layers, see page 297. To align layers via buttons on the Options bar, see page 160.)

To move layers manually:

1. On the Layers palette, click a layer (or Shift-click or Ctrl-click/Cmd-click two or more layers).

2. Choose the **Move** tool (V) ⊕ or hold down Ctrl/Cmd if another tool is chosen (for a temporary Move tool).

3. Drag in the document window. The entire layer will move. **A–B** If you move part of the layer outside the canvas area, don't worry—it will be saved with the document and you can move it back into view at any time.

➤ To move a group of layers, click the group, choose the Move tool (V), check Auto-Select and choose Groups on the Options bar, ★ then drag the group in the document window. To move an individual layer in a group, check Auto-Select and choose Layer on the Options bar, then click or drag the layer.

➤ To nudge a selected layer by one pixel at a time, choose the Move tool, then press an arrow key. Press Shift-arrow to move a layer by 10 screen pixels at a time. Don't press Alt-arrow/Option-arrow—unless you want to duplicate the layer.

➤ In the mood for Mexican food yet?

A *The type layer is being moved with the* **Move** *tool.*

B *The type layer was* **moved** *to the left.*

MOVING SMART

You can use smart guides to align the edge of a layer you're moving with the edge or center of other layers. Turn on View > Show > **Smart Guides.** Move a layer or layer group, and temporary guide lines will appear onscreen as the edge of the layer imagery you're moving encounters the edge or center of nontransparent pixels, type, or a shape on another layer.

FLIPPING OUT

On the Layers palette, click a layer or layer group, then choose Edit > Transform > **Flip Horizontal** or **Flip Vertical.** Any layers that are linked to the selected layer(s) will flip, too.

Choosing Layers palette options

You can dramatically change the appearance of a layer and the layers below it by changing its **blending mode** and/or **opacity percentage.A** By lowering the layer opacity you lighten its contents—imagery, brush strokes, type, shape, Smart Object, or adjustment command—as well as any applied layer effects. The blending modes affect how pixels or type on a layer blend with underlying layers.

Note: This is just a brief intro to these two features. The blending modes are illustrated on pages 192–196 and discussed on pages 288–289; and the Opacity and Fill options are explored more fully on page 287. The Fill percentage comes into play when you apply layer effects.

To change the blending mode or opacity of a layer or layer group:

1. Click a layer or layer group that overlaps imagery on a layer below it so you'll be able to see the results.

2. Choose a **blending mode** from the menu at the top of the palette, or change the **Opacity** percentage (use the scrubby slider).

The **Lock Transparent Pixels** button on the Layers palette prevents or allows the editing of transparent pixels by any command or tool. By way of example, in the following instructions you'll learn how this option affects strokes that you'll apply with the Brush tool. By default, transparent pixels on a layer are represented by a gray and white checkerboard.

To limit edits by locking transparent pixels:

1. Click a layer.

2. Choose the **Brush** tool (B). (To change the brush diameter, press [or].)

3. On the Layers palette, click the **Lock Transparent Pixels** button, then draw brush strokes on the layer.**B** Only nontransparent pixels can be recolored.

4. Show the **Swatches** palette, then click a color.

5. Click the **Lock Transparent Pixels** button again (or press /) to toggle it off.

6. Paint on the layer again. Now all layer pixels can be edited, whether transparent or not.**C**

▶ The Lock Transparent Pixels option isn't available for editable type layers.

A We chose Linear Burn **mode** for the type layer and lowered the **Opacity** of the "Limes" layer to 55% (compare with the image on the previous page).

B With the **Lock Transparent Pixels** option on, only nontransparent pixels are affected by our brush strokes.

C With the **Lock Transparent Pixels** option off, brush strokes can be applied anywhere on the layer.

CUSTOMIZE THE CHECKERBOARD

To change the size or color of the checkerboard pattern (grid) that represents transparent pixels, or to hide the checkerboard, visit Preferences (Cmd-K/Control-K) > **Transparency & Gamut.**

PALETTE ICONS IN OTHER CHAPTERS

Button	Icon	Ch.
Link button	⇔	19
Layer Style menu	*fx.*	20
Add Layer Mask button	◻	8
New Fill/Adjustment Layer menu	◐.	11

Use the **lock options** for **layers** to prevent inadvertent edits.

To lock a layer or layer group:

1. Click a layer or layer group.

2. Do any of the following:

   Click the **Lock Image Pixels** button 🖌 to prevent layer pixels from being edited. You can still move the layer, as well as choose options for it, such as layer effects, blending mode, opacity, etc.

   Click the **Lock Position** button ✛ to lock only the location of the layer. The layer can still be edited.

   Click the **Lock All** button 🔒 to prevent the layer from being moved or edited. This button is also available for layer groups.

   A lock icon **A** will appear on the palette.

To choose thumbnail options for the Layers palette:

Right-click/Control-click a layer thumbnail and choose any of the following:

A different **thumbnail size,** or No Thumbnails (turning off thumbnails boosts the program's performance but frankly, we find it impossible to work without them).

Clip Thumbnails to Layer Bounds to show only the area that encompasses the opaque pixels on the layer in the palette thumbnails (this is useful if your layers contain silhouetted shapes);**B** or **Clip Thumbnails to Document Bounds** to include surrounding transparent pixels in the thumbnails.

➤ To assign a different color to the area behind the visibility icon 👁 on a layer, click the layer, right-click/Control-click in the visibility column, and choose a color.**C**

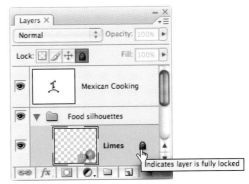

A *This layer is fully **locked** (note the dark padlock), meaning it can't be moved or edited.*

B *We chose **Clip Thumbnails to Layer Bounds** and **Medium Thumbnails** for our Layers palette. Why is it prettier than yours? See the next figure.*

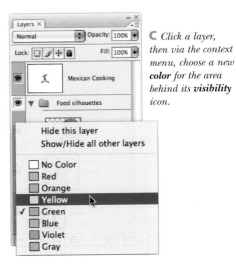

C *Click a layer, then via the context menu, choose a new **color** for the area behind its **visibility** icon.*

Merging layers

The merge commands—**Merge Down, Merge Layers,** and **Merge Visible**—merge two or more selected layers into one layer (the bottommost of the selected layers). You can apply any of these commands periodically during the editing process, both to reduce the file size of your document and to keep the Layers palette from getting overly cluttered. (The Flatten Image command, discussed on page 116, is normally used as a final step before outputting a file.)

To merge layers:

1. Do one of the following:

   Click the **upper** layer of two layers you want to merge.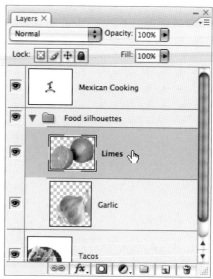 The bottom layer must be an image layer.

   Ctrl-click/Cmd-click **nonconsecutive** layers. The layers can be solo, in a group, or a combination thereof.

   Click a **group.** All the layers in the group will be merged.

   Notes: You can merge an image layer with an adjustment layer, shape layer, or editable type layer. When a type or shape layer is merged, it becomes rasterized.

2. Do either of the following:

   Right-click/Control-click the selected layer and choose **Merge Down;** or choose **Merge Layers** if multiple layers are selected; or choose **Merge Group** if you selected a group.

   Press **Ctrl-E/Cmd-E.**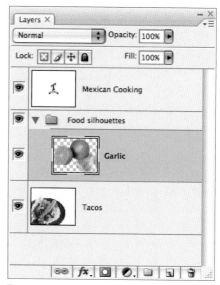

   If the underlying layer contains a layer mask, an alert dialog box will appear; click Preserve or Apply, as you wish.

   If you merged a group, the group icon will disappear from the palette.

➤ If you want to merge layers while preserving access to a copy of the original, separate layers, follow the instructions on the next page.

➤ Adjustment layers can't be merged with each other.

➤ The Merge Down command isn't accessible when the selected layer is locked.

A *We clicked the "Limes" layer.*

B *The **Merge Down** command merged the "Limes" layer into the "Garlic" layer.*

The **Merge Visible** command merges all the currently visible layers into the currently selected layer but doesn't discard hidden layers. By hiding the layers you don't want to merge before choosing this command, you can control which ones will be merged.

To merge only visible layers:

1. Make sure only the layers you want to merge are visible (have eye icons) and hide any layers (including the Background, if desired) that you don't want to merge.

2. Click any one of the layers or layer groups to be merged.**A** Note: If you merge an editable type layer, shape layer, or adjustment layer, it will no longer be editable.

3. Right-click/Control-click one of the layers and choose **Merge Visible** (Ctrl-Shift-E/Cmd-Shift-E).**B**

The commands in the following instructions **copy** and **merge** ("Stamp") two or more selected layers into one new layer in one easy step, while preserving the original, separate layers. If you want to test out some edits (e.g., filters, transformations) on multiple layers instead of just one layer, use one of these commands first, then apply your edits to the merged layer.

To copy and merge layers:

1. Ctrl-click/Cmd-click the layers you want to merge.

2. Do either of the following:

   Hold down Alt/Option as you choose **Merge Layers** from the palette menu (don't release the mouse until you see the new layer appear on the palette). The new layer name will contain the word "(merged)" and the latest state on the History palette will be "Stamp Layers."

   To copy only visible layers, hold down Alt/Option as you choose **Merge Visible** from the palette menu.

► You can also merge layers while preserving access to the originals by creating a Smart Object layer (see pages 302–304).

A In this document, the "Tacos" layer is **hidden**.

B The **Merge Visible** command merged all the layers except "Tacos," which remains hidden.

Flattening layers

Aside from conserving storage space, the main reason for flattening all the layers in a file is to prepare it for output or export. At the present time, the only formats that support multiple layers are Photoshop PDF, Photoshop, Large Document Format, and TIFF. Some applications can read such files, but if the application you're exporting your file to does not, you'll have to either flatten it or save a flattened copy of it using File > Save As. The **Save As** method (which we use) preserves the layered version of the file so you can overwork it to death at a later time.

To save a flattened copy of a file:

1. Choose File > **Save As.** The Save As dialog box opens.

2. Do all of the following:

    Change the file name.

    Check **As a Copy.**

    Uncheck **Layers.**

    Choose from the **File Type/Format** menu.

    Click **Save.**

    Note: The layered version will remain open.

▶ The File > Scripts > Export Layers to Files script saves each layer in a document to a separate file.

If you're the cocky sort and you're sure your image is totally done, *finis*, you can use the **Flatten Image** command instead of saving a flattened copy. This command merges the currently visible layers into the bottommost visible layer—and discards hidden layers!

To flatten layers:

1. Make sure all the layers and layer groups you want to flatten are visible (have eye icons). It doesn't matter which layer is selected. The file in figure **A** contains an adjustment layer, a layer style, and a layer mask, all of which, in addition to the type layer and image layers, the Flatten Image command will rasterize, apply to the image, and flatten.

2. Right-click/Control-click any layer name and choose **Flatten Image.** If the file contains any hidden layers, an alert dialog box will appear; click OK.**B**

    Any formerly transparent areas in the bottom-most layer will now be white.

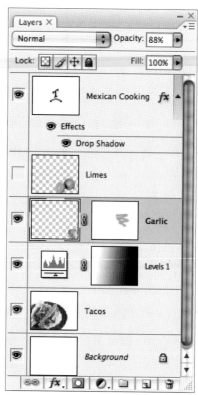

A *When you choose the **Flatten Image** command, it doesn't matter which layer is selected. Here, the "Limes" layer is hidden.*

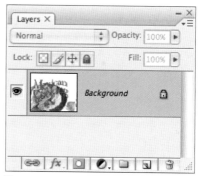

B *All the visible layers were flattened into the Background and the hidden layer ("Limes") was discarded.*

When you select part of a layer, only that area can be edited, and the rest of the layer is protected.
Apply a filter, for example, and only the currently selected pixels will be affected. Selections are represented onscreen by a marquee of "marching ants."

In this chapter, you'll learn how to create selections using the Marquee, Lasso, Quick Selection, and Magic Wand tools, and the Color Range command. You'll also learn how to refine selection edges; modify, move, hide, and transform selection marquees; save selections to the Channels palette; and "paint" selections in Quick Mask mode.

Before or after creating a selection, you also need to let Photoshop know which layer the selection will protect (by clicking a layer). If you move a selection of pixels on a layer (Move tool), the exposed area will be replaced with transparency; if you move a selection on the Background, the exposed area will fill automatically with the current Background color.

Creating layer-based selections

To select all the pixels on a layer:

On the Layers palette, do either of the following:

Click a layer or the Background, then choose Select > **All** (Ctrl-A/Cmd-A). A marquee will surround the entire layer.

To select only nontransparent areas on a layer, Ctrl-click/Cmd-click the **layer thumbnail, A–B** or right-click/Control-click the layer thumbnail and choose **Select Pixels.** ★

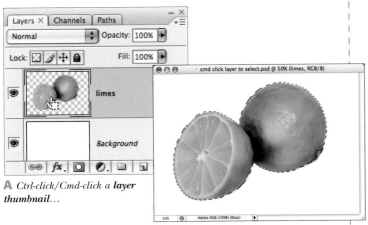

A Ctrl-click/Cmd-click a **layer thumbnail**…

B …to select only the **nontransparent pixels** on that layer.

Creating selections by dragging

To create a rectangular or elliptical selection:

1. Click a layer.

2. Choose the **Rectangular Marquee** 🔲 or **Elliptical Marquee** ⭕ tool (M or Shift-M).

3. *Optional:* To soften the selection edges, choose a Feather value greater than zero on the Options bar. For a smoother edge on an elliptical selection, check Anti-alias on the Options bar.

4. Drag diagonally.**A** A marquee will appear. Shift-drag to create a square or circular selection.

5. *Optional:* To add to the selection, Shift-drag again; to subtract from it, Alt-drag/Option-drag.

➤ To move the marquee while the mouse button is still down, drag with Spacebar down. To move the marquee after releasing the mouse, drag inside it with any selection tool.

➤ As you draw a marquee, its dimensions will be listed in the W and H areas on the Info palette.

➤ To create the thinnest possible selection, choose the Single Row Marquee or Single Column Marquee tool, then click on the image.

To create a selection using a fixed ratio:

1. Choose the **Rectangular Marquee** 🔲 or **Elliptical Marquee** ⭕ tool (M or Shift-M).

2. On the Options bar, from the **Style** menu, choose **Fixed Ratio**, then enter **Width** and **Height** values for the desired width-to-height ratio of the selection (e.g., 5 to 7).**B**

   ➤ Click the ⇄ button to swap the Width and Height values.

3. Drag diagonally on the image.**C**

To create a selection of specific dimensions:

1. Choose the **Rectangular Marquee** 🔲 or **Elliptical Marquee** ⭕ tool (M or Shift-M).

2. From the **Style** menu on the Options bar, choose **Fixed Size**, then enter the desired **Width** and **Height** values.

3. Click on the image.**D**

➤ To change the unit for the Width or Height field, right-click/Control-click the field and choose a unit from the context menu.

A *Drag* diagonally with the **Rectangular Marquee** tool.

B We chose **Fixed Ratio** for the **Rectangular Marquee** tool and entered a **Width** to **Height** ratio of 5 to 7.

C With the **Fixed Ratio** option chosen, any size selection marquee you draw will keep that ratio.

D Enter **Fixed Size** values, then **click** the image to make the marquee appear. You can drag the marquee to reposition it, as shown here.

The **Lasso** is a good tool to use for selecting an area loosely, say, to limit subtle color adjustments to a general area. We also use this tool to clean up selections made with other tools, such as the Magic Wand or Magnetic Lasso.

To create a free-form selection:

1. Click a layer.

2. Choose the **Lasso** tool (L or Shift-L).

3. **Drag** around an area on the layer. Your initial selection doesn't have to be precise, as you'll be able to refine it in the next step. When you release the mouse, the open ends of the selection will join automatically.

4. *Optional:* To add to the selection, Shift-drag around the area you want to add.**B** To subtract from the selection, Alt-drag/Option-drag around the area to be removed.**C–D** We get the best results by starting with our pointer inside an existing selection when adding or outside the selection when subtracting.

➤ To create a straight side using the Lasso tool, with the mouse button still down, Alt-click/ Option-click to create corners. To resume drawing a free-form selection, drag, then release Alt/Option.

➤ To feather the edge of an existing selection, see page 126.

To create a straight-edged selection:

1. Click a layer.

2. Choose the **Polygonal Lasso** tool (L or Shift-L).

3. To create straight sides, **click** to create points.**E** To draw a side on the horizontal or vertical axis, hold down Shift.

4. To **join** the open ends of the selection, do either of the following:

   Click the starting point (a small circle will appear next to the pointer).

   Ctrl-click/Cmd-click or double-click anywhere in the document window.

➤ Alt-drag/Option-drag to draw a free-form segment as you create a polygonal selection. Release Alt/Option to resume drawing straight sides.

➤ While using the Polygonal Lasso, press Backspace/Delete to erase the last corner.

A *With the **Lasso** tool, we selected the top and sides of the ice cream first.*

B *Then, using **Shift**, we're adding to the existing selection to complete the shape.*

C *We want to **remove** the pistachio nut from the selection...*

D *...so we **Alt-drag/Option-drag** with the **Lasso** tool.*

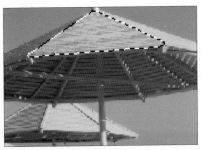

E *We created this straight-edged selection with the **Polygonal Lasso** tool.*

Creating selections based on color

The features we're going to discuss next—the Quick Selection tool, Magic Wand tool, and Color Range command—create selections more automatically. Because Photoshop does the work of detecting the color boundaries for you, the resulting selections tend to be very precise.

To select an irregular area, instead of using a lasso tool, try using the new **Quick Selection** tool. Instead of tediously drawing a precise contour, with this tool you merely drag across a shape and watch as it detects and selects that shape's color boundary. You can enlarge a selection to include an adjacent color boundary or push a selection back to select a smaller area. This is our favorite tool for selecting distinct shapes.

To use the Quick Selection tool:★

1. Choose the **Quick Selection** tool (W or Shift-W).

2. On the Options bar:

   Click the **New Selection** button to deselect any existing selections (or press Ctrl-D/Cmd-D).

   Check **Auto-Enhance** for improved edge detection.

   From the Brush picker, choose an appropriate **Diameter** for the area you want to select. Or to change the brush diameter via the keyboard, press] or [.

3. Drag within the area of the image you want to select.**A** The selection will expand to the first significant color or shade boundary that the tool detects. The selection will preview as you drag, and become more precise when you release the mouse.

4. Do any of the following optional steps:

   To **enlarge** the selection, click or drag in an adjacent area; the selection will enlarge to include it.**B–C**

   To **subtract** from the selection, Alt-drag/Option-drag across it (**A–B**, next page). Alt-drag/Option-drag along the edge of the selection to contract it inward (or click the Subtract From button on the Options bar, then drag without holding down Alt/Option).

   ► To block an adjacent area from becoming selected as you enlarge the selection, Alt-click/Option-click that area, release Alt/Option, then

A We selected the kumquat in the center by dragging the **Quick Selection** tool across it.

B Next, we enlarged the brush diameter, then clicked the kumquat to the right to add it to the selection.

C Then we dragged across the green leaf above the kumquats. The selection spread beyond the edge of the leaf to include some of the background area.

drag to enlarge the selection area. The block will remain in effect only until you click that area again with the Quick Selection tool.**C–E**

To undo the last click or drag of the Quick Selection tool, press Ctrl-Z/Cmd-Z.

➤ To save any selection as an alpha channel, see page 133.

➤ To modify a Quick Selection, you can use any other selection tool, such as the Lasso.

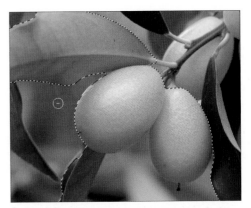

A *We Alt-dragged/Option-dragged below the leaf to* **subtract** *that area from the selection…*

B *…and did the same thing to subtract the area below the kumquats.*

C *We zoomed in, reduced the Brush diameter, then Alt-clicked/Option-clicked areas around the stems to* **block** *them from becoming selected.*

D *We dragged along the stems to select them, then Alt-clicked/Option-clicked the background areas between the stems to* **remove** *them from the selection.*

E *Finally, we cleaned up the selection of the stems and added the kumquat tip to complete the selection.*

With the **Magic Wand** tool, you simply click a color in the image and the tool selects all adjacent pixels of the same (or a similar) shade or color. Like the Color Range command (discussed next), the Magic Wand lets you control the range of pixels the tool selects, but unlike Color Range, with this tool you also have the ability to add non-similar colors to the selection.

To select a color area with the Magic Wand tool:

1. Click a layer.

2. Choose the **Magic Wand** tool (W or Shift-W).

3. On the Options bar:

   Check **Anti-alias** to allow the tool to add semi-transparent pixels along the edge of a shape, thereby creating smoother edge transitions for recoloring or editing.

   Check **Contiguous** to limit the selection to areas that are connected to the first pixel you click, or uncheck this option to allow the tool to select noncontiguous (unconnected) areas of a similar color throughout your image with the same click.

   Choose a **Tolerance** value (use the scrubby slider) to control the range of colors the tool selects (try a starting value between 30 and 40).

   To select possible occurrences of a similar color on all visible layers, check **Sample All Layers,** or uncheck this option to select colors only on the current layer.

4. Click a color in the image.

5. Unless your image contains nothing but totally flat color areas (unlikely), you'll have to do some extra work to refine the selection. Do any of the following:

   To **add** to the selection, Shift-click any unselected areas. **B** To **subtract** any areas from the selection, Alt/Option-click them. You could also perform either task using the Lasso tool with Alt/Option held down. **C**

   To select additional, noncontiguous areas of a similar color or shade automatically, based on the current Tolerance value, right-click/Control-click in the document window and choose **Similar.** (This command works the same whether Contiguous is checked or not.)

A *With the **Magic Wand** tool (**Tolerance 25; Contiguous checked**), we clicked the upper left corner of the image, then Shift-clicked a couple of stray unselected areas in the lower right.*

B *Next, we Shift-clicked the area shown above, but part of the airplane became selected, so we used the Undo command, lowered the **Tolerance** to **15**, then Shift-clicked there again.*

C *Finally, we used the **Lasso** tool with Alt/Option held down to remove parts of the airplane from the selection.*

If you want to turn the selection into a silhouette, follow the next set of instructions.

➤ You can change the Tolerance value between clicks. For example, for greater control when adding unselected shades or colors along the edge of a selection, lower the Tolerance value incrementally. Try clicking with a Tolerance of 30–40 first, lower it to 15–20 and click again, then finally lower it to 5–10 and click once more to further refine the selection edge. To select only one color or shade, use a Tolerance of 0 or 1.

➤ To undo the last click with the Magic Wand tool or to undo the Similar command, press Ctrl-Z/Cmd-Z.

To turn a selection into a silhouette:

1. On the Layers palette, click an image layer. Or click the Background, press Ctrl-J/Cmd-J to copy it, and keep the copy selected.

2. Use any method (Magic Wand tool or other) to select the background area behind an object or shape.

3. Press Backspace/Delete,**A** then choose Select > **Deselect** (Ctrl-D/Cmd-D).

4. *Optional:* Copy/paste or drag and drop a new image into the layer below the silhouette layer. **B–C** (see pages 145 and 148).

➤ To turn a selected object or shape into a silhouette, switch the selected/unselected areas by choosing Select > Inverse (Ctrl-Shift-I/Cmd-Shift-I), then follow steps 3–4, above.

A *We pressed **Delete** to remove the selected pixels.*

B *To create a more dramatic background, we drag-copied a cloud layer from another file (the image of the skier), and stacked it below the silhouetted plane layer.*

TO ANTI-ALIAS, OR NOT?

Before using a selection tool, check **Anti-alias** (if available) on the Options bar to fade the edge of the selection to transparency, or uncheck this option to create a crisp, hard-edged selection.**D–E** The effect of anti-aliasing won't be visible until you edit the pixels inside the selection.

D *The **Anti-alias** option was **on** when this selection was created.*

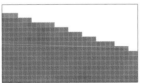

E *The **Anti-alias** option was **off** when this selection was created.*

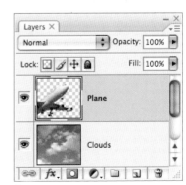

C *This is the Layers palette for the image shown above.*

Creating selections via a dialog box

With the **Color Range** dialog box open, you can click a color area in either the preview or the document window, and the command will select all occurrences of that color or a range of related colors. The dialog box also gives you controls for widening or narrowing the range. After closing the dialog box, you can further refine the selection using any selection tool.

To create a selection using the Color Range command:

1. Click a layer.**A** (The more flat the color areas in an image, the more effectively the Color Range command works.) The command samples colors from all the currently visible layers, but of course only the current layer can be edited.

2. Choose Select > **Color Range**, or if you have a selection tool chosen, right-click/Control-click in the document window and choose Color Range. The Color Range dialog box opens.**B**

3. Choose from the **Select** menu to limit the selection to Sampled Colors (shades or colors you'll click on with the Color Range eyedropper); to a specific preset color range (e.g., Reds, Yellows); or to a luminosity range (Highlights, Midtones, or Shadows).

4. If you chose Sampled Colors in the previous step, click with the **eyedropper** in either the dialog box preview or the document window to sample colors in the image.

   To **add** more **colors** or shades to the selection, Shift-click in the document window or in the preview;**C** or Alt-click/Option-click to remove colors or shades from the selection.

   To expand the range of selected colors, move the **Fuzziness** slider to the right. Or if too many color areas are selected, as shown in the preview, move the slider to the left to narrow the range.

5. Choose a **Selection Preview** option for the selection in the document window: None for no preview; Grayscale to see a larger version of the dialog box preview; Black Matte to see the selection against a black background; or White Matte to see the selection against a white background. Try either of the latter two options to judge how successfully the edges have become selected.

A We chose the **Color Range** command, then with the eyedropper, clicked the blue sky at the top of the image.

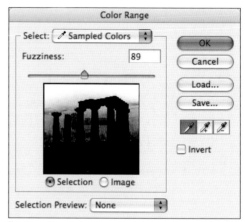

B The white in the preview represents the area of sky that became selected, gray represents partially selected pixels, and black represents unselected pixels.

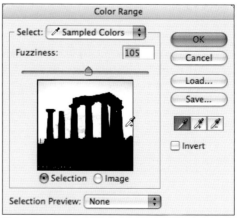

C By Shift-clicking a lower section of the sky in the Preview and raising the **Fuzziness** value to 105, we were able to select the entire sky and background.

6. Click OK.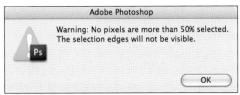A If you chose a preset color range and the image contains only low levels of that color, an alert dialog box will inform you that the selection marquee will be in effect but invisible.B Try selecting another color or range.

➤ To swap the selected and unselected areas, check Invert in the Color Range dialog box. You can use this option to select a complex area of an image indirectly: Select a large, flat color area first, then invert the selection.

➤ To add or subtract colors from a selection, click the + or – eyedropper in the Color Range dialog box, then click in the image or preview without holding down Shift or Alt/Option.

NOT SURE WHICH SELECTION METHOD TO USE?

Don't get overwhelmed by the sheer number of selection methods available in Photoshop. Granted, each method represents the protected versus editable pixels differently; a **selection** uses a marquee, a **channel** uses black and white areas, and a **Quick Mask** uses red and clear areas. But all the methods serve basically the same function: they let you protect part of a layer from editing and signal to Photoshop which area of that layer you're ready to edit. To help you choose which selection method is best suited for the edit you're going to perform, use our handy chart of selection methods on page 140.

A *In the final* **Color Range** *selection, the entire blue sky and distant background are selected, including the noncontiguous areas between the columns.*

B *If this alert appears, it means the color that you tried to select isn't present in sufficient quantity in the image.*

Refining selection edges

Using the new **Refine Edge** command, you can fine-tune your selection edges to remove unwanted background pixels or change the feather value —with five dynamic preview options.

To refine the edge of a selection: ★

1. Create a selection and choose a selection tool, then click **Refine Edge** on the Options bar (or right-click/Control-click and choose Refine Edge from the context menu). The Refine Edge dialog box opens.**A**

2. Check Preview (P). If necessary, zoom in—up to 300%—so you'll be able to see the selection edges clearly (Ctrl-click/Cmd-click the image).

3. To change how the selection previews in the document window, click a **Preview** button (use the tool tips and Description info to learn more):

   Standard for normal marquee display.

   Quick Mask to view the selection as a Quick Mask (useful for judging whether the selection includes all the desired areas).

   On Black to view the selection in color against a black background (useful if you're going to copy the selection to a dark background or if the unselected areas are light in color).

   On White to view the selection in color against a white background (useful if you're going to copy the selection to a light background).

   Mask to view the selection as a grayscale mask.

   ► We usually use On Black or On White.

4. We suggest using the Refine Edge options in the following order (use the scrubby sliders):

   To smooth out small bumps or jagged edges, raise the **Smooth** value.

   To soften the transition between pixels located just inside and outside the selection edge, raise the **Feather** value.

   To shrink the selection inward or expand it outward by a few pixels from the edge, change the **Contract/Expand** value.

   To increase the width of the selection border to incorporate small details (pixels just outside the current edge), raise the **Radius** value slightly.

   To heighten the contrast between pixels only within the selection border to produce a crisper edge, raise the **Contrast** value.

5. Click OK.

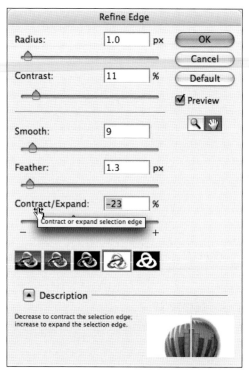

A In the **Refine Edge** dialog box, you can use one of five preview options as you refine your selection edges.

SHORTCUTS FOR REFINE EDGE

With the **Refine Edge** dialog box open, you can use any of these shortcuts:

Toggle preview on/off	P
Toggle current preview/ normal image	X
Cycle through the 5 preview modes	F
Zoom in	**Ctrl-click/Cmd-click** in document window
Zoom out	**Alt-click/Option-click** in document window
Open the Quick Mask Options dialog box	**Alt-click/Option-click** the Quick Mask button
Restore the default settings	Click **Default**
Restore settings from when the dialog box was opened	Alt/Option click **Reset**

REFINE A SELECTION EDGE TO INCLUDE A MINIMUM OF BACKGROUND PIXELS ★

A *We're using the kumquats and leaf selection, which is also illustrated on pages 120–121. In the **Refine Edge** dialog box, click Default, then click the **On White** preview button. Zoom in to 200–300%.*

B *Raise the **Smooth** value to 15 to remove jagged bumps from the selection edge; edges on the stems will become smoother. Raise the **Feather** value to 3 px, note the soft transition into unselected areas (shown here), then reset the Feather to 1 px.*

C *Lower the **Contract/Expand** value to –35% to shrink the selection edge inward, thereby removing background pixels from the selection.*

D *Raise the **Radius** value to 7 px to include more edge pixels (shown here). At this value, the edge is too soft, causing some background pixels to be selected; lower the Radius to 1.5 px to eliminate them.*

E *Raise the **Contrast** value to 40% to sharpen the edge. The contrast at the edge is now too strong (shown here), and there's a hard, noticeable color outline.*

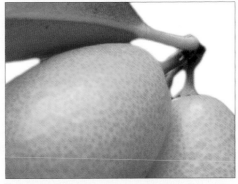

F *Lower the **Contrast** to 16% to soften the hard edge. Now the object is selected accurately. To save the selection to the Channels palette, see page 133.*

REFINING A SMALL, SOFT-EDGED SELECTION

Are there any guidelines for choosing settings in the Refine Edge dialog box? It depends on the kind of shapes you've selected. Large, well-defined shapes, such as those shown on the previous page, require different slider settings than small, soft-edged shapes, such as foliage.**A–B**

▶ To prevent narrow shapes from becoming deselected by the Refine Edge command, keep the Contrast value below 10% and the Contract/Expand value near 0%.

A *We used the **Refine Edge** command to fine-tune the selection of these small, soft leaf shapes.*

B *For the image shown at left, we used these settings: very low Radius and Contrast to include as few background pixels as possible; a low Smooth setting to preserve the naturallly rough edges; a Feather setting of 1 px to soften the edge slightly while excluding background pixels; and a Contract/Expand value just below 0 to prevent narrow shapes from becoming deselected.*

To expand a selection via a command:

Choose Select > **Grow** or **Similar**.**C–D** These commands use the current Tolerance setting for the Magic Wand tool (Options bar). You can repeat either command to further expand the selection. If the Magic Wand tool is selected, you can access these commands via the context menu.

WHY WORK HARDER THAN YOU HAVE TO?

Although you have every right to use the Smooth, Expand, Contract, and Feather commands on the Select > Modify submenu to modify selection edges, we recommend using the all-inclusive **Refine Edge** command instead. Not only does it offer slider equivalents to the above-mentioned commands, it also lets you monitor your changes instantly via a preview.

C *We clicked the blue sky area with the Magic Wand tool (Tolerance 35), Shift-clicked once on the clouds...*

D *...then chose Select > **Similar**. The current Tolerance setting determines what range of pixels is added to the selection.*

Working with selections

If you don't like having to retrace your steps (we sure don't), **deselect a selection** only when you're sure you're done using it. Selections are registered as states on the History palette, but the history is short-lived. To preserve a selection for future use, save it in an alpha channel (see page 133.).

To deselect a selection:

Do one of the following:

Choose any **selection** tool (except Quick Selection), then click **inside** the selection.**A**

Press **Ctrl-D/Cmd-D.**

Right-click/Control-click and choose **Deselect.**

To reselect the last selection:

Do one of the following:

Press **Ctrl-Shift-D/Cmd-Shift-D.**

With any selection tool except the Magic Wand chosen, right-click/Control-click and choose **Reselect.**

Click the state on the **History** palette that bears the name of the tool or command that was used to create the selection.

If you **delete** selected pixels from a layer,**B** the area within the selection will become transparent.**C** If you delete selected pixels from the Background, the area within the selection will fill with the current Background color.**D**

To delete selected pixels:

1. On the Layers palette, click a layer or the Background. If you click the Background, also choose a Background color (see Chapter 12).

2. Do one of the following:

   Press **Backspace/Delete.**

   Choose Edit > **Cut** (Ctrl-X/Cmd-X) to place the selection on the Clipboard.

   Choose Edit > **Clear.**

A Click **inside** a selection to **deselect** it.

B We selected the blue sky, then pressed Backspace/ Delete.

C Because the deleted pixels were on a selected **layer,** they were replaced by **transparency.**

D Here, the deleted pixels were on the **Background** (not a layer), and so were replaced with the current **Background color** (in this case, red).

Follow these instructions to **move** a **selection marquee** without moving its contents.

To move a selection marquee:

1. *Optional:* To help you position the marquee at a particular location, choose View > Show > Smart Guides; or drag a guide from the horizontal or vertical ruler and turn on View > Snap To > Guides.

2. Choose any selection tool (except Quick Selection).

3. Do either of the following:

   Drag inside an existing selection. To constrain the movement to a multiple of 45°, hold down Shift after you start dragging.

   Press any **arrow** key to nudge the marquee by one pixel at a time.

➤ With a selection tool, you can drag a selection marquee from one document window into another.

The **Transform Selection** command affects only the selection marquee—not its contents.

To transform a selection marquee:

1. Choose any selection tool (except the Magic Wand), then right-click/Control-click the image and choose **Transform Selection.A**

2. Drag a handle to scale, rotate, skew, or distort the selection (see pages 298–299).**B–C**

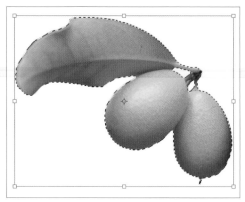

A *We selected a silhouetted image, then chose* **Transform Selection** *to display the transform controls (bounding box and handles).*

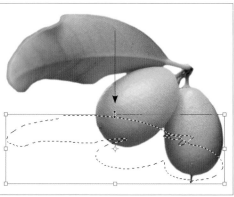

B *Next, we pulled the top center control handle downward to make the selection shorter, then double-clicked to accept the change.*

C *We created a new layer below the image layer, filled the selection with a gray, deselected, then applied Filter > Blur > Gaussian Blur.*

To switch the selected and unselected areas:

Do either of the following:

With any selection tool chosen, right-click/Control-click the image and choose **Select Inverse.A–B**

With any tool chosen, press **Ctrl-Shift-I/Cmd-Shift-I** (or choose Select > Inverse).

Choose the same command or shortcut again to switch back to the original selection.

If your **selection edges** (those "marching ants") become distracting or downright annoying, you can **hide** them temporarily. If you do so, remember that the selection remains in effect even when you can't see it!

To hide/show a selection marquee:

Press **Ctrl-H/Cmd-H.** If this command doesn't work, make sure View > Show > **Selection Edges** has a check mark.**C–D**

Note: The Ctrl-H/Cmd-H shortcut hides/shows whichever options are currently checked on the Show submenu. If all Show options are hidden, you can show any individual option by choosing it from the View > Show submenu.

➤ If an option is unchecked in the View > Show > Show Extras Options dialog box, you can turn it on or off only via the Show submenu, not with the Ctrl-H/Cmd-H shortcut.

➤ To verify that a selection is present in your document, click the Select menu. If most of the commands on the menu are available, a selection is present.

➤ You can hide or show selection edges (via the shortcut) while some Image > Adjustments dialog boxes are open.

A *The original selection*   **B** *The **inverse** of the selection*

C *We applied the Texture > Grain filter (Speckle option) to the inverse of the selection.*

D *Then we **hid** the **selection edges** to help us gauge the effect.*

With the Rectangular Marquee or Elliptical Marquee tool, you can create a **selection** in the **shape of a frame**, either at the edge of the canvas area or floating somewhere within it. You can then apply filters or adjustment commands to the frame-shaped selection, or turn it into an adjustment layer mask (don't worry, we'll teach you all these tricks later in the book).

To create a selection in the shape of a frame:

Method 1 (at the edge of the canvas area)

1. Click a layer.

2. Choose the **Rectangular Marquee** ⬚ or **Elliptical Marquee** ◯ tool (M or Shift-M).

3. In the document window, drag a marquee to define the inner edge of the frame selection.

4. *Optional:* For a soft-edged frame, click Refine Edge on the Options bar, click the On White preview button, adjust the Feather value to achieve the desired softness, then click OK.

5. Right-click/Cmd-click in the document window and choose **Select Inverse.A–B**

Method 2 (within the image)

1. Click a layer.

2. Choose the **Rectangular Marquee** or **Elliptical Marquee** tool (M or Shift-M), then drag to define the outer edge of the selection.

3. Alt-drag/Option-drag inside the first selection to create the inner edge of the frame selection.**C**

A *We created the inner selection with the **Rectangular Marquee** tool, applied a Feather of 25 px (the image is 300 ppi), then chose Select > **Inverse.***

B *We created a Levels adjustment layer to lighten the area within the **frame selection** (see pages 180–181), then added an editable type layer. The type is easier to read on a light background.*

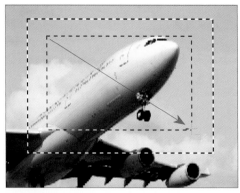

C *Alt-drag/Option-drag one rectangular selection **inside** another.*

The **intersection** of **two selections** is the area where they overlap.

To select the intersection of two selections:

1. With a selection present, choose a selection tool.

2. Do either of the following:

3. Click the **Intersect with Selection** button  on the Options bar, then create a new selection that overlaps the current one; or without clicking the button, Alt-Shift-drag/Option-Shift-drag.**A–B**

A *Alt-Shift-drag/Option-Shift-drag from* **inside** *an existing selection…*

B *…to select only the* **intersection** *of the existing selection and the new one.*

Saving and loading selections

One trademark characteristic of Photoshop pros is that they use the minimum number of steps to accomplish their tasks without redoubling their efforts. Among the most tedious of tasks, even considering the large number of tools and commands at your disposal, is creating selections. You'll be reassured to know that that intricate selection you created with the Magic Wand tool or Color Range command—then painstakingly refined—can be saved for future use. Once saved in an **alpha channel**, a selection can be loaded onto the document at any time, and can be copied to other documents. Any selection that would be time-consuming to re-create is a logical candidate for this procedure.

After learning how to save and load alpha channel selections, you can delve further into this topic by learning how to delete and duplicate alpha channels and to reshape alpha channel masks with the Brush tool.

To save a selection to a channel:

1. Create a selection.**C**

2. Display the **Channels** palette, then click the **Save Selection as Channel** (second) button  at the bottom of the palette. A new alpha channel will appear on the Channels palette.**D**

➤ To delete an alpha channel, click it, click the Delete Current Channel button, then click Yes.

➤ You can save alpha channels with a document in most formats, such as Photoshop, BMP, Large Document, Photoshop PDF, PICT, and TIFF. To do this, check Alpha Channels in the File > Save As dialog box.

C *Create a selection, then click the* **Save Selection as Channel** *button on the* **Channels** *palette.*

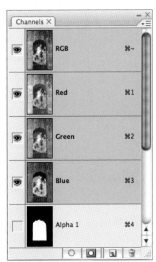

D *The* **alpha channel** *appears on the Channels palette.*

You can **display** an **alpha channel** in the document window without loading it as a selection, just to see what it looks like.

To display a channel selection:

1. Click an **alpha channel** name on the Channels palette. The selected area will be white, the protected area black.**A**

2. To restore the normal document display, click the topmost (composite) channel name on the palette (not the visibility icon) or press Ctrl-~(tilde)/Cmd-~.

➤ If a selection that you saved as an alpha channel had a Feather value greater than zero, the feathered area will be gray and will be only partially affected by editing.

➤ To rename an alpha channel for easier reference, double-click the name on the palette, type the desired name in the selected field, then click OK.

You can **duplicate** an **alpha channel** in the same file, or drag an alpha channel from the Channels palette to another document (a copy will appear on the palette in the target document).

To duplicate an alpha channel:

Do either of the following:

Drag the name of the channel you want to duplicate over the **New Channel** button ⬛ or into another document window.

Right-click/Control-click an alpha channel name, then choose **Duplicate Channel** from the context menu. The Duplicate Channel dialog box opens. Change the channel name (in the As field), if desired, then click OK.

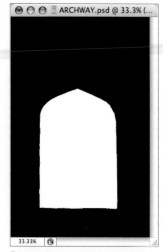

A *We clicked an alpha channel name on the Channels palette to make our* ***alpha channel*** *appear in the document window. The selection area is white, the protected area black.*

To load an alpha channel onto an image as a selection:

On the Channels palette, do either of the following:

Ctrl-click/Cmd-click the alpha channel you want to load. Your selection will reappear in the document window.

Drag the channel name over the **Load Channel as Selection** button.

To combine two alpha channel selections:

1. Create a selection in the document to combine with the existing channel.**A**

2. Choose Select > **Load Selection.** The Load Selection dialog box opens.**B**

3. From the **Channel** menu, choose an alpha channel.

4. Click **Operation: Add to selection.**

5. Click OK.**C**

A *We're going to combine this selection with our existing alpha channel selection.*

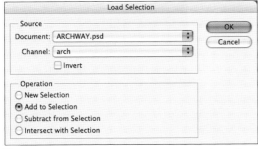

B *In the **Load Selection** dialog box, choose a **Channel** and an **Operation** option (we're choosing Add to Selection).*

C *The **alpha channel selection** (palm trees and sky) is combined with our initial selection (the top of the arch).*

Just as you can switch the areas a selection protects with the areas it does not, you can also **invert** an **alpha channel.**

To reverse the masked and unmasked areas in an alpha channel:

1. Click an alpha channel on the Channels palette.**A**

2. Press **Ctrl-I/Cmd-I** or choose Image > Adjustments > **Invert.B**

SLIM DOWN YOUR FILE SIZES

One drawback to using alpha channels is that they make your files slightly larger, so try to create and keep only the ones you need. To conserve storage space, as an alternative to alpha channels for preserving selections: convert the selection to a **layer mask** and store it on the Layers palette (see page 292).

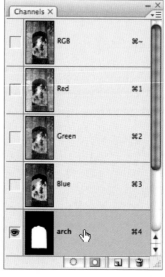

A *Click an* **alpha channel** *on the* **Channels** *palette.*

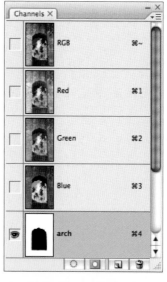

B *The channel is* **inverted.**

You can superimpose an **alpha channel** selection as a **colored mask** (or rubylith, for folks with traditional design training) over an image and then reshape the mask using the Pencil or Brush tool.

To reshape an alpha channel mask:

1. Make sure nothing is selected in your document.

2. Display the Channels palette.

3. Click in the **visibility** column for the alpha channel to make a visibility (eye) icon appear. **A** A colored mask will cover the whole image except over the white areas in the alpha channel.

4. Click the alpha channel.

5. Choose the **Brush** tool (B or Shift-B).

6. On the Options bar, do the following:

   Click the **Brush Preset** picker arrowhead, then click a brush in the picker.

   Choose **Mode**: Normal.

   Choose 100% **Opacity** and 100% **Flow** to create a full mask or a lower Opacity to create a partial mask.

7. Do either or both of the following:

   To enlarge the **masked** (protected) area, draw brush strokes with black. **B–C**

   To enlarge the **unmasked** area, press X to swap the Foreground and Background colors, then draw brush strokes with white. **D**

8. To hide the mask, click the visibility icon for the alpha channel. To edit the image (not the alpha channel), click the topmost channel on the Channels palette.

To delete an alpha channel:

Do either of the following:

Right-click/Control-click a channel name and choose **Delete Channel.**

On the Channels palette, drag the channel you want to delete over the **Delete Channel** button.

A *On the **Channels** palette, both the **alpha channel** and the **composite** RGB channel should have a visibility icon, and the alpha channel should be selected.*

B *This is the original **alpha channel mask**.*

C *Paint with **black** to enlarge the **masked** area.*

D *Paint with **white** to enlarge the **unmasked** area. We're touching up areas that we overzealously masked (as shown in the previous figure).*

Using Quick Masks

With your document in **Quick Mask** mode, you can paint a mask onto the parts of your image that need protection. If you create a selection first, the mask will cover just the unselected areas. In either case, you can reshape (add to or remove from) the mask using the Brush or Pencil tool. By default, the mask is semitransparent red, as in a traditional rubylith. The Quick Mask itself can't be saved, but when you put your document back into Standard (non-Quick Mask) mode, the mask will turn into a selection automatically and can either be saved as an alpha channel or turned into a layer mask.

To reshape a selection by using a Quick Mask:

1. Select an area of a layer.**A**

2. Click the **Edit in Quick Mask Mode** button 🔳 on the Tools palette (Q). A mask will cover the unselected areas of the image.**B** (If it doesn't, double-click the same button, click Color Indicates: Masked Areas, then click OK.) Also, "Quick Mask" will become a temporary listing on the Channels palette and in the title bar of the document window.

3. Choose the **Brush** tool (B or Shift-B). ✏️

4. On the Options bar, do the following:

   Click the **Brush Preset** picker arrowhead, then click a brush on the picker.

   Choose **Mode:** Normal.

   Set the **Opacity** and **Flow** to 100%.

5. Do one of the following:

   Draw strokes with **black** as the Foreground color to enlarge the masked (protected) area.

   Draw strokes on the mask with **white** as the Foreground color to enlarge the unmasked area.**C** (Press X to swap the Foreground/ Background colors.)

   Draw strokes with your brush **Opacity** below 100% (Options bar) to create a partial mask. When you edit the selected pixels, that area will be only partially affected by the modifications.

6. Click the **Standard Mode** button 🔳 on the Tools palette (Q) when you're done working in Quick Mask mode. The unmasked areas will become a selection. (If you want to preserve the selection, save it as an alpha channel.)

A *Select an area of a layer.*

B *The unselected area is covered with a red* **Quick Mask.**

C *We're unmasking the helmet using the Brush tool in* **Quick Mask** *mode.*

In these instructions, you'll **paint the mask directly** in the document without creating a selection first. You can use this technique to select areas for retouching, such as eyes or teeth in a portrait photo.

To paint a Quick Mask:

1. Choose the **Brush** tool, ✐ and choose tool options as per step 4 on the previous page.

2. Double-click the **Edit in Quick Mask Mode** button ▣ on the Tools palette.

3. Click Color Indicates: **Selected Areas**; click OK.

4. Paint with **black** on the image. (The mask you're creating will become a selection when you return to Standard mode.) Paint with white if you need to remove any areas of the mask.

5. Press **Q** to return to Standard mode.

A *We painted a mask on this image in **Quick Mask** mode to protect the critical areas—eyes, nostrils, and mouth—from further edits.*

Via the **Quick Mask Options** dialog box, you can control whether the mask covers the protected or unprotected areas and also change the mask color and opacity.

To choose Quick Mask options:

1. Double-click the **Edit in Quick Mask Mode** button ▣ on the Tools palette. The Quick Mask Options dialog box opens.

2. Do any of the following:

   Choose whether **Color Indicates:** Masked Areas or Selected Areas.

   Click the **Color** swatch, then choose a new color for the Quick Mask.

   Change the **Opacity** of the mask color.

3. Click OK.

➤ To toggle the mask color between the selected and masked areas without opening the Quick Mask Options dialog box, Alt-click/Option-click the Edit in Quick Mask Mode button.

B *When we put the image back into **Standard** mode, the mask turned into a selection. (We'll Feather the selection slightly via the Refine Edge dialog box to soften the transitions before editing.)*

MORE WAYS WITH MASKS

➤ Convert any active selection into a **layer mask.** Only pixels on the current layer that fall within the selection area will be visible (see pages 292–295).**C**

➤ Create an **adjustment layer mask** (page 175).

➤ To **swap** the black and white areas in a layer mask, click the mask thumbnail, then press Ctrl-I/Cmd-I.

➤ Use **type shapes** as a layer mask (page 359).

➤ Create a layer **clipping mask** (page 296).

C *We saved our selection (shown in the previous figure) as a **layer mask.***

CHOOSING A SELECTION METHOD

Now that you're acquainted with a wide array of selection methods, you can use this list to help you choose the most appropriate one for the task at hand.

	Tool or command	What it's good for selecting
SELECT BY DRAGGING	Rectangular and Elliptical Marquee tools	Rectangular and round shapes; can specify a specific width-to-height ratio or dimensions
	Lasso tool	Irregular areas; indispensible for cleaning up selections created with other tools or commands
	Add or subtract with selection tools	Shift to add; Alt/Option to remove; Alt-Shift/Option-Shift to select intersection of existing and new selection
	Polygonal Lasso tool	Straight-edged shapes
SELECT BASED ON CONTRAST/COLOR	Magnetic Lasso tool	Objects or figures that are clearly delineated from their background in tonality or color
	Quick Selection tool	Well-defined shapes, including irregular areas; creates selections automatically by detecting color boundaries
	Magic Wand tool	Color areas based on a Tolerance range; good for selecting backgrounds, such as sky or water; use the Lasso tool afterward to add areas or remove stray areas from the selection
	Color Range command	Discrete color areas; via a dialog box, lets you select all occurrences of one color or a range of tonal values
MODIFY SELECTIONS	Refine Edge command	Refine the smoothness, sharpness, and precision of a selection edge; preview the selection on different backgrounds
	Grow, Similar commands	Enlarge selections based on current Tolerance setting of Magic Wand tool; Similar command is good for selecting noncontiguous, but similar, areas
OTHER RELATED TECHNIQUES	Extract command*	Select intricate shapes by using masking tools in a dialog box; creates a new layer containing just the extracted pixels
	Convert selection to path*	Reshape the former selection using anchor points; convert back to a selection after reshaping or store as a path for later conversion
	Trace shape with Pen tool*	Create smooth, precise paths, then convert it to a selection
	Quick Mask mode	Paint a mask onto an image "by hand" in Quick Mask mode (and easily remove areas of the mask where necessary); converts to a selection automatically upon return to Standard mode
	Save/load selections	Save selections as alpha channels to preserve for later use; you can combine an alpha channel selection with an existing selection

This technique is not covered in this book.

If we had to pick one chapter that represents the heart and soul of Photoshop, this would be it. Here you'll learn how to copy selections and layers within the same document and between documents, and use layer masks to blend images together. You'll also learn about the Pattern Stamp tool, the Photomerge command, and features for positioning and aligning layers. You'll be amazed at how easy (and how much fun) it is to create composite images!

Moving selection contents

In the instructions on this page, you'll **move a selection** of pixels in the same file. (To move a selection marquee but not its contents, see page 130.)

To move selection contents:

1. Create a selection. *Optional:* To help you position the selection, choose View > Show > Smart Guides to display alignment guides; or display the rulers, then drag a guide from either ruler. Also turn on View > Snap To > Guides.

2. Do either of the following:

   On the Layers palette, click the **Background**, then choose a Background color (see pages 185–188). The area you expose (in step 4) will fill with this color.

   Click a **layer.** The area you expose will fill with transparent pixels automatically.

3. Choose the **Move** tool (V). (Ctrl/Cmd accesses this tool when most other tools are selected.)

4. Position the pointer over the selection, then drag. Imagery within the selected area will move. **A–B** When you deselect the selection, its contents will drop back into its original layer (but in the new location), regardless of which layer is selected.

➤ With the Move tool chosen, press an arrow key to nudge a selection in 1-pixel increments, or press Shift-arrow to nudge a selection in 10-pixel increments.

A *A selection is moved on a layer.*

B *A selection is moved on the Background.*

Duplicating selections

To drag-copy a selection in the same document:

1. Click a layer and create a selection.

2. Do either of the following:

   Choose the **Move** tool (V),⊹ then **Alt-drag/ Option-drag** the selection.**A** The duplicate pixels will remain selected.**B**

   With any other tool selected, **Ctrl-Alt-drag/ Cmd-Option-drag** the selection.

➤ Include Shift with either shortcut listed above to move the selection at an increment of 45°.

A *Create a **selection** on a layer or the Background (we selected the window with the Rectangular Marquee tool), then Alt-drag/Option-drag it with the **Move** tool.*

C *We created a selection.*

B *A copy of the window is made.*

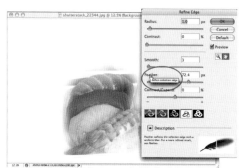

D *We used the Refine Edge command to **feather** the edge of the selection.*

E *The **feather** becomes visible when we **drag-copy** the selection.*

REFINE EDGE IN ACTION ★

The **Feather** option in the **Refine Edge** dialog box fades a selection edge by a specified number of pixels. With a selection active,**C** right-click/Control-click in the document window and choose Refine Edge (or click Refine Edge on the Options bar). Click Default, then choose a Feather value.**D** The higher the document resolution, the higher the Feather value needed (for a 300 ppi image, try a value between 35 and 65 px, depending on how soft you want the edge to be). The feather will preview while the dialog box is open, disappear when you click OK, then become visible again in the document when you move, drag-copy,**E** copy/paste, or apply edits to (paint, filter, etc.) the selection.

When you **drag and drop a selection** of pixels from one document to another, presto, a duplicate of those pixels appears on a new layer in the target document. This method doesn't use the Clipboard, so it's not memory-intensive.

To drag and drop a selection between documents:

1. Open the source and target documents, and arrange the windows so you can see some of each one.

2. In the source document, create a selection on a layer or the Background.

3. Choose the **Move** tool (V). (Ctrl/Cmd accesses the Move tool when most other tools are selected.)

   With the Move tool selected, you can check **Show Transform Controls** on the Move Options bar to make visible the bounding box that surrounds the selection.

4. Drag the selection into the target document window, and release the mouse where you want the pixels to be dropped.**A–B** Or Shift-drag to have the selection appear in the exact center of the target document, regardless of where you release the mouse.

   The duplicate imagery will appear on a new layer automatically; you can reposition it using the Move tool.

➤ Does the imagery that you dragged and dropped look larger or smaller? Read the sidebar on the next page.

➤ To drag-copy a layer between documents, see page 148.

➤ Press Alt-arrow/Option-arrow to duplicate a selection and offset it by 1 pixel, or press Alt-Shift-arrow/Option-Shift-arrow to duplicate and offset a selection by 10 pixels.

A *Drag a selection from one document to another.*

B *When you release the mouse, a **copy** of the **selected** pixels will appear in the target document; the source document stays the same.*

DE-MATTE OR CONTRACT

➤ Let's say you select imagery on a black or dark background with Anti-alias on, then move or paste it. You could try choosing the one-step Layer > Matting > **Remove Black Matte** command to remove unwanted remnants from the black background. Or to remove remnants from a white background, choose Layer > Matting > **Remove White Matte.** You're more likely to notice the change if the selection had a feathered edge.

➤ By using the **Contract/Expand** slider in the **Refine Edge** dialog box, ★ you can contract a selection (remove edge pixels) to achieve a cleaner edge — with a preview to boot. (This method is more flexible than the Defringe command.)

Using the Clipboard

You can use the Edit > **Cut**, **Copy**, or **Copy Merged** command to put a selection in a temporary storage area in memory, called the Clipboard, then use Edit > **Paste** or **Paste Into** to paste the Clipboard pixels into another layer in the same document or in another document. These commands are available only while a selection is active in your document.

If you Cut a selection from the Background, the exposed area will fill with the current Background color automatically. If you cut a selection from a layer, the area left behind will be replaced with transparency. (The same thing happens when you move pixels on a layer.)

The Edit > Paste command automatically pastes the Clipboard contents into a new layer. If you paste into a document of smaller pixel dimensions, any pasted pixels that extend beyond the canvas area will be preserved (and will save with the document) and can be moved into view with the Move tool (see the sidebar on the next page).

You can paste the same Clipboard contents as many times as you like. Only one selection can be stored on the Clipboard at a time, though, and it will be replaced by new contents each time you choose the Cut, Copy, or Copy Merged command. With **Export Clipboard** checked in Preferences > General, the Clipboard contents will stay in temporary system memory even if you exit/quit Photoshop (but only until you shut down your computer).

➤ The dimensions in the File > New dialog box automatically match the dimensions of the current contents of the Clipboard, if any.

➤ The Edit > Clear command empties a selection area without using the Clipboard.

➤ To slightly soften the edge of imagery that you cut/copy and paste, check Anti-alias on the Options bar for your selection tool before using it. Or use the Refine Edge dialog box after creating a selection to refine the edge.

HONEY, WHO SHRANK MY PICTURE?!

When you paste or drag and drop a selection between documents, the copy is rendered in the **resolution** of the **target document.** If the resolution of the target document is higher than that of the source imagery, the copy will look smaller; **A** if the resolution of the target document is lower than that of the source document, the copy will look larger. To prevent this size discrepancy when copying to a higher-resolution file, before creating the copy, increase the resolution of the target document (Image > Image Size) to match the source document, and to avoid confusion, set both document windows to the same zoom level. (To match the dimensions of two images with the Crop tool, see page 147.)

A *These two documents have the same width and height and the same zoom levels, but the pasted image looks* **smaller.** *Why? Because the source document (top) has a* **lower resolution** *than the target document (bottom).*

When using the **Clipboard** commands (Cut, Copy, or Copy Merged, then Paste), if the dimensions of the selection you copy are larger than those of the target document, some pixels will paste outside the canvas area and will be hidden from view. You can move the layer with the Move tool to bring hidden pixels back into view.

To copy and paste a selection:

1. Click a layer or the Background, then create a selection. *Optional:* To refine the selection edge, use the Refine Edge dialog box.

2. Choose one of the following commands:

   Edit > **Copy** **A** (Ctrl-C/Cmd-C) to copy pixels from the current layer within the selection area.

   Edit > **Copy Merged** (Ctrl-Shift-C/Cmd-Shift-C) to copy pixels from all visible layers in the document, within the selection area.

   Edit > **Cut** (Ctrl-X/Cmd-X) to cut the selection out of the layer.

3. Click in any document window.

4. Choose Edit > **Paste** (Ctrl-V/Cmd-V). The pasted pixels will appear in a new layer. **B** You can restack the new layer or move it with the Move tool (see also the sidebar below).

NEW LAYER VIA COPY OR CUT

As an alternative to the copy-and-paste method, you can get imagery onto a new layer in the same file by using an easy one-step command. Create a selection, then right-click/Control-click in the document window and choose either of the following:

Command	Shortcut	What it does
Layer Via Copy	Ctrl-J/Cmd-J	Puts a copy of the selected pixels on a new layer
Layer Via Cut	Ctrl-Shift-J/ Cmd-Shift-J	Removes selected pixels from the original layer and puts them on a new layer

---

A *We created a selection, then chose Edit > Copy.*

PIXELS OUTSIDE THE CANVAS AREA

➤ If you apply an image-editing command, such as a filter, to a **layer,** it will also apply to any pixels outside the live canvas area.

➤ To **enlarge** the canvas area to include hidden pixels, choose Image > **Reveal All.**

➤ To **select all** nontransparent pixels on a layer, including any pixels outside the live canvas area or that are hidden by a layer mask, Ctrl-click/Cmd-click the layer thumbnail on the Layers palette. (Don't use Select > All, which selects just the canvas area.)

➤ To **remove** pixels that extend outside the live canvas area, click the layer in question, choose Select > All, then choose Image > **Crop.** This will help reduce the file size.

➤ If a layer contains hidden pixels outside the live canvas area and you **merge** it with the Background (not with another layer), the hidden pixels will be deleted.

B *We used the Paste command in a new document. The Clipboard contents appear on a new layer.*

If you use the **Paste Into** command to paste the Clipboard contents inside a selection, a new layer will be created automatically and the active marquee will become a layer mask. The pasted imagery can then be repositioned within the layer mask, or the mask itself can be reshaped to reveal more or less of the imagery.

To paste into a selection:

1. Select an area of a layer.**A**

2. Choose Edit > **Copy** (Ctrl-C/Cmd-C) to copy pixels from only the currently selected layer, or choose Edit > **Copy Merged** (Ctrl-Shift-C/Cmd-Shift-C) to copy pixels within the selection area from all the currently visible layers.

3. Click a layer in the same document or in another document.

4. Select the area (or areas) that you want to paste the Clipboard contents into.**B** (Click Refine Edge and adjust the selection edge, if desired.)

5. Choose Edit > **Paste Into** (Ctrl-Shift-V/Cmd-Shift-V).**C** A new layer and layer mask will appear on the Layers palette.

6. Related options to explore:

   The entire Clipboard contents were pasted onto the layer, but the layer mask may be hiding some of those pixels. To move the layer contents within the mask, click the **layer** thumbnail (on the left), then drag in the document window with the **Move** tool (V). Or to move the layer mask relative to the layer, click the **layer mask** thumbnail (on the right), then drag in the document window with the Move tool.

   Click the layer mask thumbnail, then with the **Brush** tool (B or Shift-B), paint on the **layer mask** in the document window with white to expose more of the pasted image or with black to hide more of the pasted image.

   To move the layer and layer mask as a unit, click between the layer and layer mask thumbnails to **link** them together, choose the Move tool (V), then drag in the document window. (Click the link icon to unlink.)

   ➤ A large Clipboard selection usurps program memory. To empty the Clipboard at any time to reclaim memory, choose Edit > Purge > Clipboard, then click OK.

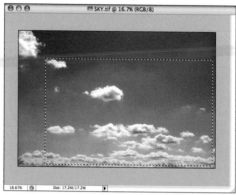

A *Select an area of an image. In this image, we used the Rectangular Marquee tool.*

B *Select an area in another image. We used the Polygonal Lasso tool to select the sky.*

C *We pasted the contents of the Clipboard into the selection via the **Paste Into** command.*

Matching image dimensions

In order to prevent a size discrepancy when copying a larger image into a smaller image, you can make sure the two documents have the **same dimensions** first by using the Crop tool.

To match the dimensions of two files, then drag and drop a layer:

1. Open the source and target documents, then click in the target document window. (In our example, the source document is larger than the target document.)

2. Choose the **Crop** tool (C).

3. On the Options bar, click **Front Image**.**A** The dimensions of the smaller document will display on the Options bar.

4. Click in the source document window, marquee as much of the larger image as you can,**B** then double-click inside the marquee to accept the crop. The source image will now have the same resolution and dimensions as the target image.

5. Choose the **Move** tool (V), then Shift-drag and drop the source layer from the Layers palette into the target document window.**C** It should fit neatly.**D**

6. *Optional:* To scale the new layer slightly to make it fit better, choose the Move tool, check Show Transform Controls on the Options bar, then Shift-drag a corner handle on the bounding box.

7. Close the source document without saving it, but save the target document.

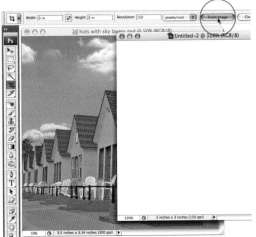

A *Choose the* ***Crop*** *tool, then click* ***Front Image*** *on the Options bar to record the dimensions of the smaller document.*

B *With the* ***Crop*** *tool, drag a marquee to crop the larger image to the dimensions that were recorded on the Options bar.*

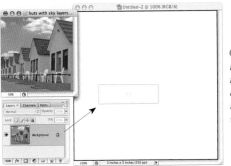

C *Shift-drag the layer from the source document into the target document window.*

D *Now the source image fits neatly in the target document window.*

Copying layers between files

If you **drag** a **layer**, multiple layers, or a layer group from the Layers palette in one document into the window of another document, the layers are **copied automatically.** In addition to being quick and easy, unlike copy/paste, this method includes pixels outside the live canvas area.

To drag and drop a layer between files:

1. Open the source and target documents, and arrange the windows so you can see some of each window.

2. Click in the **source** document window, then on the **Layers** palette, click the layer, Background, or layer group that you want to duplicate, or Ctrl-click/Cmd-click multiple layers. (Any tool can be selected.)

3. Shift-drag the layer or layer group from the Layers palette into the target document

window.**A** The new layer(s) will be centered in the target document (thanks to the Shift key) and will be stacked above the previously selected layer in the target document. If you dragged the Background, it will appear as a layer.

Note: An alert dialog box will appear if you try to copy a layer from an 8-bits-per-channel document to a 16-bits-per-channel document. Click Yes to accept a reduction in image quality, or click No to cancel the duplication.

4. If the image you dragged is larger than the target document, choose the **Move** tool (V), click **Show Transform Controls** on the Options bar to display the bounding box, press Ctrl-0/ Cmd-0 to enlarge the document window, then Shift-drag a corner handle to scale the layer to the desired size.**B**

A *Click in the* ***source*** *document window, then drag a layer, multiple layers, a layer group, or the Background into the* ***target*** *document window.*

B *If necessary, press Ctrl-0/Cmd-0 to enlarge the target document window, then Shift-drag a corner handle to* ***scale*** *the layer to the desired size.*

Pattern stamping

To use the Pattern Stamp tool:

1. *Optional:* To create a custom pattern, click in a document window (or with the Rectangular Marquee tool, select an area of a layer), choose Edit > Define Pattern, type a Name in the Pattern Name dialog box, click OK, then deselect (Ctrl-D/Cmd-D).

2. Choose the **Pattern Stamp** tool (S or Shift-S).

3. On the Options bar:

   Click the **Brush Preset** picker arrowhead, then click a brush.

   Choose a blending **Mode**, **Opacity** percentage, and **Flow** percentage.

   Click the **Pattern** picker arrowhead or thumbnail, then click a pattern on the picker.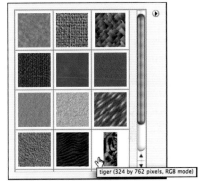 If you created a pattern (step 1), it will be the last pattern on the picker.

   Check **Aligned** to stamp pattern tiles in a perfect grid, regardless of how many separate strokes you make; or uncheck Aligned if you don't want the tiles to align perfectly.

   Optional: Check **Impressionist** to create a soft, mushy version of the pattern.

4. In the same document or in another document, click a layer, then click or drag to stamp the pattern in the image.**C**

➤ You can change Options bar settings between strokes with the Pattern Stamp tool, or layer multiple patterns at different opacities.

A *Select an area of an image, then choose Edit > **Define Pattern**.*

B *Click the new pattern (or any other pattern) in the **Pattern** picker.*

C *You can apply the pattern in any document. Here, we chose different opacities for the **Pattern Stamp** tool.*

Blending imagery using layer masks

One very effective approach to compositing is to drag and drop images to a target file that contains a white or solid-color Background or a faint, low-contrast image. Then, using a **layer mask**, you **fade** the edge of each new image layer softly into the background or into underlying layers. The image layers can also be scaled or moved individually to create a pleasing composition. If we had to pick one technique that embodies the magic of Photoshop, this would be it.

To blend images using layer masks:

1. Open several images, one of which will be used as a background (target) image for the whole composition. **A–B** The target image should be the largest of the bunch. (To make your job easier, make sure all your images have the same resolution.)

2. Click in one of the images to be copied, then drag the source layer from the Layers palette into the target document window. Repeat for any other images to be added (**A**, next page).

3. Choose the **Move** tool (V). In the target image, select one of the new image layers, then resize and reposition it as desired. Keep the layer selected.

4. Click the **Add Layer Mask** button at the bottom of the Layers palette.

5. Keep the layer mask thumbnail selected (not the layer thumbnail), and choose the **Gradient** tool (G). On the Options bar, click the Linear Gradient (first) button, then click the "Black, White" thumbnail in the Gradient picker.

6. In the document window, start dragging horizontally or diagonally from where you want the complete fadeout to be, and stop dragging where you want the image to remain fully opaque (hold down Shift to constrain the movement to an increment of 45°). The gradient will fill the layer mask, and the imagery on that layer will fade to transparency (black areas in a layer mask hide layer pixels) (**B**, next page).

   ➤ To redo the fade effect, make sure the layer mask thumbnail is still selected, then drag with the Gradient tool.

7. Repeat steps 3–6 for the other layers (**C**, next page). Note: To touch up the seams, see page 156.

A *We started by opening some theme-related images, just to get our creative juices flowing and see how they look together. We're going to create a banner to advertise vacation travel to Thailand.*

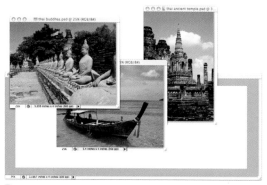

B *We narrowed our choice down to three images and created a larger, blank image to become the background for the duplicate layers.*

A *Drag a layer from each source image onto the target image (then resize and reposition the new image layers, as needed).*

B *Create a **layer mask** for each new layer and fill each layer mask with the **"Black, White" gradient** to partially mask the edge of the layer imagery.*

C *Type adds the finishing touch to our **composite image**.*

Using the Clone Source palette ★

With the **Clone Stamp** tool, you clone imagery (by dragging) from one layer to another within the same document or from one document to another. It's useful for retouching (see pages 272–273), collaging, or even for eliminating seams after using the Photomerge command.

The new **Clone Source** palette expands the power of the Clone Stamp tool by letting you keep track of up to five different clone sources (represented by a row of source buttons at the top of the palette); assign different sources; clone repeatedly from the same source; and scale, rotate, or reposition the source pixels before or while cloning them.

To use the Clone Stamp tool and the Clone Source palette: ★

1. Open one or more RGB documents to use as source imagery, and create or open a document to clone to.**A** (You can also clone within the same document.)

2. Choose the **Clone Stamp** tool (S or Shift-S), then from the Options bar, choose a brush preset and Mode, choose Opacity and Flow percentages, and check Aligned.

3. Display the **Clone Source** palette.**B** By default, the first clone source button is selected.

4. Check **Show Overlay** and **Auto Hide**, then set the **Opacity** to 35–40% (use the scrubby slider) so you'll be able to preview the clone source as you work.

5. In the document you're going to clone to, create a new layer.

6. Click in the document you want to clone from, then from the **Sample** menu on the Options bar, choose **Current Layer, Current & Below,** or **All Layers**, depending on where you want to clone from, and if necessary, click a layer.

   Alt-click/Option-click an area to set the source point for cloning. The document and layer name will be assigned to, and listed below, the first clone source button on the palette.

7. *Optional:* If you're cloning to another document, click in that window now.

8. To position the clone, move the pointer over the image without clicking (a faint overlay of the source will appear below the pointer), then drag to start cloning. The overlay will disappear temporarily (because you checked Auto Hide),

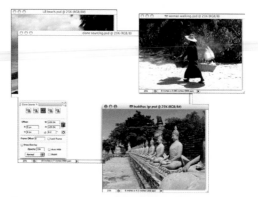

A *Open the images you want to clone from, and create or open an image to clone to.*

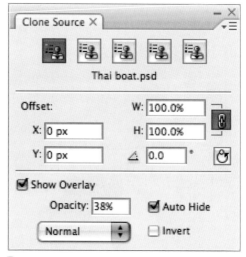

B *Use the **Clone Source** palette to keep track of and transform imagery from multiple clone sources.*

then reappear when you release the mouse. (When you start dragging, the position of the source overlay becomes fixed. To reposition it, see the instructions on the next page.)

9. To clone from another source, click the second source button, create a new layer in the target document if desired, then in any document, Alt-click/Option-click another area. Drag to clone. Repeat to clone from yet more sources.

   Note: The Clone Source palette keeps a link active only while the source document is open. Close a source document, and the link to the Clone Source palette is **broken!**

To switch between clone sources when using the Clone Stamp tool: ★

Click any of the **source** buttons at the top of the **Clone Source** palette. The new source will display as the overlay in the document window.

You can **scale**, **flip**, or **rotate** a **clone source** before or during cloning. These changes will apply only to the source that's currently selected on the palette.

To scale the source imagery while cloning: ★

Before or while cloning, change the **W** or **H** value on the Clone Source palette (use the scrubby slider);**A–B** or hold down Alt-Shift/Option-Shift and press [or]. Note the new scale of the overlay, then drag in the document window. Select the Link button to preserve the current aspect ratio as you change the W or H value. To flip the source, enter negative W and/or H values. We don't recommend scaling beyond 150 or –150%.

To rotate the source imagery: ★

At any time while cloning, change the **Rotate** value △ on the Clone Source palette; or hold down Alt-Shift/Option-Shift and press < or >. Note the new angle of the source overlay, then drag to clone at the chosen angle. (To restore the default scale and rotation settings, click the Reset Transform button.↺)

As soon as you start cloning, the position of the source overlay becomes fixed. You can clone the source imagery in a new location by **repositioning** the **source overlay**.

To reposition the source overlay after you've started cloning: ★

1. With an overlay displaying in the document you're cloning in, change the **Offset** X and/or **Y** value on the Clone Source palette; or Alt-Shift-drag/Option-Shift-drag the overlay, then release.

2. Click, then drag to clone in the new location.

A *We're using one of the scaling controls (W) on the **Clone Source** palette to shrink the overlay image (the woman) so it's more in keeping with the scale of the statues.*

B *We created this composite image by cloning from three different source files. For the Clone Stamp tool, we chose an Opacity of 70%, a Flow of 90%, and turned on the Airbrush option.*

➤ *A panoramic format worked well for our imagery, but you can clone to an image of any shape, and you can clone onto a blank background or on top of existing imagery.*

Stitching photos together

The **Photomerge** feature combines a series of two or more photos into a single panoramic image. Each photo becomes an individual layer, with a layer mask that creates a smooth, seamless edge between photos. The new Layout and "Blend images together" options make creating a panorama easier and more automatic.

To merge photos via the Photomerge command: ★

1. In Bridge, rearrange the images for the panorama so they're sequential (we like to group ours in a stack), then multiple-select them. All the source files must have a bit depth of 8 bits/channel but they can be in different formats (e.g., PSD, TIFF, JPEG). Although you can use Raw photo files, you'll get faster results with Photomerge by converting them to JPEG or PSD.

2. Choose Tools > Photoshop > **Photomerge.** The Photomerge dialog box opens. **A**

3. In the **Layout** area, click one of the first 4 layout options (**A–C**, next page): **Auto** (the program determines the best layout option), **Perspective, Cylindrical,** or **Reposition Only** (you can't preview these options). For the Interactive option, which lets you arrange the photos yourself, see Photoshop Help.

4. Check **Blend Images Together** to have Photomerge correct any slight differences in exposure where the photos overlap to produce a more seamless panorama. Click OK.

   Sit tight as Photomerge opens and duplicates the source files, aligns and blends them into a panorama, and fixes your lunch.

5. The finished panorama will appear onscreen. Note that on the Layers palette, each layer has its own layer mask. You can use the **Crop** tool ✄ to crop away any transparent areas from the edges of the panorama. Save the file in the PSD format.

6. Zoom in and inspect the image for any noticeable seams. You can use the **Clone Stamp** tool ♨ (choose Sample: All Layers) to manually clean up any visible seams.

➤ You can also get to Photomerge from Photoshop (File > Automate > Photomerge), but it's a convoluted path, so we use Bridge.

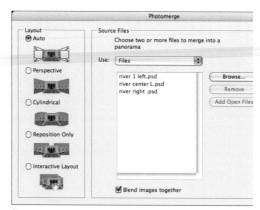

A *The new, improved* **Photomerge** *command has more aligning and blending power.*

SHOOTING PHOTOS FOR A PANORAMA

➤ Use a **tripod** for more accurate alignment and less distortion from photo to photo.

➤ **Overlap** the view area in each shot by approximately 25%.

➤ Use the same **exposure** for all your shots. Set the camera exposure mode to Shutter-Priority (fixed shutter speed), Aperture-Priority (fixed f-stop), or Manual (you set the shutter and f-stop). (Too complex? Just use the Auto exposure mode —the results will probably be satisfactory.) Although the Blend Images Together option will try to even out exposure discrepancies among your photos, to get good results, you still have to supply Photomerge with properly exposed photos.

➤ In Bridge, arrange your photos in the correct **sequence** for the layout; the images will appear in that order in the Photomerge dialog box. This way, if Photomerge doesn't figure out the correct order of photos (it usually does), you'll get your intended results. Plus, Photomerge will produce the final image more quickly if the original photos are in the correct order at the outset.

LAYOUT OPTIONS IN PHOTOMERGE

*We'll use **Photomerge** to create a panorama from these three **source** photos.*

A *The **Perspective** option shrank the images in the center, creating more depth. It also produced some distortion on the right side and a lot of transparency at the top and bottom. This option is best for creating a narrower panorama with just 2 photos.*

B *The **Cylindrical** option made the images in the center larger—producing a flatter-looking panorama—and also yielded less transparency along the edges. This option is good for creating a wide-angle panorama with 3 or more photos.*

C *The **Reposition Only** option simply placed the images in a row without scaling them, making it a good choice for maps or other flat imagery. Note that Photomerge omitted our center photo from the scene.*

Blending seams manually

To soften the seams between imagery on different layers, you can apply **brush strokes** to a **layer mask**. We like this method because you only have to edit the mask—not the layer imagery. Note: Before following these instructions, read the sidebar at right for an even simpler solution that might just do the trick!

To blend seams on a layer mask with the Brush tool:

1. Open a document that contains multiple layers; at least one layer should have a layer mask.**A**

2. Choose the **Brush** tool (B or Shift-B).

3. On the Options bar, choose a large, soft-edged brush, and also choose Opacity and Flow percentages. For partial (subtle) masking, choose an Opacity of 50% or less.

4. On the Layers palette, click the thumbnail for the layer mask you want to edit. Press X, if necessary, to make the Foreground color white.

5. Drag across the area you want to mask.**B** You can change the brush opacity and diameter between strokes. To restore part of the mask, press X to make the Foreground color black.**C**

6. When you're done editing the mask, click any layer thumbnail to resume normal image editing.

MOVING THE GRADIENT IN A LAYER MASK

If your layer mask contains a **gradient,** you can move the mask to adjust the blending effect. On the Layers palette, click the thumbnail for the layer mask, click the link icon 🔗 to unlink the mask from the layer, choose the **Move** tool (V),⊹ then drag in the document window. Depending on where you position the gradient, the imagery will fade more or less gradually. When you're done moving the mask, click the space between the mask thumbnail and the layer thumbnail to make the link icon reappear, then click any layer thumbnail to resume normal image editing.

A *Although we used layer masks successfully to merge layers in this composite image (see pages 150–151), the left side could still use some hand blending.*

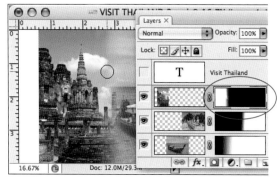

B *We clicked a **layer mask** thumbnail, chose a large, soft brush and an Opacity of 50% for our **Brush** tool, and are painting with white to soften the edge of the mask.*

C *Now the seams, although still visible, look smoother.*

Using alignment features

Sometimes successful composite images come together in a serendipitous way without a lot of forethought or careful alignment. At other times, you may need to plan ahead—or position objects more precisely by using such layout features as grids, rulers, and guides.

The **rulers** are handy for positioning objects and for creating guides.

To show/hide the rulers:

To show/hide the rulers, choose View > **Rulers** (Ctrl-R/Cmd-R). Rulers will appear on (or disappear from) the top and left sides of the document window, and the current location of the pointer on the image will be indicated by a dotted marker on each ruler.**A** Move the pointer, and you'll see what we mean.

If you created a composite image, try moving a layer to a specific location (with the Move tool) based on the markers on the rulers.**B**

➤ To change the ruler units quickly, right-click/Control-click either ruler and choose a unit from the context menu. Or to get to the Units & Rulers panel in the Preferences dialog box quickly, where you can also change the units, double-click either ruler.

➤ To change the ruler origin to measure from a specific location in the image, from the upper left corner where the two rulers meet, drag diagonally into the document.**C** To restore the default origin, double-click in the upper left corner.

CHOOSE YOUR EXTRAS

The View > **Extras** command (Ctrl-H/Cmd-H) shows/hides whichever document features are currently enabled on the View > **Show** submenu. Among the Show submenu features that you can show/hide are Layer Edges, Selection Edges, the Grid, (ruler) Guides, and Smart Guides. These choices affect only the current document window (and any documents you subsequently open).

A *The current **location** of the **pointer** is indicated by a dotted marker on each ruler.*

B *As we move a type layer, the current **location** of the **pointer** is indicated on each ruler.*

C *Drag the **ruler origin** to a new location.*

If the **Smart Guides** feature is on and you move an item (selection border, layer, path, type, or shape), temporary guide lines will appear onscreen, designating the top, middle, or bottom of another layer.

To move a layer using smart guides:

1. Make sure View > Show > **Smart Guides** has a check mark.

2. Click a layer (in a document that contains more than one layer).

3. Choose the Move tool, then drag the layer. Magenta (default color) lines will appear, designating the top, middle, or bottom of visible imagery or type on other layers.**A–B** Snap the item to a guide or a pair of intersecting guides.

➤ In the Guides, Grid & Slices pane of the Preferences dialog box, you can change the color of guides, smart guides, and the grid, and choose other related options.

The **grid** is a nonprinting framework that you can snap image elements to, and it can be displayed or hidden as needed.

To show/hide the grid:

To show/hide the grid,**C** choose View > Show > **Grid** (Ctrl-'/Cmd-'). This option can be turned on or off for individual files. With View > Snap To > Grid on, a selection, layer, path, or shape will snap to a grid line if you move it within 8 screen pixels of the line.

When View > **Snap** is on (and depending on which document features are enabled on the View > Snap To submenu), as you move a selection border, layer, path, type, or shape near a guide, grid line, layer, or the edge of the canvas area, the pointer or item will snap (to the item) with a subtle tug. (Hint: We prefer to use smart guides...)

To use the Snap feature:

1. Choose View > Snap To > **Guides, Grid, Layers, Slices, Document Bounds,** or **All** (of the above); or to turn off all of the above, choose None. Note: For the Snap To > Guides, Grid, or Slices option to be available, that feature must be showing (have a check mark on the View > Show submenu).

2. Make sure View > **Snap** is on (has a check mark) (Ctrl-Shift-;/Cmd-Shift-;). This command enables whichever options are currently checked on the Snap To submenu.

A *Using **smart guides,** the type layer is being aligned horizontally to the left edge of the boat layer and vertically to the midpoint of that layer.*

B ***Smart guides** are being used again, but this time the top of the type is being aligned to the midpoint of the boat layer.*

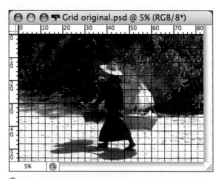

C *The **grid** is displayed.*

If you find the grid to be overbearing but still yearn for guides that stay onscreen, try working with **ruler guides.** You can place ruler guides wherever you need them and remove them individually at any time—plus they have the same "Snap To" behavior as the grid.

To create ruler guides:

1. Make sure the rulers are showing (Ctrl-R/Cmd-R), then drag from the horizontal or vertical **ruler** into the document window.**A–B** A guide will appear where you release the mouse.

2. As you create guides, you can do the following:

   Snap a guide to a **selection** or a **selected layer.**

   Make sure View > Snap is checked, then Shift-drag slowly to snap a guide to a **ruler** increment.

   Make sure the grid is showing and View > Snap To > Grid is on, then snap a guide to a grid line.

➤ You can move any existing guide with the Move tool (the pointer will become a double arrow), provided guides aren't locked.

➤ Alt-drag/Option-drag as you create a guide to switch its orientation from vertical to horizontal (or vice versa).

When **guides** are **locked,** they can't be moved with the Move tool.

To lock/unlock all ruler guides:

Choose View > **Lock Guides** (Ctrl-Alt-;/Cmd-Option-;). Rechoose the command to unlock.

➤ Guides will keep their relative positions if you resize your image, provided they're not locked.

To create a ruler guide at a specific location:

1. Choose View > **New Guide.** The New Guide dialog box opens.

2. Click **Orientation: Horizontal** or **Vertical,** enter a **Position** relative to the 0 (zero) point on that axis, in any measurement unit used in Photoshop, then click OK.

To remove ruler guides:

Do either of the following:

To remove **one** guide, choose the **Move** tool (V), ➤⊕ then drag the guide out of the document window (this works only if guides aren't locked). Don't press Delete!

To remove **all** guides, choose View > **Clear Guides.**

A *We're dragging a **guide** downward from the horizontal ruler.*

B *We created four **ruler guides** to surround this type layer. (Via the Guides, Grid & Slices pane of the Preferences dialog box, we changed the guide color to red to contrast better with this image.)*

Similar to the way you might align objects in a drawing program, you can **align** the visible parts of one layer to another layer—or align multiple layers to one another—via buttons on the Options bar.

To align layers to one another:

1. Choose the **Move** tool (V), then check **Auto Select** and choose **Layer** on the Options bar.

2. Click one image or type layer, then Ctrl-click/ Cmd-click another layer or layers.**A**

3. Click one of the six **Align** buttons on the Options bar (use tool tips to identify them).**B–C**

➤ Before using these buttons, you can click a layer that one or more other layers are linked to; the other layers will align to the layer you click.

➤ To align to a selection, create the selection before step 1 above.

The **Distribute** buttons equalize the spacing among multiple selected or linked layers. You must select three or more layers first.

To equalize the spacing among layers:

1. Choose the **Move** tool (V), then check **Auto Select** and choose **Layer** on the Options bar.

2. Click a layer, then Ctrl-click/Cmd-click at least two other layers (not the Background).

3. Click one of the six **Distribute** buttons on the Options bar (use tool tips to identify them).**D–E**

➤ You clicked the wrong button? Undo the last command before applying a new one.

The **Ruler** tool ★ (formerly called the Measure tool) is a simple measuring device.

To measure the distance and angle between two points:

1. Choose the **Ruler** tool (I or Shift-I).

2. Drag in the document window. The angle (A) and length (L) of the measure line will be listed on the Options bar. You can Shift-drag to constrain the angle to a multiple of 45°.

3. Choose another tool when you're done using the Ruler; choose the Ruler tool again, and the measure line will redisplay. A document can have only one measure line at a time.

➤ To remove the measure line, choose the Ruler tool, then click Clear on the Options bar.

➤ With the Ruler tool, you can move a measure line to another area of the document, or drag an endpoint to change the angle of the line.

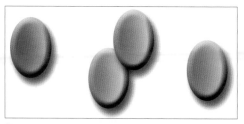

A *We selected four layers and chose the **Move** tool.*

Align Top Edges Align Vertical Centers Align Bottom Edges

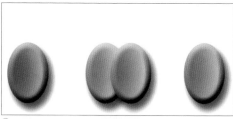

Align Left Edges Align Horizontal Centers Align Right Edges

B *The **Align** buttons on the Options bar*

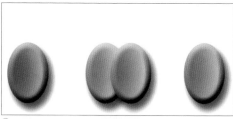

C *After clicking **Align Bottom Edges***

Distribute Top Edges Distribute Vertical Centers Distribute Bottom Edges   Auto-align layers

Distribute Left Edges Distribute Horizontal Centers Distribute Right Edges

D *The **Distribute** buttons on the Options bar*

E *After clicking **Distribute Horizontal Centers***

Using the History palette, you can selectively undo or restore previous stages (called "states") of a work session. In this chapter, you'll learn how to restore, delete, and clear previous states; preserve states by using snapshots; create a new document from a state or snapshot; and restore areas of an image to a prior state by using the History Brush or by filling a selection or layer with a history state.

Using the History palette

The **History** palette displays a list of the most recent states (edits) made to the currently open document, with the bottommost state being the most recent. Click a prior state, and the document is restored to that stage of the editing process. What happens to your document when you do this depends on whether the palette is in linear or nonlinear mode,**A** so you need to learn the difference between the two modes.

To toggle between modes, choose History Options from the palette menu, then in the History Options dialog box, check or uncheck **Allow Non-Linear History**. You can switch between modes at any time during an editing session.

Continued on the following page

HISTORY

10

Source for the **History Brush** *tool*

History ✕	Actions
⬜ 🏠	for History.tif
⬜ 🏠	Snapshot 1
⬜ 📄	Open
✎ 📄	Layer Via Copy
⬜ ➡📄	Levels 1 Layer
⬜ 📄	Hue/Saturation 1 Layer
⬜ T	Type Tool

— *The current history state*

History *state slider*   **Create New Document** *from Current State*   **Create New** *Shapshot*   **Delete Current** *State*

A *The* **History** *palette shown here is in* **linear** *mode. Note that all the steps below the current state are dimmed. The palette shown on the next page is in nonlinear mode.*

In **linear mode** (Allow Non-Linear History unchecked), if you click an earlier state and resume image editing from that state or delete it, all subsequent (dimmed) states will be discarded. **A**

In **nonlinear mode**, if you click or delete an earlier state, subsequent states won't be deleted (or become dimmed). In this mode, if you resume image editing with an earlier state selected, your next edit will show up as the latest state on the palette, and all the states in between will be preserved. The latest state will incorporate the earlier stage of the image plus your newest edit. If you change your mind, you can click any in-between state whenever you like and resume editing from there. This makes nonlinear the more flexible of the two modes. **B** Let's say you want to try out some strokes with the Brush tool in three different colors without having to paint one on top of another. Apply the first stroke, click the prior state, paint a stroke with your second color choice, click the prior (non-stroke) state again, and repeat for the third color. At any time, you can click a "Brush Tool" state and work from that point forward.

All of the above notwithstanding, nonlinear mode can be confusing or disorienting. If you find this to be the case, work in linear mode instead and you'll have the option to revert back to an earlier state with a nice, clean break.

The last option in the History Options dialog box, **Make Layer Visibility Changes Undoable**, controls whether the hiding/showing of layers (via the visibility icon) on the Layers palette is listed as a state on the History palette. We prefer to leave this option off.

To specify the number of states that can be listed on the palette per editing session, go to Preferences (Ctrl-K/Cmd-K) > Performance and enter a **History States** value (1–1000; default 20). If the maximum number of history states is exceeded during an editing session, earlier steps will be removed automatically to make room for the new ones. The maximum number of states may be limited by various factors, including the image size, the kind of edits that are made to the image, and currently available memory. Each open document has its own list of states. Regardless of the preference setting, when you close a document, all the history states are **deleted!**

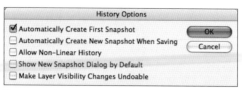

A *In the **History Options** dialog box, choose whether or not to **Allow Non-Linear History**.*

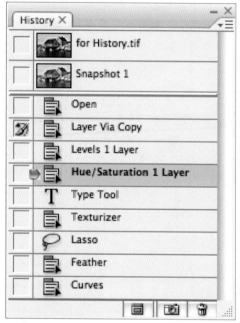

B *Because this **History** palette is in **nonlinear** mode, all of the states are available, even those listed below the current state.*

Changing history states

To summarize, if the History palette is in **linear** mode (the Allow Non-Linear History option is off) and you click an earlier state, all the states below the one you click will become dimmed. If you then delete the state you clicked or continue editing the image with that earlier state selected, all the dimmed states will be deleted. (If you change your mind, you can choose Undo immediately to restore the deleted states.) In **nonlinear** mode, if you click an earlier state and then perform an edit, the new edit will become the latest state, but the prior states won't be deleted.

To change history states:

1. Perform some edits on an image.
2. Do one of the following:

    Click a **state** on the History palette. **A–B**

    On the left side of the palette, drag the **History State slider** upward or downward to the desired state.

    To **Step Forward** one state, press Ctrl-Shift-Z/ Cmd-Shift-Z; or to **Step Backward** one state, press Ctrl-Alt-Z/Cmd-Option-Z.

➤ You can Alt-click/Option-click a state to create a duplicate, but it will be listed generically as "Duplicate History State," and thus will be hard to identify (you can't rename it).

➤ When you choose File > Revert, it becomes a state on the History palette, and as with any state, all the states preceding it are preserved. You can restore a whole image to a state prior to the Revert command being applied or restore portions of a state selectively with the History Brush tool (see pages 168–169).

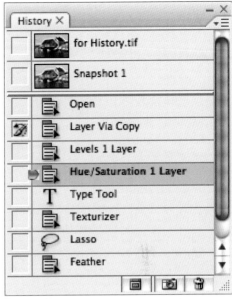

A *After clicking a prior state with the History palette in nonlinear mode*

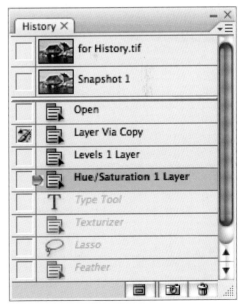

B *After clicking a prior state with the History palette in linear mode*

Deleting and clearing history states

If Allow Non-Linear History is checked and you **delete a state**, only that state is deleted. If Allow Non-Linear History is unchecked and you delete a state, that state and all subsequent states are deleted (you can choose Edit > Undo to restore them).

To delete a state:

Do one of the following:

Right-click/Control-click a state and choose **Delete** from the context menu,**A** then click Yes when the alert dialog box appears.**B**

To bypass the alert prompt, drag the state to be deleted over the **Delete Current State** button 🗑 on the History palette.

To delete consecutive states from the current state backward, click a starting state, then Alt-click/Option-click the **Delete Current State** button (and keep clicking). Note that the Undo command can only restore the last deleted state.

To clear the History palette:

To clear all the states (not the snapshots) from the History palette for all currently open documents in order to free up memory, choose Edit > Purge > **Histories**, then click OK. This command can't be undone!

To clear all states (not snapshots) from the History palette for just the current document, Right-click/Control-click any state and choose **Clear History**. This command can be undone.

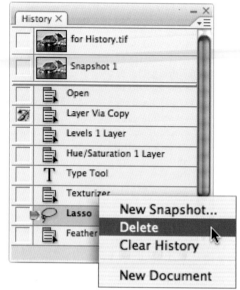

A *Right-click/Control-click a state and choose Delete from the context menu, then click Yes in the alert dialog box.*

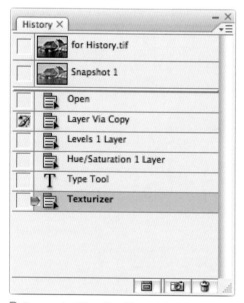

B *Because the **Allow Non-Linear History** option was **unchecked** when we deleted the "Lasso" state, subsequent states were deleted in addition to that state.*

Using snapshots

A snapshot is like a copy of a history state, with one major difference: unlike a state, a snapshot remains on the palette even if the state from which it was created is deleted because the maximum number of history states was reached or the palette is cleared or purged. All snapshots are deleted when a document is closed.

In these instructions, you'll choose **snapshot options**, which affect all Photoshop files; on the next page, you'll learn how to create snapshots for a particular file.

To choose snapshot options:

1. Choose **History Options** from the History palette menu. The History Options dialog box opens. **A**

2. Check/uncheck any of the following options:

   Automatically Create First Snapshot to have Photoshop create a snapshot each time you **open** a file (this option is checked by default).

   Automatically Create New Snapshot When Saving to have Photoshop create a snapshot every time you **save** a file. The time of day that the snapshot was created will be listed next to the snapshot thumbnail.

   Show New Snapshot Dialog by Default to have the **New Snapshot** dialog box appear whenever you click the New Snapshot button, allowing you to choose options.

3. Click OK.

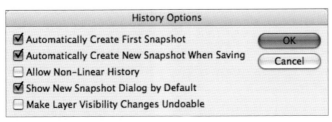

A *There are three snapshot options to decide on in the **History Options** dialog box.*

If the Automatically Create New Snapshot When Saving option is off, get in the habit of **creating snapshots** periodically as you work and before running any actions on your document. If you use the New Snapshot dialog box (the second method below), you'll be able to choose whether the snapshot is made from the full document, from merged layers, or from just the current layer.

To create a snapshot of a state:

Method 1 (without choosing options)

1. On the History palette, click the state that you want to create a snapshot of.

2. If the Show New Snapshot Dialog by Default option is off in the History Options dialog box, click the **New Snapshot** button.📷 If the dialog option is on, Alt-click/Option-click the New Snapshot button. A new snapshot thumbnail will appear after the last snapshot in the upper section of the palette.

Method 2 (choosing options)

1. To create a snapshot of a layer, click that layer on the Layers palette.

2. Right-click/Control-click a history state and choose **New Snapshot.A** The New Snapshot dialog box opens.**B**

3. Type a **Name** for the snapshot.

4. Choose **From: Full Document** to create a snapshot that preserves all the layers on the Layers palette at that state; or **Merged Layers** to create a snapshot that merges all layers on the Layers palette at that state; or **Current Layer** to make a snapshot of only the currently selected layer in its current state.

5. Click OK.**C**

➤ If the Show New Snapshot Dialog by Default option is on in the History Options dialog box, you can also open the New Snapshot dialog box by clicking a state, then clicking the New Snapshot button at the bottom of the palette. Or if the dialog option is off, Alt-click/Option-click the New Snapshot button to open the dialog.

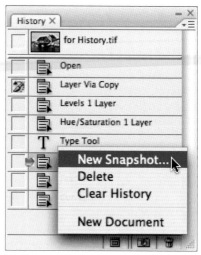

A *Right-click/Control-click a state and choose* **New Snapshot** *from the context menu.*

B *In the* **New Snapshot** *dialog box, enter a name and choose which part of the image you want the snapshot to be created from.*

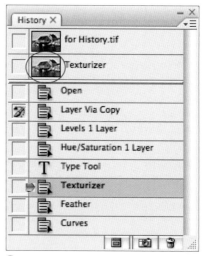

C *A thumbnail for the new* **snapshot** *appears on the History palette.*

To make a snapshot become the current state:

Do either of the following:

Click a **snapshot thumbnail**. If the Allow Non-Linear History option is off and edits were made to the document after that snapshot was taken, the document will revert to the snapshot stage of editing and all the states will be dimmed; resume editing, and all dimmed states will be deleted. If Allow Non-Linear History is on, subsequent states will remain on the palette.

Regardless of the Allow Non-Linear History option setting, you can **Alt-click/Option-click** a **snapshot thumbnail** to have the other states remain available and that snapshot become the latest state. This is a very useful option for preserving edits.

To delete a snapshot:

Do either of the following:

Click the snapshot, right-click/Control-click and choose **Delete** (or click the Delete Current State button), then click Yes.

To bypass the prompt, drag the snapshot to the **Delete Current State** button.

Creating documents from states

Using the **New Document** command, you can spin off versions of your current document based on any state or snapshot.

To create a new document from a history state or snapshot:

Do either of the following:

Right-click/Control-click a snapshot or a state, then choose **New Document** from the context menu.**A**

Drag a snapshot or a state over the **New Document from Current State** button, (or click a snapshot or a state, then click the button).

A new document window will appear onscreen bearing the title of the snapshot or state from which it was created, and "Duplicate State" will be the name of the starting state for the new document.**B** Save this new document!

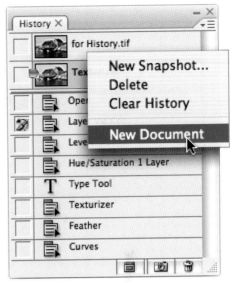

A *Right-click/Control-click a snapshot or state and choose* ***New Document.***

B *The History palette for the new document*

Restoring areas selectively

When you draw strokes on a document with the **History Brush** tool, pixels below the pointer are restored from whichever state or snapshot you have designated as the history source.

Note: The History Brush tool can't be used on an image if you have changed its pixel count since it was opened (such as by cropping it, by changing the document color mode or canvas size, or by adding or deleting layers). Furthermore, the tool can't restore deleted or modified layer effects, vector data (type or shapes), imagery from a deleted layer, or the effects of an adjustment layer. Moral: Keep your layers!

To use the History Brush tool:

1. Open an image, and make some edits. (For the image shown at right, we duplicated an image layer via Ctrl-J/Cmd-J, renamed the duplicate, and applied a filter to it.) **A–C**

2. Choose the **History Brush** tool (Y or Shift-Y).

3. On the Options bar:

   Click the Brush Preset picker arrowhead, then click a **brush** on the picker.

   Choose a blending **Mode**, **Opacity** percentage, and **Flow** percentage. Click the **Airbrush** button, if desired, for soft strokes.

4. On the **History** palette, click in the leftmost column for the state or snapshot to be designated as the source for the History Brush tool; the history source icon will appear.**D**

A *The original image*

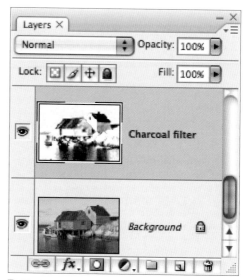

B *We duplicated the image layer, then applied the Charcoal filter to the duplicate layer.*

C *The Charcoal filter is applied to a duplicate image layer.*

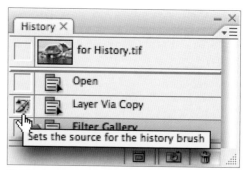

D *We clicked to set the **History Source** icon to a state prior to the filter edit (in this case, the state called "Layer Via Copy") but after the layer addition.*

5. On the **Layers** palette, click the layer that you want to restore pixels to, and make sure Lock Transparent Pixels is off.

6. Draw strokes on the image. Pixel data from the prior state of that layer will replace the current data where you apply strokes. **A–C**

➤ Say you apply some brush strokes to a layer, then decide a few editing steps later to remove the strokes. If you click the state above the one labeled "Brush Tool," the edits that you want to keep will be deleted when you resume editing. Instead, set the source for the History Brush tool as the state above "Brush Tool," click the layer on the Layers palette that you applied brush strokes to, then with the History Brush tool, "paint out" your strokes in the document window.

SNAPSHOT AS HISTORY BRUSH SOURCE

To use a snapshot instead of a state as the source for the History Brush tool, do the following: Modify a layer (e.g., apply a filter or Image > Adjustment command, draw brush strokes), make a snapshot of the current state, then click the prior state. Set the **History Source** icon to the **snapshot,** then with the **History Brush** tool, draw strokes over areas of the layer where you want to restore the modifications selectively.

➤ When using a snapshot as the source for the History Brush, you can choose which layer you restore pixels to if you chose the **Full Document** or **Merged Layers** option in the New Snapshot dialog box when you created the snapshot. If you chose Current Layer in the New Snapshot dialog box, you'll be able to paint only on the single layer that was preserved in the snapshot.

A *On the duplicate layer that we applied the filter to, we applied strokes with the **History Brush** tool (55% Opacity and a big scratchy Spatter brush).*

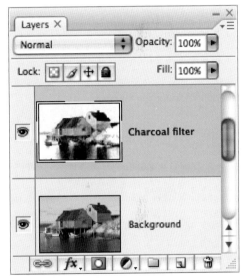

B *In the Layers palette for the final image (shown below), you can see that the original color was restored to some areas of the duplicate layer.*

C *The final image*

The **Fill** command, when used with the History option, fills a layer or selection with pixels from a designated history state or snapshot. The Note on page 168 also applies to this command.

To fill a selection or layer with a history state or snapshot:

1. Edit your document, and click an image layer. **A**

2. *Optional:* Create a selection. Leave the selection edges sharp, or use Refine Edge to feather them. **B**

3. On the History palette, click in the leftmost column for the state or snapshot you want to use as the fill data. The History Source icon will appear where you click.

4. Choose Edit > **Fill** (Shift-Backspace/Shift-Delete). The Fill dialog box opens. **C**

5. Choose **Use: History.**

6. Choose a **Blending Mode** and an **Opacity** percentage.

7. Check **Preserve Transparency** to replace only existing pixels, or leave it unchecked to allow pixels to appear anywhere on the current layer. This option is available only if the layer contains transparent pixels.

8. Click OK. **D**

A *The original image*

B *We applied the Conté Crayon filter to a duplicate image layer, selected the bottom of that layer, and feathered the selection using Refine Edge.*

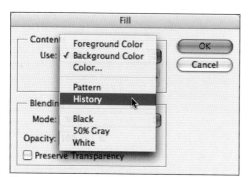

C *In the* **Fill** *dialog box, choose* **Use: History,** *and change the Blending Mode and Opacity, if desired.*

D *The selection is filled with the unedited imagery at an Opacity of 75%.*

You're happy with the composition of a photo, but it has too much contrast or looks a bit dull? Enter the digital darkroom. Photoshop offers so many commands for adjusting images, we couldn't fit them all into this chapter! First, we'll show you how to use adjustment layers—a flexible method for applying adjustment commands. After that you'll learn how to use the Threshold and Posterize commands, the Histogram palette, the Levels command, and the Brightness/Contrast command. In the last task in this chapter, you'll learn how to burn (darken) or dodge (lighten) areas of an image via a neutral color layer.

Applying adjustment commands

First, a few general pointers for applying adjustments:

➤ Although adjustment commands can be applied directly to any layer via the Image > **Adjustments** submenu, for flexibility, we prefer to apply them via editable and removable **adjustment layers.** We're so keen on this method, it's the only one we list in the instructions in this chapter.

➤ To restrict the effect of an adjustment command to a specific area, create a **selection** before choosing the command.

➤ To **restore** the settings that were in place when you opened the dialog box, hold down Alt/Option and click Reset.

➤ To see how an adjustment will affect your image, check **Preview** in the adjustment dialog box; uncheck Preview to view the unadjusted image.

➤ To change how an adjustment layer affects your document, **restack** it above a different layer.

TONAL ADJUSTMENTS

11

IN THIS CHAPTER

ADJUSTMENT COMMANDS TO EXPLORE IN OTHER CHAPTERS

Command	Page	Command	Page
Black & White	200–201	Levels (for color)	208–209
Color Balance	203–204	Match Color	270–271
Curves	210–213	Photo Filter	250
Desaturate	202	Replace Color	274–276
Hue/Saturation	205	Shadow/Highlight	247–249

Using adjustment layers

The command in an **adjustment layer** affects all the layers below it, but the changes don't become permanent until you decide to merge it downward. Commands applied via the Image > Adjustments submenu, on the other hand, cause permanent changes to the current layer. We recommend using adjustment layers because they're flexible, meaning you can change their settings as often as you like, restack or hide/show them at any time, and even drag-copy them from one file to another. When you're done using them, you can either merge them downward or toss them out. Easy.

To create an adjustment layer:

1. Click a layer. The adjustment layer is going to appear above the layer you click.

2. From the **New Fill/Adjustment Layer** menu ⬯. at the bottom of the Layers palette, choose an adjustment command.**A**

3. The dialog box for the chosen command opens. Make the desired adjustments, then click OK. The adjustment layer will appear on the Layers palette, with a thumbnail icon for that particular command and an editable mask.**B**

➤ You can also create an adjustment layer by choosing a command from the Layer > New Adjustment Layer submenu.

To change the settings for an adjustment layer:

1. On the Layers palette, double-click the **adjustment layer thumbnail** (the thumbnail on the left).

2. Make the desired changes in the adjustment dialog box, then click OK.

➤ While any adjustment dialog box is open, you can Ctrl-Spacebar-click/Cmd-Spacebar-click to zoom in or Alt-Spacebar-click/Option-Spacebar-click to zoom out. If the image is magnified, you can drag it in the document window while holding down the Spacebar.

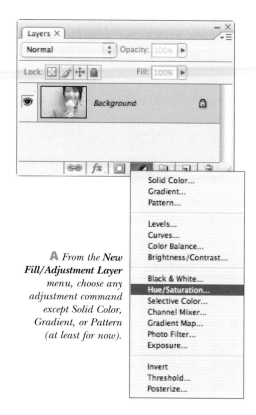

A *From the New Fill/Adjustment Layer menu, choose any adjustment command except Solid Color, Gradient, or Pattern (at least for now).*

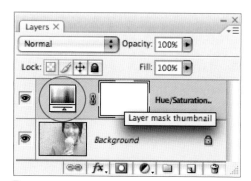

B *Each **adjustment** command has a unique icon in its **layer** thumbnail.*

You can keep an adjustment layer right where it is but **change** which **adjustment command** it contains (e.g., change Levels to Curves or change Hue/Saturation to Color Balance).

To change the command in an adjustment layer:

1. Click an adjustment layer on the Layers palette.

2. From the Layer > **Change Layer Content** submenu, choose a replacement command.

3. Make the desired adjustments, then click OK.

➤ To discard an adjustment layer, drag it to the Delete Layer button. 🗑

When you **merge down** an adjustment layer, the adjustments become permanent for the image layer below it. If you change your mind, you can either choose Edit > Undo (right away) or click the prior state on the History palette.

To merge an adjustment layer:

Do either of the following:

Click the adjustment layer you want to merge downward,**A** then press **Ctrl-E/Cmd-E.B**

Right-click/Control-click near the adjustment layer name and choose **Merge Down.**

➤ Adjustment layers don't contain pixels, so you can't merge them with one another. However, you can merge multiple adjustment layers into an image layer (or layers) by using either the Merge Visible or Flatten Image command (see pages 115–116).

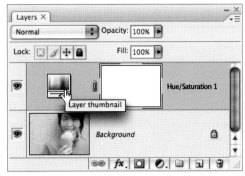

A *Click the adjustment layer you want to merge downward.*

B *The **Merge Down** command applied the **Hue/Saturation** values from the adjustment layer to the layer below it—in this case, to the Background. (We used Hue/Saturation to change the woman's sweater from blue to pink.)*

Adjustment layer techniques

▶ Click an adjustment layer, then choose a different **blending mode** from the menu on the Layers palette. By changing the blending mode for an adjustment layer, you can dramatically change how it affects underlying layers. Try Saturation mode to heighten the saturation, Luminosity to adjust light and dark values but not the color, Darken to darken the image, or Lighten to lighten it.

▶ Stack several different adjustment layers, then hide **A** or lower the **opacity** of each one to see how it affects the underlying image.

▶ To compare different settings for the same command, **duplicate** an adjustment layer (such as Levels) a few times, then change the settings slightly for each one. Hide all the adjustment layers, and then show/hide them one by one.

▶ To limit the area an adjustment layer affects, create a **selection** before choosing the adjustment command. The selection area will be represented by white in the layer mask thumbnail.**B–F** (See also the following page.)

▶ **Paint, or fill** an area on an adjustment layer with **black** to **hide** the adjustment effect, or with **white** to reveal it again. Your strokes will display in the layer mask thumbnail.

▶ To **prevent** an underlying layer from being affected by an adjustment layer, drag it above the adjustment layer.

▶ You can use a **clipping mask** to limit the effect of an adjustment layer to just the layer below it instead of all the underlying layers (see page 296). If you Alt-click/Option-click the New Fill/Adjustment Layer menu when you create an adjustment layer, the New Layer dialog box opens; check **Use Previous Layer to Create Clipping Mask** to create a clipping mask right off the bat.

▶ And finally, let's say you have a series of photos of the same scene or subject that were taken under the same lighting conditions. Create an adjustment layer to enhance or correct one of the images first, then **drag and drop** the adjustment layer from the Layers palette onto each of the other document windows to quickly apply the same adjustment.

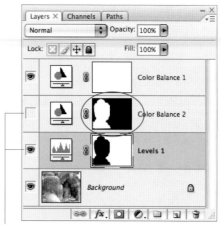

A *Hide/show different adjustment layers to compare their individual or cumulative effects.*

B *If you create a **selection** before creating an adjustment layer, the selection shape will appear in the **layer mask**.*

C *The original image has a magenta cast.*

D *We used a **Color Balance adjustment layer** to neutralize the color cast.*

E *We selected the large Buddha on the left with the Magnetic Lasso tool, then used a **Color Balance adjustment layer** to make it warmer.*

F *We reselected the Buddha on the left, chose Select > Inverse, then used a **Levels adjustment layer** to darken the background.*

By default, all new adjustment layers have a layer mask. You can ignore the mask or you can use it to control which area of the image the adjustment layer affects. In these instructions, you'll **edit** the **adjustment layer mask** either by creating and filling a selection or by applying brush strokes.

To partially mask an adjustment layer:

1. Click an adjustment layer.

2. Press D to choose the default colors, then press X to switch to black as the Foreground color (note the two color squares on the Tools palette).

3. To mask the adjustment layer effect, do either or both of the following:

   Create a **selection** using any selection tool (e.g., Rectangular Marquee, Lasso, or Magic Wand), choose Edit > Fill (Shift-Backspace/Shift-Delete), choose Use: Foreground Color, then click OK.

   Choose the **Brush** tool (B or Shift-B). On the Options bar, choose a brush tip, Mode: Normal, and Opacity 100% (or a lower opacity to create a partial mask), then paint on the image. **A–C**

4. *Optional:* To restore the adjustment layer effect by painting out the black mask, press X to switch the colors again (the Foreground color is now white), then draw brush strokes in the document window.

▶ To remove the entire mask, deselect, click the adjustment layer, choose Edit > Fill, choose Use: White, then click OK.

▶ To allow the adjustment layer to affect only a small area, fill the entire mask with black, then paint with white.

A *We applied the **Posterize** command to an image via an adjustment layer first.*

B *Then we applied **brush strokes** to the **layer mask** to soften the harsh highlights in the background.*

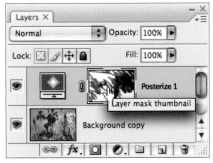

C *On the **Layers** palette for the previous figure, you can see our brush strokes on the **adjustment layer mask** thumbnail.*

LAYER MASK SHORTCUTS

To turn off any of the features listed below, simply repeat the shortcut.

View the mask in the document window	Alt-click/Option-click the layer mask thumbnail
View the mask in the Quick Mask color (default color is red)	Alt-Shift-click/Option-Shift-click the layer mask thumbnail
Deactivate/activate the mask	Shift-click the layer mask thumbnail
Convert the unmasked area into a selection	Ctrl-click/Cmd-click the layer mask thumbnail

Two-step adjustment commands

Next we'll show you how to use a couple of easy two-step commands that produce dramatic changes: Threshold and Posterize. To increase your editing flexibility when applying these commands, apply them via an adjustment layer.

The **Threshold** command makes the current layer high-contrast by converting all colors to either black or white.

When applying this command, keep an eye on the histogram in the dialog box, which diagrams the distribution of pixels in your image. (To learn more about histograms, see pages 178–179.)

To apply the Threshold command:

1. Click a layer or the Background. **A**

2. From the New Fill/Adjustment Layer menu ⬤. at the bottom of the Layers palette, choose **Threshold.** The Threshold dialog box opens. **B**

3. Raise the **Threshold Level** (1–255) to increase the number of black pixels, or lower it to increase the number of white pixels (use the scrubby slider). Pixels that are lighter than the Threshold Level will turn white; darker pixels will turn black.

4. Click OK. **C–D**

➤ To have the Threshold command convert midtones into linework, before choosing the command, apply Filter > Other > High Pass to the selected layer (try a Radius setting of around 4 or 5).

A *The original image*

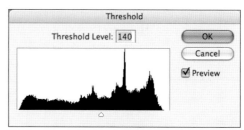

B *The slider in the **Threshold** dialog box controls the cutoff point for black/white values.*

C *After applying the **Threshold** command*

D *To restore some of the original image colors, we lowered the adjustment layer Opacity to 50%. The light colors now look softer than the dark colors.*

The **Posterize** command reduces the number of color or value levels in an image to a specified number. When applied at a low number of Levels, this command produces the look of a silkscreen. You may also find Posterize useful for reducing the number of colors in a file before optimizing it in the GIF format (for Web output).

To apply the Posterize command:

1. Click a layer or the Background.**A**

2. From the New Fill/Adjustment Layer menu ⬤. at the bottom of the Layers palette, choose **Posterize.** The Posterize dialog box opens.

3. Make sure **Preview** is checked, then choose the desired number of Levels (2–255). To make the layer look like a poster or silkscreen, choose a low value (try 4, 5, or 6).

4. Click OK.**B–D**

➤ If you apply an adjustment command directly to a layer (not via an adjustment layer), you can lessen its effect via the Opacity slider in Edit > Fade (Ctrl-Shift-F/Cmd-Shift-F)—provided you do so immediately after applying the command. We prefer to use an adjustment layer and lessen its effect by changing the adjustment command settings or by lowering the adjustment layer Opacity.

A *The original image*

B *The **Posterize** command applied at **4 Levels***

C *The **Posterize** command applied at **5 Levels***

D *The **Posterize** command applied at **6 Levels***

Using the Histogram palette

The **Histogram** palette is fully accessible whenever an adjustment command or adjustment layer dialog box is open. It displays a graph of the current light and dark tonal values in an image, which updates dynamically as you edit your document. By monitoring changes to the histogram as you apply adjustments, you'll be better equipped to gauge their impact.

After opening a scanned image or digital photo in Photoshop—but before you begin editing—study the histogram to evaluate the existing distribution of tonal values. The horizontal axis on the graph represents the grayscale or color levels between 0 and 255; each vertical bar represents the number of pixels at that particular level; and the overall shape of the graph represents the current tonal range of the image.

From the Histogram palette menu, choose a view for the palette: **Compact View** (just the histogram);**A** **Expanded View** (the histogram plus access to individual channels);**B** or **All Channels View** (a histogram for every channel).

While a large file is being edited, Photoshop maintains the redraw speed of the Histogram palette by reading from the cache data for the histogram—not from the actual image data. As this is occurring, a **Cached Data Warning** icon ⚠ appears on the palette. Be sure to keep updating the palette—even while an adjustment dialog box is open—so it continues to reflect the current tonal values of the image. You can specify a **Cache Levels** value (1–8) in Preferences > Performance. Relaunch Photoshop to activate the new setting.

To update the Histogram palette:

Do one of the following:

Double-click anywhere on the **histogram.**

Click the **Cached Data Warning** icon. ⚠

Click the **Uncached Refresh** button. 🔄

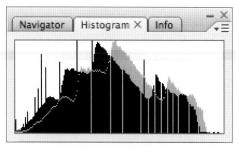

A *The black areas on the **Histogram** palette represent the tonal and color changes being made to the image. The gray areas, which display if you apply an adjustment command to a layer directly (not via an adjustment layer), represent the distribution of pixels prior to any adjustment. The palette shown here is in **Compact View.***

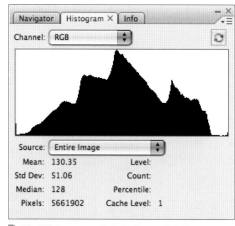

B *The **Histogram** palette in **Expanded View***

Interpreting the Histogram palette

A histogram is a dynamic graph of the tonal range (distribution of pixels) of an image. Pixels are represented by black areas, with shadows on the left, midtone pixels in the middle, and highlight pixels on the right.

If an image is low key (relatively dark, such as a night scene), pixels will be clustered primarily on the left side of the histogram. If an image is average key (has balanced lights/darks), the distribution of pixels will be more uniform across the histogram. And if an image is high key (light, with little or no shadow areas, such as a polar bear in snow) pixels will be clustered primarily on the right.

If an image has a wide tonal range (which is optimal), pixels will stretch from the leftmost to rightmost edges of the graph, and will be distributed fairly equally in the shadow, midtone, and highlight zones. The graph will be mostly solid and will have a relatively smooth (not spiky) contour.**A**

If an image lacks detail in a particular tonal range, the graph will exhibit gaps and/or spikes, like teeth on a comb:

➤ If an image is average key but **underexposed**, pixels will be clustered primarily on the left side of the histogram, indicating that the image lacks detail in the highlights.**B**

➤ If an image is **overexposed**, pixels will be clustered mostly on the right side of the histogram, indicating that the image lacks detail in the shadows.**C**

➤ If pixels were **clipped** (details discarded) from the extreme shadow or highlight areas in an image, a line or cluster of pixels will rise sharply off the left or right edge of the histogram.**D**

➤ If an image has lost detail as a result of editing (say from applying filters or adjustments), there will be **gaps** or **spikes** in the histogram.**E** Gaps indicate a loss of specific tonal or color levels; spikes indicate that pixels from different levels have been averaged together and assigned the same value (the bar becomes taller at that level). Whereas a few gaps or spikes are an acceptable result of editing, large gaps signify posterization and a loss of too many continuous tonal values (bad for photos). On the other hand, a lousy-looking histogram doesn't always signify failure—it can be thrown off by something as simple as adding a white border. If you like the way the image looks, ignore the histogram.

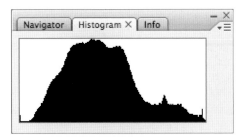

A *This image has a **good tonal range**.*

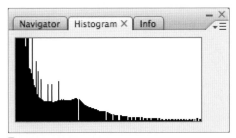

B *This image is **underexposed**.*

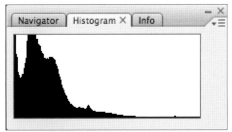

C *This image is **overexposed**.*

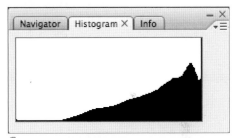

D *This histogram has **clipped shadow pixels**.*

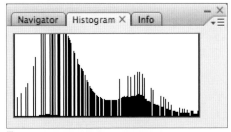

E *This histogram has **gaps** and **spikes**.*

Using the Levels command

Now that you know what a "good" histogram looks like, you're ready for the **Levels** command. We invariably use this command when we bring a photograph into Photoshop, then often use it again during the course of editing. In these instructions, via the Input Levels and Output Levels sliders, you'll adjust highlight, midtone, and shadow values to intensify or diminish contrast.

To correct the light/dark balance of an image:

1. Click a layer, **A** then from the New Fill/ Adjustment Layer menu ◑. at the bottom of the Layers palette, choose **Levels.** The Levels dialog box opens.

2. Do any of the following: **B**

   To enhance the contrast, move the white **Input Levels** highlights slider to the left to brighten the highlights and move the black **Input Levels** shadows slider to the right to darken the shadows. Any pixels located to the left of the black slider will be shifted to the darkest tonal value; any pixels located to the right of the white slider will be shifted to the lightest tonal value. This shifting of values is called "clipping."

   Another way to figure out where to position the highlights and shadows sliders in a Grayscale or RGB image is to hold down Alt/Option, then drag the highlights or shadows slider. This will activate **Threshold** mode (a high-contrast clipping display of the image). As you drag the highlights slider, release the mouse when only a few areas of color or white appear **C**; these pixels will become the lightest tonal value. Then drag the shadows slider, releasing the mouse when only a few areas of color or black appear (**A**, next page); these pixels will become the darkest tonal value.

3. With the shadows and highlights sliders in their proper place, now move the gray **Input Levels** midtones slider to lighten or darken the midtones separately from the shadows or highlights.

A *The original image looks dull (lacks contrast).*

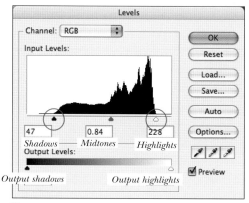

B *The histogram in this **Levels** dialog box doesn't extend to the edges, signifying that our photo has a narrow tonal range. To correct it, we moved the shadows and highlights Input Levels sliders inward to align with the outer edges of the histogram (to expand the tonal range), and moved the midtones slider to darken the midtones.*

C *This is **Threshold mode** as we Alt-drag/Option-drag the white **Input Levels** (highlights) slider.*

4. Click OK.**B–C**

➤ To apply the current Levels settings to other open images (images that were taken under similar lighting conditions, perhaps, that require the same adjustments), drag the adjustment layer into each document window. The adjustment layer will be copied to the Layers palette for each target document. To learn about the Options button, see page 206.

➤ The Shadow/Highlight command, another of our favorite commands, gives you even more options and controls for adjusting lights and darks in an image than Levels. See pages 247–249.

A *This is* **Threshold** *mode as we Alt-drag/Option-drag the black* **Input Levels** *(shadows) slider.*

B *Our* **Levels** *adjustments enhanced the light/dark* **contrast,** *as reflected in the histogram shown in the next figure.*

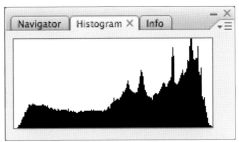

C *The histogram after the Levels adjustments shows that the tonal range of the image was expanded (the graph now extends to the edges), with the result being stronger shadows and highlights (better contrast).*

Printing dark text on top of a photo can be tricky. The picture has to be light enough to allow the text to be readable, yet visible enough to be interpreted as an image. **Screening back imagery** is yet another great use for the **Levels** command.

To screen back a layer:

1. Open an image.

2. *Optional:* To limit the screened-back effect to a specific area of the image, create a selection.

3. Click an image layer or the Background,**A** then from the New Fill/Adjustment Layer menu ⊘. at the bottom of the Layers palette, choose **Levels**. The Levels dialog box opens. Check Preview.

4. To reduce contrast in the image, move the **Input Levels** highlights (white) slider slightly to the left, and the **Output Levels** shadows (black) slider to the right.

5. To lighten the midtone values in the image, move the **Input Levels** midtones (gray) slider to the left.

6. Click OK.**B–C**

A *The original document contains an editable type layer and an image layer.*

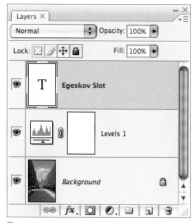

B *We used a **Levels** adjustment layer to lighten the image, shown at right.*

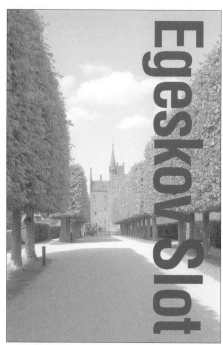

C *With the image screened back, the type is more prominent and easier to read.*

Adjusting brightness and contrast

Good news! Adobe has improved the **Bright-ness/Contrast** command so that it no longer dis-cards pixel data from the entire tonal range of an image. After adjustment, the histogram displays only minor shifts and redistribution of the tonal range—not the major changes seen in past versions of Photoshop. We can now safely recommend it as one of the more useful commands for applying minor brightness and/or contrast adjustments.

To adjust brightness and contrast: ★

1. Click a layer or the Background.

2. From the New Fill/Adjustment Layer menu ●. at the bottom of the Layers palette, choose **Brightness/Contrast.** The Brightness/Contrast dialog box opens.

3. To brighten or increase contrast, move the slid-ers to the right. To darken or lower contrast, move the sliders to the left.

4. Click OK.**A–D**

➤ Don't check the Use Legacy option! Doing so will allow the command to shift all the tonal values and remove tonal levels (bad).

A *The original image is a bit dull (lacks contrast and saturation).*

B *Using the **Brightness/Contrast** settings shown at left, we increased the brightness of the overall image and increased the contrast to make the colors more saturated.*

C *The skin tones in the original image look a bit washed out.*

D *Using the settings shown at left, we decreased the **brightness** of the overall image, and also increased the **contrast** to make the skin tones more saturated.*

Dodging and burning

If you need to lighten (or darken) pixels by hand in small areas, the Dodge (or Burn) tool might seem like an obvious contender. However, both tools permanently alter layer pixels, which we strenuously try to avoid doing. A good alternative technique is to **dodge** and **burn** areas of an image with the Brush tool on a removable, editable, neutral color layer, as per these instructions.

To dodge and burn colors using a neutral color layer:

1. If the document isn't already in RGB Color mode, choose Image > Mode > **RGB Color.**

2. Click a layer, **A** then Alt-click/Option-click the **New Layer** button 🔲 on the Layers palette. The New Layer dialog box opens.

3. Choose Mode: **Overlay**, check **Fill with Overlay-Neutral Color (50% gray)**, and click OK.

4. Choose the **Brush** tool (B or Shift-B). 🖌 From the Options bar, choose a large, soft-edged brush and an Opacity of 20%. Press D to reset the default colors to black and white.

5. Paint with **black** to darken areas of the image. Press X to swap the Foreground/Background colors, then paint with **white** to lighten areas. **B–C**

   If you're not happy with the results in a specific area, choose **60% gray** (use tool tips to find it on the Swatches palette), then paint over that area. This will remove any dodge or burn effect and restore the neutral gray. (Yes, 60%—the neutral gray—isn't 50% gray.)

➤ To lessen the overall dodge/burn effect, click the neutral gray layer on the Layers palette, then lower the layer Opacity or choose Soft Light as its blending mode.

A *The center of this image, where the focal point should be,* **lacks contrast.** *We'll adjust the reflected light on the cobblestones to draw attention to the figure.*

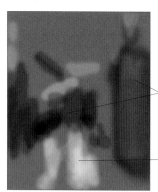

B *This is the* **neutral gray layer** *(the other layers are hidden).*

We painted with **black** *to* **darken** *the shadows on the sides of the houses.*

We painted with **white** *to* **lighten** *the cobblestones around the figure.*

C *We painted on the* **neutral gray layer** *to* **dodge** *the road and* **burn** *the houses, then lowered the layer Opacity to 78% to soften the overall effect.*

In the first part of this chapter, you'll learn how to choose colors to use with various tools and commands. The last part of this chapter is a reference guide to the blending modes, which are available for tools, layers, and commands. In other chapters, you'll learn how colors are applied.

Choosing colors

The current **Foreground color** is applied when you draw strokes with the Brush or Pencil tool, create type, enlarge the canvas area, or use other tools and commands. The current **Background color** is applied by other procedures, such as when you apply a transform command to, or move a selection on, the Background.

These two colors are displayed in the Foreground and Background color squares on the Tools palette **A** and Color palette.**B** (Written with an uppercase "F" or "B," these terms refer to the two colors, not to the foreground or background areas of a picture.) On the following pages, you'll learn the following methods for choosing Foreground and Background colors:

➤ Enter values or click the large color square in the **Color Picker**

➤ Pluck a color from an image with the **Eyedropper tool**

➤ Choose a premixed color from a matching system via the **Color Libraries** dialog box

➤ Enter values or move sliders on the **Color palette**

➤ Click a swatch on the **Swatches palette**

*The **Default Foreground and Background Colors** button (D) makes the Foreground color black and the Background color white.*

*The **Switch Colors** button (X) swaps the current Foreground and Background colors.*

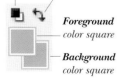

Foreground color square

Background color square

The currently selected square has a black border.

Foreground color square

Background color square

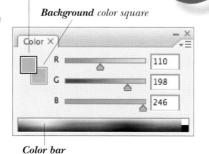

Color bar

A *The color controls on the **Tools** palette*

B *Use the **Color** palette to mix colors.*

(OLORS & BLENDING MODES)

12

To choose a color using the Color Picker:

1. Do one of the following:

   Click the Foreground or Background color square on the **Tools** palette.

   Click the Foreground or Background color square on the **Color** palette, if it's already selected (has a black border).

   Double-click the Foreground or Background color square on the **Color** palette, if it's not already selected.

   Note: If the square you click contains a custom color from a matching system, the Color Libraries dialog box opens. Click **Picker** to get to the Color Picker dialog box.

2. *Optional:* In the Photoshop Color Picker, check Only Web Colors to make only Web-safe colors available.

3. Do one of the following:

   Click a color on the vertical color slider to choose a **hue**, then click a variation of that hue in the large square.**A**

   To mix a specific process color for print output, enter C, **M**, **Y**, and K percentages from a printed color matching system swatchbook (you can use the scrubby sliders).

   For onscreen output, enter R, G, and B values (0–255). Entering 0 in all three fields produces black; entering 255 in all three fields produces white.

4. Click OK. The color will appear in the Foreground or Background color square on the Tools and Color palettes. To save the color to the Swatches palette for future use, see page 189.

▶ To access your system's color picker, in Preferences > General, choose Color Picker: Windows/Apple; or to use the Photoshop Color Picker (the default picker), choose Adobe. Only one color picker can be accessed at a time.

▶ You can also enter numbers in the **H**, **S**, and **B** or **L**, **a**, and **b** fields.

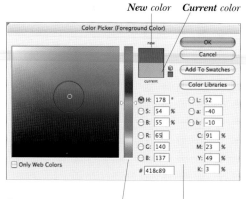

New color   **Current** *color*

A *Click a color on the color slider, then click a color in the large square...*   *...or enter percentages in the **HSB**, **RGB**, **Lab**, or **CMYK** fields.*

ARE YOUR COLORS OUT OF GAMUT?

An **out-of-gamut** icon ⚠ in the Color Picker or Color palette signifies that the current color is outside the printable gamut, meaning it can't be printed with inks. If you're planning to print your Photoshop file, you should change any out-of-gamut color to an in-gamut color or click the exclamation point to let Photoshop substitute the closest printable color (shown in the swatch next to or below the exclamation point). Keep in mind that when your image is converted to CMYK Color mode, all the image colors are brought into the printable gamut. The out-of-gamut range is defined by the CMYK output profile, which is specified in Edit > Color Settings on the Working Spaces: CMYK menu.

A **non-Web-safe** icon 🔲 in the Color Picker signifies that the chosen color isn't Web-safe. Click the swatch below the cube to have Photoshop substitute a similar Web-safe color. Note that with the proliferation of 16-bit monitors, you probably won't need to restrict yourself to Web-safe colors.

Custom colors are formulas specified by third-party companies (such as PANTONE and FOCOLTONE). For each color library or system, you can buy a printed matching system guide or fan book. For Web publishing or small-scale desktop printing, you don't need to refer to such a printed book, but commercial printing is an entirely different story. In the latter case, you can't just go picking colors willy-nilly based on whether they look good onscreen, because even the most carefully calibrated display won't show matching system colors with perfect accuracy.

Before choosing colors in Photoshop for print output, the first step is to ask your commercial printer which brand of ink they're planning to use. Get the printed fan book for that system, and flip through it to decide which colors you're going to use. To choose those colors in Photoshop, you'll use the **Color Libraries** dialog box.

To choose a color from a color library:

1. Do one of the following:

   Click the Foreground or Background color square on the **Tools** palette.

   Click the Foreground or Background color square on the **Color** palette, if it's already selected (has a black border).

   Double-click the Foreground or Background color square on the **Color** palette, if it's not already selected.

2. If the color square you clicked on isn't a custom color, the Color Picker dialog box will open. Click **Color Libraries** to open the Color Libraries dialog box.

3. From the **Book** menu, choose the matching system that your commercial printer recommends.**A**

4. Do either of the following:

   Without clicking anywhere, type the number assigned to the desired color (refer to your swatch book); that swatch will become selected.

   Click a color on the vertical color slider, then click a swatch on the left side of the dialog box.**B**

5. Click OK.

➤ To load a library of matching system colors onto the Swatches palette, see page 190.

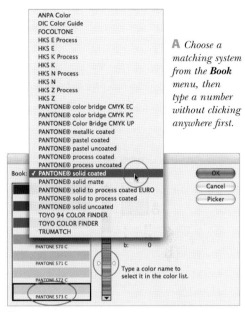

A *Choose a matching system from the Book menu, then type a number without clicking anywhere first.*

Type a color name to select it in the color list.

B *Or click a color on the vertical color slider, then click a swatch at left.*

CHOOSING A LIBRARY FOR PRINT OUTPUT

➤ ANPA colors are used in newspaper printing.

➤ DIC Color Guide and TOYO Color Finder colors are used in Japan.

➤ FOCOLTONE is a process color system that was developed to help prevent registration problems; it can be used in the U.S.

➤ HKS process colors and HKS spot colors (with no "Process" in the name) are used primarily in Europe.

➤ PANTONE process colors and PANTONE spot colors (with no "Process" in the name) are widely used in the U.S.

➤ TRUMATCH is a process color system with a different organizational system than PANTONE. You can also use this system in the U.S.

SPOT OR PROCESS?

By default, when color-separating an image for printing, Photoshop separates all colors — process and spot colors — into the C, M, Y, and K process colors. If you want to output a spot color to a separate plate from Photoshop, you have to create a spot color channel for it (see page 407).

For Web output, you can mix **RGB** or **HSB** colors directly on the **Color** palette, by using the color bar, sliders, or fields.

To choose an RGB or HSB color using the Color palette:

1. Click the Foreground or Background color square, if the desired square isn't already selected.**A**

2. From the top of the Color palette menu, choose a color **model** for the sliders.**B** For Web output, choose RGB Sliders, HSB Sliders (hue, saturation, and brightness), or Web Color Sliders (for Web-safe colors).

3. Do any of the following:

   Move any of the **sliders.**

   Click on or drag across the **color bar.**

   Enter values in the **fields.**

➤ To choose a different spectrum style for the color bar or to quickly access the Make Ramp Web Safe command, right-click/Control-click the color bar.

➤ Alt-click/Option-click the color bar to choose a color for whichever color square isn't currently selected.

➤ If Dynamic Color Sliders is checked in Preferences (Ctrl-K/Cmd-K) > General, colors inside the slider bars will update interactively as you drag in the color bar.

➤ In the RGB model, white (the presence of all colors) is produced when all the sliders are at the far right, black (the absence of all colors) is produced when all the sliders are at the far left, and gray is produced when all the sliders are aligned vertically with one another at any other location.

A *Click the* **Foreground** *or* **Background** *color square. The currently selected square has a black border.*

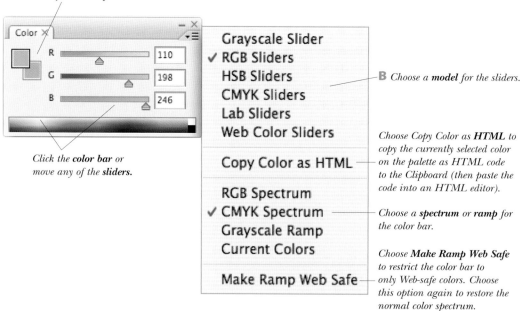

Click the **color bar** *or move any of the* **sliders.**

B *Choose a* **model** *for the sliders.*

Choose Copy Color as **HTML** *to copy the currently selected color on the palette as HTML code to the Clipboard (then paste the code into an HTML editor).*

Choose a **spectrum** *or* **ramp** *for the color bar.*

Choose **Make Ramp Web Safe** *to restrict the color bar to only Web-safe colors. Choose this option again to restore the normal color spectrum.*

Using the Swatches palette

You may want to detach the Swatches palette from the Color palette group before following these instructions.

To choose a color from the Swatches palette:

Do either of the following:

To choose a color for the currently selected color square, **click** a color swatch.

To choose a color for the square that isn't currently selected, **Ctrl-click/Cmd-click** a color swatch.

➤ To append other libraries of swatches to the palette or replace the existing swatches, follow the instructions on the next page.

Colors you **add** to the **Swatches palette** stay there unless you delete them or reset the palette, and are available for all your documents.

To add a color to the Swatches palette:

1. Mix or choose a **Foreground** color by using the Color palette or the Color Picker.

2. On the Swatches palette, do either of the following:

Click the blank area below the swatches on the palette (paint bucket pointer) **A** or right-click/ Control-click any existing swatch and choose **New Swatch.** Name the swatch, then click OK.

To create a new swatch without entering a custom name, click the **New Swatch of Foreground Color** button at the bottom of the Swatches palette.

Regardless of which method you use, the new swatch will appear as the last swatch on the palette.

➤ To rename a swatch, double-click it, change the name, then click OK. To see the swatch name, use the tool tip, or choose Small List or Large List from the palette menu.

You can't undo the **deletion** of a **swatch,** so proceed with caution.

To delete a color from the Swatches palette:

Alt-click/Option-click the swatch to be deleted (scissors pointer), or right-click/Control-click a swatch and choose **Delete Swatch.B**

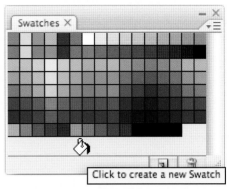

A *To **add** a color to the **Swatches** palette, click the blank area below the swatches.*

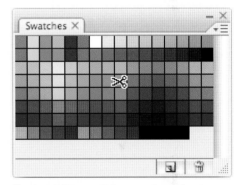

B *Alt-click/Option-click a swatch to **delete** it.*

If you **save** the current **swatches as a library**, you'll be able to load that group of swatches onto the palette whenever you need it.

To save the current swatches as a library:

1. Make sure all the colors you want to save in the new library are on the Swatches palette, then choose **Save Swatches** from the palette menu.

2. In the **File Name/Save As** field, enter a name for the library (keep the .aco extension).

3. Choose a location in which to save the library (see the sidebar on this page).

4. Click Save.

➤ To edit an existing user-created library, follow the instructions above, except retype the same name for the library. When the alert dialog box appears, click Replace.

You can **load** any user-created library or any of the **preset swatch libraries** that ship with Photoshop into the Swatches palette. You can either replace the existing swatches with the new ones or append the additional swatches while keeping the existing ones on the palette.

To replace or append a swatches library:

1. From the lower portion of the Swatches palette menu, choose the desired library name.

2. Do either of the following:

Click **Append** to add the new library of swatches to the current palette.

Click **OK** to replace the current swatches with the new ones. A prompt may appear, giving you the option to save the existing swatches on the palette as a library.**A**

➤ If you want to use your current swatches in another Creative Suite 3 application, save them via the Save Swatches for Exchange command on the Swatches palette menu.

➤ If you do interior design work, you may already know that some paint companies let you download swatches from their website (such as benjaminmoore.com, under Professional > Architects and Designers). Install the files in the default location, as listed in the sidebar at right, then relaunch Photoshop. The new category of swatches can be loaded from the Swatches palette menu.

You'll need to follow these instructions to **load** a **swatches library** only if the library isn't in the default location (as listed in the sidebar below); otherwise, follow the previous set of instructions.

To load a swatches library:

1. From the Swatches palette menu, choose **Load Swatches**.

2. Locate and click the desired library.

3. Click **Load**. The newly loaded swatches will appear below the existing swatches.

To restore the default swatches:

Choose **Reset Swatches** from the Swatches palette menu, then click OK. A prompt may appear, giving you the option to save the existing swatches as a library.

WHERE TO STORE YOUR SWATCH LIBRARIES

To have your color swatch libraries appear automatically on the Swatches palette menu, you need to store them in the following location:

➤ In Windows, in Program Files\Adobe\Adobe Photoshop CS3\Presets\Color Swatches.

➤ In the Mac OS, in Applications/Adobe Photoshop CS3/Presets/Color Swatches.

A *This prompt will appear in the Mac OS if you replace your current Swatches palette colors with a new library and the current swatches haven't yet been saved. In Windows, the buttons are Yes, No, and Cancel.*

Using the Eyedropper tool

Being able to pluck a color from an image is useful for color matching, when, say, retouching a photo or adding type. For this, you use the **Eyedropper** tool.

To choose a color from an image using the Eyedropper:

1. Choose the **Eyedropper** tool (I or Shift-I).
2. When you do either of the following, the sampled color will appear in the currently selected color square on the Tools and Color palettes:

   Click a color in any open document window.**A**

   Drag in any document window. The Foreground color square will change dynamically as you drag. Release the mouse when the pointer is over the desired color.

➤ Alt-click/Option-click or drag in the document window with the Eyedropper tool to choose a Background color when the Foreground color square is selected or a Foreground color when the Background color square is selected.

Copying colors as hexadecimals

For Web output, you can **copy colors** as **hexadecimal values** from a file in Photoshop and paste them into an HTML file.

To copy a color as a hexadecimal value:

Method 1

1. Choose the **Eyedropper** tool (I or Shift-I).
2. Right-click/Control-click a color in the document window, then choose **Copy Color as HTML.** The color you selected will be copied to the Clipboard as a hexadecimal value.
3. To paste the color into an HTML file, display the HTML file in your HTML-editing application, then choose Edit > Paste (Ctrl-V/Cmd-V).

Method 2

1. Choose a **Foreground** color via the Color palette, Color Picker, or Swatches palette.
2. From the Color palette menu, choose **Copy Color as HTML.** The Foreground color will be copied to the Clipboard as a hexadecimal value.
3. To paste the color into an HTML file, open the destination application, display the HTML file, then choose Edit > Paste (Ctrl-V/Cmd-V).

A *Sampling a color from an image with the* **Eyedropper** *tool*

CHOOSING A SAMPLE SIZE

To change the size of the area the Eyedropper tool samples from, on the Options bar, choose **Sample Size: Point Sample** (the exact pixel you'll click on) or one of the **Average** options (e.g., an average within a 5-by-5-pixel square).**B** You can also right-click/Control-click in the document window with the Eyedropper tool and choose a sample size from the context menu. 3 by 3 Average and 5 by 5 Average are useful for sampling continuous tones, such as skin tones in a portrait photo or the background area in a landscape. 11 by 11 Average through 101 by 101 Average are four new options that work with files of all bit depths. ★

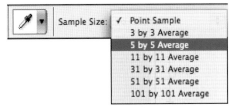

B *Choose a* **Sample Size** *for the* **Eyedropper** *tool from the Options bar (or from the context menu).*

Choosing blending modes

The **blending mode A** that you choose for a tool or a layer affects how that tool or layer modifies underlying pixels. You can choose from a list of blending modes in many locations in Photoshop, such as the Options bar (for most painting and editing tools), the Layers palette, and the Layer Style dialog box.

In the text that accompanies the figures in this section, the colors of underlying pixels are called the **base colors**; the color that you choose for a layer or apply with a tool (such as the Brush), and that you choose a mode for, is called the **blend color**. In the images, we used the same three color squares, as shown in the first figure below. To avoid confusion, we kept the blend layer opacity at 100% (except for Dissolve mode).

➤ For most blending modes, Photoshop compares the colors of the two layers (or the layer and the paint color being applied by a tool) on a channel-by-channel basis. For example, the lightness of a pixel in the Red channel of the blend layer would be compared to the lightness of a corresponding pixel in the Red channel of the base layer.

➤ When choosing an Opacity percentage for a tool via the Options bar, keep in mind that the impact of the tool is also affected by the opacity of the layer that you apply strokes to. For example, strokes applied with the Brush tool at a 50% opacity on a layer opacity of 50% will appear lighter than the same strokes on a layer opacity of 100%.

Normal Dissolve Behind Clear	*Basic*
Darken ✓ Multiply Color Burn Linear Burn Darker Color	*Darken*
Lighten Screen Color Dodge Linear Dodge (Add) Lighter Color	*Lighten*
Overlay Soft Light Hard Light Vivid Light Linear Light Pin Light Hard Mix	*Contrast*
Difference Exclusion	*Comparative*
Hue Saturation Color Luminosity	*Component*

A *The* **blending modes** *are organized in groups based on their function.*

CYCLING THROUGH THE MODES

To cycle through the **blending modes** for the current painting or **editing tool,** or for the currently selected **layer** if a nonediting tool is selected (such as the Move tool or a selection tool), press **Shift - +** (plus) or **Shift - –** (minus).

Basic blending modes **replace** the base colors

Normal
All base colors are modified. When an image is in Bitmap or Indexed Color mode, this mode is called Threshold.

Dissolve (50% Fill)
Creates a chalky, dry-brush texture using the blend color. The higher the pressure or opacity of the tool or the higher the opacity of the layer, the more solid the color.

Darken blending modes **darken** the base colors

Darken
The blend color darkens lighter pixels in the base colors; darker pixels aren't changed. Contrast is lowered in the blend color.

Multiply
A dark blend color produces darker base colors; a light blend color merely tints the base colors. All base colors are darkened. (Good for creating semitransparent shadows.)

Color Burn
Increases contrast in the base colors by making the shadow areas darker and the highlights lighter.

Linear Burn
Uses the blend color to darken the base colors by decreasing the brightness.

Darker Color ★
The blend color replaces base colors lighter than itself without affecting darker base colors. The blend color is fully opaque. Use to "paint out" light colors on a figure or object without having to use a selection.

*The light blue strokes were applied to a blank layer above the image layer. **Darker Color** blending mode is chosen for the layer that contains the brush strokes.*

Lighten blending modes **lighten** the base colors

Lighten
Modifies only base colors that are darker than the blend color, not base colors that are lighter than the blend color.

Screen
A light blend color produces lighter, bleached base colors; a dark blend color lightens the base colors less.

Color Dodge
A light blend color lightens the base colors by decreasing the layer's contrast; a dark blend color tints the base colors slightly.

Linear Dodge
A light blend color lightens the base colors by increasing the layer's brightness; a dark blend color tints the base colors slightly.

Lighter Color ★
The blend color replaces base colors darker than itself without affecting lighter base colors. The blend color will be fully opaque. Use to "paint out" dark colors around a light figure or object without having to use a selection.

*The light blue strokes were applied to a blank layer above the image layer. **Lighter Color** blending mode is chosen for the layer that contains the brush strokes.*

Contrast blending modes increase or decrease overall **contrast**

Overlay

Multiplies (darkens) dark base colors and screens (lightens) light base colors while preserving luminosity (light and dark) values. Black and white pixels aren't changed, so details are preserved.

Soft Light

Softens and fades by lowering contrast in the blend color. Preserves luminosity values in the base colors.

Hard Light

Screens (lightens) the base colors if the blend color is light; multiplies (darkens) the base colors if the blend color is dark. Increases contrast in the blend color. Good for composite effects or for painting glowing highlights.

Vivid Light

Burns (darkens) the base colors by increasing contrast if the blend color is dark; dodges (lightens) the base colors by decreasing contrast if the blend color is light.

Linear Light

Burns (darkens) the base colors by decreasing its brightness if the blend color is dark; dodges (lightens) the base colors by increasing brightness if the blend color is light.

Pin Light

The blend color replaces the base colors, depending on its relative brightness. A blend color lighter than 50% gray replaces only dark base colors; a blend color darker than 50% gray replaces only light base colors.

Contrast blending modes (continued)

Hard mix
Posterizes (reduces) the base colors to approximately 5–8 flat colors. A dark blend color produces more black in the base colors; a light blend color produces more white in the base colors.

Comparative blending modes **invert** the base colors

Difference
Inverts the base and blend colors. The lighter the blend color, the more saturated the inverted color.

Exclusion
Grays out the base colors where the blend color is dark; inverts the base colors where the blend color is light. Lowers contrast.

HSL modes apply a specific **color component**

Hue
Applies the hue of the blend color without changing saturation and luminosity values in the base colors.

Saturation
Applies the saturation of the blend color without changing hue and luminosity values in the base colors.

Color
Applies the saturation and hue of the blend color without changing light and dark (luminosity) values in the base colors. Details are preserved, making this a good mode to use for tinting.

Luminosity
Replaces luminosity values in the base colors with luminosity values from the blend color without changing hue and saturation values in the base colors.

> **BEHIND AND CLEAR MODES**
>
> ➤ **Behind** mode lets you modify only transparent areas (not existing base colors). It will appear as if you're painting on the reverse side of the current layer, which is good for creating shadows. To access this mode, make sure both the Lock Image Pixels and Lock Transparent Pixels buttons are off for the current layer. You can choose this mode from the Options bar for the painting tools, cloning tools, and Gradient tool. You can't choose it for a layer or use it on the Background.
>
> ➤ To access **Clear** mode for a tool (e.g., the Brush), make sure both the Lock Image Pixels and Lock Transparent Pixels buttons are off. The base colors are erased where strokes are applied. You can also choose Clear mode in the Fill, Stroke, or Fill Path dialog box. You can't choose it for a layer or use it on the Background.

From professional-level correction to exotic color shifts, Photoshop has an adjustment command to suit your needs. First try to figure what needs correcting, then decide which command will help you achieve your goal. For figurative photography, that goal will probably be color fidelity, whereas for a montage, you might aim for a unified color "temperature" that strikes the right mood. Some commands (such as Color Balance and Levels), are easier to get the hang of than others (Curves, Hue/Saturation), but when you forego simplicity, you gain more options and greater control.

In lieu of choosing adjustment commands directly from the Image > Adjustments submenu, we urge you to apply them via individual adjustment layers. An adjustment layer affects all the visible layers below it but doesn't actually change pixels until you merge it with the underlying layer (if you're not comfortable using adjustment layers yet, see pages 172–175).

Important note: Make sure your monitor is calibrated before performing any color adjustments! See pages 33–35. Also, unless we're working with a CMYK scan, we always perform our color adjustments in RGB Color mode (digital camera images are already in this mode). Should you need to make adjustments for a specific CMYK output device, it's a good idea to copy your original file first.

COLOR ADJUSTMENTS

13

SETTING THE STAGE FOR COLOR ADJUSTMENTS

The first thing we suggest you do before performing color corrections is to put your workspace in **Maximized screen mode** (use the Screen Mode menu at the bottom of the Tools palette). The document window will expand to meet the edges of your palette docks and a neutral gray backdrop will display around your image, enabling you to better judge your color adjustments. In this mode, you can zoom in and out via keyboard shortcuts (see pages 85–86).

Or if you prefer to work on a neutral gray background without the window border, choose **Full Screen Mode With Menu Bar.** Use the Hand tool (H) 🖐 to reposition the image on the gray background.

► To get back to Standard screen mode, press Shift-F.

Creating fill layers

Like an adjustment layer, a fill layer affects the layers below it, except in this case it applies a solid color, gradient, or pattern. Like adjustment layers, fill layers can be edited or removed easily, and their content can be changed at any time. We'll explore two common uses for **fill layers:** applying a **pattern/texture** (below) and applying a color tint (next page).

To add a texture using a pattern fill layer:

1. On the Layers palette, click the layer that you want the fill layer to appear above.**A**

2. From the New Fill/Adjustment Layer menu ⬤. on the Layers palette, choose **Pattern**. The Pattern Fill dialog box opens.

3. Click the pattern thumbnail.**B** The **Pattern** picker opens.

4. From the picker menu (click the arrowhead), choose a pattern library. When the alert prompt appears, click Append to add the library to the current picker.

5. Click a pattern thumbnail in the picker. You can move the pattern by dragging in the document window.

6. Click OK.

7. With the fill layer still selected, change the layer blending mode and opacity.**C**

➤ Click the fill layer, then paint with black in the layer mask to block the effect of the fill layer, with white to restore it, or with a low-opacity brush to block it partially.

➤ To create a custom pattern, select an area of an image layer with the Rectangular Marquee tool (Feather value of 0), choose Edit > Define Pattern, enter a Name, click OK, then deselect all (Ctrl-D/Cmd-D). Your new pattern will appear on the Pattern picker. You can also use the Pattern Maker filter to create custom patterns (see pages 343–344).

➤ To limit the effect of an adjustment layer to just the layer directly below it, Alt-click/Option-click the line between the two (this creates a clipping mask).

A *The original image*

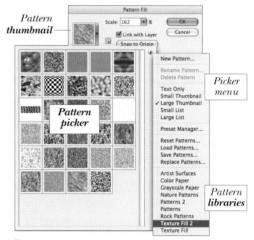

B *Using the **Pattern picker** menu, you can open a new pattern library and append it to the current picker. (We're choosing the Texture Fill 2 library.)*

C *A pattern **fill layer** (Weave 5, Scale 162) above the image layer is creating the paper texture. The fill layer Opacity is 50%.*

If you apply a color to a layer (or to a selection on a layer) via a **Solid Color fill layer**, you'll have the option to edit or remove it at any time. When first applied, a Solid Color fill layer is completely opaque. If you wish, you can use the opacity controls on the Layers palette to lighten the fill layer or change the blending mode for the fill layer to make it interact differently with the underlying layers. This is a simple but effective way to correct a color cast or to apply a color tint to a whole image—or more typically, to part of an image.

To apply a tint using a color fill layer:

1. *Optional:* To restrict the color/tint to part of the image, create a selection.**A**

   (We chose the **Quick Selection** tool (W) and a brush Diameter of 10 px on the Options bar, then dragged across the sky. Next, we clicked the sky area below each arm, then Alt/Option dragged to deselect any selected snow areas.)

2. From the New Fill/Adjustment Layer menu ⊘. on the Layers palette, choose **Solid Color.** The Color Picker dialog box opens.**B**

3. Choose a color for the tint. Don't sweat it: You can change this color later if you wish. Click OK.

4. *Optional:* With the fill layer selected, choose a blending mode via the Layers palette.**C** You could also lower the layer opacity to lighten the color fill.

▶ To change the tint for a color fill layer, double-click the adjustment layer thumbnail; the Color Picker reopens.

▶ Although you can apply a tint, gradient, or pattern, respectively, via the Color Overlay, Gradient Overlay, or Pattern Overlay layer effect, you can't limit layer effects to a specific area with a mask, whereas you can limit areas with the mask on a fill layer.

▶ You can also apply a tint via a Photo Filter adjustment layer (see page 250).

A *We selected the sky before creating a **Solid Color** fill layer.*

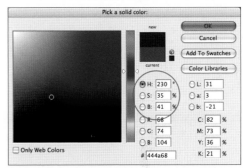

B *Choose a color in the **Color Picker** (we chose H: 230, S: 35, B: 41).*

C *Via a **Solid Color** fill layer, we applied a blue tint to the selection to enliven the sky. (We also changed the adjustment layer blending mode to Vivid Light to restore some definition to the clouds.)*

Converting layers to grayscale

We'll show you three ways to strip color from a layer without changing the document color mode. Our favorite method is the **Black & White** command. By using this command to convert color in a layer to grayscale, you can control how the R, G, B and C, M, Y color channel values contribute individually to the resulting gray levels. Although we use the word "conversion" in these instructions, it's not a true conversion, as this command preserves the original document color mode.

To convert an RGB image to grayscale using the Black & White command: ★

1. Click a layer or the Background.**A**

2. From the New Fill/Adjustment Layer menu on the Layers palette, ⊘. choose **Black & White**. The Black & White dialog box opens and the image becomes grayscale.

3. To control the grayscale conversion of an RGB image, try adjusting the Reds, Greens, and Blues sliders first. If you like, you can click Auto to have the program choose settings for you, then use that conversion as a starting point for the adjustments.**B** Move the **Reds, Greens,** and **Blues** sliders to control how each color is converted to a particular gray level (**A–B**, next page). Drag a slider to the left to produce a darker gray for that color or to the right to produce a lighter gray.

   ➤ If you want to preserve the existing overall light/dark balance in the image, keep the combined sum of the Reds, Greens, and Blues values close to 100%; if you want to alter the overall tone, ignore the combined total (**C–D**, next page).

4. Fine-tune the conversion by adjusting the **Yellows, Cyans,** and **Magentas** sliders. You can use the Yellows slider to lighten/darken a portrait or to correct a landscape image that contains a lot of green.

5. Move the mouse over a gray area in the image that you want to adjust. Press the mouse, and it becomes a scrubby slider, which in turn shifts the slider for the most dominant color in that area (the swatch for that slider will also be highlighted).

   ➤ To reset an individual slider to its default setting, Alt-click/Option-click its color swatch.

A *The central figure commands our attention in this color image because of her position and outstretched hands, the light on her face and hands, and the stripes on her sweater.*

B *The **Auto** setting in the Black & White adjustment layer produced an adequate grayscale conversion, but we'll adjust the gray values next to draw more attention to the central figure, as in the color image.*

To reset all the sliders to their defaults, hold down Alt/Option and click Reset. Neither reset can be undone.

6. *Optional:* To apply a tint to the whole image, check Tint, move the Hue slider to choose a color, and move the Saturation slider to control the color intensity. (Or click the color swatch in the Tint area to open the Color Picker, drag the vertical Hue slider to choose a color, then drag horizontally in the large square to set the Saturation, and vertically to set the Brightness.)

7. Click OK.

8. *Optional:* To restore some of the original color uniformly to the whole layer, lower the opacity of the adjustment layer. Or to restore color by hand, click the adjustment layer mask, choose the Brush tool, make the Foregound color black, then draw strokes on the image.

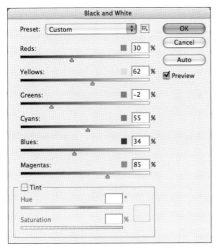

A *We reduced Reds and Yellows to darken the man's jacket, reduced Cyans and Blues to darken the women's clothing, and reduced Greens to darken the stripes on the sweater.*

B *With the slider settings shown at left, the three figures are darker and more uniformly gray except for the face and cupped hands of the central figure, which are lighter. Now the focus is where we intend it to be, but the central figure could use more punch.*

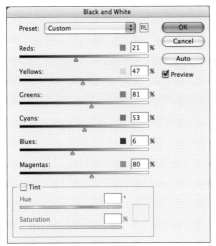

C *We reduced Reds, Yellows, and Blues to darken the outer figures and increased Greens to lighten the stripes on the sweater.*

D *As an experiment, we used the slider settings shown at left to enhance the contrast in the striped sweater. Now the central figure clearly commands the most attention, as in the color version.*

SAVE YOUR ADJUSTMENT SETTINGS ★

The Custom dialog box settings for your adjustment layer will be lost if you choose None or another preset from the Preset menu. To save your custom settings for future access, from the **Preset Options** menu, choose **Save Preset** (keep the .blw extension and keep the default Black and White folder as the location). The preset will appear on the Preset menu.

► Choose **Load Preset** from the Preset Options menu to load a saved preset. Choose **Delete Current Preset** to delete the currently listed user preset.

ORCHESTRATE THE SCENE

In our environment, as in art and photography, colors define spatial and shape relationships and draw our eye to specific parts of a scene. When converting an image to grayscale, you can orchestrate visual movement using lights and darks instead of color. Choose gray levels based on how you want to reinterpret the composition and which areas you want to draw the viewer's attention to. For example, if there was a bright red shape in the center of the original composition, you could lighten or darken the shape to make it stand out from the surrounding grays.

Here are two simpler methods for converting a layer to grayscale.

To convert a layer to grayscale:

1. Click a layer or the Background.

2. Choose Image > Adjustments > **Desaturate** (Ctrl-Shift-U/Cmd-Shift-U). Easy does it.

To convert a color layer to grayscale and restore the color selectively:

1. Click a layer in a color document.

2. From the New Fill/Adjustment Layer menu ⊘. on the Layers palette, choose **Hue/Saturation**. The Hue/Saturation dialog box opens.

3. Move the **Saturation** slider all the way to the left (to –100), then click OK.**A**

4. Choose the Brush tool. Press D for default colors, then press X to swap them.

5. Click the adjustment layer, then apply strokes where you want to restore the original colors.**B–C** To restore colors partially, lower the brush opacity; to restore grayscale areas, press X and paint with white. To restore color uniformly to the whole layer, lower the adjustment layer opacity.

A *To remove the color from this image, we **lowered** the **Saturation** to –100 via a **Hue/Saturation** adjustment layer.*

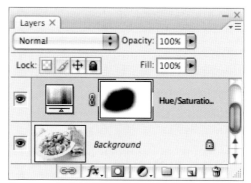

B *We applied brush strokes to the **adjustment layer mask** to restore color in the center of the image.*

C *The color is visible only in the center of the image.*

Using the Color Balance command

You can use the **Color Balance** command to apply a warm or cool cast to an image or to neutralize an unwanted cast. Each slider in the dialog box affects a pairing of cool/warm colors, so you'll be able to see how the overall image is affected as you add or reduce individual colors. For example, moving a slider toward green reduces magenta, adding yellow reduces blue, and so on.

(Note: With this command, you adjust a whole tonal range at a time: shadows, midtones, or highlights. To make adjustments to a narrower tonal range, use Curves or Hue/Saturation.)

A *The original image has a harsh magenta cast.*

To use the Color Balance command to make an image cooler or warmer:

1. Click a layer or the Background **A**, and show the Histogram palette.

2. From the New Fill/Adjustment Layer menu on the Layers palette, ⬤. choose **Color Balance**. The Color Balance dialog box opens.

3. In the **Tone Balance** area, click a range to adjust: **Shadows, Midtones,** or **Highlights B–C** (and **A–D**, next page).

   Optional: Keep Preserve Luminosity checked to preserve lightness values as you make corrections; or keep this option unchecked to apply soft color adjustments when adjusting highlights, such as in skin tones. (For the image shown on this page and next, our adjustments were more successful with this option off.)

4. In the **Color Balance** area, cool colors are paired opposite warm colors. Move a slider toward any color you want to add more of or away from any color you want to reduce, noting how the image is affected.

   ➤ To make the image warmer or cooler, move multiple sliders toward similar colors. For example, to add a cool cast, you could move the first slider toward Cyan and the third slider toward Blue.

5. Click any other Tone Balance button, then adjust the color sliders for that range, unchecking and rechecking Preview as you do this to evaluate your adjustments.

6. Click OK.

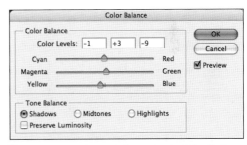

B *Increasing Yellow and Green via the **Color Balance** dialog box removed Magenta from the Shadows, and increasing Cyan and Green neutralized the Shadows.*

C *A **Shadows** adjustment (using the settings shown above) produced a subtle change. If you look carefully at the dark shadows on the columns, you'll see that they're slightly more gray than before.*

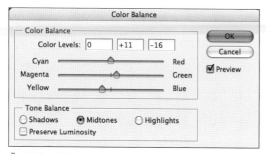

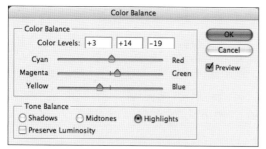

A *Adding Yellow and Green removed Magenta from the* **Midtones** *too, and adding Green also helped lighten the Midtones.*

B *An adjustment to the* **Midtones** *using the settings shown at left added blue to the sky and distant landscape and made the stone lighter and more neutral. However, the highlights still contain too much Magenta.*

C *Adding Yellow and Green removed Magenta from the* **Highlights,** *adding Green helped lighten the Highlights, and adding Red warmed the yellow-green of the stone.*

D *An adjustment to the* **Highlights** *using the settings shown at left finished neutralizing the Magenta cast. Now the clouds are whiter and the stone is a warm, natural-looking cream.*

Using the Hue/Saturation command

For making precise hue and saturation corrections without having to make a selection, the **Hue/Saturation** command is a better choice than Levels or Curves. It lets you target a specific range of colors, then shift just those colors to a different hue or adjust their saturation or lightness. This command is especially handy for swapping out colors in a product or fashion shot.

To apply the Hue/Saturation command:

1. Click a layer.**A**

2. From the New Fill/Adjustment Layer menu ⬙. on the Layers palette, choose **Hue/Saturation**. The Hue/Saturation dialog box opens. Check Preview.

3. To specify the range of colors to be adjusted, do either of the following:

   To change all the document colors, keep **Master** as the choice on the **Edit** menu.

   To limit the adjustment to a color range,**B** choose that range from the **Edit** menu, then pinpoint the color to be edited by clicking in the document window. The menu will list the color you clicked, and the adjustment slider will shift over to that color on the color bar.

   ➤ To see which image colors are in the chosen range, drag the **Hue** slider to one extreme end or the other. Colors in the chosen range will shift in hue (this is called a "false" preview). Drag the Hue slider back to 0 before proceeding. This technique works for any Edit range except Master.

4. To adjust the image, do any of the following:

   Move the **Hue** slider to shift the selected colors to a different hue.

   Move the **Saturation** slider to adjust the saturation.

   Move the **Lightness** slider to lighten or darken. After adjusting the Lightness, you may need to increase the Saturation to revive any colors that are too light or dark.

5. Click OK.**C**

   ➤ You don't need to use this command to correct out-of-gamut colors for print output. That correction will occur when the document is converted to CMYK Color mode.

A *In this image, we want to change the **blue** napkin to yellow to coordinate better with the lemons on the left side.*

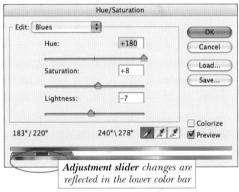

Adjustment slider changes are reflected in the lower color bar

B *In the **Hue/Saturation** dialog box, choose a preset color range from the **Edit** menu first. We chose Edit: Blues, clicked the blue of the napkin to select that color range, moved the **Hue** slider into the yellow range, increased the **Saturation,** and lowered the **Lightness**.*

C *Now the napkin is **yellow.***

Applying Auto Color Correction

The **Auto Color Correction Options** command adjusts the color, tonal range, and contrast in an image using preset algorithms (formulas) or, better yet, by using target values that you specify for the midtones. To achieve good results, we recommend the latter approach.

To apply Auto Color Correction options:

1. Open an image,**A** and show the Histogram palette. Click an image layer, then choose Image > Adjustments > **Levels.** The Levels dialog box opens.

2. Click **Options.** The Auto Color Correction Options dialog box opens.**B** Move it out of the way, if necessary, so you'll be able to monitor the Levels histogram as you choose options.

3. Click the **Find Dark & Light Colors algorithm** (the algorithms are described in the sidebar on the next page).

4. Check **Snap Neutral Midtones.** Photoshop will adjust any colors that are close to neutral to match the Midtones target color swatch in the dialog box.

5. To change which color values are assigned to midtones, click the **Midtones** swatch. The Select Target Midtone Color dialog box opens.**C**

6. Click the **H** button in the **HSB** group. On the vertical Hue bar, click a red-yellow hue to warm up the overall temperature of your image, or a green-blue hue to cool it down. To change the midtone brightness, drag the circle slightly upward or downward in the large square (keep the **B** value around 45–55), or to apply your chosen color to the midtones, drag the circle slightly to the right (keep the **S** value around 10–30). Note how the histogram updates in the Levels dialog box as you do this.

   Note: Midtones is the only swatch you need to adjust; the other two swatches will adjust automatically when the document colors are converted to a printer profile.

7. Click OK three times: to close the Select Target Midtone Color dialog box, the Auto Color Correction Options dialog box, and finally the Levels dialog box (**A**, next page). When the alert dialog box appears, click No (we'd rather choose settings on a case-by-case basis than establish global default settings).

A *The original image looks overly cool, due to a blue-green cast in the midtones.*

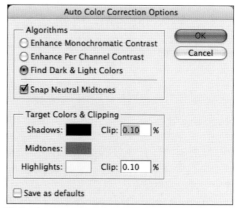

B *In the **Auto Color Correction Options** dialog box, we'll specify target values via the **Target Colors & Clipping** options.*

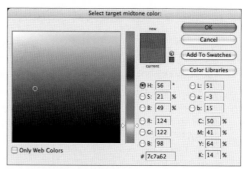

C *This dialog box opens when you click the **Midtones** swatch. We're choosing a warmer yellow-green for the moss, sand, and evergreens in our photo.*

➤ For the most control when redefining the mid-tone color, we recommend editing the Midtones swatch via the Auto Color Correction Options dialog box, as per the instructions on the previous page. A less reliable method would be to adjust the midtones using the gray point (middle) eyedropper in the Levels or Curves dialog box—less reliable because the results vary depending on where you click. If you can locate (and click) a neutral gray area, fine and dandy, but doing that is harder than it sounds. **B–C**

➤ We don't recommend using a Levels adjustment layer for the Auto Color Correction because it doesn't give you the editing flexibility that you'd expect: If you reopen the Auto Color Correction Options dialog box, the settings are reset to their defaults. We also don't recommend checking Save As Defaults, which would apply the same settings to all your photos.

A *As a result of a **Midtones** adjustment by way of the **Auto Color Correction Options** dialog box, the image now has a warmer, more naturalistic tone.*

B *Clicking in the original image with the gray eyedropper from the **Levels** dialog box in the location shown above set the midtone color to a cool gray, which wasn't the change we were aiming for.*

THE AUTO COLOR CORRECTION ALGORITHMS

➤ **Enhance Monochromatic Contrast** moves the black and white Input Levels sliders inward, resulting in lighter highlights and darker shadows. The sliders are moved by the same amount for each channel, so color relationships among the channels are preserved. (The Auto Contrast command uses this algorithm.)

➤ **Enhance Per Channel Contrast** moves the Input Levels sliders inward by a different amount for each channel, resulting in more noticeable color shifts and changes in contrast. (The Auto Levels command uses this algorithm.)

➤ **Find Dark & Light Colors** positions the black and white Input Levels sliders in each channel based on the average darkest and lightest pixels in the image, resulting in heightened contrast. This is the algorithm we prefer. (The Auto Color command uses this algorithm.)

(These algorithms are also accessible when you click Options in the Curves dialog box.)

C *Clicking in the original image in the location shown above with the gray eyedropper from Levels also failed to correct the cool cast in the midtones.*

When we need to apply comprehensive color adjustments, we turn to Levels or Curves because with these commands, we can make corrections to individual color channels. Which one should you use? It depends on what needs correcting. Before opening either dialog box, study the image to figure out what the exact problem is. Is it under- or over-exposed? If so, we suggest using Levels because it lets you correct broad ranges of color, especially in the midtones. Or perhaps the image has an unnatural color cast. For this, Curves would be a better choice because it lets you correct not only a broad color range (such as the color in a sky) but also a specific color cast, say, in the midtones.

We'll discuss the **Levels** command first. The instructions below are general, whereas the captions below the figures apply specifically to that image.

Using the Levels command

To adjust colors in an RGB image using the Levels command:

1. Study the image and try to figure out which color component(s) (R, G, and/or B) need correction. **A** You'll adjust those colors in step 4.

2. From the New Fill/Adjustment Layer menu ●. on the Layers palette, choose **Levels.** The Levels dialog box opens. Check Preview.

3. Correct any exposure problems in the full RGB channel first (see **B–C** and pages 180–181).

4. To begin removing a color cast, do as follows:

   Choose **Red** from the **Channel** menu.

   To reduce red in the midtones, move the gray Input Levels slider to the right (this increases green and blue); or to increase red, move the slider to the left.

   To add red to the highlights, move the white Input Levels slider to the left. To reduce red in the shadows, move the black Input Levels slider to the right.

5. Choose the **Green** channel, then the **Blue** channel, and in each case increase/decrease the amount of that color by moving the sliders as in the previous step (**A–D**, next page).

   ▸ Don't overadjust any single channel or you'll throw off the color balance of the whole image. Also, we don't recommend moving the Output Levels sliders to adjust an individual color channel; this can actually create a color cast.

A *The original image is* **underexposed** *and has a greenish* **cast.**

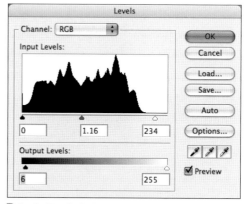

B *In the* **Levels** *dialog box, we moved the gray Input Levels slider to the left to lighten the midtones, moved the white Input Levels slider inward to brighten the highlights, and moved the black Output Levels slider inward to lighten the shadows.*

C *Adjustments to the RGB channel (see the previous figure) made the image lighter. So far, so good.*

6. To finalize the correction, switch back and forth between the color channels to readjust them, if necessary, then click OK.

7. *Optional:* To remove the adjustment in specific areas, with the adjustment layer mask selected, paint on the image with the Brush tool, Foreground color black.

➤ As contrast increases, so does color saturation. To reduce oversaturation from a Levels or Curves adjustment layer, choose Luminosity as the blending mode for the adjustment layer.

USING LEVELS ON CMYK IMAGES

When adjusting individual color channels via the Levels command in a **CMYK** document, to decrease or increase the amount of a color, move the sliders in the opposite direction from our instructions (step 4, previous page). For instance, for the Cyan channel, you would move the gray Input slider to the left to decrease cyan or to the right to increase it.

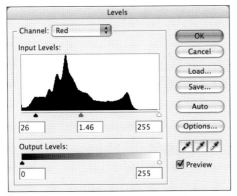

A *Red channel: We added red to the midtones (moved the gray Input Levels slider to the left) and removed red from the shadows (moved the black slider to the right).*

B *Adjustments to the **Red** channel removed a greenish cast from the bricks and stones, but that area now looks too rosy, and the sky and water still look dull. For the **Green** channel (not shown), we moved the gray slider to 1.04 to make the bricks less pink.*

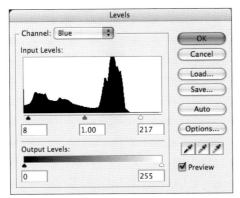

C *Blue channel: We moved the black Input Levels slider to the right to remove blue from the shadows and moved the white Input Levels slider to the left to add blue to the highlights (sky, path, and water).*

D *Adjustments to the **Blue** and **Green** channels successfully removed the green cast, but the castle, path, and other stone work are still too pink. In the next section, we'll use Curves for the same correction, which will work better for this image.*

Using the Curves command

The **Curves** command is even more powerful than Levels because it lets you make adjustments to a narrowly defined tonal range, such as highlights, quarter tones, midtones, three-quarter tones, or shadows. As with Levels, you can apply precise corrections to the composite channel (all the channels combined) or to individual color channels.

To adjust the color in an RGB image using the Curves command: ★

Part 1: Apply tonal adjustments

1. Open an image that needs color adjustment.**A** (We'll apply Curves to the same image that we used for our Levels adjustment so you can compare the results from the two commands.)

2. From the New Fill/Adjustment Layer menu ⊘. on the Layers palette, choose **Curves.** The Curves dialog box opens. (If you're following along with our illustrations, expand the dialog box to display the Curve Display Options, then check the four Show options; see the sidebar at right.)

3. First, adjust the shadows and highlights by doing any of the following:

   The Input sliders affect the lightest and darkest tonal values in the image. To **increase** the **contrast**, drag the black shadow Input slider and white highlight Input slider inward to align with the ends of the histogram.**B** ★ This will darken the shadows and brighten the highlights (the steeper the curve, the greater the contrast).

   To set the lightest/darkest values (and thus increase the contrast) in **Threshold** mode—a high-contrast display of clipping—Alt-drag/Option-drag the black slider until a few areas of black appear and Alt-drag/Option-drag the white slider until a few areas of white appear.★ (The Levels dialog box has this feature, too.)

   To **lessen** the **contrast**, drag the lower left part of the curve upward (to lighten the shadows) and drag the upper right part of the curve downward (to lessen the highlights). The middle of the curve should now be less steep.

4. A point is created when you move any part of the curve. As you do this, note the **Input** value, which is the current brightness value of the pixel you're adjusting, and the **Output** value, which is the value of that pixel after

A *The original image is underexposed and has a greenish cast.*

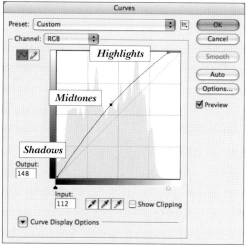

B *In the **Curves** dialog box, we moved the white slider inward toward the right end of the histogram to brighten the highlights and moved the middle of the curve upward to lighten the midtones.*

DISPLAY OPTIONS IN CURVES ★

The four **Show** options in the **Curves** dialog box are as follows:

Channel Overlays	The color channel curves and the composite curve
Histogram	Histogram for the image
Baseline	Straight diagonal line representing no adjustments, for comparison
Intersection Line	Axis guides that appear as you move a point on the curve

Click the large grid button ⊞ to display large, quarter-tone grid lines, or click the small grid button ▦ to display a finer grid.

adjustment. If the Output value is higher than the Input value, you've lightened that pixel; if Output is lower than Input, you've darkened it.

To **lighten** the **midtones,** drag the middle of the curve upward; to **darken** the midtones, drag the middle of the curve downward.**A–B**

You can use the arrow keys to nudge a selected point. To remove a point, click it, then press Backspace/Delete; or Ctrl-click/Cmd-click it.

► To associate a part of the curve with a color area in an RGB image, press the mouse on the image—a small circle will appear on the curve—then Ctrl-click/Cmd-click the image

to make a corresponding point appear on the curve. (We placed the selected point shown in **A** by Ctrl-clicking/Cmd-clicking a light area of the brick; now we can adjust the lightness of that area.)

Note: When moving a point, be careful not to create a sharp bend in the curve, or you'll posterize the colors in the areas corresponding to that part of the curve.**C–D** To straighten out a curve to remove the posterization, move the point back toward the diagonal baseline.

Don't click OK yet. To correct the color, follow the instructions on the next page.

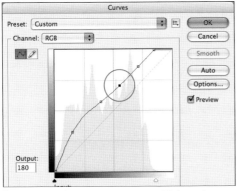

A *On the **RGB** channel curve, we added a point to the lower left to lighten the shadows in the trees, a point in the middle to lighten the midtones on the brick and stone, the currently selected point to lower the light on the bricks, and a point in the upper right to recover details in the sky and path.*

B *Our adjustments to the RGB channel improved the light/ dark balance, but the image still has a greenish cast and could use more saturation.*

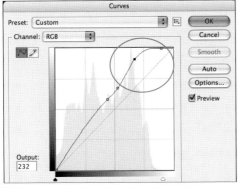

C *This curve bends too sharply; colors corresponding to that part of the curve will be posterized.*

D *The gray areas in the brick are posterized from the sharp curve.*

Part 2: Correct the color

1. With the Curves dialog box still open, from the **Channel** menu, choose **Red** to adjust that channel separately.

2. Drag the midpoint of the curve upward to add more **red** to the **midtones,** or downward to reduce red (this adjustment will also affect red in the shadows and highlights slightly). Usually this midtone adjustment is all that's required.

   You can also add/reduce red in the shadows by dragging the lower part of the curve or add/reduce red in the highlights by dragging the upper part of the curve. **A–B**

   ➤ Don't add too many points; try to keep your color curve as smooth as possible.

3. Choose the **Green** channel, then the **Blue** channel, increasing or decreasing the amount of each color in the image by moving the curves, as in the previous step.

4. Switch back and forth between color channels to readjust them as needed, then click OK (**A–E**, next page).

5. *Optional:* You can lower the opacity of the Curves adjustment layer to lessen its impact. Or to remove the adjustment in specific areas, click the adjustment layer mask, then paint on the image with the Brush tool, with the Foreground color set to black.

➤ Ctrl-Shift-click/Cmd-Shift-click in the document window to place a corresponding point on all the color channel curves (alas, no point will be placed on the RGB curve).

➤ The Preset menu and Preset Options button are described in the "Save Your Adjustment Settings" sidebar on page 201.

USING CURVES ON CMYK IMAGES

Features in the Curves dialog box work the opposite way for a **CMYK** Color image than for an RGB image:

➤ Readouts from the Curves graph are listed as percentages of ink. Black is 100%; white is 0%.

➤ Shadow values are in the upper right part of the curve, and highlights are in the lower left. Drag the curve downward to lighten a tonal value (by applying less ink), or upward to darken it. Similarly, for each individual color channel, you can drag the curve upward to add more of a color or downward to reduce it.

➤ Color opposites (cyan/red, magenta/green, yellow/blue) work in tandem. For example, lowering cyan adds red, lowering magenta adds green, and lowering yellow adds blue.

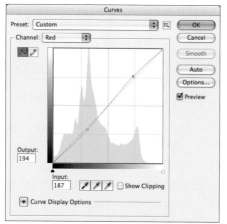

A *We dragged the bottom part of the curve downward slightly to reduce red in the shadows and moved the upper part of the curve upward to add red to the highlights.*

B *Our adjustments to the **Red** channel via the **Curves** command were successful. We were able to add red just where we need it: the light areas on the building facade, sky, and path.*

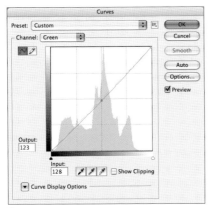

A *We dragged the* **Green** *channel curve downward slightly to reduce green throughout the image.*

B *Reducing green via adjustments to the Green channel added more red and blue to the image, which was our aim.*

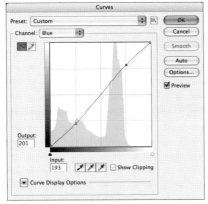

C *We dragged the lower part of the* **Blue** *curve downward to reduce blue in the shadows and raised the upper part to increase blue in the sky.*

D *This is the cumulative result of all our adjustments in the* **Curves** *dialog box.*

WHICH COMMAND DID A BETTER JOB?

▶ Curves **D** brought out more detail in the shadows in the trees on the right side, whereas Levels **E** left those areas fairly flat.

▶ Using Curves, we were able to control the color of the brick more precisely (neither too red nor too green), whereas Levels made the brick too pink.

▶ Using Curves, we were able to adjust specific highlights and achieve a better balance between red and blue in the sky and path, while keeping the stone railing neutral. Levels left those areas too red.

E *For comparison, this is the final result of our adjustments using the Levels command.*

To correct several images using the same adjustment layer:

1. Say you have a series of photos that were shot under the same lighting conditions and require the same color correction. Adjust one of the photos via an adjustment layer.

2. Open all the files that need correction.

3. Drag and drop the adjustment layer from the Layers palette of the document you corrected into the document window of the other open images.**A**

AVOID THE SPONGE! (SORRY, SPONGE BOB)

With the Sponge tool, you can drag across color areas on the current layer to increase or reduce saturation. You may get uneven color changes with this tool, though, because you can't control which color range is being edited. Besides, when you use color profiles to control the conversion from RGB to CMYK, out-of-gamut colors are reined into the designated output gamut automatically. For performing color corrections, the adjustment commands offer much more power and control (and who doesn't love power and control?).

A *We're dragging a **Levels adjustment layer** from the Layers palette in one document into another open document behind it. A copy of the adjustment layer will appear in the target document.*

FURTHER YOUR STUDIES

You've probably gathered by now that color correction is a complex — and often confusing — subject. For more in-depth coverage of related topics, such as tonal adjustment, color correction, and output, we recommend these titles (all from Peachpit Press):

➤ *Real World Adobe Photoshop CS3,* by David Blatner, Conrad Chavez, and Bruce Fraser

➤ *Real World Color Management, Second Edition,* by Bruce Fraser, Chris Murphy, and Fred Bunting

➤ *Microsoft Windows XP Color Management,* by Joshua Weisberg

To take it straight from the horse's mouth, you could also read "Making Color and Tonal Adjustments" in Photoshop Help.

You'll need to choose brush settings when using the Brush tool, and also for many other tasks, such as when editing a Quick Mask or layer mask "by hand" or when using the History Brush or Healing Brush tool. In this chapter, you'll master the Brush tool; use the Brush Preset picker and Brushes palette to customize your brush settings; smudge colors with the Smudge tool; and erase parts of a layer with the Eraser and Magic Eraser tools.

Using the Brush tool

Before getting into the complexities of custom brush presets, take a few minutes to get acquainted with the **Brush** tool. In these instructions, you'll choose an existing brush preset (brush tip) for the Brush tool and choose Options bar settings to control the tool's behavior. In the next section, you'll learn how to customize brush presets via the Brushes palette.

To use the Brush tool:

1. Click an image layer (or create a new layer).
   Optional: Create a selection if you want to restrict your brush strokes to a specific area.

2. Choose the **Brush** tool (B or Shift-B).

3. Choose a **Foreground** color.

4. On the Options bar, do the following:

   Click the **Brush Preset** picker arrowhead or thumbnail, then click a preset.**A**

   Choose a blending **Mode** (see pages 192–196).

   Choose an **Opacity** percentage. At 100%, the stroke will completely cover underlying pixels.

   Choose a **Flow** percentage to control how fully and smoothly the brush will apply the paint.

   Continued on the following page

*Click to open the **Brush Preset** picker.*

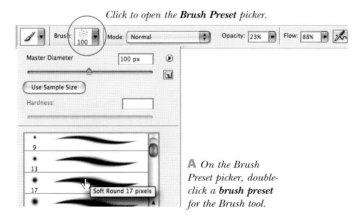

A *On the Brush Preset picker, double-click a **brush preset** for the Brush tool.*

Click the **Airbrush** button to have paint spread and build up when you hold down the mouse, as in traditional airbrushing.

5. Draw strokes in the document window. If the Airbrush option is on and you press and hold in one spot, the paint drop will gradually widen (up to the maximum diameter of the brush) and become more dense and opaque.**A–B** Feel free to change Options bar settings between strokes.

➤ On the Layers palette, click the Lock Transparent Pixels button for the current layer to allow the tool to recolor only nontransparent pixels.

➤ To draw a straight stroke, hold down Shift while dragging; or click in a starting location, then Shift-click to end the stroke.

➤ To sample colors with a temporary Eyedropper while using a painting tool, Alt-click/Option-click anywhere in the document window.

Choosing temporary brush settings

Each brush preset has its own built-in **Master Diameter** and **Hardness** settings, but you can make temporary changes to either setting via a context menu or the Options bar.

To choose temporary settings for a brush preset:

1. Choose any tool that uses brush presets, such as the Brush, Pencil, Dodge, Burn, or Eraser tool.

2. Right-click/Control-click in the document window, then change the **Master Diameter** and, if available, the **Hardness** setting.**C** These settings can also be changed on the Brush Preset picker.

3. Press Enter/Return or just start dragging in the document window. This setting will remain in effect only until you choose a different preset.

A *A brush stroke created with the **Airbrush** option **off***

B *A brush stroke created with the **Airbrush** option **on***

SHORTCUTS FOR CHANGING TOOL SETTINGS

These shortcuts work with any tool for which the option or feature is available, such as the Brush, Paint Bucket, Pencil, Smudge, Dodge, or Burn tool:

Cycle through the **blending Modes** for the tool	Shift- + (plus) *or* Shift - - (minus)
Decrease/increase the **Master Diameter** for a brush preset	[*or*]
Change the **Opacity, Exposure,** or **Strength** percentage* (Shift-press a number to change the Flow level**)	0–9 (e.g., 2 = 20%), *or* quickly type a percentage (e.g. "38")

*If the Airbrush option is on, press a number to change the Flow percentage or Shift-press a number to change the Opacity percentage.

**When Shift-pressing in Windows, use the numbers on the main keyboard, not on the keypad.

C *You can change the **Master Diameter** and **Hardness** for a preset quickly via the context menu.*

Using the Brushes palette

The **Brushes** palette offers a huge assortment of options for customizing brush presets. The presets, in turn, are available for the Brush, Pencil, History Brush, Art History Brush, Clone Stamp, Pattern Stamp, Eraser, Blur, Sharpen, Smudge, Dodge, Burn, and Sponge tools.

The first step is to familiarize yourself with the Brushes palette. This is "Brushes Palette 101." In the next set of instructions, you'll explore palette settings.

To use the Brushes palette:

1. Choose one of the tools listed in the first paragraph above.

2. To show the Brushes palette, click the palette tab or icon ✎; or choose Window > Brushes (F5); or click the Toggle Palette button ☰ in the middle of the Options bar.

3. If you don't see a list of option sets on the left side of the palette, **A** choose **Expanded View** from the palette menu. (To resize the palette, drag the lower right corner or any edge.)

4. Check the **box** for any of the first six option sets to **activate** the features for that set. If a set name is dimmed, it means it's not available for the current tool. The option sets are discussed in depth in the next set of instructions.

5. To display the **options** for an option set, click the set **name**, such as Scattering or Texture. The bottom five options can be switched on and off, but you can't choose settings for them.

6. To choose a different **display** type for the palette, click **Brush Presets** in the upper left corner of the palette, then from the palette menu, choose Text Only, Small Thumbnail, Large Thumbnail, Small List, Large List, or Stroke Thumbnail. The "Small" choices make the list more compact; the "Large" choices enable you to see the brush tips more easily.

➤ To learn how to load additional brush preset libraries onto the picker, see pages 394–397.

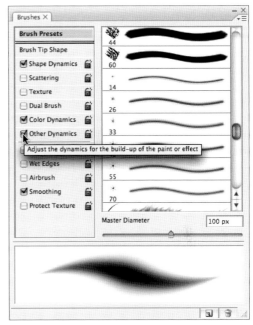

A *Use the **Brushes** palette to **choose** and **customize** brush **presets**.*

Customizing brushes

The options that you use to **customize a brush preset** are organized into sets on the Brushes palette, except for a handful of options that you simply switch on or off. Some features apply specifically to stylus and airbrush input devices. Your choices for customizing brush presets are infinite, but we'll make the job manageable for you by listing the features we use most often separately from the ones we rarely touch (writing a book isn't fun unless you can reveal your biases). You can pick and choose among the various options to create your dream brush.

Note: Custom settings you choose for a preset are lost as soon as you choose another preset. In step 9, we'll show you how to save your custom brush as a new preset. Note also that brush presets are used with many other tools besides the Brush. Keep this in mind when you see the word "pigment" in our instructions.

To customize a brush preset (main course):

1. Choose a tool that uses brush presets, and show the Brushes palette. 🖌

2. Click **Brush Presets A** in the upper left corner of the Brushes palette, then click a preset (scroll down the list, if necessary).

3. To change basic shape or size settings for the preset, click **Brush Tip Shape** at the top of the list, **B** then keep an eye on the brush preview at the bottom of the palette as you make any of these changes:

   To change the **Diameter** (brush size), move the slider or enter a value (1–2500 pixels).

   To change the **Angle** (brush slant), use the scrubby slider; drag the arrowhead around the circle; or enter a new Angle.

   To change the **Roundness** (brush shape), **C** use the scrubby slider (0–100%) or drag either of the two tiny dark circles on the ellipse inward or outward.

   To change the **Hardness** (feather or sharpen the edge of the brush), **D** move the slider or enter a value (0–100%). This option isn't available for all brush tips.

   To control the distance between brush tips within the stroke, check **Spacing**, then move the slider (1–1000%). **E–F**

A Click **Brush Presets** on the left side of the Brushes palette, then click a preset on the right.

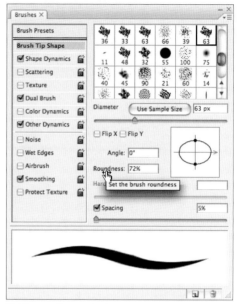

B The *preview* at the bottom of the **Brushes** palette updates dynamically as you change settings.

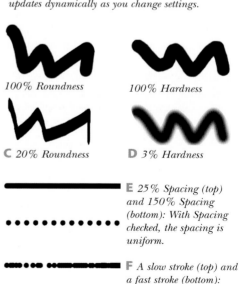

C 20% Roundness   **D** 3% Hardness

100% Roundness   100% Hardness

E 25% Spacing (top) and 150% Spacing (bottom): With Spacing checked, the spacing is uniform.

F A slow stroke (top) and a fast stroke (bottom): With Spacing unchecked, the spacing is uneven.

4. To control how much variation is allowable in the brush tip shape, click **Shape Dynamics** (click the words—the box will become checked automatically), then do any of the following:

Change the **Size Jitter,** **A** **Angle Jitter,** and **Roundness Jitter** values to establish variation parameters for those attributes. "Jitter" is the amount of random variation allowable for that option.

From the **Control** menus, choose a feature for your stylus to control that option's variation directly. Variations will occur even if you choose Off.

Change the **Minimum Diameter** value for the brush size variations.

Change the **Minimum Roundness** value.

5. To control the placement of pigment in the stroke, click **Scattering**, then do any of the following:

Check **Both Axes** **B** to scatter pigment along and perpendicular to the path you draw, or uncheck Both Axes to scatter pigment perpendicular to, but not along, the path. Also choose a Control option, if desired.

Change the **Scatter** value (1–1000%) to control how far pigment can veer off the path you draw. The lower the Scatter value, the more solid the stroke.

Change the **Count** value (1–16) to control the overall density (amount of pigment) in the stroke.

Change the **Count Jitter** value **C** (0–100%) to control how much the Count (density) can vary.

6. To control how randomly the overall stroke opacity can vary as you paint, click **Other Dynamics**, then do any of the following:

Change the **Opacity Jitter** (0–100%) **D–F** for the amount the opacity can vary. Choose a Control option to control fading.

Change the **Flow Jitter** (0–100%) to control how smoothly the pigment is applied. A high Flow Jitter makes for a blotchy stroke, but maybe that's what you want. Choose a Control option.

Continued on the following page

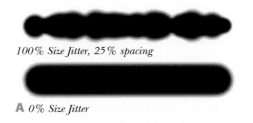

100% Size Jitter, 25% spacing

A *0% Size Jitter*

0% Scatter, 100% Spacing

500% Scatter, Both Axes option checked

B *500% Scatter, Both Axes option unchecked*

0% Count Jitter, 100% Spacing

C *100% Count Jitter: The Count varies randomly from 1% to 100% of the Count value.*

0% Opacity Jitter

D *100% Opacity Jitter*

E *100% Opacity Jitter, Control off: The Opacity varies randomly from 1% to 100%.*

F *0% Opacity Jitter, Control set to Pen Pressure: The Opacity is controlled by the amount of pressure exerted on the tablet by the stylus.*

7. And last but not least (you're almost done!), check any or all of these options:

Noise to add random grain to your brush strokes to make them look more rough.

Wet Edges to simulate the buildup of pigment at the edges of brush strokes, as in traditional watercoloring.**A–D**

Airbrush to allow a stroke to build up for as long as the mouse button is held down in the same spot. Clicking the ✍ button on the Options bar does the same thing.

Smoothing to draw smoother curves.

Protect Texture to apply the same texture pattern and scale to other brushes that currently use a texture option, or to which you add a texture option, thereby creating a uniform surface texture on the entire canvas.

8. *Optional:* Click an open lock icon 🔓 next to the name of any option set to prevent the current settings for that set from being edited, even if you change presets (note the closed lock icon). Locked settings are applied, but not saved, to any other preset you choose. Click a closed lock icon to make those settings editable again. (To unlock all locked settings, choose Reset All Locked Settings from the palette menu.)

9. Changes made to a preset remain in effect only until you choose a different preset. To save your custom preset for future use, click the **New Brush** button 📄 at the bottom of the palette or choose **New Brush Preset** from the palette menu. Change the name in the Brush Name dialog box, if desired, then click OK. To learn about saving and managing brush preset libraries, see pages 394–397.

A *This image was created with the **Brush** tool using various presets and settings.*

B *The **Wet Edges** option also created the "pooling" effect in this image.*

C *A stroke made with **Wet Edges unchecked***

D *A stroke made with **Wet Edges checked***

To customize a brush preset (side dishes):

1. Choose a tool that uses brush presets, and show the Brushes palette.

2. To use the texture from a pattern in your brush strokes, click **Texture** on the left side of the palette, **A** then monitor the preview as you do any of the following:

   Click the **Pattern Preset** arrowhead, then click a pattern in the picker.

   Check **Invert** to swap the light and dark areas in the pattern.

   Change the **Scale** of the texture (1–1000%).

   Check **Texture Each Tip** to allow the Depth (see below) to vary within each stroke, or uncheck to keep the Depth value constant.

   Choose a blending **Mode** to control how the texture mixes with the brush stroke.

   Choose a **Depth** value (0–100%) **B** to control how deeply paint sinks into the texture. At a high Depth value, paint will be applied only to the high points in the texture, making the texture look more prominent.

   If you checked Texture Each Tip, you can choose a **Minimum Depth** to keep the texture from looking too flat. Some brushes reveal texture more than others. Also choose a **Depth Jitter** value to control how much the Depth can vary, and choose an option from the Control menu to specify if and how the stroke can fade.

3. To make the brush preset more interesting, you could add another tip to it. Click **Dual Brush,C** click a tip; choose a Mode to control how the two tips interact with each other, then choose Diameter, Spacing, Scatter, and Count values.

4. To control how much the color can vary as you use the brush, click **Color Dynamics**, then do any of the following:

   Choose a **Foreground/Background Jitter** value **D** for the amount of allowable variation between the Foreground and Background colors. Choose an option from the Control menu to specify if and how colors can fade.

   Choose **Hue Jitter**, **Saturation Jitter**, and **Brightness Jitter** values to establish variation parameters for those attributes.

   Choose a **Purity** value to control the level of saturation in the stroke.

BACK TO BASICS

➤ To turn off all the Brush Tip Shape options temporarily for the current preset, choose **Clear Brush Controls** from the Brushes palette menu.

➤ To restore the default settings to a saved preset, simply **reselect** the preset.

*A Strokes drawn using a texture preset, with **Pen Pressure** chosen as the **Opacity Jitter Control***

50% Texture Depth

B 100% Texture Depth

Primary brush tip

Secondary brush tip

C Tips combined using the Dual Brush option, Linear Burn mode

0% Foreground/Background Jitter

D 100% Foreground/Background Jitter

Smudging colors

To smudge colors:

1. Click a layer.

2. Choose the **Smudge** tool (R or Shift-R). 🖐 (It's on the Blur tool menu).

3. On the Options bar, do the following:

   Click a brush preset on the **Brush Preset** picker.

   Choose a blending **Mode: Normal** smudges all shades or colors; **Darken** pushes dark colors into lighter ones; **Lighten** pushes light colors into darker ones; **Hue, Saturation,** and **Color** smudge color attributes without changing tonal (light/dark) values; and **Luminosity** smudges tonal values without changing colors.

   Choose a **Strength** percentage to control how forcefully the stroke smudges pixels.

   Check **Sample All Layers** to smudge colors found on all the currently visible layers and send the results to the active layer (uncheck Finger Painting if you use this option); or uncheck Sample All Layers to smudge colors from only the currently selected layer.

   To start the smudge with the Foreground color, check **Finger Painting;** or leave this option unchecked to have the smudge start with the color under the pointer where the stroke begins.

   ➤ Hold down Alt/Option to toggle the Finger Painting option on or off.

4. Drag across any area of the image.**A–D** Pause between strokes, if necessary, for the screen to redraw.

A *The original image*

B *Smudge, Normal mode: All colors smudge.*

C *Smudge, Lighten mode: Only light colors smudge.*

D *Smudge, Color mode: Colors smudge, luminosity values in the image are preserved.*

Erasing

The **Eraser** tool is handy for removing stray blobs, perhaps to tidy up after deleting most of the background area behind an object, or for erasing part of a layer in an isolated area.

Note: The Eraser tool results are permanent, so you may want to work on a duplicate layer. As an alternative to using this tool, you can block out part of a layer with an editable and removable layer mask (see page 292).

To use the Eraser tool:

1. Choose the **Eraser** tool (E or Shift-E).

2. On the Options bar, do the following:

   Choose a brush preset from the **Brush Preset** picker.

   Choose **Mode: Brush**, **Pencil**, or **Block** (square shaped eraser).

   Choose an **Opacity** percentage.

   For the Brush mode, you can choose a **Flow** percentage. The lower the Flow, the thinner the erasure stroke.

   Click the **Airbrush** button off.

3. Click a layer or the Background (or create a duplicate layer).

4. Decide whether to click **Lock Transparent Pixels** on or off.

   If Lock Transparent Pixels is on for the currently selected layer (or you clicked the Background), the area you erase will fill with the current Background color; choose that color now. **A**

   If Lock Transparent Pixels is off for the current layer, the erased area will fill with transparency.

5. Click on or drag across any area of the image. **B–C**

A We used the **Eyedropper** tool to sample the white background color first, then pressed **X** to swap the Foreground and Background colors.

B Next, we're using the **Eraser** tool (80% Opacity) to erase four of the "dots" of sauce. Because we clicked **Lock Transparent Pixels** on for the layer, the erased area is being replaced by the current **Background** color (the color we sampled with the Eyedropper).

C The final image

With the **Magic Eraser**, you erase only by clicking with the mouse, not by dragging. The tool erases pixels that are similar in color to the pixel you click on, within a user-defined tolerance range. Unlike the Background Eraser, you can lower the Magic Eraser tool opacity to render areas of a layer semitransparent.

To use the Magic Eraser tool:

1. Click an image layer; or click the Background, duplicate it, and keep the duplicate selected.**A** If you work on a layer with transparency unlocked, the erased pixels will be replaced with transparency; if you work on a layer with transparency locked, choose a Background color to replace the erased pixels.

2. Choose the **Magic Eraser** tool (E or Shift-E).

3. On the Options bar, do the following:

   Choose a **Tolerance** value (you could start with a value of around 30). The higher the Tolerance, the wider the range of colors the tool can erase. To erase only colors that are very similar to the color you click on, choose a lower Tolerance of around 5–8; to erase just one color, make the Tolerance 0.

   Check **Anti-alias** to slightly soften the edges of the erasure.

   Check **Contiguous** to erase only pixels that are adjacent to one another, or uncheck this option to erase similarly colored pixels throughout the currently selected layer.

   Check **Sample All Layers** to erase colors found on all the currently visible layers, or uncheck this option to erase colors found only on the current layer. It's easier to control what you're erasing with this option unchecked.

   Choose an **Opacity** percentage of 100% to replace colored pixels with transparent ones, or choose a lower opacity to replace them with semitransparent pixels.

4. In the document window, click the area that you want to erase.**B–C** To make it easier to position the pointer, press Caps Lock to turn the pointer into a crosshair.

➤ If you erase too large or small an area, undo (or click a prior state on the History palette), change the Tolerance value on the Options bar, then click again in the document window.

A *The sky in this image is mostly uniform in color and is lighter than any of the adjacent areas, so the **Magic Eraser** tool should be able to remove it with just a couple of clicks. Our first step was to duplicate the Background.*

B *The first click with the **Magic Eraser** tool removed most of the sky (tool settings of Tolerance 38, Contiguous on, and Opacity 100%), and a click on the remaining section of sky finished the job.*

C *After removing the sky, we created a new layer, restacked the new layer below the duplicate image layer, then filled the new layer with a solid color.*

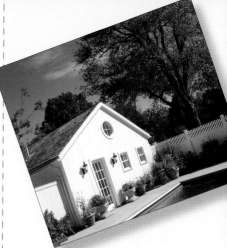

The beauty of the Adobe Camera Raw plug-in is that it lets you apply corrections to your photos before you open them in Photoshop. In this chapter, in addition to learning how to open digital photos via the Camera Raw plug-in ("Camera Raw," for short), you'll also use the many tabs in Camera Raw to correct photos for exposure, color, and lighting deficiencies.

Why use Camera Raw?

Whereas amateur-level digital cameras store images in the JPEG or TIFF format, advanced amateur and pro models offer the option to save images as Raw files, which offers substantial advantages. For the JPEG or TIFF format, the camera also performs internal processing operations, such as sharpening, setting the white balance, and making color adjustments. With Raw files, you get only the raw information that the lens captured onto its digital sensor, so you have full control over subsequent image processing and correction. Each camera manufacturer creates its own version of a Raw file. (See our comparison of JPEG vs. Raw on page 227.)

The following are some key features of the **Camera Raw** plug-in:

► Camera Raw processes **Raw** files from most of the current camera manufacturers, as well as **TIFF** and **JPEG** files.

► Camera Raw offers powerful features for **correcting deficiencies** in your photos, such as exposure, color, tonal range, and noise, and you can monitor your adjustments via a large preview.

► For Raw files, Camera Raw edits (instructions) are saved in a "sidecar" file or the Camera Raw database and in the file's metadata; for TIFFs and JPEGs, the instructions are saved in the file itself. In either case, when you open a file from Camera Raw into Photoshop, the instructions are applied to a **copy** of the file; the original digital files are preserved (like traditional film negatives).

► Camera Raw lets you **convert** photos to a few standard formats, such as PSD or TIFF. You can also save your files in any standard format *after* opening them in Photoshop.

Note: Don't confuse Raw files from a camera with Photoshop Raw, which is available as a file type/ format in File > Save/Save As.

Continued on the following page

CAMERA RAW

15

IN THIS CHAPTER

More reasons to use Camera Raw

The Camera Raw plug-in offers some powerful and unique features that you won't find in Photoshop. In case you're not fully convinced, we'll outline some compelling reasons for using the Camera Raw plug-in instead of opening your digital photos directly into Photoshop.

Raw preview: The only way to preview the actual Raw photo (not the JPEG version of a file) is via a Raw converter, such as Camera Raw.

Less destructive: Exposure, white balance, and color adjustments that you apply in Camera Raw cause less destruction to an image than adjustment commands in Photoshop. Remember, your goal is to preserve as much original data as possible.

16 bits per channel: To preserve the full tonal range of your Raw photo, you can use Camera Raw to convert it to 16 bits per channel. Starting with all the original data at the outset helps offset the data loss that image edits cause in Photoshop, and the end result is a better-quality image.

Tonal redistribution: A bonus feature of Camera Raw is that it fixes a "problem" inherent in all digital photos: the fact that the camera's digital sensor records data in a linear fashion. A light value of 50% gray, for example, is recorded as a pixel value of 127 (midtone gray). The camera captures the full tonal range in about 6 discrete levels, or stops, but more pixels are used to record the lighter tones than the darker tones. In **A**, you can see that the graph for an original linear capture is straight.

The human eye is more sensitive to lower levels of light than to brighter levels. That is, we're more likely to notice a lack of detail in the shadows and less likely to discern details from extra pixels in the highlights. Camera Raw redistributes captured pixels into the midtone and shadow range to produce an image that more closely approximates human vision. The graph of this restribution is curved rather than straight.**B** Tonal adjustments in Photoshop cause posterization and a loss of detail when there is insufficient data in the shadow areas, so Camera Raw images are better able to weather such edits.

CAPTURING TONAL VALUES: A CAMERA VERSUS THE HUMAN EYE

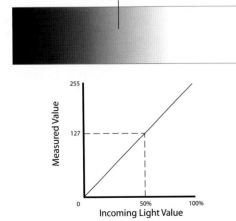

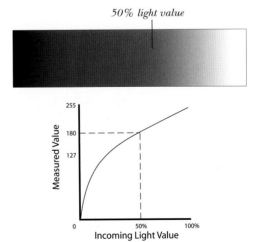

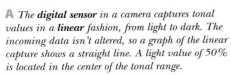

A *The **digital sensor** in a camera captures tonal values in a **linear** fashion, from light to dark. The incoming data isn't altered, so a graph of the linear capture shows a straight line. A light value of 50% is located in the center of the tonal range.*

B *Camera Raw performs tonal redistribution to shift data to the **lower levels.** Incoming data is altered, so the graph is now curved. The 50% light value is now shifted to the right of center (of the tonal range). There is now more detail in the lower levels, which is the range the human eye is more sensitive to.*

Noise reduction: The noise reduction features in Camera Raw are simpler, less destructive, and more effective than related commands in Photoshop.

You're halfway there: Camera Raw features that you'll use to adjust the tonal and color balance in your photos are similar to adjustment commands (such as Levels, Curves, and Hue/Saturation) that you learned about in earlier chapters, so you'll be able to build on your skills.

The skinny: To correct and enhance digital photos in preparation for work in Photoshop, Camera Raw is an ideal launching pad.

Raw, JPEG, or TIFF?

In addition to **Raw** files, photos that a camera saves as **JPEG** or **TIFF** can also be opened and edited in Camera Raw. ★ We recommend shooting Raw photos whenever possible so you can take advantage of all the features the Camera Raw plug-in has to offer, but if your camera won't let you create Raw photos or you acquire JPEGs or TIFFs from other sources, you can still use Camera Raw to process them. Except where noted, the instructions in this chapter apply to Raw, JPEG, and TIFF files.

Unfortunately, Camera Raw can't correct deficiencies in JPEG and TIFF photos as fully it can in Raw photos, for several reasons. First, the camera reduces the tonal range of a photo to fit the 8-bits-per-channel depth of JPEGs and TIFFs. Second, color and tonal processing is applied to JPEGs and TIFFs by the camera ("in camera"). Camera Raw reinterprets this processed data, with less successful results than when it has access to the raw, unprocessed data. And finally, the editing instructions are saved in the files themselves (processing is applied to the original pixels), not in the sidecar or database file, as is the case with Raw.

Nonetheless, you can use the many outstanding correction and adjustment features in Camera Raw to improve your JPEG and TIFF photos.

Note: In this chapter, we focus only on processing Raw and JPEG files in Camera Raw—not TIFFs, and we mention the JPEG format in our steps only when a command behaves differently for JPEGs.

JPEG...

JPEG pluses

JPEG files are smaller in storage size than Raw files, so your digital camera can store more of them.

JPEG files have shorter transfer speeds, so they can be created and stored more quickly by a camera than Raw files. This allows for faster shot sequencing—a necessity for sports, nature, and other quick-motion photography.

Most software programs can read JPEG files.

JPEG drawbacks

JPEG compression methods lower the image quality and can produce defects, such as artifacts, banding, and loss of detail.

Cameras that process and save photos as JPEG perform in-camera image-processing operations that alter the original pixel data. The camera also reduces the original tonal range to fit the 8-bits-per-channel JPEG format. Although you can apply adjustments to your photos in Camera Raw, you can't retrieve any of the original pixel data.

...VERSUS RAW

Raw pluses

The Raw compression methods are lossless.

Raw preserves the original, unprocessed pixel information that was captured by your camera.

Raw files can be opened as 16-bits-per-channel files in Photoshop.

Raw files contain the full range of tonal levels that were captured by the camera.

Because the white point setting isn't applied to Raw pixels when the photo is shot (it's just stored in the metadata of the file), you can adjust this setting in Camera Raw.

In Camera Raw, higher-quality adjustments can be made to Raw files than to JPEG files.

Camera Raw does a better job of redistributing tonal values in Raw files, which makes them better suited for editing in Photoshop.

Raw drawbacks

Digital cameras create and store Raw files more slowly than JPEG files.

Raw files have larger storage sizes than JPEG files.

The bottom line

Although JPEG offers the advantage of speed, which is useful for action photography, for most purposes, Raw is the clear winner.

Getting JPEG and TIFF files into Camera Raw ★

To get your JPEGs and TIFFs to open directly into Camera Raw instead of Photoshop, you need to set the appropriate Preference:

In Bridge, if **Prefer Adobe Camera Raw for JPEG and TIFF Files** is checked in Preferences > **Thumbnails** and you click a JPEG or TIFF thumbnail, choosing File > Open in Camera Raw (or pressing Ctrl-R/Cmd-R) will open the file in Camera Raw. Make the desired adjustments in Camera Raw, then click Open Image to open the image into Photoshop, or click Done to close Camera Raw. In either case, if you made any adjustments in Camera Raw, a Camera Raw edit badge 🔄 will display in the top right corner of the thumbnail in Bridge, and your adjustments will be reflected in both the thumbnail and the preview.

➤ Unfortunately, to make the Open in Camera Raw command work, and for the edit badges and adjustments to show up for JPEG file previews in Bridge, you have to force Bridge to regenerate all the thumbnails for the folder by choosing Tools > Cache > Purge Cache for Folder [current folder name]. Or to save time, you can move or copy any JPEGs that were edited in Camera Raw into a new folder in Bridge. Bridge will generate new thumbnails as you move or copy the files.

If you want to open a JPEG or TIFF directly into Photoshop (and the file hasn't been edited in Camera Raw), press Ctrl-O/Cmd-O.

In Bridge, if the currently selected file has been edited in Camera Raw, the Metadata panel will have a Camera Raw category.

Who's hosting Camera Raw?

In Bridge, choose Edit (Bridge, in the Mac OS) > Preferences (Ctrl-K/Cmd-K), then click General ★ on the left side. If **Double-Click Edits Camera Raw Settings in Bridge** is checked and you double-click a Raw file thumbnail in Bridge, the file will open into the Camera Raw dialog box, hosted by Bridge.*

If **Prefer Adobe Camera Raw for JPEG and TIFF Files** is also checked in Bridge Preferences, a JPEG or TIFF file that you double-click will open in Camera Raw, hosted by Bridge. With the Double-Click Edits... preference unchecked, you can double-click the thumbnail for a Raw or edited JPEG file to open the file into Camera Raw, hosted by Photoshop.*

In Photoshop (or in Bridge, if you click a Raw thumbnail first), if you choose File > **Open** (Ctrl-O/Cmd-O), the Raw file will always open into Camera Raw, hosted by Photoshop.

With Bridge as the host for Camera Raw, the default button for exiting the dialog box is "Done"; with Photoshop as the host for Camera Raw, the default button is "Open Image."

HOW WE DO IT

If you find the instructions on this page to be confusing, well, so do we! If you want to follow along with our Preferences choices, do as follows:

➤ If you open all your files from Bridge, don't check any Camera Raw-related Preferences in Photoshop.

➤ In Bridge, check only the Prefer Adobe Camera Raw for JPEG and TIFF Files preference (not the Double-Click Edits... preference).

This way, your Raw files always open in Camera Raw and your JPEG and TIFF files open in Camera Raw only via Ctrl-R/Cmd-R.

THE CAMERA RAW SETTINGS

➤ When you open a file into Camera Raw, by default, it's adjusted as per the built-in profile for your **camera model.** To assign a different collection of settings to your file, or to restore the original settings, choose a setting from the Camera Raw Settings menu:

➤ **Image Settings** to restore the settings that were attached to the file from either the initial photo shoot or a prior Camera Raw session. When you first open a Raw file, these settings will match the Camera Raw Defaults settings.

➤ **Camera Raw Defaults** to remove any custom settings and reapply the built-in default settings for the current camera model.

➤ **Previous Conversion** to apply the settings from the last Raw image you adjusted.

➤ **Custom Settings** to reapply the settings chosen during the current Camera Raw session.

➤ The name of any applied **user-saved preset** appears next on the menu.

Camera Raw: The basic steps

Before we get into the specific tabs in Camera Raw, we'll outline the **basic steps** for using this plug-in, just by way of introduction.

To open a digital photo via the Camera Raw plug-in:

1. Launch Bridge. Each digital camera model attaches a different extension to its Raw file names, such as .nef for Nikon, .crw or .cr2 for Canon, and .dcr for Kodak. If a file has been opened and edited previously in Camera Raw, it will have a badge ⚑ in the top right corner of the thumbnail. To open a Raw photo in Camera Raw, double-click the thumbnail; or click it, then press Ctrl-R/Cmd-R. To open a JPEG into Camera Raw, make sure the appropriate preferences have been set first (see the previous page).

2. The Camera Raw dialog box opens. **A** An alert symbol displays in the upper right of the preview window while the image data is reading in, and disappears when it's completed. Information about your photo (taken from the metadata the camera stores in the photo) is listed in the following locations: the camera

model in the title bar at the top of the dialog box; the file name below the preview; and the camera settings used to take the photo (aperture, shutter speed, ISO sensitivity, and focal length) below the histogram on the right side. The color space/bit depth/dimensions/resolution link below the preview gets you to the Workflow Options dialog box.

The image adjustment options are distributed among 8 tabs — Basic, Tone Curve, Detail, HSL/Grayscale, Split Toning, Lens Corrections, Camera Calibration, and Presets. ★ You'll use sliders in each tab to correct your photo (**A–B**, next page).

3. When you're satisfied with how the photo looks, click Open. Camera Raw will convert and open a copy of your image using your chosen settings, leaving the original data untouched.

A *The **Camera Raw** dialog box*

*Link to open **Workflow Options** dialog box*

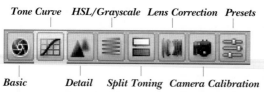

Tone Curve   HSL/Grayscale   Lens Correction   Presets

Basic   Detail   Split Toning   Camera Calibration

A *Click the **tab** icons to access related settings.*

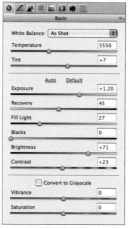

*Use the **Basic** tab to adjust the white balance and exposure (see pages 234–237).*

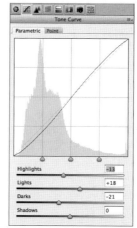

*Use the **Tone Curve** tab to fine tune the exposure (see pages 238–240).*

*Use the **HSL/Grayscale** tab to adjust colors individually (see pages 240–241).*

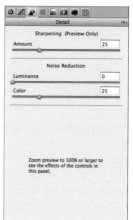

*Use the **Detail** tab to reduce noise (see page 242).*

B *4 of the 8 tabs in Camera Raw are illustrated here. We do most of our correction work in the Basic, Tone Curve, and HSL/Grayscale tabs.*

STAYING CURRENT

Of the many proprietary Raw "formats," some are unique to a particular manufacturer (e.g., Nikon, Canon) and some are unique to a particular camera model. To make sure you're using all the latest **interpreters** for the Raw formats that Camera Raw supports, periodically visit **www.adobe.com** and download any Camera Raw updates that are available for your camera.

Using the Camera Raw tools

To use the simple "one-click" tools:

In the toolbox in the upper left corner of the dialog box, **A** click the **Zoom** tool (Z), then click the image preview to zoom in or Alt-click/Option-click it to zoom out.

From the **Zoom Level** menu below the image preview, choose a preset zoom percentage, or click the – or + zoom level button.

If the image preview is magnified, you can use the **Hand** tool (H) to move it in the preview window.

➤ Double-click the Zoom tool to change the zoom level to 100%, or double-click the Hand tool to change the zoom level to Fit in View.

➤ You can also use the same shortcuts to zoom-click in and out as you would in the document window: Ctrl-Spacebar/Cmd-Spacebar and Ctrl-Alt-Spacebar/Cmd-Option-Spacebar.

For information about the **White Balance** tool, see page 234.

Choose the **Color Sampler** tool (S), then click in the image preview to place up to nine samplers. Readouts of the RGB components for the pixels below each sampler display below the toolbox, and update as you make color and tonal adjustments to the photo. To reposition a sampler, drag with the Color Sampler tool. To remove all samplers, click Clear Samplers.

Click the **Open Preferences** button ≣ (Ctrl-K/Cmd-K) ★ to open the Camera Raw Preferences dialog box.

Click the ↺ button (L) to **rotate** the photo 90° counterclockwise or the ↻ button (R) to rotate it 90° clockwise. The rotation will preview in the dialog box.

Check **Preview** (P) to preview changes made in all the tabs; uncheck it to see changes made in all tabs except the current one (that is, to turn off the adjustments made in the currently displayed tab).

Click the **Toggle Full Screen Mode** button (F) ⤢ to have the dialog box fill the entire screen; ★ click it again to restore the previous dialog box size.

Continued on the following page

A *The Camera Raw toolbox*

KEY TOGGLES

You can change the function of a button or tool in the Camera Raw dialog box by holding down one of the following keys:

Alt/Option	Cancel becomes **Reset,** which restores the original dialog box settings; Save Image… becomes **Save Image,** which bypasses the Save Options dialog box
Alt/Option	Lets you zoom out with the **Zoom** tool; also changes the Hand tool to a temporary **zoom out** tool
Ctrl/Cmd	Changes the Hand tool to a temporary **zoom in** tool
Spacebar	Changes any tool to a temporary **Hand** tool
Alt/Option	Open Image becomes **Open Copy** (see page 245)

Using the **Crop** tool, you can control which portion of the Camera Raw image opens in Photoshop. You can readjust the crop marquee at any time, and it will remain available even after you click Save, Done, or Open. The Raw pixels are preserved.

To crop the image:

1. Choose the **Crop** tool (C). ⊡
2. Drag a marquee on the preview image.**A** The area within the marquee will import; areas below the gray shield won't. To move the marquee, drag inside it; to resize it, drag a handle.
➤ To remove the crop marquee from the preview, with the Crop tool selected, press Esc.

To straighten out a crooked photo:

1. Choose the **Straighten** tool (A). ⊿
2. Drag across the preview along an edge in the photo that you want to align to the horizontal or vertical axis.**B** A crop marquee will display, aligned to the angle you drew.**C** When you open the image in Photoshop, that edge will be aligned with the document window.

To touch up blemishes or imperfections: ★

1. Choose the **Retouch** tool (B). ⊿
2. Drag in the preview; a red and white **target** circle will display.**D** Drag inward or outward to scale the target circle to cover the blemish (the Radius slider will move accordingly). Release the mouse, and a green and white source circle will appear, linked to the target circle.
3. Drag the **source** circle over an area to copy those pixels to the target circle.**E**
4. From the **Type** menu, choose **Heal** to blend source pixels into the luminosity of the target pixels or **Clone** to perform an exact copy of the source pixels (pause to preview).

   You can also drag the edge of either circle to resize them simultaneously, add more circle pairs to correct other blemishes, or reposition them at any time. They'll remain available even after you click Save, Done, or Open; the original Raw pixels aren't altered. To hide the circles, choose a different tool. To remove a pair, click inside a circle, then press Backspace/Delete; to remove all pairs, click Clear All.
➤ The Red Eye Removal tool (E) ⊙ ★ works like the Red Eye tool in Photoshop (see page 286).

A *Drag with the **Crop** tool in the preview window of the Camera Raw dialog box.*

B *With the **Straighten** tool, drag across the preview along an edge that you want to align with the horizontal axis.*

C *The **Straighten** tool created a crop marquee around part of the photograph.*

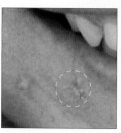
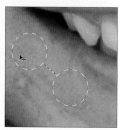

D *With the **Retouch** tool, drag to scale the **target** circle over a blemish...*

E *...then drag to position the linked **source** circle. Source pixels will copy to the target circle.*

Using the Workflow options

The **Workflow** options let you change the color space, dimensions, bit depth, and resolution of a photo before opening it into Photoshop (the original digital file is unaltered).

To change a color space, dimensions, bit depth, and resolution:

1. Follow step 1 on page 229 to open your photo into Camera Raw. At the bottom of the Camera Raw dialog box, click the underlined link that lists the color space, file dimensions, etc. ★ The **Workflow Options** dialog box opens.

2. From the **Space** menu, choose the color profile to be used for converting the Raw file to RGB: Adobe RGB (1998), ColorMatch RGB, ProPhoto RGB, or sRGB IEC61966-1 ("sRGB," for short). In Chapter 2, you assigned Adobe RGB as the default color space for color management, so we recommend that choice.

3. From the **Depth** menu, choose a color depth of 8 Bits/Channel or 16 Bits/Channel (see page 49). If you have a large hard drive and a fast system with a lot of RAM, go ahead and choose 16 Bits/Channel. With the extra pixels, more of the original tonal levels in your photo will be preserved as it's edited in Photoshop.

4. If you need to resize the image, from the **Size** menu, choose a preset size (in megapixels) that matches the proportions of your Raw image. (The default image size has no – or + after it.) Resampling will occur if you choose a larger size than the original. If a crop marquee is present, the crop size will be the default size. (Experts disagree on whether it's better to resample an image in Camera Raw or in Photoshop. Until they reach a consensus, take your pick.)

5. Enter a **Resolution**. This value affects only the print output size of the photo. (By way of example, a resolution of 240 to 300 would be appropriate for a 2000 x 3000 pixel image for printing on an inkjet printer or even on a commercial press.)

6. Click OK. The new document info will be listed below the preview.

➤ To learn about the Open in Photoshop as Smart Objects option, see page 246.

GETTING BACK TO THE DEFAULTS

➤ **Double-click** a slider to restore the default setting to just that slider.

➤ Click **Default** in the Basic or HSL/Grayscale tab to reset the sliders in just that tab to their default settings (no adjustments).

➤ Choose **Camera Raw Defaults** from the Camera Raw Settings menu to reset the sliders in all the tabs to their default settings.

Using the Basic tab ★

As you use the **Basic** tab to perform white balance, exposure, and other tonal adjustments, keep your eye on the histogram so you can monitor changes in the distribution of tonal values in your photo.**A** The histogram graphs the red, green, and blue pixels in an image, superimposed upon one another at each tonal level. Shadow pixels are on the left, highlights are on the right, and the white areas indicate where all three colors are present.

For the first round of adjustments, we recommend using the Basic sliders in the order in which they appear.

To apply white balance adjustments:

1. Click the **Basic** tab ⚙ (**A**, next page), and choose **Fit in View** as the zoom level for the preview.

2. You'll adjust the white balance (color temperature) first, because this setting affects the overall photo. Unlike the color adjustment controls in Photoshop, these sliders cause minimal destruction to image pixels. Do either of the following:

    From the **White Balance** menu, choose a preset setting that best describes the lighting conditions in which the photo was taken (for Raw files only). Choose As Shot at any time to restore the initial camera settings.**B** As soon as you move the Temperature or Tint slider, Custom becomes the menu listing.

    To correct the color temperature more specifically, move the **Temperature** slider to the left to add blue (make the image cooler),**C** or to the right to add yellow (make the image warmer).**D** To fine-tune the temperature correction, drag the **Tint** slider slightly to the left (–) to add green or to the right (+) to add magenta.

    To learn about the other sliders in the Basic tab, see pages 236–237.

    ➤ To quickly adjust the white balance based on a sampled area, you could choose the White Balance tool (I), 🖋 then click a grayish white area that contains some detail. However, since deciding which area to click on can be tricky, we use the Temperature and Tint sliders instead.

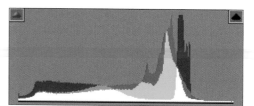

A *The Camera Raw* **histogram** *charts the number of pixels at each tonal level in a photo for red, green, and blue. As in all the histograms you'll find in Photoshop, shadow pixels are on the left and highlight pixels are on the right.*

WHITE BALANCE IN DIGITAL PHOTOGRAPHY

The color temperature of the environment or lighting in which a photo is shot determines the relative amounts of red, green, and blue that the camera records. A digital camera uses a technique called **white balance** to balance red, green, and blue to create an accurate white, and adjusts other colors in the photo based on that value.

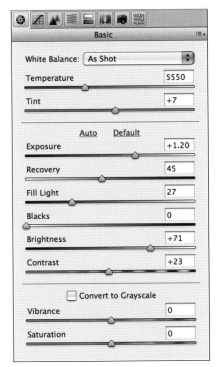

A Use the **Basic** tab to apply white balance, exposure, and other adjustments.

B With **As Shot** chosen on the **White Balance** menu, the color temperature is well balanced.

C With the **Temperature** slider moved to the **left,** the overall temperature is **cooler.** The metal is noticeably blue and the light on the ground also looks cooler.

D With the **Temperature** slider moved to the **right,** the overall temperature is **warmer.** The metal is warmer and the ground is more yellow.

To make tonal adjustments: ★

1. When Camera Raw first opens, the tonal sliders in the **Basic** tab—Exposure, Recovery, Fill Light, Blacks, Brightness, and Contrast—are set to their default values (the word Default is dimmed). You can click **Auto** to see which slider settings Camera Raw deems appropriate for your photo, but for even better results, we recommend making custom adjustments. Click **Default** to reset the above-mentioned sliders to their default settings, then follow the remaining steps.

2. The **histogram** reflects the current Camera Raw settings and redraws as you change those settings. Study the graph to see if any highlight or shadow pixels are being pushed to the edge (clipped). Clipping occurs if the tonal range of a scene is wider than the range the camera can capture. Your goal will be to bring the pixels into the range of your chosen RGB color space, thereby minimizing clipping. (In our own setup, both the camera and Camera Raw are set for the Adobe RGB color space.)

3. To minimize the clipping of highlight and shadow pixels, do the following:

    In the top left corner of the histogram, click the **Shadow Clipping Warning** button (U) to display a representation of any shadow clipping in the preview; and in the top right corner, click the **Highlight Clipping Warning** button (O) to display any highlight clipping.**A** ★ With the clipping warnings for reference (blue for shadows, red for highlights), your corrections will be better informed.

    Use the Exposure and Recovery sliders as a pair to improve highlight detail. Move the **Exposure** slider to the left and the **Recovery** slider well to the right until only a trace remains of the red highlight warning color.

    Use the Blacks and Fill Light sliders as a pair to improve shadow detail. Move the **Fill Light** slider slightly to the right and the **Blacks** slider to the left until only a trace remains of the blue shadow warning color.

    To minimize clipping another way, Alt-drag/ Option-drag the **Exposure** and/or **Recovery** slider and release the mouse when small amounts of white (representing all three color channels) display in the black preview and Alt-drag/Option-drag the **Blacks** slider and release the mouse when small amounts of black display in the white preview. Color areas, if any, represent clipping in those channels.

4. Use the **Brightness** slider to control detail in the midtones, and the **Contrast** slider to increase or decrease contrast.

To adjust the color saturation:

Use the **Vibrance** ★ or **Saturation** sliders in the Basic tab to adjust the color saturation (to the right to increase saturation). Note that these sliders produce different results. The Saturation slider can cause oversaturation and highlight clipping (move it to the right, and your photo will start looking unnatural). The Vibrance slider, on the other hand, doesn't cause oversaturation, so of course we prefer it. In fact, Vibrance goes so far as to prevent slightly oversaturated skin tones from becoming even redder.

➤ To adjust the saturation of individual colors, see pages 240–241.

Shadow Clipping Warning button   *Highlight Clipping Warning button*

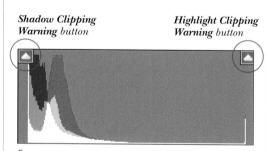

A *Click either or both of the **Clipping Warning** buttons above the histogram (a white frame around a button means that warning is on). This is the histogram for the original photo, shown in **A** on the next page. Most of the pixels are clustered at the left edge on the graph, signifying that the image is underexposed.*

CORRECTING AN UNDEREXPOSED PHOTO

A *The original photo is **underexposed**, as shown by the blue and red clipping warning colors in **A** on the previous page.*

B *We moved the **Exposure** slider to the right to lighten and recover detail in the highlights and midtones. We also moved the **Recovery** slider to recover some detail in the metal highlights, but we'll leave some clipping because the specular lighlights on these bright, metallic surfaces are supposed to be pure white, without details.*

C *We used the **Fill Light** and **Blacks** sliders to recover detail in the shadows (on the lower front area of the car and in the grass). The blue and red clipping warnings are now minimized.*

D *We moved the **Brightness** slider to the right to recover more detail in the midtones and moved the **Contrast** slider to the right to increase contrast (and thereby intensify the shadows).*

E *Finally, we moved the **Vibrance** slider to the right to increase the color saturation. Now this classic MG really shines!*

Using the Tone Curve tab ★

After making adjustments in the Basic tab, the next step is to use the **Tone Curve** tab to fine-tune a specific section of the tonal range (highlights, midtones, or shadows). You can adjust the curve in either of two ways: by manually placing points, employing the same techniques that you'd use in the Curves dialog box (see pages 210–213), or by using the parametric sliders. We'll show you the latter method because we think it produces higher-quality corrections. It offers a slider for each part of the tonal range (no need to guess which part of the curve to bend), and it protects against posterization by preventing you from misshaping the curve. The parametric curve and sliders were first introduced in Adobe Photoshop Lightroom, and they're the adjustment method of the future.

To make tonal adjustments using the Parametric sliders:

1. Click the **Tone Curve** tab,  then click the nested **Parametric** tab.**A–B** Behind the curve is a static image of the current histogram.

2. Drag the **Highlights, Lights, Darks,** or **Shadows** slider to the right to lighten that tonal range (and thus raise the corresponding portion of the curve above the diagonal line) **C** or drag any slider to the left to darken that tonal range (and thus lower that portion of the curve below the diagonal line) (**A–B**, next page).

   ► We recommend using these sliders to adjust one or two sections of the tonal range (say, just the midtones and highlights or just the midtones and shadows), and moving no more than three sliders. Remember, you're just fine-tuning the exposure.

3. After adjusting the sliders, move a **region control** (located below the graph) to expand or contract the range of any slider adjustment. The left region control affects the Shadows slider, the right region control affects the Highlights slider (**C–F**, next page), and the middle region control affects the Lights and Darks sliders (**A–B**, page 240). The more a control moves the curve away from the diagonal line, the more adjacent tonal ranges are affected; the more a control moves the curve closer to the diagonal line, the fewer adjacent tonal ranges are affected.

A *The highlights in this photo lack detail, and the midtones lack contrast.*

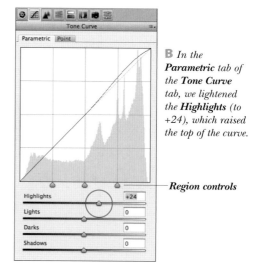

B *In the **Parametric** tab of the **Tone Curve** tab, we lightened the **Highlights** (to +24), which raised the top of the curve.*

Region controls

C *Now the **highlights** are lighter, particularly in the clouds. We'll darken the midtones next.*

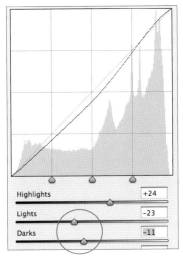

A *We moved the* **Lights** *and* **Darks** *sliders to the left, which lowered the middle of the curve.*

B *The* **Lights** *and* **Darks** *adjustment darkened the midtones.*

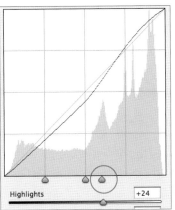

C *We moved the* **right region control** *to the* **left**, *which raised the top and middle sections of the curve.*

D *The control adjustment expanded the effect of the lightened highlights to the midtones, which isn't our aim.*

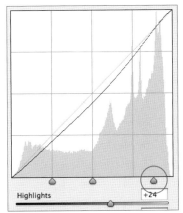

E *We moved the* **right region control** *to the* **right**, *which lowered the top and middle of the curve.*

F *The control adjustment narrowed the lightening effect of the Highlights slider to just the highlights and recovered details in the clouds.*

Illustrations continue on the following page

*A Finally, moving the middle **region control** to the right lowered the middle of the curve slightly.*

B *The last control adjustment expanded the darkening effect of the Lights and Darks sliders and produced more contrast in the midtones. Now the exposure is just right.*

Using the HSL/Grayscale tab ★

In the **HSL/Grayscale** tab, you can adjust the hue, saturation, or luminance of colors individually. This tab is powerful!

To adjust individual colors:

1. Click the **HSL/Grayscale** tab ☰ and choose Fit in View as the zoom level for the preview.

2. Click the nested **Hue** tab. Move a slider to shift that color toward its adjacent hues, as shown in the bar. For example, shifting the greens in a photo toward yellow makes the scene warmer; shifting greens toward aqua cools it down.

3. Click the **Saturation** tab (**A–C**, next page). Move a slider to the left to desaturate a color (make it grayer) or to the right to make it more saturated (more pure). Try not to oversaturate colors, or your photo will look unnatural.

   ► To make a sky more vivid, increase the saturation of Blues and Aquas. For a warm sunset effect, increase the saturation of Yellows or Greens. To make the lighting gray and hazy, lessen the saturation of Yellows or Greens.

4. Click the **Luminance** tab (**D–E**, next page). Move a slider to the left to make that color darker (add black) or to the right to make it lighter (add white). Don't overlighten a color, or you'll end up clipping the highlights.

Highlights   +24

APPLYING HSL ADJUSTMENTS TO A PHOTO

A *In the original photo, the sky lacks contrast and the greens and yellows in the field are too overpowering.*

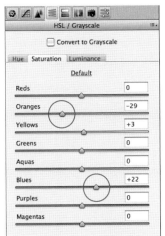

B *Via the **Saturation** tab of the **HSL/ Grayscale** tab, we lowered the saturation of Oranges and increased the saturation of Blues.*

C *Using the **Saturation** sliders, we lowered the intensity of oranges in the field and made the blues in the sky richer.*

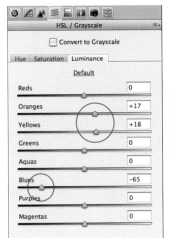

D *Via the **Luminance** tab, we lightened the Oranges and Yellows and darkened the Blues.*

E *Using the **Luminance** sliders, we were able to change the quality of light in the field from orange-yellow to a crisp, neutral light. We also darkened the blues in the sky. In summary, by desaturating the colors in the field and enriching the saturation and contrast in the sky, the photo is now richer and more balanced.*

Using the Detail tab

Via sliders in the **Detail** tab, you can preview and adjust the sharpness of your photo, make smoothing adjustments, and reduce color noise.**A**

To make smoothing adjustments and reduce color noise:

1. Click the **Detail** tab  **B** and choose a zoom level of 100%–200% for the preview.

2. The **Sharpening** slider controls edge defini-tion. We prefer to make as many adjustments as possible in Camera Raw, but in this case we recommend leaving the Sharpening slider at the default value of 25 and, if need be, using a sharpening filter in Photoshop instead—such as our current favorite, Smart Sharpen.

   To forego sharpening your photo in Camera Raw but still preview the effect of sharpening, click the **Open Preferences** button ☰ on the toolbox, then in the Camera Raw Preferences dialog box, choose **Apply Sharpening To: Preview Images Only.** The words "(Preview Only)" will appear above the Amount slider.

3. All digital cameras produce some undesirable noise, such as visible artifacts and stray pixels. Budget cameras tend to produce the most noise, but noise can also result from using high ISO (light sensitivity) settings with high-end cameras in poorly lit scenes. Noise can become accentuated by image editing, so if possible, it should be removed before opening your photo into Photoshop. To reduce noise in the dark areas, move the **Luminance** (smoothing) slider (try a value between 10 and 15).

   ➤ The higher the Luminance value, the more you'll need to sharpen the photo afterward in Photoshop.

4. Finally, move the **Color** (noise reduction) slider to the right to eliminate color artifacts and random speckling from all the tonal levels of the photo.**C** These defects tend to be most noticeable on solid-color surfaces, especially in shadow areas. The default value is 25, but you can raise it to 40–60, depending on the type of photo you're working with (figure, landscape, interior, etc.).

A *In this photo, the sky and background are showing too much* **color noise.**

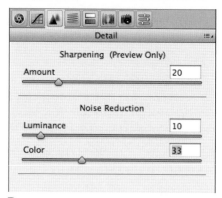

B *In the* **Detail** *tab, we moved the* **Luminance** *and* **Color** *sliders to the right.*

C **Eliminating noise** *from the sky and background made those areas look smoother (as a final step, we'll resharpen the photo in Photoshop).*

Saving and applying Camera Raw settings

After carefully choosing custom settings for a photo in Camera Raw, it's good to know that you can save those settings for future access. Once you save a collection of settings as a **settings preset**, it can then be applied it to other files (say, from the same photo session) that need the same or similar corrections. Your settings preset can be applied to a single image via Camera Raw, to multiple selected thumbnails via Bridge, or to multiple files via batch processing.

To save Camera Raw settings as a preset: ★

1. With your corrected image open in Camera Raw, choose **Save Settings** from the Settings menu. The Save Settings dialog box opens.**A**

2. Check which settings you want saved to the settings file; or to narrow the selection, choose a single settings category (tab name) from the **Subset** menu.

3. Click Save. In the Save Settings dialog box, enter a name (preferably one that describes the type of settings being saved), keep the .xmp extension and leave the location as the Settings folder, and click Save.

4. The saved settings preset can now be chosen in the Presets tab for any photo (see the next set of instructions).

You can apply a **user-defined preset** (saved collection of settings) to any photo in Camera Raw.

To choose a Camera Raw preset: ★

In Camera Raw, do either of the following:

Click the **Presets** tab, ▦ then click the preset you want to apply.

From the **Apply Preset** submenu on the Settings menu, choose the desired preset.

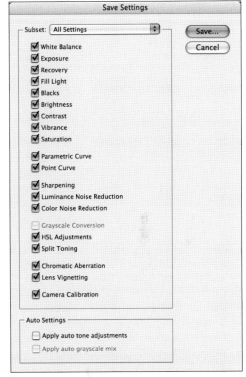

A *In the **Save Settings** dialog box, specify which of your custom Camera Raw settings will be saved in a preset.*

When you open multiple photos simultaneously into Camera Raw, the files are represented by thumbnails in a filmstrip panel on the left side of the dialog box. In theory, you could, say, open multiple files from the same photo shoot into Camera Raw, choose settings, then click **Synchronize** to apply those settings to all the photos. In practice, it's unlikely that all the adjustments for one photo will work perfectly on the rest. The Synchronize option is useful, however, for applying settings incrementally. For example, you could apply some Basic adjustments to all your photos (perhaps white balance and exposure), then select smaller batches of thumbnails and make more targeted adjustments. In each case, you'll click Synchronize to apply the changes to all the currently selected thumbnails.

To synchronize the Camera Raw settings of multiple files:

1. In Bridge, select two or more Raw file thumbnails that were shot under the same lighting conditions and that need the same type of correction. Double-click one of the selected thumbnails.

2. In Camera Raw, the filmstrip panel will display.**A** Click one of the thumbnails.

3. Make the necessary adjustments to the selected image, including cropping, if you want to crop all the images the same way.

4. Click **Select All** at the top of the filmstrip panel or Ctrl-click/Cmd-click multiple thumbnails, then click **Synchronize**. The Synchronize dialog box opens. (This dialog box is very similar in appearance and layout to the Save Settings dialog box, which is shown on the previous page.)

5. Either check the setting(s) you want to apply or choose a category from the Synchronize menu.

6. Click OK to apply the current settings to all the selected thumbnails.

A *If you open two or more Raw files simultaneously (whether via Bridge or via File > Open in Photoshop), image thumbnails will display in the **filmstrip** panel on the left side of the **Camera Raw** dialog box. Click the thumbnail for the photo you want to either apply corrections to or open.*

Opening and saving Camera Raw files

Still with us? Great! Finally, you get to **open** your **Camera Raw file** in Photoshop. (After reading this page, be sure to see our instructions for opening a Camera Raw file as a Smart Object layer on the next page.)

To open a Camera Raw file, saving settings:

When you're done choosing settings in the Camera Raw dialog box, click **Open** to convert and open the corrected file in Photoshop. The current settings will be saved as instructions for converting the Raw or JPEG file without changing the original Raw or JPEG file itself.

Note: The settings for a Raw photo will be saved either as part of the internal Camera Raw database in your system or as a hidden sidecar .xmp file in the same folder as the Raw file. This internal file is different from any user-created settings file that you may have created via the Save Settings command on the settings menu.

➤ To close Camera Raw without opening your file, click Done; your current settings will still be saved as instructions for modifying the file.

You can also open a **copy** of a Camera Raw file **without** recording the settings into the metadata of the Raw file or into the actual JPEG file.

To open a copy of a Camera Raw file:

In the Camera Raw dialog box, hold down Alt/Option and click **Open Copy.** The file will be converted using the current settings and will open in Photoshop, but those settings won't be recorded over any existing instructions in the Raw or JPEG file.

You can rename your photo files and **convert** them to the DNG (digital negative), JPEG, TIFF, or Photoshop format without having to open them in Photoshop.

To save a file via Camera Raw:

1. In the Camera Raw dialog box, click **Save Image.** The Save Options dialog box opens.

2. Choose a location, enter a file name, choose a format, then click Save.

➤ Via the Save Image button, you can save more than one version of a photo, each with a different set of adjustments (such as two different exposure adjustments). In this case, in the Save Options dialog box, simply change the file name.

WHAT IS DNG?

Photographers often ask which is the best file format for saving their digital photos — for the present and also for the future — so they'll be able to access and reprint them 20 or 30 years from now. **DNG,** an open-standard file format that was developed by Adobe, may be the answer. The DNG format preserves all the raw, unprocessed pixel information as recorded by the camera. Adobe has made the code for DNG publicly available ("open-standard") to other interested companies in the hope that they'll be adopted for a wide range of hardware devices and software applications. In the future, hopefully, DNG files will be universally readable.

Opening and placing photos as Smart Objects

If you open or place a Camera Raw file into Photoshop as a **Smart Object,** you'll have the option to readjust it at any time via Camera Raw. To learn more about Smart Objects, see pages 302–304.

To convert a Camera Raw file into a Smart Object: ★

Method 1 (open as a new document)

When you're done applying your Camera Raw edits, hold down Shift and click **Open Object.** A new file will open in Photoshop, with the image on a Smart Object layer.

➤ To have Camera Raw open all files as Smart Objects, click the underlined link to open the Workflow Options dialog box, then check Open in Photoshop as Smart Objects; or uncheck to open your photos as non–Smart Object layers.

Method 2 (place into an existing document)

1. Open a Photoshop document.

2. In Bridge, click the thumbnail for a Raw or JPEG photo that was previously edited in Camera Raw.

3. Choose File > Place > **In Photoshop.** The Camera Raw dialog box opens.

4. Make any adjustments to the photo, if desired, then click **OK.** It will appear on its own layer in the currently active Photoshop document, within a transform box.

5. Apply any scale or shape transformations, then press Enter/Return or double-click inside the transform box to accept the placed image. It's now a **Smart Object** layer.

To edit a Smart Object photo:

1. Double-click a Smart Object layer thumbnail to reopen an embedded copy of the photo into the Camera Raw dialog box.**A**

2. Make any desired adjustments, then click OK to apply your edits to the Smart Object layer. The original file won't be affected by your edits.

➤ You can also scale a Smart Object layer at any time. Photoshop will use the pixel data from the original file to scale the image, so its quality won't be diminished (that is, provided you don't enlarge it beyond its original size).**B–D**

A *To change the Camera Raw settings for a* **Smart Object** *image, double-click the layer thtumbnail.*

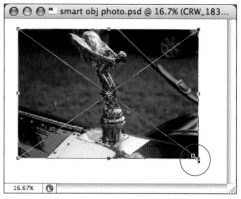

B *To* **scale** *a* **Smart Object** *layer, choose the Move tool, then Shift-drag a corner handle of the transform box.*

C *This photo was opened in Photoshop as a normal layer. When we enlarged it, it lost its crispness.*

D *The same photo on a* **Smart Object** *layer and enlarged by the same amount: the details are crisp and the image quality remains high.*

When you first open a photograph in Photoshop, take a few minutes to study it. Does it have any overall deficiencies or problems? Is it over- or underexposed? Does it have a color cast (ghostly blue, sickly green)? There are a number of commands that you can use to rectify these kinds of problems. If you captured the photo as a Raw file or in the JPEG or TIFF format, you were able to apply exposure corrections via the Camera Raw plug-in. If you didn't use Camera Raw, you can apply exposure corrections in Photoshop.

In this chapter, you'll perform shadow and high-light corrections; adjust the color temperature to compensate for improper lighting; correct over- or underexposure by rebalancing light and dark values; correct for the failure to use a flash; and apply lighting effects.

Using the Shadow/Highlight command

The **Shadow/Highlight** command is one of our favorite adjustment tools because it's nondestructive. It adjusts the luminance of each individual pixel depending on the darkness or lightness of neighboring pixels, and it lets you apply corrections in a specific tonal range without overadjusting other areas of the image. And by recovering details in the shadows and highlights, it can prove to be invaluable for correcting overexposed and underexposed areas, such as subjects that may be in shadow as a result of strong side or back lighting.

Because Shadow/Highlight preserves the full range of tonal values, it's superior to Levels and Curves, which are powerful commands but discard pixel data. This can be verified by viewing the Histogram palette while using the Shadow/Highlight command (**A**, next page). And because Shadow/Highlight lets you pinpoint the tonal ranges that need adjusting, it saves you from having to use layers or masks (as you do when using Levels and Curves).

The Shadow/Highlight command works on CMYK, RGB, LAB, Grayscale, and Duotone images, and with 8-bit and 16-bit files. Its only glaring flaw, as far as we can tell, is that it can't be applied via an adjustment layer. We don't tend to fill our books with superlatives, but we can't praise this feature enough!

Continued on the following page

EXPOSURE

16

To apply the Shadow/Highlight command:

1. Click a layer or the Background, **B** and display the **Histogram** palette so you can monitor the tonal adjustments.

2. Choose Image > Adjustments > **Shadow/Highlight.** The Shadow/Highlight dialog box will open and the image will be adjusted automatically using preliminary settings.

3. For the **Shadows,** move the Amount slider to the right to lighten the shadows. You may find that the default setting of 50% does a decent job of correcting underexposed shadow areas. You can increase this value slightly (but not to 100%) for stronger shadow correction, such as foreground subjects that are underexposed due to strong backlighting, and to extend those corrections into the midtones and highlights.

4. Increase the **Highlights** Amount to darken the highlight areas (0% produces no darkening). By lowering the brightness of the highlights, you'll recover detail in those areas and also allow the midtones to stand out more. **C–D**

5. Uncheck, then recheck **Preview** to compare the original and adjusted images.

6. *Optional:* Check **Show More Options,** and do any of the following:

   Change the **Tonal Width** value for the Shadows and/or Highlights to expand/reduce the range of tones (adjacent to the shadow or highlight areas) that the command affects. To limit the adjustment to only very dark shadows or very light highlights, keep the Tonal Width value low.

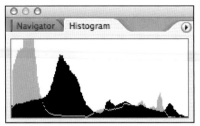

A *No gaps or spikes appear on the **Histogram** palette as we apply **Shadow/Highlight** because the command preserves all the tonal ranges.*

B *Exposing the original image for the sky **underexposed** the buildings (it's hard to see details).*

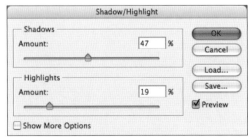

C *In the **Shadow/Highlight** dialog box, we increased the **Shadows** Amount to restore detail to the buildings. We also increased the **Highlights** Amount slightly to restore the cloud shapes and reduce brightness in the sky.*

D *After our initial **Shadow/Highlight** adjustments, the photo still needs work.*

Raise/lower the **Radius** value **A** to expand/ reduce how many neighboring pixels will be compared to a specific pixel in a shadow or highlight area to produce the adjustment.

➤ An overly high Radius value may actually reduce contrast because too many pixels will be compared, thus minimizing any adjust- ment. An overly high Tonal Width or Radius could also produce unreal glows (halos) around the edges of shapes in the midtones.

If raising the Shadows Amount caused oversatu- ration, you can desaturate the image by moving the Adjustments: **Color Correction** slider to the left. Or to increase the saturation, move the slider to the right.

Move the **Midtone Contrast** slider to the right to increase contrast in the midtones or to the left to decrease contrast in the midtones.

7. *Optional:* To save your Shadow/Highlight set- tings to use with any image, click Save, enter a descriptive name (keep the .shh extension), choose a location, then click Save again. To load previously saved settings, click Load.

8. Click OK.**B–C**

➤ To restore the default Shadow/Highlight settings while the dialog box is still open, hold down Alt/Option and click Reset.

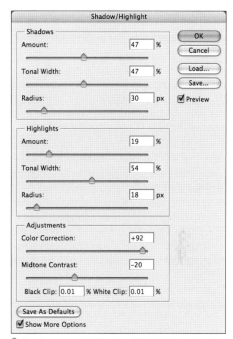

A *In the expanded **Shadow/Highlight** dialog box, we used the **Shadows Tonal Width** and **Radius** settings to restore just the right amount of detail to the shadows and midtones (a high Tonal Width value would have washed out shadow details) and **Highlights Tonal Width** and **Radius** settings to restore contrast in the sky (a low Tonal Width or high Radius value would have reduced contrast and reduced detail in the sky).*

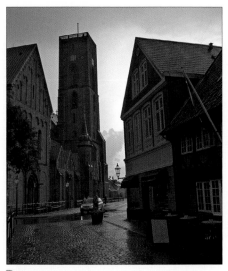

B *The final results of the **Shadow/Highlight** adjustments*

C *To lighten the image further, we copied the image layer, then for the layer copy, chose Color Dodge as the blending mode and an Opacity of 25%.*

Using the Photo Filter command

To change the color temperature of a scene (make a shot look warmer or cooler), photographers use colored lens filters at the time of the photo shoot. The **Photo Filter** command in Photoshop simulates the effect of these camera filters. You can choose one of the 20 ★ preset filter tints or choose your own color via the Color Picker, and best of all, you can apply the command via an adjustment layer. When using this feature, go for subtle or extreme, but not in between.

To apply the Photo Filter command:

1. Click a layer or the Background. **A**

2. From the New Fill/Adjustment Layer menu ⦿. on the Layers palette, choose **Photo Filter.**

3. The Photo Filter dialog box opens. **B** Check Preview.

4. Do either of the following:

    Click **Filter**, then from the menu, choose a warming or cooling filter or a preset filter color. The color you choose will appear in the swatch.

    Click the **Color** swatch, choose a color for the filter from the Color Picker, then click OK.

5. Using the slider or scrubby slider, choose a **Density** (opacity percentage) for the tint. Between 10 and 25% should be fine. You can also lower the adjustment layer opacity after clicking OK.

6. Check **Preserve Luminosity** to preserve the overall brightness and tonal range of the image. With this option unchecked, the contrast will be softer in the highlights; for portraits, you may prefer the results with this option unchecked.

7. Uncheck, then recheck Preview to compare the original and adjusted images, then click OK. **C**

➤ To restore the original settings in the Photo Filter dialog box while it's still open, hold down Alt/Option and click Reset.

A *The original image has a magenta cast.*

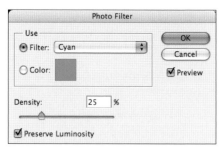

B *In the **Photo Filter** dialog box, we chose Cyan from the Filter menu and set the Density to 25%.*

C *The **Photo Filter** command toned down the magenta while preserving the warmth of the afternoon sun.*

Exposure correction via the Layers palette

Here's a quick and easy way to correct an **over-** or **underexposed** photo: Choose a lightening or darkening blending mode for an adjustment layer, then duplicate the adjustment layer multiple times. It's not the most precise method in the world, but if it works, it works (and if it makes your art director happy, maybe you can go home early).

To correct over- or underexposure via the Layers palette:

1. Open an over- or underexposed photo,**A** and click the Background or a layer.

2. From the New Fill/Adjustment Layer menu on the Layers palette, choose **Levels.**

3. The Levels dialog box opens. Don't change any settings; just click OK.

4. With the adjustment layer selected, choose a **blending mode** from the Layers palette. To darken an overexposed image, try **Multiply** mode; to lighten an underexposed image, try **Screen** mode.

5. If the image is still too light or dark, duplicate the adjustment layer (Ctrl-J/Cmd-J).**B** Continue to duplicate the layer until you reach Nirvana—actually, until you reach a point where the image is overcorrected and you need to step it back a bit.

6. Lower the opacity of the topmost adjustment layer until the exposure is just right.**C**

7. The extra adjustment layers won't increase the file size, but when you're done editing the image, you can choose a merge or flatten command to merge all the adjustment layers into the original Background or layer (use the context menu or press Ctrl-Shift-E/Cmd-Shift-E).

A *The original image is very* **underexposed.**

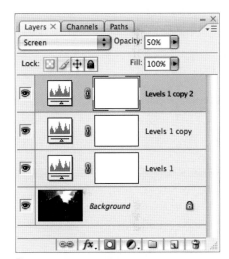

B *We created an* **adjustment layer,** *chose* **Screen** *blending mode for the new layer, then* **duplicated** *it twice.*

C *The final corrected image*

Correcting for lack of flash

If you have a photo in which the main subject is partially in shadow because of backlighting (that is, the photographer neglected to use a flash), the best way to correct it is via the Fill Light slider in the Basic panel of Camera Raw. An alternative method is to **correct underexposed areas by hand** by applying brush strokes to a layer mask, as per these instructions.

To correct for the lack of a flash:

1. Click the Background or a layer, then press Ctrl-J/Cmd-J to duplicate it.**A**

2. With the duplicate layer selected, choose Image > Adjustments > **Levels** (Ctrl-L/Cmd-L). The Levels dialog box opens.**B**

3. Move the midtones (Input Levels) slider to the left to lighten the midtones, move both the white and black Input Levels sliders inward slightly to lighten the highlights and add contrast, then click OK. (Our photo now looks too light. We'll fix that next.)

4. Alt-click/Option-click the **Add Layer Mask** button ⬚ on the Layers palette. The Levels adjustment is now fully masked from the image. Keep the layer mask thumbnail selected.

5. Make the Foreground color white (D).

6. Choose the **Brush** tool (B or Shift-B), ✐ then on the Options bar, do the following:

    Click the **Brush** thumbnail, then choose a soft-edged brush and an appropriate Diameter. For a high-resolution image (1800 x 2400 pixels or larger), choose a Diameter of at least 100 pixels.

    Choose **Mode:** Normal.

    Choose an **Opacity** of 90–100%.

7. Draw strokes on the underexposed areas of the image. Where you drag, the layer mask will be removed and the Levels effect will be exposed.**C** Continue to paint until the desired correction is achieved.**D**

8. If you overlighten any areas, press X to switch the Foreground color to black, then paint over the same area, thereby masking the Levels effect. Or to create a subtle transition between the properly exposed and underexposed areas, use the Brush tool at a low opacity (Options bar).

A *The original image*

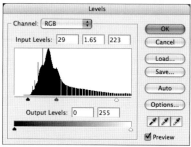

B *We used these settings in* **Levels.**

C *Paint with* **white** *on the* **mask** *of the lightened layer to* **expose** *the Levels effect. Our mask reveals the Levels effect on just the face.*

D *The corrected image*

Applying the Lighting Effects filter

The **Lighting Effects** filter offers a wide assortment of lighting effects. You can place up to 16 light sources in your image, and you can assign a different color, intensity, and angle to each source.

To cast a light on an image:

1. Click a layer in an RGB document.**A** *Optional:* To preserve the option to readjust the filter settings later, convert the layer into a Smart Object.

2. Choose Filter > Render > **Lighting Effects.** The Lighting Effects dialog box opens.**B**

3. From the **Style** menu, choose Default or a preset lighting effect.

4. In the **Light Type** area:

   Check **On** to access the Light Type options.

   From the **Light Type** menu, choose Directional, Omni, or Spotlight.

   Move the **Intensity** slider to adjust the brightness of the light.

   Continued on the following page

A *The original image has diffused light (no noticeable highlights).*

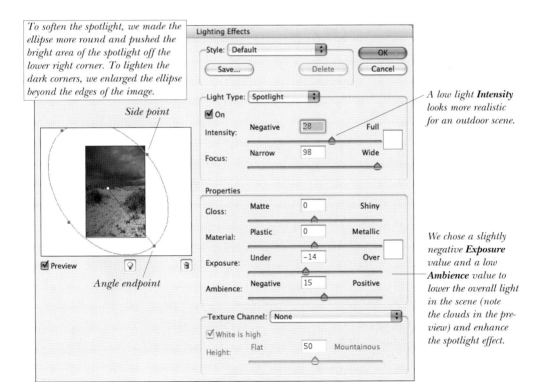

To soften the spotlight, we made the ellipse more round and pushed the bright area of the spotlight off the lower right corner. To lighten the dark corners, we enlarged the ellipse beyond the edges of the image.

*A low light **Intensity** looks more realistic for an outdoor scene.*

*We chose a slightly negative **Exposure** value and a low **Ambience** value to lower the overall light in the scene (note the clouds in the preview) and enhance the spotlight effect.*

B *To produce its effect, the **Lighting Effects** filter darkens the whole layer; the only lighting comes from the filter.*

For the Spotlight Light Type, you can move the **Focus** slider to adjust the size of the beam that fills the ellipse.

To change the **color** of the light, click the color swatch, then choose a color from the picker.

5. In the preview window, do any of the following:

To **move** the entire light, drag the center point.

To **rotate** the ellipse without reshaping it, Ctrl-drag/Cmd-drag any point.

To **intensify** the light, drag the angle endpoint toward the center.

To change the **direction** of the light on an ellipse or to **widen** or **narrow** it, drag either side point.

6. Use the **Properties** sliders to adjust the surrounding light conditions on the current layer:

Gloss controls the amount of surface reflectance on the lighted surfaces.

Material adjusts the relative amount of color that emanates from either the light source (Plastic) or the image (Metallic).

Exposure lightens/darkens the whole layer.

Ambience controls the balance between the light source and the overall light in the layer.

You can also click the **Properties** color swatch to choose a different color for the ambient light around the spotlight.

7. Do any of these optional steps:

To add the current configuration of settings to the Style menu for use with other images, click Save, enter a name, then click OK.

To add more light sources, drag the light bulb icon 💡 into the preview window.

To delete a light source, drag its center point over the trash icon. 🗑 A minimum of one light source must remain.

To duplicate a light source, Alt-drag/Option-drag its center point.

8. Click OK.**A–B**

➤ The last-used settings of the Lighting Effects filter will remain in the dialog box until you change them or exit/quit Photoshop. To restore the default settings, choose Default from the Style menu. To remove the current Style choice, click Delete, then click Delete again in the alert dalog box.

A *To add a bright foreground light, we applied the **Lighting Effects** filter using the settings shown on the previous page.*

B *In a copy of the original landscape, we used the **Lighting Effects** filter, Style: **Soft Omni**, for an even more dramatic effect.*

Photographers use focusing techniques to orchestrate a scene, such as blurriness to convey motion or a wide depth of field to contrast an in-focus subject with its background. In Photoshop, you can apply similar special effects (blur areas that were previously in focus) or correct for photographic errors (sharpen an image that lacks focus). In this chapter, you'll apply the Lens Blur filter and use vignettes to create a focal point in your photo; apply the Motion Blur filter to simulate motion; apply the Lens Correction filter to correct for lens distortion; and apply the Smart Sharpen and Unsharp Mask filters to sharpen.

Using the Lens Blur filter

When you use a camera, you know that, like it or not, some parts of a scene end up being more in focus than others. If your camera lets you adjust exposure and shutter settings (as opposed to the "point-and-shoot" type of camera), you can control how much of the image will be in focus via the f-stop, or depth of field, setting. Objects that fall outside the depth of field—either in front of it or behind it—will be blurred. The appearance of the blurred area will vary depending on the individual camera lens and camera model. For example, blurred white highlights, which photographers call specular highlights, can vary in shape and brightness.

The **Lens Blur** filter in Photoshop attempts to replicate this type of blurring. What formerly required the use of multiple channels, gradients, and editing steps can now be accomplished via this single command. All of this number crunching comes at a price, though: it can be slow when applied to a large image.

To apply the Lens Blur filter:

1. Click an image layer (or duplicate the Background via Ctrl-J/Cmd-J), then click the **Add Layer Mask** button on the Layers palette.

2. With the layer mask thumbnail selected, choose the **Gradient** tool (G or Shift-G), click the Gradient Picker arrowhead on the Options bar, click the "Foreground to Background" preset, then click OK. Drag across the document window to apply a gradient. The Lens Blur filter will place this gradient over the photo invisibly. Keep this in mind when you choose a Blur Focal Distance

Continued on the following page

REFOCUS

17

setting in step 5. (Don't worry where the white and black areas of the gradient land; you'll be able to swap them in the Lens Blur dialog box.)

3. Shift-click the layer mask thumbnail to disable the layer mask (you don't want to mask out the imagery). Click the layer thumbnail, then choose Filter > Blur > **Lens Blur.** The Lens Blur dialog box opens (resize it, if you like).**A**

4. At any time while making adjustments, you can uncheck, then recheck **Preview** to compare the original and blurred images.

Click a **Preview** speed. For a large file (over 100 MB), click **Faster;** for a smaller file, click **More Accurate.**

You can also change the **zoom level** for the preview via the zoom buttons or menu in the lower left corner of the preview window. We recommend the Fit in View setting.

5. The grayscale values in a depth map will control where the blur is applied, mimicking the depth of field in a camera. In the **Depth Map** area:

From the **Source** menu, choose **Layer Mask** as the source for the depth map. The change in grayscale values in the source will control which areas remain in focus. (A setting of None blurs the whole image uniformly.)

To set the **Blur Focal Distance,** either specify which grayscale value (from 0, black, to 255, white) in your depth map will remain in full focus via the scrubby slider, or in the preview, click the area that you want to keep in focus. In either case, what you're doing is choosing a grayscale value from the hidden gradient in the layer mask (**A,** next page). Shades lighter or darker than this value will become progressively more blurry. You'll see the change more readily after moving the Radius slider in the next step.

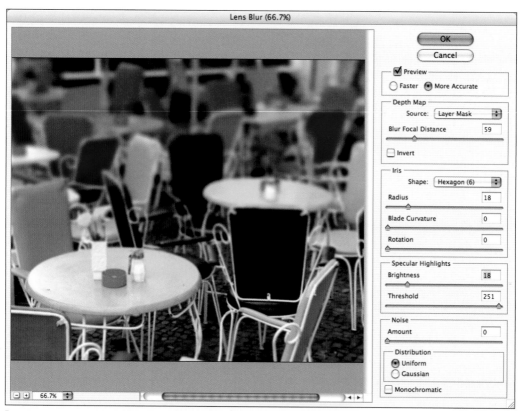

A *Before opening the* **Lens Blur** *dialog box, with the Gradient tool and the layer mask thumbnail selected, we dragged upward from the bottom of our image.*

Optional: Check Invert to swap the white and black areas in the depth map, and thereby swap the areas in focus with the areas that are not.

6. In the **Iris** area, use the **Radius** value to control the intensity of the blur. This produces the most pronounced effect of any option in the dialog box. (The other Iris sliders are used for creating intricate "photographic" highlights).

7. Blurring averages the values of neighboring pixels and tends to gray out white specular highlights. In the **Specular Highlights** area, you can use the **Brightness** slider to brighten highlight areas that have become blurred and use the **Threshold** slider to control which tonal range the current Brightness setting affects. At 255, only pure white pixels will be affected; at low settings, most of the pixels in the blurry areas will be brightened.

8. Blurring can also affect the film grain in an image, producing a nonuniform texture. To add noise back to the blurred areas, do any of the following:

Move the **Noise: Amount** slider slightly.

Click **Distribution: Uniform** or **Gaussian**.

Check **Monochromatic** to limit the noise to just grayscale pixels instead of color pixels.

9. Click OK. **B–C**

Light *grayscale values will produce total blurring in this part of the photo.*

Intermediate *grayscale values will produce partial blurring in this part of the photo.*

Because we chose a **dark** *grayscale value (59) as our* **Blur Focal Distance,** *no blurring will occur in this part of the photo.*

Image

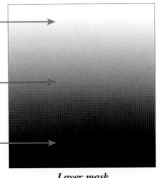

Layer mask

A *When you click the preview in the Lens Blur dialog box or move the Blur Focal Distance slider, you're choosing a grayscale value in the layer mask, which in turn becomes the* **Blur Focal Distance** *value. Pixels at that grayscale value will stay in focus; the remaining pixels will become progressively more blurry.*

B *The original image*

C *We used a layer mask in conjunction with the* **Lens Blur** *filter to blur the background of this photo. Our settings are shown in the figure on the previous page, and our layer mask is shown in the figure above.*

Using the Motion Blur filter

To create an illusion of motion, you'll use the **Motion Blur** filter (in this case, as a Smart Filter). In these instructions, you'll blur the whole image first, then paint on the filter mask to remove the blurring from an object to bring it back into focus.

To apply the Motion Blur filter to part of an image:

1. Click an image layer and duplicate it by pressing Ctrl-J/Cmd-J.**A**

2. With the duplicate layer selected, choose Filter > **Convert for Smart Filter**, then click OK if an alert dialog box appears; or choose Convert to Smart Object from the Layers palette menu.

3. Choose Filter > Blur > **Motion Blur.** The Motion Blur dialog box opens.**B**

4. Choose an **Angle** value (use the scrubby slider or move the dial), choose a **Distance** for the degree of blurring, then click OK.**C** For a high-resolution image (300 ppi), a Distance of 80–100 will substantially blur the image while preserving some recognizable details in the background.

5. On the Layers palette, click the Smart Filter mask thumbnail.

6. Choose the **Brush** tool (B or Shift-B).

7. On the Options bar, choose a medium-sized, soft-edged tip and an Opacity of 80%. Press X, if necessary, to make the Foreground color black.

8. Paint over the area(s) of the image that you want to keep in focus.**D–E** Painting with black will hide the blur effect on the object and create a visual separation between the object and the background. Paint over an area more than once to hide more of the motion blur.

   If you hide too much of the motion blur, press X to switch the Foreground color to white and draw strokes to restore the effect of the filter.

9. *Optional:* Double-click the Motion Blur listing on the Layers palette.**F** In the Motion Blur dialog box, change the Angle or Distance settings, then click OK. The beauty of Smart Filters is that you can readjust the settings!

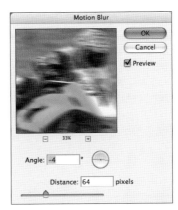

B *We used these settings in the **Motion Blur** dialog box. We set the Angle dial to match the angle and direction of the motorcycle.*

A *The original photo*

C *Apply the **Motion Blur** filter to the whole image first.*

D *Click the **Smart Filter mask** thumbnail, then paint with black where you want to **hide** the Motion Blur effect.*

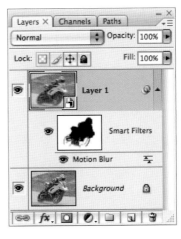

F *The Layers palette shows our **Smart Object** layer (Layer 1), **Smart Filter**, and **filter mask**.*

E *The final results convey fast motion. We were careful not to remove the Motion Blur from the tires, since they would be moving too fast to be in focus.*

Creating vignettes

In these instructions, you'll create an area of focus by using a Smart Filter and Smart Filter mask. An advantage of this method is that you can modify the filter settings and edit the mask to change which part of the image is in focus.

To create an area of focus (vignette) by using a mask:

1. Open an image in which you want to emphasize the center.**A**

2. On the Layers palette, click an image layer or the Background, then press Ctrl-J/Cmd-J to duplicate it.

3. Select the area of the image that you want to **emphasize** (keep in focus). For example, you could use the Elliptical Marquee tool (M or Shift-M) then Alt-drag/Option-drag to create an oval (as we did), or use the Lasso tool to create an irregular selection.

4. On the Options bar, click **Refine Edge.** In the Refine Edge dialog box, check Preview, choose an appropriate **Feather** value, then click OK.

5. Press Ctrl-I/Cmd-I (Select > Inverse). Now the areas outside the marquee are selected.**B**

6. Choose Filter > **Convert for Smart Filters,** then click OK if an alert dialog box appears.

7. Choose Filter > Blur > **Gaussian Blur.** The Gaussian Blur dialog box opens. Click the zoom out (–) button so you can see the whole image in the preview window, increase the **Radius** to blur the image, then click OK.**C–D**

➤ To change the Radius amount, double-click the Gaussian Blur (Smart Filter) listing on the Layers palette. The dialog box reopens.

A *The original image is entirely in focus.*

B *We created an oval* **selection,** *used Refine Edge to* **feather** *it (Feather value of 40 px for this 300 ppi photo), and chose Select > **Inverse**. Now everything outside the oval marquee is selected.*

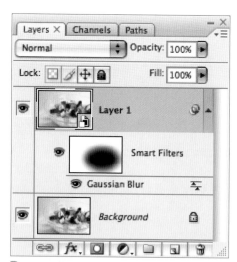

D *The Layers palette shows our **Smart Object** layer (Layer 1), **filter mask,** and **Smart Filter.***

C *For our focus vignette, we used a blur **Radius** value of 5.7 pixels.*

Another way to create a **vignette** is by manipulating light and dark values. In this case, you'll use (and move) the layer mask on a **Levels** adjustment layer to control the position of the vignette on the image.

To create a darkening vignette via Levels:

1. Open an image in which you want to emphasize an area in or near the center.

2. Follow steps 2–4 on the previous page.

3. With the duplicate layer selected, from the New Fill/Adjustment Layer menu ⊘. on the Layers palette, choose **Levels**, then click OK in the Layers dialog box (ignore the settings for now).

4. With the adjustment layer thumbnail selected, press Ctrl-I/Cmd-I to **invert** the mask.

5. Double-click the **Levels** adjustment layer thumbnail. In the Levels dialog box, move the white **Output Levels** slider to the left to darken the image.

6. Click OK.**A–B**

7. *Optional:* To change the location of the darkening vignette, on the Layers palette, click the Levels adjustment layer, click the Link Layer Mask icon 🔗 to unlink the mask from the adjustment layer, then with the Move tool (V), ⊹ drag the mask shape to the desired location in the document window.**C–D** Click again between the layer mask thumbnail and the adjustment thumbnail to make the link icon reappear.

A *We darkened Layer 1 via a **Levels** adjustment layer (we moved the white Output Levels slider to 180).*

B *For a more dramatic lighting effect, we changed the blending mode of the Levels adjustment layer to **Difference** and lowered the layer **Opacity** to 80%.*

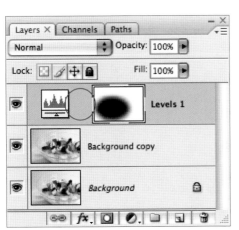

C *We unlinked the **layer mask** from the adjustment layer thumbnail (no link icon now), then, with the Move tool, moved the layer mask to the left.*

D *Because we moved the layer mask to the lower left, the light area (the area blocked by the mask) is now on the left side.*

Using the Lens Correction filter

The **Lens Correction** filter lets you correct many types of lens distortion, such as when the top of a tall building or column appears to be tilting away from the camera (called "keystoning"); color fringes along the edges of shapes (chromatic aberrations); under- or overexposure along the edges of a photo (vignetting); and horizontal or vertical perspective. The filter combines aspects of the Pinch filter and the Transform commands.

To correct lens distortion:

1. Open an RGB image.**A** On the Layers palette, click an image layer or the Background, then press Ctrl-J/Cmd-J to duplicate it.

2. With the duplicate layer selected, choose Filter > **Convert for Smart Filters**, then click OK if an alert dialog box appears.

3. Choose Filter > Distort > **Lens Correction**. The Lens Correction dialog box opens.**B** You can use the sliders or scrubby sliders for these steps.

4. In the **Settings** area, do any of the following:

   Lower the **Remove Distortion** value to spread the image out (expand the midsection) **C** or raise it to pinch the image inward.

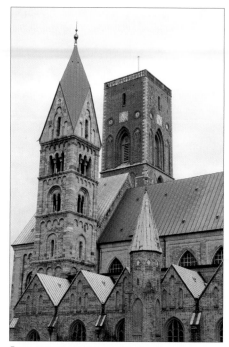

A *In the original image, the church towers are leaning toward the center of the image.*

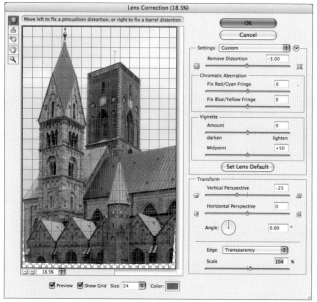

B *The* **Lens Correction** *dialog box lets you correct various types of optical distortion. The final settings we used are shown here.*

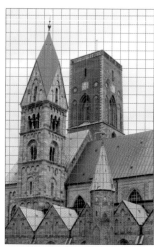

C *We moved the* **Remove Distortion** *slider to the left to keep the horizontal elements (such as the red brick in the foreground) level.*

Use the **Chromatic Aberration** sliders to correct color fringes along high-contrast edges.

➤ If the grid is distracting, uncheck Show Grid below the preview window.

Use the **Vignette** sliders to help correct for under- or overexposure on the outer edges of the image.

5. In the **Transform** area, do any of the following:

Lower the **Vertical Perspective** value to widen the top of the image **A** or raise it to widen the bottom. You may have to readjust the Remove Distortion value to keep horizontal shapes level.

Lower the **Horizontal Perspective** value to widen the left edge of the image or raise it to widen the right edge of the image.

To rotate the image, change the **Angle** via the scrubby slider (which gives you more control than the dial).

6. If empty canvas areas appear at the edges of the image, from the **Edge** menu, choose whether those areas will fill with an Edge Extension (extension of the image), Transparency, or the current Background Color.

You can also enlarge or shrink the image by moving the **Scale** slider, or crop the image after exiting the dialog box.

7. Use any of the options below the preview window:

Click the **zoom in/out** buttons or choose a preset zoom level from the menu.

Check/uncheck **Preview** to compare the original and edited images.

Choose a grid size from the **Size** menu, or click the **Color** swatch to change the grid color.

8. *Optional:* To save the current settings, from the settings menu choose Save Settings, enter a name (keep the .lcs extension), then click Save. Saved settings can be chosen from the Settings menu for any image.

9. Click OK.**B**

➤ To learn about any tool in the Lens Correction dialog box, rest the pointer on it and read the usage description above the preview window.

➤ To change the results, double-click the Lens Correction (Smart Filter) listing on the Layers palette; the dialog box reopens.

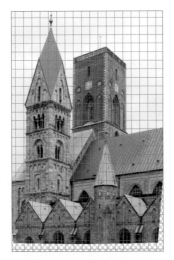

A *We moved the **Vertical Perspective** slider to the left to widen the tops of the towers; now they align better vertically.*

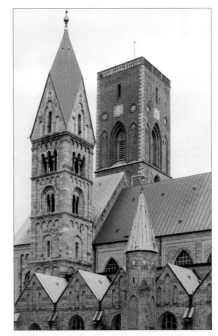

B *In the corrected (and slightly cropped) photo, the horizontals and verticals are properly aligned.*

Using the sharpening filters

Deciding which sharpening filter to use

Most digital photos need sharpening, and the need is accentuated if you change a document's dimensions or resolution with the Resample Image option checked, convert your document to CMYK Color mode, or apply a transformation command. You can correct unwanted blurring by using the **Smart Sharpen** filter **A** or the **Unsharp Mask** filter (the latter, despite its name, has a focusing effect).

These filters can add noise to an image, and therefore should be applied at the end of the image-editing/color and correction cycle—unless your image source is a scan, in which case we recommend applying some minimal sharpening before editing and once again after editing.

High-resolution printing also causes some minor blurring due to dot gain. You can anticipate and compensate for this by applying sharpening to the image when you prepare your file for output. Experience will teach you how much sharpening is needed.

(Note: We don't recommend using the Sharpen tool because it creates unwanted artifacts. Instead, if you want to confine the sharpening effect, select an area before applying the Smart Sharpen filter.)

Although the Unsharp Mask filter has been an industry standard for years and is a powerful sharpening tool, Smart Sharpen may very well replace it in your workflow because it offers many advantages.

➤ **More control:** The Tonal Width sliders extend sharpening through a broader tonal range. Also, Smart Sharpen gives you the ability to sharpen, then fade the sharpening, in the shadow and highlight areas separately; Unsharp Mask doesn't give you that control.

➤ **More power:** The More Accurate option in Smart Sharpen performs multiple sharpening passes on the image automatically.

➤ **Fewer halos:** With the ability of Smart Sharpen to detect edges, fewer color halos are produced.

➤ **Flexibility:** Smart Sharpen offers three algorithms (to correct Gaussian Blur, Lens Blur, or Motion Blur), whereas Unsharp Mask corrects just Gaussian blur.

➤ **Better workflow:** Smart Sharpen lets you save and reuse settings, for improved workflow and consistency.

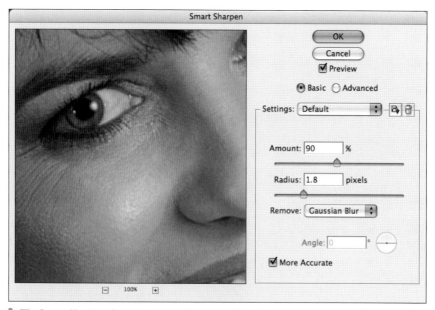

A *The **Smart Sharpen** filter gives you a lot of control over how tonal areas in an image are sharpened, making it a good choice for sharpening portraits.*

Let's say you're starting off with a slightly blurry photo or you tried to smooth skin irregularities or soften surface features in a photo by using the Gaussian Blur filter—but you overdid it. You can resharpen the image by using the **Smart Sharpen** filter.

To apply the Smart Sharpen filter:

1. Open a photo that needs sharpening.**A** On the Layers palette, click an image layer or the Background, then press Ctrl-J/Cmd-J to duplicate it. Choose Filter > **Convert for Smart Filters**, then click OK if an alert dialog box appears.

2. Choose Filter > Sharpen > **Smart Sharpen**. The Smart Sharpen dialog box opens (**A**, previous page). Leave the preview zoom level at 100%.

3. Check **More Accurate** to produce a high-quality sharpening effect by allowing multiple passes of the filter. This takes longer, but it's worth it.

4. From the **Remove** menu, choose an algorithm for correction: Gaussian Blur is a good, all-purpose choice; Lens Blur sharpens details with fewer halos resulting; Motion Blur is useful if the blurring is due to movement of the camera or subject.

5. Try a **Radius** value between 1 and 2.5 pixels, and an **Amount** of 60–110% (you can use the scrubby slider for all the sliders in this dialog box). The image should now look slightly oversharpened;**B** you'll fade the effect next.

6. To control the amount of sharpening in the shadow and highlight areas, click **Advanced**, then click the **Shadow** tab.**C** Drag in the preview to display an area of the image that contains both shadows and midtones. Do the following:

   Choose a **Radius** value between 5 and 10 to control how many neighboring pixels will be compared to a specific pixel. The higher the Radius, the larger the area to be compared.

   Change the **Tonal Width** value to control the range of midtones to be affected by the Fade Amount. The higher the width, the wider the range of midtones affected and the more evenly the sharpening will fade into the shadows.

   Move the **Fade Amount** slider until you see the desired reduction of oversharpening in the shadows. If the Tonal Width value is too low, it will limit the effectiveness of this slider.

Continued on the following page

A *The original 300 ppi resolution image is blurry.*

B *The settings we used in the **Basic** pane of the **Smart Sharpen** dialog box (shown on the previous page) properly sharpened the eyes, teeth, and lips (details) but oversharpened the skin.*

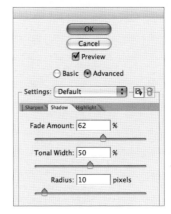

C *In the **Shadow** tab of the **Smart Sharpen** dialog box (Advanced), we used a high **Fade Amount** to soften the sharpening in the shadows (particularly around the eyes) and a moderate **Tonal Width** amount to make the fade affect the shadows fully and the midtones slightly.*

7. Click the **Highlight** tab.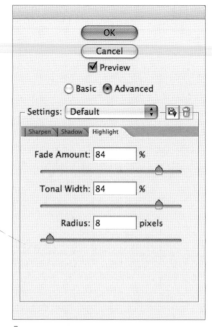 Drag the image in the preview to display an area that contains both highlights and midtones. Adjust the **Radius, Tonal Width,** and **Fade Amount** values, as per the previous step.

8. Hopefully, sharpness is now restored to the details (such as the eyes and mouth in a portrait) but not to the flatter areas (cheeks, forehead). If the overall image now looks too sharp, click the **Sharpen** tab and lower the **Amount** value slightly. After making adjustments in one pane, you may need to readjust the settings in the other two tabs.

9. Click OK.**B–C**

▶ To save the current settings, click the Save a Copy button, ✎ enter a name, then click OK. Saved settings can be chosen from the Settings menu for any image.

▶ To compare the unsharpened and sharpened images, press on the dialog box preview, then release.

▶ To restore all options in the dialog box to their default settings, hold down Alt/Option and click Reset or choose Default from the Settings menu.

▶ To modify the Smart Sharpen results, double-click the Smart Sharpen listing on the Smart Object layer; the dialog box reopens. Your changes will affect the original blurry image, not the already sharpened one.

A *In the **Highlight** tab of the **Smart Sharpen** dialog box, we used a high Fade Amount again to soften the sharpening on the broad, flat highlight areas of the skin (to make them look smoother) and a high Tonal Width amount to allow the fade to affect the highlights and the lighter midtones.*

B *Finally, we used the sliders in the **Shadow** and **Highlight** panes to soften the sharpening on the cheeks, nose, and forehead and around the eyes.*

C *The original image (for comparison)*

To enhance sharpness in an image, the **Unsharp Mask** filter increases the contrast between adjacent pixels. You can specify how much the contrast increases (the Amount), the number of surrounding pixels that the filter affects (the Radius), and the degree of contrast adjacent pixels must have to be affected by the filter (the Threshold).

To apply the Unsharp Mask filter:

1. Choose a zoom level of 100% for your image, then duplicate an image layer (Ctrl-J/Cmd-J).**A**

2. Right-click/Control-click the duplicate layer and choose **Convert to Smart Object.**

3. With the Smart Object layer selected, choose Filter > Sharpen > **Unsharp Mask.** The Unsharp Mask dialog box opens.**B**

4. Choose an **Amount** value for the percentage increase in contrast between pixels. Use a low setting (try 80–100) for figures or natural objects or a higher setting (150–170) if the image contains sharp-edged objects. For a high-resolution image (say, 2000 x 3000 pixels and higher), try an Amount of 130–170.

   Uncheck, then recheck Preview to compare the original and sharpened images.

5. The **Radius** controls how many pixels surrounding high-contrast edges will be modified. Choosing an appropriate Radius can be tricky, as you need to consider the total number of pixels and the subject matter of the image.**C** The more pixels the image contains, the higher the Radius value needed to achieve the desired result. For a low-contrast image that contains large, simple objects and smooth transitions, try a high Radius of 2 (you'll rarely need to use a higher value); for an intricate, high-contrast image with sharp transitions, use a lower Radius (around 1).

   Note: The Amount and Radius settings are interdependent, meaning if you raise the Radius, you'll need to lower the Amount, and vice versa.

6. Choose a **Threshold** value (0–255) for the minimum amount of contrast an area must have to be affected by the filter (**A**, next page). Start with a Threshold of 0 (which sharpens the entire image), then raise it. At a Threshold of 5–10, high-contrast areas will be sharpened, and areas of lesser contrast will be sharpened less. When raising the Threshold, you can also

Continued on the following page

A *The original 300 ppi image is slightly blurry.*

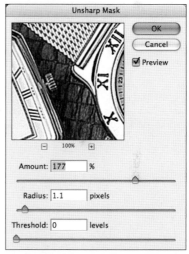

B *A high **Amount** value for the **Unsharp Mask** filter produced halos along the edges of the watches.*

C *And a high **Radius** value (3.3) produced halos around the watch hands and numerals.*

increase the Amount and Radius to sharpen edges (thankfully, the filter won't oversharpen the low-contrast areas).

7. Click OK.**B** You can double-click Unsharp Mask on the Layers palette at any time to reopen the dialog box and adjust the settings.

➤ With the Unsharp Mask dialog box open, if you click in the document window, that area will display in the preview window.

➤ Sharpening can produce color halos along the edges of objects. To correct this, right-click/Control-click the Unsharp Mask listing, choose Mode: Luminosity, then click OK. Now the sharpening is confined to just luminosity and removed from the hue and saturation.

SUGGESTED SETTINGS FOR UNSHARP MASK

We suggest these values for a 3000 x 2000 pixel image:

Landscapes and other soft-edged subjects	Amount 100–150, Radius 1–1.5, Threshold 10–15
Portraits	Amount 100–120, Radius 1.5–2, Threshold 4–6, or to the point where skin areas start looking smoother
Buildings and objects for which contrast is a priority	Amount 150–200 or more, Radius 1.5–2, Threshold 1–3

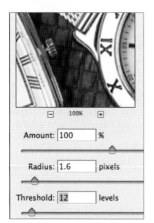 

A At a high **Threshold** value (12) for the **Unsharp Mask** fiter, only high-contrast edges are sharpened. The watch bands and background are still blurry.

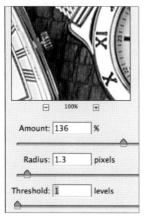 

B We used the values shown above (a lower Threshold value) to produce this final sharpened image.

Photoshop has a tool to fix every kind of small imperfection, from blemishes and crow's feet to creases or stains in precious vintage photos. We're seeing more middle-aged fashion models nowadays, but the pursuit of perfection persists. To a design director, even a seemingly perfect portrait may need some repair—perhaps the model has a birthmark or a slightly imperfect smile—horrors! Or perhaps you have an old, damaged family photo that you want to salvage. In this chapter, you'll perform color changes—such as changing product colors or whitening teeth—using the Match Color command, the Replace Color command, and the Color Replacement tool; clone areas with the Clone Stamp tool; smooth textures, such as skin, using the Surface Blur filter; smooth or remove wrinkles with the Healing Brush and Spot Healing Brush tools; repair tears, dust marks, and creases with the Patch tool; **A–B** and remove red-eye with—yup! You guessed it—the Red Eye tool.

RETOUCH

18

A *The original photo has some creases.*

B *The **Patch** tool magically repaired them.*

IN THIS CHAPTER

Using the Match Color command

You can use the **Match Color** command to match the overall color and tonal values in one document with those in another document. This is useful, say, for correcting a series of product shots that were shot under slightly different lighting conditions or with different camera settings, and thus have different color values. Match Color works best on images of the same subject matter (e.g., food, figures) or of similar content, such as a series of landscapes.

To use the Match Color command:

1. Open a one-layer RGB document to be used as the source for the desired color and tonal values, and a second one-layer RGB document to be the recipient (target) of the color match.**A–B**

2. *Optional:* Show the Histogram palette to observe a graph of the tonal changes.

3. With the target document active, on the Layers palette, drag the Background over the **New Layer** button. Keep the duplicate layer selected.

4. Choose Image > Adjustments > **Match Color.** The Match Color dialog box opens. Make sure Preview is checked.

5. From the **Source** menu, choose the name of the source document that you opened in step 1.**C** The target document will adopt the color tones of the chosen source document immediately.

A *The original images include a scene with bright midday sunlight...*

B *...and a misty scene with overcast light.*

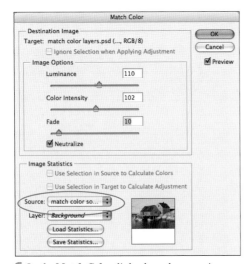

C *In the **Match Color** dialog box, choose an image from the **Source** menu.*

D *Using the **Match Color** command, we made the "overcast" image adopt the warmer tones of the "midday sun" image.*

6. In the **Image Options** area, do any of the following:

   Move the **Luminance** slider to adjust the overall brightness of the image.

   Move the **Color Intensity** slider to adjust the color saturation.

   Move the **Fade** slider to restore some of the original color to the image, blending the old and the new.

   Check **Neutralize** to remove any color casts from the target document. If this causes too great a color shift, try lessening the effect via the Fade slider.

7. Readjust any of the sliders as needed, then click OK (**D**, previous page).

➤ To limit the choice of colors you match from to help prevent peculiar color shifts from occurring in the target image, create a selection in the source document before choosing Match Color. In the Match Color dialog box, check Use Selection in Source to Calculate Colors.

Another use for the Match Color dialog box is to quickly **remove** a **color cast** from an image. It doesn't always work, but when it does, it works beautifully.

To remove a color cast in one step:

1. Open an RGB image.**A** Choose Image > Adjustments > **Match Color.** The Match Color dialog box opens.**B** Make sure Preview is checked.

2. Don't select a Source document. Just check **Neutralize.**

3. Do any of the following (you can use the scrubby sliders):

   Adjust the **Luminance** and **Color Intensity** as needed.

   If the color correction is too severe, adjust the **Fade** value to restore some of the original image color.

4. Click OK.**C**

A *The original image has a cool **blue** cast.*

B *In the **Match Color** dialog box, we checked Neutralize and used the Image Options sliders to make minor adjustments.*

C *The cool **color cast** is **corrected**.*

Cloning

You can use the **Clone Stamp** tool to clone imagery on the same layer, from one layer to another within the same document, or from one document to another.

To clone imagery:

1. Open an RGB document.**A**

2. Choose the **Clone Stamp** tool (S or Shift-S).

3. On the Options bar,**C** do the following:

   Click the **Brush Preset Picker** arrowhead, then click a brush that's an appropriate size for the area you want to clone.

   Choose a blending **Mode.**

   Choose an **Opacity** percentage.

   Choose a **Flow** percentage to control the rate of application.

   Check **Aligned** to maintain the same distance between the source point and the area that you drag across, even if you release the mouse, switch modes, or switch brushes between strokes (to clone a large area smoothly); or uncheck Aligned to sample from the original source point each time you release the mouse (to produce repetitive clones of a smaller area).

   From the **Sample** menu, ★ choose **All Layers** to sample pixels from all the currently visible layers that you Alt-click/Option-click over (see the sidebar on the next page).

4. Create a new layer in the target document, and keep it selected.

5. Alt-click/Option-click the area you want to clone from to establish a source point.**B**

6. Drag the Clone Stamp tool back and forth where you want the clone to appear.

   Two pointers will appear onscreen: a pointer over the source point and a pointer where you drag the mouse (**A**, next page). Imagery from the source point will appear where you drag, replacing any underlying pixels (**B**, next page).

7. If you want to establish a new source point to clone from, Alt-click/Option-click a different area in the source document (**C–D**), next page.

A *We want to remove the metal pipes from the side of the building (wall) and add more leaves to fill in the front of the trellis.*

B *We Alt-clicked/Option-clicked with the **Clone Stamp** tool to sample a blank area of the wall.*

Brush: • 10 | Mode: Normal | Opacity: 90% | Flow: 100% | ☑ Aligned | Sample: All Layers

C *The Options bar for the **Clone Stamp** tool*

8. Because your cloning results are on a separate layer, you can show/hide—or even erase—your edits on that layer at any time without affecting the original image.

➤ You can change Options bar settings for the Clone Stamp tool between strokes.

➤ To create a "double-exposure" effect, choose a low Opacity percentage for the tool. The underlying pixels will partially show through the cloned pixels.

➤ Be sure to read about the Clone Source palette (pages 152–153), which lets you keep track of source points in multiple documents when using the Clone Stamp tool.

SAMPLING LAYERS

With the **Sample All Layers** option checked or chosen on the Options bar for the current editing tool, the tool will sample pixels from all the visible layers and send the results to the current layer. If the current layer is a new, blank layer, you'll be able to show and hide your edits—or erase any unwanted edits—at any time.

A *We're dragging with the* **Clone Stamp** *tool to replace the pipe with pixels from the blank wall.*

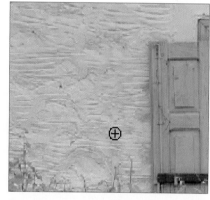

B *We're continuing to sample the wall and clone away the pipe.*

C *We're* **sampling** *the vine leaves because we want to add more leaves to the trellis.*

D *Our final results*

Using the Replace Color command

Using the **Replace Color** command, you can adjust the hue, saturation, or lightness of colors in specific areas that you click in either the document window or the dialog box—without using any selection tools. This powerful command works best for adjusting soft-edged areas, such as in a landscape, that don't require a sharp-edged selection.

To use the Replace Color command:

1. *Optional:* For an RGB document that you're going to send to a commercial printer, choose View > Proof Setup > Working CMYK to see a soft proof of the image in CMYK color.

    Once you've made a choice from the Proof Setup submenu, you can toggle the proof on and off while the Replace Color dialog box is open by pressing Ctrl-Y/Cmd-Y. Regardless of whether the proof is on or off, the Color and Result swatches in the Replace Color dialog box display in RGB.

2. Click a layer or the Background.**A**

3. *Optional:* Create a selection to restrict color replacement to that area.

4. Choose Image > Adjustments > **Replace Color.** The Replace Color dialog box opens.

5. Initially, the preview window will be all or mostly black. In the document window, click on or drag across the color that you want to replace.**B** That color will appear in the **Color** swatch at the top of the dialog box.**C**

    Click **Selection** to preview the current selection in the preview window, or click **Image** to display the entire document. You can press/release Control to toggle between the two display modes.

6. Do either of the following:

    To add more color areas to the selection, choose the first **eyedropper**, then Shift-click or drag in the preview window or document window.

    Move the **Fuzziness** slider to the right to add similar colors to the selection or to the left to narrow the range of selected colors.

    (To start over, choose the eyedropper and click without holding down Shift.)

7. If you've added colors to the selection that you now want to subtract, with the first eyedropper, Alt-click/Option-click or drag in the preview

A *We want to replace the red on the three watering cans in the middle of this image with a soft tan.*

B *We click the small red can…*

C *…to initiate the selection in the preview window in the* **Replace Color** *dialog box.*

window or document window. Or choose the 🖉 eyedropper, then click or drag without holding down Alt/Option.**A–B**

8. To replace the selected colors, do either of the following:

   In the **Replacement** area, choose a replacement **Hue, Saturation,** and **Lightness.** The Result swatch will update as you move the sliders or scrubby sliders.

   Click the **Result** swatch, choose a color from the Color Picker, then click OK. The sliders will shift to reflect the attributes of the new color.

   Note: The Replacement sliders will stay put, even if you click a different area of the image or add to or subtract from the selection.

9. Click OK.**C–D**

➤ The Result swatch color in the Replace Color dialog box also displays in the currently active square on the Color palette. If you choose a nonprintable color, the out-of-gamut warning ⚠ will display on the Color palette.

➤ The Replacement sliders won't change the amount of Black (K) in a color for a CMYK document. That component is set separately by the Black Generation feature in Photoshop.

➤ To restore the original settings to the dialog box, hold down Alt/Option and click Reset.

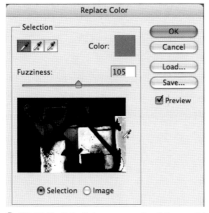

A *We Shift-clicked the can on the right to add that color area to the selection.*

B *When we clicked the red watering can on the right, the color on the orange can in the background was selected and replaced—which wasn't our intent.*

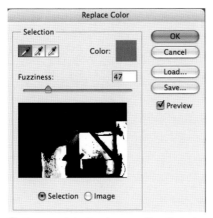

C *We lowered the **Fuzziness** to 47 to limit the selection to just the red watering cans.*

D *As you can see in the final image, only the red was replaced.*

Another use of the Replace Color command is for **whitening teeth** or the whites of the **eyes.** By selecting those problem areas in an image before using the Replace Color command, you can quickly correct any discoloration.

To whiten teeth or eyes:

1. Open a portrait photo that you want to correct, and choose the **Lasso** tool. Zoom in on the teeth or eye area.

2. Drag to create a tight selection of the teeth **A** or of the white area on one of the eyes.

3. On the Options bar, click **Refine Edge.** In the Refine Edge dialog box, click **Default,** choose a **Feather** value of 6–12 px, then click OK.

4. Choose Image > Adjustments > **Replace Color.** The Replace Color dialog box opens.**B**

5. With the **eyedropper** from the dialog box, click the preview or click the selection in the document window.

6. To add related shades of white to the selection, move the **Fuzziness** slider or Shift-click on, or drag across, any unselected areas.

7. Lower the **Saturation** to desaturate the selected area and remove the off-white tinge (you can use the scrubby slider), and raise the **Lightness** slightly to brighten the selected area.

8. Click OK. Deselect the selection.**C**

9. If you're whitening eyes, repeat the steps above to select and whiten the remaining off-white areas.

➤ An alternative method would be to select the area you want to correct and create a Hue/ Saturation adjustment layer. In the Hue/ Saturation dialog box, choose Edit: Yellows, lower the Saturation, and raise the Lightness. Personally, we think it's easier to select the desired color range with the eyedropper and Fuzziness slider in the Replace Color dialog box.

A *Use the **Lasso** tool to select the teeth.*

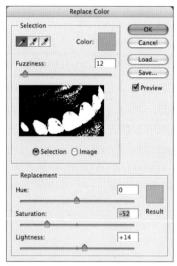

B *Use the eyedropper in the **Replace Color** dialog box to refine the selection.*

C *We whitened the **teeth** using the settings shown above—no toothbrushing required.*

Using the Surface Blur filter

The **Surface Blur** filter makes an easy job of smoothing skin or mottled surfaces.

To smooth skin or other surfaces:

1. Press Ctrl-J/Cmd-J to duplicate the Background in an image that needs surface smoothing.**A**

2. Choose Filter > Blur > **Surface Blur.** The Surface Blur dialog box opens.

3. Choose a low **Threshold** value (try 3–6) to blur only low-contrast areas, such as the cheeks and forehead in a portrait, while preserving contrast in details, such as facial features.

4. To soften skin (cheeks, forehead again), choose a **Radius** of around 6–12. Increase the Radius just enough to produce the desired smoothing effect. A Radius that's too low can produce posterization and make skin look blotchy.

5. Readjust the **Threshold** to either increase or decrease the amount of blurring in low-contrast areas. Too much smoothing could make a face look artificial—but then again, this whole task is a lesson in artifice!

6. Click OK.**B**

➤ To restore some surface details from the original image, choose a slightly lower opacity for the duplicate layer.

➤ If we had created a Smart Object layer and applied the Surface Blur filter as a Smart Filter, we would have had to do any further touchups on the Smart Object content, where the skin smoothing effect isn't displayed.

If the Surface Blur filter caused too much blurring, you can **restore details** with a mask and brush.

To selectively restore details after using the Surface Blur filter:

1. With the duplicate layer selected, click the **Add Layer Mask** button on the Layers palette.

2. Choose the **Brush** tool (B or Shift-B).

3. On the Options bar, choose a small, soft-edged tip and choose an Opacity of 80–90%.

4. With black as the Foreground color, draw strokes on the areas you want to restore sharpness to (e.g., lips, eyes, eyebrows, hair),**C** or paint with white to restore the blur filter effect.

A *The pores on this woman's skin are too prominent.*

B *With a **Radius** setting of 7 pixels and a **Threshold** setting of 5 levels (our file is 300 ppi), the **Surface Blur** filter successfully smoothed the skin texture while keeping the facial details crisp. Compare the cheeks and under-eye areas in this image with the image above.*

C *Paint with black on a **layer mask** to restore details from the underlying layer (in this case, to the face).*

Using the Color Replacement tool

Like the Replace Color command, the **Color Replacement** tool lets you change color, hue, saturation, and luminosity values. But here, instead of using a dialog box, you'll apply changes manually with a brush. You can also specify mode, sampling, limits, and tolerance parameters for the tool. And unlike the Brush tool, which applies flat colors, the Color Replacement tool tries to preserve the original texture as it changes colors. This tool, like the Replace Color and Match Color commands, is a boon for advertising and catalog designers.

To use the Color Replacement tool:

1. Open an RGB image.

2. Choose the **Color Replacement** tool (B or Shift-B).

3. Do either of the following to choose a **replacement** color:

   Choose a Foreground color from the Color or Swatches palette.

   Alt-click/Option-click with the Color Replacement tool to sample a color in the image (temporary Eyedropper).

4. Add the new color to the Swatches palette by clicking the **New Swatch of Foreground Color** button at the bottom of the palette. Now you'll be able to reselect that color at any time.

5. From the Options bar (**A**, next page) choose parameters for the tool:

   Click the **Brush Preset Picker** arrowhead and choose a suitable Diameter, a high Hardness value, and a low Spacing value.

   To control which color characteristics the tool applies, choose a blending **Mode: Hue, Saturation, Color,** or **Luminosity.** We recommend Color mode.

   Click the **Sampling: Continuous** button to apply the current Foreground color to all pixels the brush passes over (we prefer this option because it lets us replace both light and dark colors); or **Sampling: Once** to sample the first pixel the brush crosshair clicks on and then apply the Foreground color only to pixels that match that initial sampled color (this option gives you the most control but may not replace both light and dark colors); or **Sampling: Background Swatch** to replace only colors that match or are similar to the current Background color (choose a Background color for this option).

   Choose **Limits: Discontiguous** to recolor only pixels under the pointer; or **Contiguous** to recolor pixels under the pointer plus adjacent pixels; or **Find Edges** (our favorite option) to recolor pixels under the pointer while keeping the color replacement within discrete shape edges. For all three choices, the tool replaces only pixels that fall within the current Sampling parameters.

   To control the range within which a color can differ from the sampled color and yet still be recolored, choose a **Tolerance** value (1–100%). A high Tolerance value permits a wide range of colors to be recolored; a low value limits recoloring to only pixels that closely match the sampled color.

   Optional: Check Anti-alias to smooth the transitions between the original and replacement colors.

6. Click a layer, then drag across the areas you want to recolor (**B–E**, next page). Only pixels that fall within the Mode, Sampling, Limits, and Tolerance parameters that you just established will be recolored. To vary the results, change the Options bar settings between strokes.

A *Choose settings for the **Color Replacement** tool from the Options bar.*

B *The original image*

C *With the **Color Replacement** tool, using the tool settings shown in the Options bar above, we're painting light blue (our current Foreground color) over the light green on the sweater.*

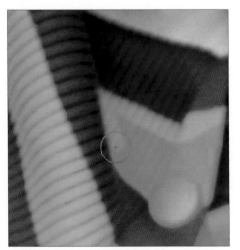

D *Next, we zoom in to paint smaller areas. At a **Tolerance** of 40%, we're able to replace both highlights and shadows on the green stripes. To replace the green along the edge of the stripes, but not the darker stripes, we'll lower the Tolerance to 15%, then paint again with light blue.*

E *With **Limits: Contiguous** as the setting, we were more likely to—and did—accidentally recolor the dark stripes. To repair our mistakes, we'll Alt-click/Option-click to sample the original color in the darker stripe (shown here), then paint the dark color. Last of all, we'll click the light blue swatch that we saved to the Swatches palette, then continue to apply light blue to replace the green.*

The three tools discussed next sample a texture, apply it to the target area, then recolor the texture with the color and brightness values of the target area, blending it seamlessly into the surrounding pixels. With these tools, it's easy to fix imperfections such as facial blemishes and paper creases.

With the **Healing Brush** tool, you Alt-click/Option-click an unblemished (sample) area, then apply strokes to repair the blemish.**A** The blemish pixels are replaced with the sampled pixels.

With the **Patch** tool, you select the blemish area first, then drag the selection marquee over a clean pixel area for sampling. Here again, blemish pixels are replaced with the sampled pixels.

And with the **Spot Healing Brush** tool, you simply stroke over blemishes without sampling. Pixels are magically replaced based on data from neighboring pixels.

Using the Healing Brush tool

To use the Healing Brush tool:

1. Choose the **Healing Brush** tool (J or Shift-J).

2. On the Options bar,**C** do all of the following:

   Click the **Brush Preset Picker** arrowhead, make the brush **Diameter** slightly wider than the area you want to retouch, and choose a low **Hardness** value. (Also, in Preferences > Cursors, click Full Size Brush Tip and check Show Crosshair in Brush Tip.)

   Choose **Mode:** Normal to preserve the grain, texture, and noise of the area surrounding the target; or choose a different mode if you don't need to preserve those attributes. Choose Lighten for subtle retouching or for wrinkles or creases that are very close together to prevent them from cloning onto one another.

   Click **Source:** Sampled.

   Check **Aligned** to maintain the same distance between the source point (which will change) and the target area that you drag across; or uncheck Aligned to create repetitive strokes anywhere in the image, always sampling from the same source point.

A *We think she's beautiful as she is, but advertisers might not like the crow's feet (they will like her nice, bright teeth!).*

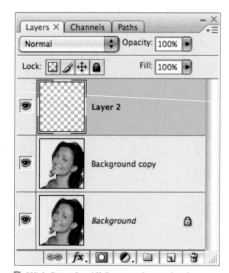

B *With **Sample: All Layers** chosen for the **Healing Brush** tool, we'll draw strokes on a new layer.*

C *The Options bar for the **Healing Brush** tool*

From the **Sample** menu, ★ we recommend choosing **All Layers** to sample pixels from all the layers below the pointer. **Current Layer** lets you sample pixels from only the current layer.

3. If you're retouching the Background, press Ctrl-J/Cmd-J to duplicate it, then click the duplicate layer.

4. Create a new, blank layer (**B**, previous page) and keep it selected. In step 6, you'll apply retouching strokes to the new layer.

5. Alt-click/Option-click the area to be used as the source texture.**A**

6. Drag across the area you want to repair.**B** When you release the mouse, the source texture will be applied to the target area and will be blended with its surrounding pixels. It will render in two stages, so be patient.**C**

7. To establish a new source point for further repairs, Alt-click/Option-click a different area, then apply more strokes.

8. *Optional:* For more realistic results, lower the opacity of the new layer slightly to blend it with the original image layer.

9. To correct any mistakes, hide the image layers below the layer you applied strokes to (to see your strokes more easily), then with the Eraser tool, erase strokes from the new layer. This is easier than using the History palette to undo your mistakes.

➤ To confine the repair to a specific area and to avoid picking up colors from surrounding areas, before using the Healing Brush tool, use the Lasso tool to select the area you want to repair.

➤ Just by way of comparison, the Clone Stamp tool simply copies a source color to a target area, whereas the Healing Brush, Spot Healing Brush, and Patch tools blend a texture into the color and brightness values of the target area.

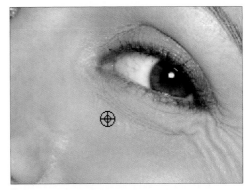

A *With the **Healing Brush** tool, Alt-click/Option-click the area you want to use as replacement pixels…*

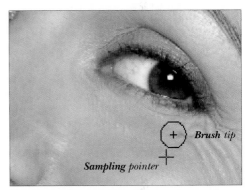

B *…then drag across the area you want to repair. A brush tip and a sampling pointer appear onscreen.*

C *We softened the lines around the right eye (we could do the same for the left).*

Using the Patch tool

The **Patch** tool is a good choice for retouching bags or wrinkles below eyes and for repairing tears, stains, and dust marks in vintage photos. With this tool, you'll select an area before applying the repair.

To use the Patch tool:

1. Choose the **Patch** tool (J or Shift-J). 🜨

2. On the Options bar, click **Patch: Source.**

3. Press Ctrl-J/Cmd-J to duplicate the Background, and keep the duplicate layer selected.

4. Drag a marquee around the area you want to repair.**A**

5. *Optional:* Add to (Shift-drag) or subtract from (Alt-drag/Option-drag) the selection as needed.

6. Drag from inside the selection to the area you want to sample from.**B** When you release the mouse, imagery from the sampled area will appear within the original selection. Deselect.**C**

7. *Optional:* When retouching a portrait, if you see a slight color change in the patched skin, try changing the blending mode of the duplicate layer to Lighten.

➤ If you're not pleased with the patch results, click the prior state on the History palette, then drag to sample a different area.

➤ To fill the Patch tool selection with a pattern, on the Options bar, click a pattern on the Pattern Preset picker, then click Use Pattern. Check Transparent if you want the fill to be semitransparent.

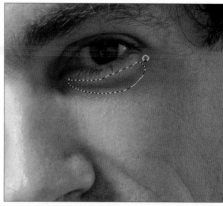

A *With the **Patch** tool, select the area to be retouched.*

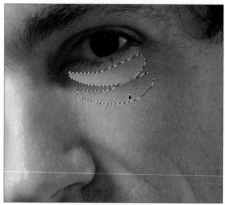

B *Drag from the selected area to the area you want to **sample** pixels **from**. To better preserve the skin texture, we're sampling an area near the eye.*

C *The patch sample is applied to the **selection**.*

REPARING A DAMAGED PHOTO WITH THE PATCH TOOL

A *The original photo has some damaged areas.*

B *With the **Patch** tool, an area is selected **for repair**.*

C *Next, the selection is dragged across an **undamaged** area, for sampling.*

D *The sampled pixels replaced the damaged area. We'll use the tool again to repair the other damaged areas.*

REMOVING DUST MARKS AND SCRATCHES

You can also use Filter > Noise > **Dust & Scratches** to quickly remove dust marks or small flecks of white from an old photo. Move the Radius slider slightly until most of the white dust marks disappear, then move the Threshold slider until some image detail is restored, but not to the point that you see dust marks again.

Using the Spot Healing Brush tool

The **Spot Healing Brush** tool is an effective blemish and wrinkle remover, and it's cheaper than Botox. Skin folds tend to be close together and have highlights and shadows, making it difficult to pick a sample area. With this tool, you correct imperfections without sampling.

To use the Spot Healing Brush tool:

1. Do either of the following:

   Press Ctrl-J/Cmd-J to duplicate the Background, and leave the duplicate layer selected.

   Create a new, blank layer to contain your correction strokes, and keep it selected.

2. Choose the **Spot Healing Brush** tool (J or Shift-J), ✐ then set the zoom level to 100%.

3. On the Options bar, do the following:

   Choose a brush that's slightly wider than the area to be retouched. (And in Preferences > Cursors, click Full Size Brush Tip and check Show Crosshair in Brush Tip.)

   Choose a **Mode**. For preserving skin tones, we find that Normal or Lighten works best. With Replace mode, the tool may pick up other facial details in the stroke, such as hair or eyelashes.

A *With the **Spot Healing Brush** tool and a small brush tip, drag in the direction of a wrinkle line (in only one direction); the stroke should follow along the fold of skin.*

B *The wrinkles we dragged over are removed.*

C *We dragged again with the **Spot Healing Brush** tool to remove more lines from the corner of the eye.*

To correct large or long facial lines, click **Type: Proximity Match**, which helps preserve tonal values in skin tones. Or to retouch a small area with a small brush tip, click **Type: Create Texture**, which helps to even out the tonal values. (Using a large brush tip with either option may produce an unnatural-looking texture.)

To allow the brush to sample pixels from all layers below the pointer, check **Sample All Layers** (check this option if you created a new, blank layer for step 1); or if you're working on an image layer, uncheck Sample All Layers to allow the brush to sample pixels from only the current layer.

4. Drag once across a wrinkle to repair it. Repeat to repair other wrinkles (**A–C**, previous page).

5. For more naturalistic results, lower the opacity of the duplicate or new layer slightly to blend it with the original photo.

If you applied strokes to a new layer, you can erase the strokes from the layer if you need to remove them. When you're done making corrections, merge the layer downward.

REMOVING FACIAL HOT SPOTS

A *You can use the **Healing Brush** tool to remove shiny hot spots, which are caused by harsh, uneven lighting. Alt-click/Option-click to **sample** a medium-toned area of skin.*

B *Choose **Mode: Darken** on the Options bar for the Healing Brush tool, then drag once or twice over a hot spot; let your stroke follow the contours of the face.*

C *The hot spot is toned down. With Darken chosen as the Mode, the tool repaired only the light areas of skin.*

Using the Red Eye tool

Red-eye in portrait photography results from light emitted by a camera-mounted or built-in electronic flash reflecting off the retina. If your camera has a built-in red-eye control, you're less likely to run into this problem. For photos taken without such controls, you can remove the red-eye with a click of the **Red Eye** tool.

To remove red-eye from a portrait:

1. Open a portrait photo, and zoom to 200%–300% view on the eye area.

2. Choose the **Red Eye** tool (J or Shift-J).

3. On the Options bar, do the following:

   Choose a **Pupil Size** for the recolored pupil; try 60–80%. You don't want the tool to enlarge the pupil.

   Choose a **Darken Amount** to control how dark the resulting pupil will be; try 30–40%. Light eyes need a lower setting than dark eyes. A setting that's too high will make the pupils overly dark.

4. Click once on the red area on each pupil. The tool will remove all traces of red. **A–B**

▶ If the tool made the pupil too large, undo the initial click, lower the Pupil Size value, then click again. Similarly, to experiment with lighter Darken Amount values, undo the initial click first.

▶ You don't need to drag across the eye with the Red Eye tool; the tool is smart enough to find the pupil area automatically with a single click.

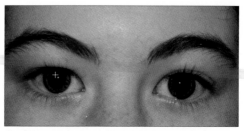

A *With the **Red Eye** tool, click once on each eye.*

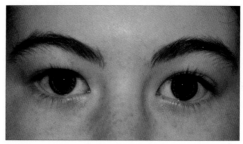

B *The red-eye is gone.*

FIXING THE IRIS

If the Red Eye tool fails to remove traces of red from the iris of the eyes (the area surrounding the pupils), do the following: Zoom in on an eye (200%–300%), then choose the **Color Replacement** tool. On the Options bar, choose a very small brush tip, Mode: Color, Sampling: Once, Limits: Contiguous, and Tolerance 30%. Alt-click/Option-click to sample an iris color to replace the red, then draw strokes to paint out the remaining traces of red.

By this point, hopefully, you've got the hang of using the Layers palette and basic layer features and are ready to explore the palette further. In this chapter, we'll show you how to blend pixels between layers; create and use layer masks; create and use clipping masks; link layers; transform layers; create and edit Smart Object layers; and fill areas with a solid color.

Changing layer opacity and fill

The **Opacity** setting on the **Layers** palette controls the opacity of a layer, including any layer effects, whereas the **Fill** setting controls the opacity of a layer, excluding layer effects (layer effects are discussed in the next chapter). Both settings are available for image, type, adjustment, Smart Object, and shape layers. Each layer can be assigned a different Opacity and/or Fill percentage.

To change the opacity or fill of a layer:

1. Click a layer (not the Background).

2. From the Layers palette, choose an **Opacity** or **Fill** percentage (you can use the scrubby slider).**A–B** The lower the opacity or fill, the more pixels from the layer below will be visible through the currently selected layer.

A *The original image contains four layers, including an editable type layer.*

B *We lowered the **Opacity** of the three image layers and lowered just the **Fill** percentage of the type layer to keep the drop shadow (a layer effect) at full opacity.*

Blending layers

The **blending mode** you choose for a layer affects how that layer blends with the layer directly below it. You can change the blending mode for any kind of layer: image, type, adjustment, shape, or Smart Object. Some modes, such as Soft Light, produce subtle effects, whereas others, such as Difference, produce dramatic color shifts. The default mode is Normal. The individual blending modes are described and illustrated on pages 192–196.

To choose a blending mode for a layer:

1. Click a layer (not the Background).**A**

2. Choose a **blending mode** from the menu in the upper left corner of the Layers palette.**B–D**

➤ If you don't have a painting or editing tool selected, you can press Shift- + (plus) or Shift - – (minus) to cycle through the blending modes for the current layer. If a painting or editing tool is selected, the same shortcut will change the mode for the tool instead.

➤ To choose a blending mode for a Smart Filter, right-click/Control-click the filter name and choose Edit Smart Filter Blending Options, then choose a mode (Blending Options dialog box).

A *We duplicated the Background in the original image.*

B *To the duplicate layer, we applied the* **Desaturate** *command to make it grayscale, then chose* **Screen** *as the blending mode.*

C *We lowered the* **Opacity** *of the duplicate layer to 70%. The type layer has its own blending mode of* **Overlay.**

D *The* **Layers** *palette for the previous figure*

In these instructions, you'll edit a duplicate layer and then **blend** the **original** and **duplicate** layers via the opacity and blending mode controls on the Layers palette. You can use this method to soften the effect of a filter or other image-editing command or to try out various blending modes. If you don't like the results, simply trash the duplicate layer (or Smart Filter) and start over.

To blend a modified layer with the original layer:

1. Click a layer, **A** then press Ctrl-J/Cmd-J to duplicate it. (Or if you know how to use Smart Filters, duplicate an image layer, then right-click/Control-click the duplicate and choose Convert to Smart Object.)

2. Modify the duplicate layer by applying one or more image-editing commands (such as filters) or adjustment commands.

3. On the Layers palette, adjust the **Opacity** of the duplicate layer to achieve the desired level of transparency **B–D** and/or choose a different **blending mode**.

A *The original image*

B *We applied the **Dry Brush** and **Grain** filters to a duplicate (Smart Object) layer, then lowered the layer **Opacity**.*

C *The original image*

D *Here, we applied the **Charcoal filter** to a duplicate (Smart Object) layer, then lowered the layer **Opacity**.*

The **Blending Options** in the Layer Style dialog box offer, in addition to the blending mode, opacity, and fill controls we've already discussed, a number of advanced settings for controlling how a layer and layer effects blend with underlying layers.

To choose blending options for a layer:

1. Double-click next to a layer name on the Layers palette, or right-click/Control-click a layer and choose **Blending Options.** The Layer Style dialog box opens, with Blending Options selected in the upper left.**A**

2. Check Preview.

3. *Optional:* In the General Blending area, change the Blend Mode or Opacity (the same options as on the Layers palette).

4. For **Advanced Blending,** do any of the following (the tool tips are helpful reminders):

   To control the opacity of the layer, excluding any layer effects, adjust the **Fill Opacity** (this has the same function as the Fill option on the Layers palette).

5. Using the **Blend If** sliders, you can control which pixels in the current layer stay visible and which pixels from the underlying layer show through the current layer (**A–E**, next page):

   Move the leftmost **This Layer** slider to the right to remove shadow areas from the current layer.

   Move the rightmost **This Layer** slider to the left to remove highlights from the current layer.

   Move the leftmost **Underlying Layer** slider to the right to restore shadow areas from the underlying layer.

   Move the rightmost **Underlying Layer** slider to the left to restore highlights from the underlying layer.

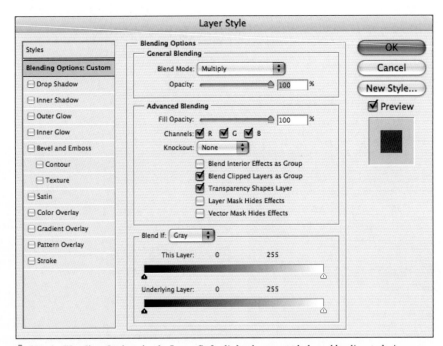

A *Use the **Blending Options** in the **Layer Style** dialog box to apply layer blending techniques.*

To adjust the midtone colors independently of the lightest and darkest colors, Alt-drag/Option-drag a slider; it will divide in two.**E**

6. Click OK.

➤ For simplicity, work with all the channels at once by leaving the Blend If menu set to Gray. If you want to experiment with blending each color channel separately, choose a channel from the Blend If menu before moving the sliders.

CONTROLLING LAYER BLENDING

A *The original image*

B *We chose black as the Foreground color and a light tan as the Background color, duplicated the Background, then applied the **Charcoal** filter to the **duplicate** layer (the filter used the colors we chose).*

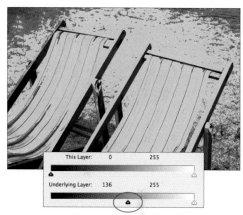

C *To allow some of the dark tones in the photo to peek through the filtered layer, we moved the black **Underlying Layer** slider in the **Blending Options** pane of the **Layer Style** dialog box.*

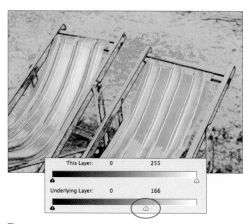

D *To restore some of the light tones from the photo, we moved the white **Underlying Layer** slider.*

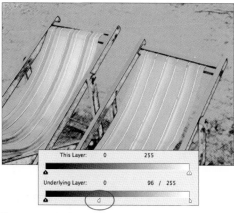

E *To restore only the midtone colors (not the lightest colors), we divided and moved the white **Underlying Layer** slider.*

Using layer masks

A **layer mask** is an 8-bit grayscale channel that hides all or some of the pixels on a layer. White areas in a layer mask permit pixels to be seen, black areas mask pixels, and gray areas mask pixels partially. With the layer mask thumbnail selected, you can edit, invert, or deactivate the mask, and move or copy it to other layers. When you're done working with the mask, you can either apply it to make the effect permanent or discard it to undo its effect completely.

To create a layer mask:

Method 1 (no selection)

1. Click a layer or layer group.

2. Do either of the following:

   To create a white mask in which all the layer pixels are **visible**, click the **Add Layer Mask** button ▢ at the bottom of the Layers palette (or choose Layer > Layer Mask > Reveal All).

   To create a black mask in which all the layer pixels are **hidden**, Alt-click/Option-click the **Add Layer Mask** button on the Layers palette (or choose Layer > Layer Mask > Hide All).

Method 2 (creating a selection first)

1. Create a selection, then select the layer that you want to apply the mask to.

2. Do either of the following:

   To **reveal** layer pixels only within the selection area, click the **Add Layer Mask** button ▢ on the Layers palette (or choose Layer > Layer Mask > Reveal Selection).**A–C**

   To **hide** layer pixels only within the selection area, Alt-click/Option-click the **Add Layer Mask** button on the Layers palette (or choose Layer > Add Layer Mask > Hide Selection).

➤ To load the mask as a selection, Ctrl-click/Cmd-click the layer mask thumbnail.

A *The original layers*

B *With the archway shape selected, we created a **layer mask** for the Tile layer, then pressed Ctrl-I/Cmd-I to invert the black and white areas in the mask. Finally, to blend the mosaic with the stone wall, we chose Pin Light mode and lowered the layer opacity.*

C *In the final image, the tile imagery is hidden by the arch-shaped **layer mask**.*

To reshape a layer mask:

1. Choose the **Brush** tool (B or Shift-B).

2. On the Options bar, click a brush on the **Brush Preset** picker, choose **Mode: Normal**, and choose 100% **Opacity** (or a lower opacity to hide layer pixels partially).

3. Do either of the following:

   To display the mask as a **colored overlay**, Alt-Shift-click/Option-Shift-click the layer mask thumbnail. **A–B** (Repeat the shortcut to restore the normal display.)

   To display the mask **by itself** in the document window, Alt-click/Option-click the layer mask thumbnail. **C–D** (Repeat the shortcut to restore the normal display.)

4. Do any of the following:

   Paint on the image with **black** as the Foreground color to **enlarge** the mask and hide pixels on the layer.

   Paint with **white** as the Foreground color to **reduce** the mask and restore pixels on the layer.

   Lower the **opacity** for the current tool to hide or restore pixels partially.

   You can change the brush diameter, hardness, or opacity between strokes. To draw straight strokes, click, then Shift-click with the tool.

5. When you're finished modifying the layer mask, click the layer thumbnail.

➤ To invert the effect of a layer mask, click the layer mask thumbnail, then press Ctrl-I/Cmd-I. Formerly hidden areas will be revealed, and formerly visible areas will be hidden.

A We're painting out areas of the mask with the mask displayed as a "rubylith" overlay on top of the image.

B In this case, we're enlarging the top of a smaller version of the mask.

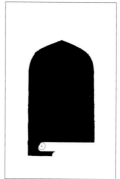 

C We're reducing the mask (adding white) with the mask displayed by itself in the document window.

D In this case, we're enlarging the mask again (adding black).

By default, a **layer** and its layer **mask** are linked and, when moved, move as a unit. If you want to move each component separately, you have to **unlink** them first.

To move the layer image or mask independently:

1. On the Layers palette, click the **link** icon 🔗 between the layer thumbnail and the layer mask thumbnail.**A–B** The icon will disappear.

2. Click either the layer thumbnail or the layer mask thumbnail, depending on which one you want to move.

3. Choose the **Move** tool (V). ⤢

4. Drag in the document window.**C**

5. Click again between the layer and layer mask thumbnails to restore the link.

To move or duplicate a layer mask to another layer:

Do either of the following:

To **move** a mask, drag a layer mask thumbnail onto another layer (not the Background).

To **duplicate** a mask, Alt-drag/Option-drag a layer mask thumbnail onto another layer.

On the previous page, we showed you how to display the mask as a colored overlay (Alt-Shift-click/Option-Shift-click the layer mask thumbnail). If you like, you can **change** the **overlay color** or **opacity** (perhaps the image contains a lot of red and it's hard to see the overlay).

To choose layer mask display options:

1. Double-click a layer mask thumbnail. The Layer Mask Display Options dialog box opens.**D**

2. Click the **Color** square, then choose a different overlay color, and/or change the **Opacity** percentage for the overlay.

3. Click OK. To see the change, display any layer mask as an overlay in the document window.

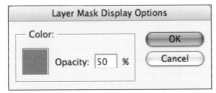

D In **Layer Mask Display Options**, change the Color and/or Opacity of the mask overlay.

A The original image contains a **layer mask,** which reveals the middle of the underlying Background imagery.

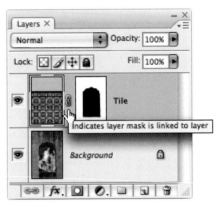

B Click the **link** icon to disengage a layer from its mask. Now you can move just the mask (or just the layer imagery) in the document window.

C When the **layer mask is moved,** a different part of the Background is revealed.

To deactivate a layer mask temporarily:

Shift-click the layer mask thumbnail on the Layers palette (the thumbnail won't become selected). A red X will appear over the thumbnail and the entire layer will be visible.**A**

(Shift-click the layer mask thumbnail again to restore the mask effect.)

One disadvantage of using layer masks is that they take up storage space, albeit a small amount, so when you're done using them, you should **apply** the ones you like to make their effects permanent and **delete** any that you don't need.

Note: Before applying or deleting any masks, use the File > Save As command to copy the file. Keep the original with layer masks in reserve for future editing.

To apply or delete a layer mask:

Do either of the following:

Right-click/Control-click a layer mask thumbnail and choose **Delete Layer Mask** or **Apply Layer Mask.**

Click the layer mask thumbnail, then click the **Delete Layer** button. An alert dialog box will appear.**B** To remove the mask and undo its effect, click Delete, or to make the mask effect permanent, click Apply.

A *Shift-click the layer mask thumbnail to* ***deactivate/ activate*** *the mask.*

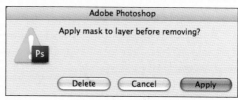

B *When you delete a mask, you can click* ***Delete*** *to delete the mask and its effect or click* ***Apply*** *to make the mask effect permanent.*

Using clipping masks

When layers are formed into a **clipping mask**, the bottommost layer, called the "base" layer, clips (limits the display of pixels on) the layers above it. The base layer also controls the mode and opacity of the clipped layers. The base layer can be a type, image, Smart Object, or shape layer.

To create a clipping mask:

1. Do either of the following:

   Alt-click/Option-click the line between two layers (the pointer will turn into two overlapping circles),**A–B** or right-click/Control-click the layer to be clipped and choose **Create Clipping Mask.**

   Note: The layers used in a clipping mask must be listed consecutively on the palette. When clipping layers in a group, all the layers must reside within the group.

   The base layer name will be underlined; the thumbnail for each clipped layer will have a downward-pointing arrow and will be indented.

2. *Optional:* Repeat the previous step to add more consecutive layers to the mask.**C–D**

➤ You can also create a clipping mask by Shift-clicking the layers to be clipped, then pressing Ctrl-Alt-G/Cmd-Option-G; the same shortcut also releases selected layers from a clipping mask.

When you **release** a layer from a clipping mask, any masked layers above the one you're releasing are released, too.

To release a layer from a clipping mask:

Do one of the following:

Alt-click/Option-click the line below the layer that you want to release.

Right-click/Control-click a layer to be released and choose **Release Clipping Mask.**

To release an entire clipping mask:

1. Click the base layer in the group.

2. **Alt-click/Option-click** the line between the base layer and the next layer above it.

A *The original image contains five layers. (An editable type layer is obscured by the image layers.)*

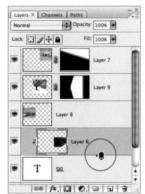

B *Alt-click/Option-click between two layers to create a **clipping mask.** The clipped layer will become indented and the base layer name will become underlined.*

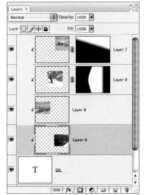

C *We Alt-clicked/Option-clicked each layer above Layer 6. All four image layers are now being **clipped** by the **base** ("ski") layer.*

D *The type layer is **clipping** the four image layers.*

Linking layers

Linked layers will move as a unit in the document window and drag-and-drop as a unit to other files. If you align, distribute, or transform (e.g., scale or rotate) a linked layer, your edit will also apply to all the layers it's linked to.

To link layers:

1. On the Layers palette, select two or more layers (Ctrl-click/Cmd-click to select nonconsecutive layers).**A–B**

2. Click the **Link Layers** button 🔗 at the bottom of the Layers palette. The layers are now linked. If you click any one of them, a link icon will appear to the right of every linked layer name.**C**

➤ To unlink a layer, click the layer, then click the Link Layers button. The link icon will disappear from that layer.

➤ To align or distribute linked layers, see the instructions on page 160.

➤ To move linked layers, choose the Move tool (V), click one of the linked layers, then drag in the document window.**D**

A *The original image*

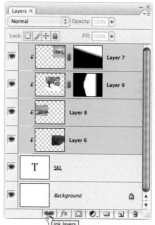

B *Select all the layers to be linked, then click the **Link Layers** button. (The layers don't have to be in a clipping mask, as they are here.)*

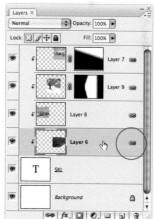

C *When you click a linked layer, the **link** icon appears for that layer and for any other layers it's linked to.*

D *We **moved** the linked image layers to the left.*

Transforming layers

In this section, you'll apply **scale**, **rotate**, **skew**, **distort**, and **perspective** transformations to a layer, layer group, selection, or linked layers. You'll apply individual transformation commands first, just to see how they work. Then you'll perform multiple transformations via the Free Transform command or Move tool—the quicker and more intuitive methods that we prefer. You can also apply transformations by entering values on the Options bar.

To transform a layer or group via an individual command:

1. On the Layers palette, click a layer or group, or Shift-select multiple layers (linked layers transform as a unit). You can scale, rotate, or skew editable type layers. To transform the Background, you must create a selection first.

2. *Optional:* For an image layer (not a group), create a selection to limit the transformation.

3. Choose Edit > Transform > **Scale, Rotate, Skew, Distort,** or **Perspective.** A transform box will surround the opaque part of the layer or the whole selection.

4. *Optional:* To transform the layer or selection from a point other than the center, drag the reference point (you can move it outside the transform box).**A**

5. To **Scale** the layer horizontally and vertically, drag a corner handle; to scale only the horizontal or vertical dimension, drag a side handle; for proportional scaling, Shift-drag a corner handle; or to scale from the reference point, Alt-drag/Option-drag.

   For **Rotate,B** position the pointer either just inside or just outside the transform box, near a handle on the box (the pointer will become a curved, double-headed arrow), then drag in a circular direction. Shift-drag to constrain the rotation to a multiple of 15°.

   For **Skew,** drag a side handle on the transform box to skew along the horizontal or vertical axis, or Alt-drag/Option-drag to skew symmetrically from the reference point (**A–B**, next page).

   For **Distort,** drag a corner handle to freely reposition just that handle, or drag a side handle to distort the side of the transform box along the horizontal and/or vertical axis.

A *A Scale transformation*

B *A Rotate transformation*

C *A Perspective transformation*

WHAT CAN YOU TRANSFORM?

You can **transform** any of the following: an image layer, type layer,* shape layer, Smart Object layer, alpha channel, selection marquee, or path.

To apply a Distort or Perspective transformation to type, you have to rasterize the type layer first.

Alt-drag/Option-drag to distort symmetrically from the center of the layer.

For **Perspective**, drag a corner handle along the horizontal or vertical axis to create one-point perspective along that axis C (and C, previous page). The adjacent corner will move symmetrically.

➤ If you're going to perform multiple transformations, apply them all (Edit > Transform) before accepting the transformation. This helps to preserve the image quality.

6. To accept the transformation, do one of the following:

Double-click inside the transform box.

Click the Commit Transform button ✔ on the Options bar.

Press Enter/Return.

(To cancel the transformation, click the Cancel Transform button ⊘ or press Esc.)

➤ To undo the last handle modification, choose Edit > Undo.

➤ To move the entire layer (or selection) while the transform box is still showing onscreen, drag inside the transform box.

➤ To rotate a layer along an angle that you define, choose the Ruler tool (I or Shift-I), 📏 drag in the document window to define an angle, then with the tool still selected, choose Edit > Transform > Rotate.

A *This editable type contains layer effects.*

B *A **skew** transformation is applied to the editable type.*

C *To apply a **perspective** transformation, you have to rasterize the type first (Layer > Rasterize > Type).*

TRANSFORM TIPS

➤ The **Image Interpolation** method setting in Preferences (Ctrl-K/Cmd-K) > General applies to transformations, among other things. The Bicubic methods, although slower, degrade the image the least. Use Bicubic Smoother when enlarging imagery, Bicubic Sharper when reducing.

➤ To repeat the last transformation, choose Edit > Transform > **Again** (Ctrl-Shift-T/Cmd-Shift-T).

➤ As you transform a layer or a selection, note how your edits are reflected in the readouts on either the **Options** bar or the **Info** palette.

WHAT'S LEFT AFTER A TRANSFORMATION?

➤ If you transform an **image** layer or a selection on an image layer, any empty space created by the transformation will be replaced with **transparency**.

➤ To transform the **Background,** you must create a selection. If you transform the Background, any empty space created by the transformation will be filled with the current **Background color**.

Now that you're acquainted with the individual Transform commands, you're ready to use the **Free Transform** command or the **Move** tool with its transform controls. Using these methods, you can apply multiple transformations without having to choose individual commands from a menu, and image data is resampled once—when you accept the edits (this helps to preserve the image quality).

To transform using the Free Transform command or Move tool:

1. Click a layer, multiple layers, or a group.  Any layers that are linked to the selected layer will also be transformed. To transform the Background, you must create a selection first.

A *The original image*

2. To display the transform controls, do either of the following:

Choose Edit > **Free Transform** (Ctrl-T/Cmd-T).

Choose the **Move** tool, ⌖ check **Show Transform Controls** on the Options bar, then click a handle.

3. Follow step 5, starting on page 298, **B** with the following exceptions:

To **Skew**, Ctrl-drag/Cmd-drag a side handle. (Include Shift to constrain the movement.)

To **Distort**, Ctrl-drag/Cmd-drag a corner handle.

To apply **Perspective**, Ctrl-Alt-Shift-drag/Cmd-Option-Shift-drag a corner handle. **C**

You can also use the **Options** bar to apply many transform settings. **D** For example, to change the reference point for the transformation, click a square on the Reference Point Location icon.

4. To accept the transformation, double-click inside the bounding box or click the ✔ on the Options bar (Enter/Return). To cancel the transformation, click the ⊘ (Esc). You must either accept or cancel to resume normal editing.

B *We selected the car, then copied it to a new layer. Here, we're scaling the new layer.*

C *We're applying perspective to make the front of the car wider than the back.*

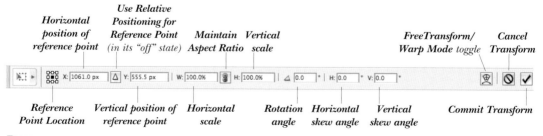

Horizontal position of reference point · Use Relative Positioning for Reference Point (in its "off" state) · Maintain Aspect Ratio · Vertical scale · FreeTransform/ Warp Mode toggle · Cancel Transform

Reference Point Location · Vertical position of reference point · Horizontal scale · Rotation angle · Horizontal skew angle · Vertical skew angle · Commit Transform

D *When you choose a **Transform** command, you can also apply **transform edits** via the **Options** bar. It's not the fastest method in the world, but it is the most accurate.*

Warping layers

The **Warp** command distorts an entire layer by using an editable grid. You can choose preset warp shapes, an orientation, and other controls for the warp via the Options bar.

To warp a layer:

1. Click a layer on the Layers palette.**A**

2. Choose Edit > Transform > **Warp**. A grid with handles will display over the layer image.

3. Do either of the following:

   To distort the layer "by hand," make sure **Warp: Custom** is chosen on the Options bar, then drag any of the squares, points, or lines on the grid, or the direction line handles in the document window.

   To apply a warp via the Options bar, choose a preset style from the **Warp** menu;**B–C** then, if desired, click the **Warp Orientation** button to toggle between horizontal and vertical distortion; or use the **Bend**, **H** (horizontal distortion), or **V** (vertical distortion) scrubby sliders to choose values for those attributes.

4. To accept the warp, press Enter/Return or click ✔ on the Options bar **D** (to cancel it, press Esc or click the ⊘). To remove a warp, use the History palette, or if it's on a Smart Object layer, rechoose the command, then choose None.

A *This image includes a type layer and an image layer.*

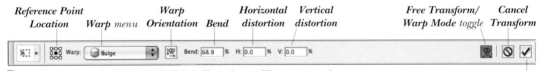

Reference Point Location | Warp menu | Warp Orientation | Bend | Horizontal distortion | Vertical distortion | Free Transform/ Warp Mode toggle | Cancel Transform

B *The Options bar after choosing the Edit > Transform > **Warp** command*

Commit Transform

C *The type layer is being warped using the **Bulge** style.*

D *We applied **Overlay mode** to the type layer to blend the type better with the lime rind.*

Using Smart Object layers

A **Smart Object** layer can contain the contents of one or more layers in the current Photoshop document or it can contain contents that you open or place into a Photoshop document (e.g., from Adobe Illustrator or Acrobat, or a Camera Raw file). If you double-click the thumbnail for a Smart Object made from Photoshop layers, a separate document window will open in Photoshop, containing the embedded layers. If you double-click the thumbnail for a Smart Object made from imported contents, the embedded file will open in the creator application. In either case, when you edit, save, and close the window for the embedded file, the Photoshop document will update automatically to reflect the new edits (pretty smart, huh?).

To create a Smart Object:

Do one of the following:

Select one or more layers (e.g., image, type, adjustment, or shape) on the Layers palette, then right-click/Control-click on the palette and choose **Convert to Smart Object** (or choose the command from the Layers palette menu).**A–B**

Via the File > **Place** command in Photoshop or Bridge, import a Raw photo, another Photoshop file, or a file from another application into the current document. Scale and position the bounding box as needed, then press Enter/Return. The file is now embedded in the document as a new Smart Object layer.

Use File > **Open as Smart Object** to open a file as a Smart Object layer in its own document. ★

➤ When you apply filters to a Smart Object layer, they become Smart Filters—meaning they can be edited or removed individually at any time, and the Smart Object will update accordingly (see pages 324–325).

To edit a Smart Object:

1. On the Layers palette, double-click the **Smart Object layer** thumbnail, then click OK when the alert prompt appears.**C**

2. If the Smart Object layer contains Photoshop layers, a separate document will open in Photoshop, containing those layers. If the Smart Object layer contains imported content (imagery or graphics), that content will appear in a document window in the creator application. Edit the document.

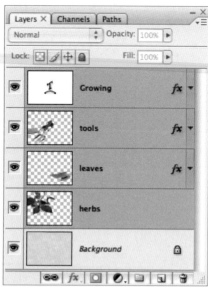

A *Select **multiple layers** in your Photoshop file for conversion into a Smart Object.*

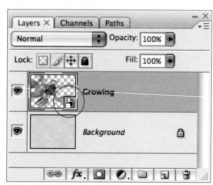

B *The layers are converted into a **Smart Object** (note the icon in the layer thumbnail). You can apply filters, layer effects, and transformations to a Smart Object layer. The individual layers will remain accessible in the embedded file.*

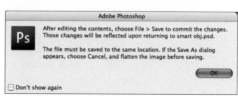

C *This alert dialog box appears if you double-click a Smart Object layer thumbnail. Click OK.*

3. Save and close the file, but don't change the file name or the location. You'll return to the Photoshop document automatically and the Smart Object layer will update to reflect your edits. Don't worry—edits applied to a Smart Object don't affect the original file.

The **Replace Contents** command lets you swap existing Smart Object content with a replacment file. This command also comes in handy if you edit the original file that the Smart Object was created from (not the embedded file).

To replace the contents of a Smart Object with another file:

1. Right-click/Control-click a Smart Object layer (not the thumbnail) and choose **Replace Contents.** The Place dialog box opens.

2. Locate the replacement file (one you've edited or an altogether new file), then click **Place.** The Smart Object updates with the new image. **A–C**

➤ Changes to Layers palette settings on a Smart Object layer, such as opacity, blending modes, masks, and effects, affect the layer appearance—not the embedded Smart Object file. If you edit or replace the contents of a Smart Object, those layer settings are preserved.

➤ If you add a mask to a Smart Object layer, it won't (and can't) be linked to the Smart Object.

Photoshop layers that are converted into a Smart Object become part of an embedded file. If you want to **reclaim** any of those **layers** (put them back into your Photoshop file), you may.

To reclaim Photoshop layers from a Smart Object:

1. On the Layers palette, double-click the thumbnail for a **Smart Object** layer, then click OK in the alert dialog box.

2. The embedded file will open in a separate document window. With that window active, drag the layers you want to reclaim from the Layers palette into the original document window.

3. Close the window for the embedded file.

4. Lower the **opacity** of the Smart Object layer. With the Move tool, reposition the reclaimed layers as needed, using the semitransparent Smart Object layer as a guide. Note: Smart Filters, transformations, and layer effects from the original Smart Object layer won't be present in the reclaimed layers.

A *We applied layer effects to this **Smart Object** layer.*

B *We edited the **original** file the Smart Object originated from (added 3 colored squares).*

C *The **Replace Contents** command replaced the contents of the Smart Object with the edited file. Note that the layer effects are preserved.*

CONTEMPLATING A MERGE?

When you're contemplating whether to merge or flatten layers, consider **grouping** them into a **Smart Object layer** instead. You'll achieve the same reduction of layers, plus you'll gain the ability to edit the original layers individually by double-clicking the Smart Object layer thumbnail.

If you **rasterize** a **Smart Object** layer (to make it a standard image layer), you'll lose the ability to access the contents of the embedded file. Before doing so, we recommend using the File > Save As command to copy the file; this way, your original Photoshop file (with its Smart Objects) will be preserved.

To rasterize a Smart Object layer:

Right-click/Control-click the Smart Object layer and choose **Rasterize Layer.**

Filling areas with a solid color

You can fill a whole layer, or a selection on a layer, with a solid color.

To fill a selection or a layer with a solid color:

1. Click a layer, or create a new layer. *Optional:* Create a selection on the layer. You could use the Select > Color Range command to select a particular area of color, or the highlight, midtone, or shadow areas in an image.

2. To choose a fill color, do either of the following:

   Choose a Foreground color via the **Color** or **Swatches** palette.

   Choose the **Eyedropper** tool (I or Shift-I), then click a color in the image.

3. Choose Edit > **Fill.** The Fill dialog box opens. **A**

4. Choose **Use: Foreground Color.** (You could also choose Color, then choose a color from the Color Picker.)

5. Check **Preserve Transparency** to recolor only opaque pixels on the layer, or uncheck this option to recolor the entire selection or layer.

6. *Optional:* Choose a Blending Mode or change the Opacity percentage for the color fill.

7. Click OK.

➤ For a more flexible way to apply a solid color, gradient, or pattern, use the New Fill/ Adjustment Layer menu on the Layers palette.

SMART WARP

If the **Warp** command is applied to a **Smart Object** layer, it remains live and can be edited or removed at any time by rechoosing the command. After converting multiple layers into a Smart Object, you can warp them in one pass.

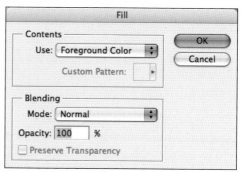

A *You can use the **Fill** dialog box to fill a selection or layer with a solid color or pattern.*

SHORTCUTS TO FILL A SELECTION OR LAYER

Windows

Fill with the Foreground color, 100% Opacity	Alt-Backspace
Fill with the Background color, 100% Opacity	Ctrl-Backspace
Fill only nontransparent pixels with the Foreground color	Alt-Shift-Backspace
Fill only nontransparent pixels with the Background color	Ctrl-Shift-Backspace

Mac

Fill with the Foreground color, 100% Opacity	Option-Delete
Fill with the Background color, 100% Opacity	Cmd-Delete
Fill only nontransparent pixels with the Foreground color	Option-Shift-Delete
Fill only nontransparent pixels with the Background color	Cmd-Shift-Delete

As a Photoshop user, you're in the business of creating illusions, and layer effects let you do so in short, easy steps. The effects that you can apply alone or in combination include Drop Shadow, Inner Shadow, Outer Glow, Inner Glow, Bevel and Emboss, Satin, Color Overlay, Gradient Overlay, Pattern Overlay, and Stroke.**A** Once applied, layer effects can be edited, hidden, or removed at any time. And best of all, when you modify layer pixels, the effects update accordingly (they should be called "smart effects"!).

In this chapter, we offer generic instructions for applying, copying, moving, and removing layer effects, instructions for applying each one, and finally, instructions for saving and applying effects combined with other Layers palette settings as styles via the Styles palette.

Applying layer effects

Layer effects can be applied to any layer (even to editable type), but not to the Background. They affect all the visible pixels on a layer and update instantly if pixels are added, modified, or deleted from the layer they're applied to. Each individual effect can be turned on/off at any time via its own visibility icon.

All the layer effects are applied and edited via the Layer Style dialog box and are listed on the Layers palette below the layer name. Before exploring the individual effects, we offer these generic instructions:

To apply layer effects (generic instructions):

1. Do any of the following:

   Double-click to the right of a layer name. (Or for an image layer—not a type, Smart Object, or shape layer—you could also double-click the layer thumbnail.)

   Click a layer, then choose an effect from the **Add Layer Style** menu *fx* at the bottom of the Layers palette.

Continued on the following page

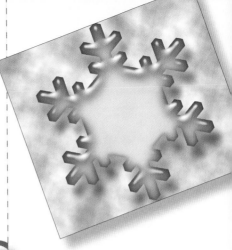

IN THIS CHAPTER

A The **Drop Shadow, Bevel and Emboss,** and **Gradient Overlay** effects, applied to editable type

The Layer Style dialog box opens. **A**

2. Click an effect name on the left side, then choose settings. Check Preview to preview the effect in the image.

3. *Optional:* Click other effect names to apply additional effects to the same layer.

4. Click OK.

5. Edit the **layer** and watch the "smart" effect update!

On the Layers palette, any layer that an effect is applied to has this icon: *fx* ★ Click the arrowhead next to the icon to expand/collapse the list of effects on that layer (**A**, next page).

To change the **settings** for an effect or to add more effects, double-click the layer or double-click the effect name nested under the layer name.

To **hide/show** one layer effect, expand the effects list for the layer in question, then click the visibility icon ☻ for the effect you want to hide.

To **hide all** the effects on a layer, click the visibility icon for the word "Effects."

➤ If you move layer pixels, any effects on that layer will tag right along with it.

➤ Alt-click/Option-click Reset to restore the settings that were in place (in all the panels) when you opened the Layer Style dialog box.

➤ Once you become familiar with the individual effects, read the helpful tips in the "Become a Layer Effects Pro" sidebar on page 311.

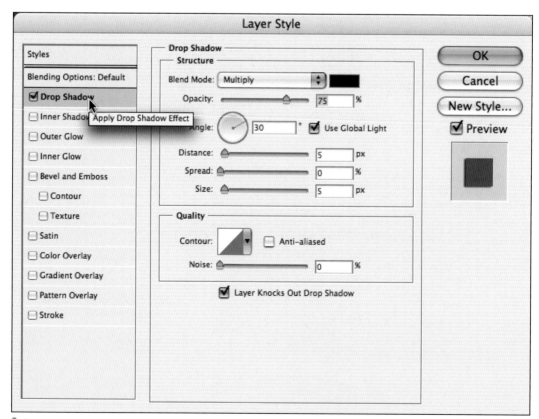

A In the **Layer Style** dialog box, click any layer effect name (the box will become checked automatically) to display settings for that effect.

What kind of imagery should you use?

➤ We recommend applying the layer effects that work inward or outward from edges—Drop Shadow, Inner Shadow, Outer Glow, Inner Glow, Bevel and Emboss, and Stroke—to a type layer, shape layer, or any layer imagery that's surrounded by transparent pixels. You can select an area of a layer, then use Layer Via Copy (Ctrl-J/Cmd-J) to isolate a subject from its background before applying a layer effect.

➤ You can apply the Satin, Color Overlay, Gradient Overlay, and Pattern Overlay effects either to fully opaque layers or to layers that contain transparency.

Note: Don't bother creating a selection before applying a layer effect; your selection will be ignored.

LAYER OPACITY AND FILL SETTINGS

A quick reminder from the previous chapter: the **Opacity** setting on the Layers palette controls the opacity of layer imagery, including any layer effects, whereas the **Fill** setting controls the opacity of just layer imagery—not layer effects.

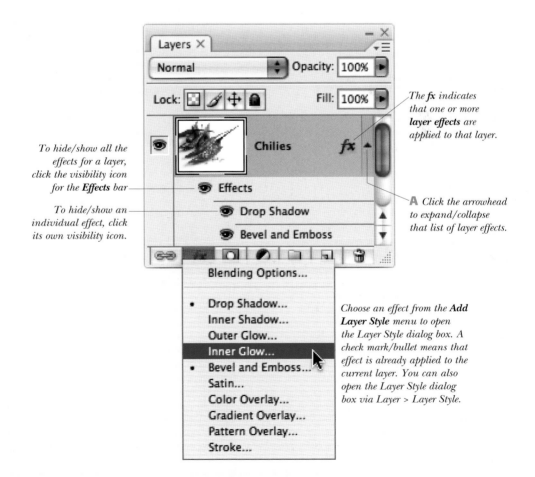

To hide/show all the effects for a layer, click the visibility icon for the Effects bar

To hide/show an individual effect, click its own visibility icon.

The fx indicates that one or more layer effects are applied to that layer.

A *Click the arrowhead to expand/collapse that list of layer effects.*

Choose an effect from the Add Layer Style menu to open the Layer Style dialog box. A check mark/bullet means that effect is already applied to the current layer. You can also open the Layer Style dialog box via Layer > Layer Style.

Layer effects in depth

You can create **drop shadows** and **inner shadows** with just a few clicks of the mouse.

To apply the Drop Shadow or Inner Shadow effect:

1. Double-click next to a layer name.**A** The Layer Style dialog box opens.

2. Click **Drop Shadow** or **Inner Shadow**.

3. Change any of the following settings:

   Choose a **Blend Mode** from the menu.

   To choose a different shadow **color**, click the color swatch, then choose a color from the Color Picker or click a color in the document window with the eyedropper (the new color will preview immediately). Click OK.

   Choose an **Opacity** percentage for the transparency level of the shadow.

   Choose an **Angle** for the angle of the shadow relative to the original layer shapes. Note: If you readjust the Angle for an individual effect while Use Global Light is checked, the angle for any other effects that utilize the Global Light option will update accordingly. This option unifies the lighting across multiple layer effects.

   Choose a **Distance** for the distance (in pixels) of a drop shadow from the original layer shapes **B** or for the width of an inner shadow.**C–D**

   ► You can also change the position of the shadow by dragging in the document window while the dialog box is open, but be aware that this will also move any other effects that utilize the Global Light option.

   Choose a **Spread** or **Choke** percentage to control the point at which the shadow starts to fade.

   Choose an overall **Size** for the shadow (in pixels).

   In the **Quality** area, click the arrowhead, then choose a preset **Contour** from the Contour Preset picker for the edge profile of the shadow. The profile can dramatically change the shape of a shadow.

   Check **Anti-aliased** to soften the jagged edges between the shadow and the layer imagery.

A *The original image consists of some garden tools on one layer and a background pattern on another layer (which we created via Filter > Render > Clouds).*

B *The **Drop Shadow** effect*

C *The original image consists of editable type on one layer and a blue-gray background pattern on another.*

D *The **Inner Shadow** effect*

Adjust the **Noise** level. Noise (speckling) can help prevent banding on print output; use a low value.

For a drop shadow, check **Layer Knocks Out Drop Shadow** to prevent the shadow from showing through the layer if the layer has a low Fill opacity.

4. Click OK. If you're not satisfied with the shape of the resulting shadow, try following the next set of instructions.

➤ When we apply the Drop Shadow effect, we usually raise the Distance, Spread, and Size values and lower the Opacity slightly from the default setting.

Depending on the time of day and the angle of the sun or other light source, cast shadows can be short or elongated. You can **reshape** a **drop shadow** via the Distort command.

To transform a Drop Shadow effect:

1. Apply the Drop Shadow effect as per the previous instructions,**A** and keep that layer selected.

2. Choose Layer > Layer Style > **Create Layer(s),** then click OK. This transfers the shadow effect to its own layer.

3. Click the new Drop Shadow layer.**B**

4. Choose Edit > Transform > **Distort**, drag the handles of the transform box to achieve the desired shape, then press Enter/Return.**C** (If you don't see all the handles, press Ctrl-0 (zero)/ Cmd-0 to enlarge the document window.) For a symmetrical distortion, hold down Ctrl-Alt-Shift/Cmd-Option-Shift as you drag a corner handle.

5. *Optional:* Change the luminosity of the shadow by choosing a different layer blending mode or opacity.

Turn on the Lock Transparent Pixels option (Layers palette) to limit any painting or fill changes to just the shadow shape.

➤ Select the shadow layer and the original image layer, then click the Link button at the bottom of the Layers palette; now you can move or transform them as a unit.

A *The original layer with a **Drop Shadow***

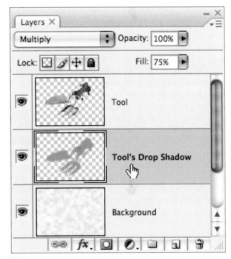

B *Click the new **Drop Shadow** layer.*

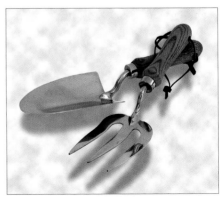

C *We **elongated** the **shadow** to make it more prominent.*

The **Outer Glow** and **Inner Glow** effects add a soft, airbrushed accent to the edges of layer imagery or type.

To apply the Outer or Inner Glow effect:

1. Display the **Swatches** palette.

2. Double-click a layer to open the Layer Style dialog box. **A**

3. Click **Outer Glow** or **Inner Glow**.

4. Choose **Structure** settings: **B**

   Choose a **Blend Mode**.

   Choose an **Opacity** level for the glow.

   Adjust the **Noise** level. Noise (speckling) helps to prevent banding on print output.

   To change the glow color, click the color square in the **Structure** area, choose a color from the Color Picker (or, while the picker is open, from the Swatches palette; or click a color in the image); then click OK. The new color will preview in the image.

   ➤ Choose a color that contrasts with the background color. It might be hard to see a light Outer Glow color against a light background.

5. Choose **Elements** settings:

   From the **Technique** menu, choose **Softer** for soft edges or **Precise** for slightly crisper edges.

   For an Inner Glow, click **Source: Center** to create a glow that spreads outward from the center of the layer pixels (this looks nice on type), or click **Edge** to create a glow that spreads inward from the inside edges of the layer imagery.

   Choose a **Spread** or **Choke** percentage to control at what point the glow starts to fade.

   Choose an overall **Size** for the glow.

6. Choose **Quality** settings:

   Click the arrowhead to choose a preset **Contour** from the Contour Preset picker to control how the glow transitions off the edge of the shape.

   Choose a **Range** to control how smoothly (high value) or abruptly (low value) the glow transitions from the contour of the shape.

7. Click OK. **C**

➤ To apply a layer effect to type, make the type large and don't apply negative tracking.

A *The original image contains a type layer and a background layer.*

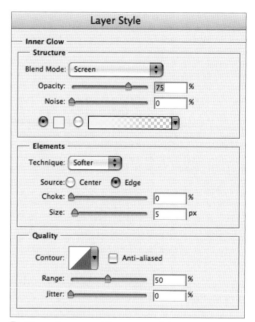

B *Choose Structure, Elements, and Quality settings for the **Inner Glow** effect in the **Layer Style** dialog box.*

C *The **Inner Glow** effect with Difference chosen as the Blend Mode, plus the **Outer Glow** effect*

BECOME A LAYER EFFECTS PRO

➤ When deciding which effect or effects to use, think about the **surface texture** you're trying to create. Stone? Metal? Paper? Embossed text that looks as if it's embedded into porous paper, or satin text that looks as if it's cast in metal? Choose an effect that will help you achieve the desired illusion.

➤ Except for Drop Shadow and Overlay, most layer effects tend look more pleasing or convincing when applied in **combination.A–D**

➤ If you achieve a layer effect or combination of effects and Layers palette settings that you like, save that collection of settings as a **style** on the Styles palette (see pages 319–320). This is a great timesaver!

➤ While the Layer Style dialog box is open, you can click **Blending Options** on the upper left side, then change any of those settings, such as the layer blending mode or Fill opacity (the same settings as on the Layers palette).

A *This is plain editable type (Bodoni Highlight font) above a background layer.*

B *The **Drop Shadow** effect*

C *The **Drop Shadow** and **Bevel and Emboss** effects — two effects are better than one.*

D *The **Drop Shadow, Bevel and Emboss,** and **Gradient Overlay** effects: Even better!*

The **Bevel and Emboss** effect creates an illusion of volume by adding a highlight and shading to layer shapes. The results can range from a chiseled bevel that looks factory-made to a pillowy emboss that looks as if it's been stamped onto porous paper. For variety, take advantage of the Contour options.

To apply the Bevel or Emboss effect:

1. Display the Swatches palette.

2. Double-click a layer **A** on the Layers palette to open the Layer Style dialog box.

3. Click **Bevel and Emboss**.

4. Choose **Structure** settings: **B**

   Choose a **Style: Outer Bevel,C Inner Bevel,D Emboss, Pillow Emboss,** or **Stroke Emboss** (**A–C**, next page).

   From the **Technique** menu, choose **Smooth, Chisel Hard,** or **Chisel Soft.**

   Choose a **Depth** for the amount the highlight and shading are offset from the layer shapes.

   Click the **Up** or **Down** button to swap the positions of the highlight and shading.

   Choose a **Size** for the depth of the bevel or emboss effect.

   Raise the **Soften** value to blur the effect.

5. Choose **Shading** settings:

   Choose an **Angle** and an **Altitude** to change the location of the light source. These settings will in turn affect the highlight and shading. Check **Use Global Light** to use the same Angle and Altitude settings for all effects that utilize the Global Light option; uncheck to use a unique setting for an individual effect. Note: If you change the Angle or Altitude for an individual effect while Use Global Light is checked, any other effects that utilize the Global Light option will update, too.

   Click the **Gloss Contour** arrowhead, then choose a profile from the Contour Preset picker.

   Choose a **Highlight Mode** and **Opacity** and a **Shadow Mode** and **Opacity** for the highlight and shading.

   To change the highlight or shading **color,** click either color swatch, then choose a color from the Color Picker (or, while the picker is open, choose from the Swatches palette or click a color in the document window). The color will preview on the image. Click OK.

A *The original image consists of two layers.*

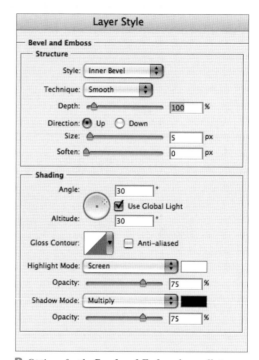

B *Options for the **Bevel and Emboss** layer effect*

C *The **Outer Bevel** effect (plus a Drop Shadow)*

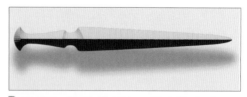

D *The **Inner Bevel** effect (plus a Drop Shadow)*

6. To add a **Contour** to the edges of the bevel or emboss, click Contour on the left side of the dialog box, below Bevel and Emboss. Click the Contour arrowhead, then click a preset contour in the picker. This can dramatically change the appearance of the effect.

Check **Anti-aliased** to soften the hard edges between adjoining areas.

For the Outer Bevel and Inner Bevel Style options, adjust the **Range** (position of the bevel on the chosen contour) to minimize or maximize the prominence of the bevel.

7. To add a texture to a bevel or emboss, click **Texture** on the left side of the dialog box, click the Texture arrowhead, choose a pattern from the picker, then do any of the following: **D**

Adjust the **Scale** of the pattern.

Change the **Depth** to adjust the contrast between the shadows and highlights in the pattern.

Check **Invert** to swap the highlight and shading. This has the same effect as changing the Depth percentage from negative to positive, and vice versa.

Check **Link with Layer** to ensure that the texture and the layer move as a unit.

Drag in the document window to reposition the texture within the effect. Click **Snap to Origin** to realign the pattern to the upper left corner of the image.

If you've changed settings for the current pattern, click the **New Preset** button to add it as a new preset.

8. Click OK.

A *The original editable type*

B *Emboss (Chisel Soft)*

C *Pillow Emboss (Smooth), plus a Drop Shadow*

D *Pillow Emboss, with a **Texture**, plus a Drop Shadow*

Use the **Satin** layer effect to apply light and dark shades to the surfaces of objects or type to make them look reflective or metallic.

To apply the Satin effect :

1. Double-click a layer **A** on the Layers palette to open the Layer Style dialog box. The default Blend Mode for this effect, Multiply, deepens some tonal values and heightens contrast, so it's a good idea to start with imagery that has a good range of tonal values.

2. Click **Satin.**

3. Do any of the following.**B**

   Change the **Blend Mode.**

   To change the overlay **color,** click the color swatch, then choose a color from the Color Picker or click a color in the document.

   Adjust the **Opacity** of the effect.

   Change the **Angle** of the effect. This angle is independent of the Global Light settings.

   Set the **Distance** and the **Size** of the effect. You can also drag in the document window to adjust the distance.

   Click the **Contour** arrowhead, then choose from the Contour Preset picker for the edge profile of the effect.

   Check **Anti-aliased** to soften the hard boundary between the effect and the underlying shape.

   Check **Invert** to swap the shadows and highlights in the effect.

4. Click OK.**C**

A *The original image contains editable type with the Bevel and Emboss effect applied.*

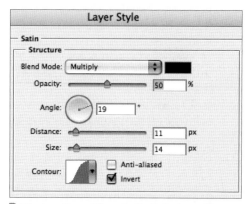

B *We chose these options for the Satin layer effect.*

C *The Bevel and Emboss and Satin layer effects combined: The Satin effect makes the surface of the letters look more reflective.*

The three overlay effects, **Color Overlay**, **Gradient Overlay**, and **Pattern Overlay**, can be applied to full image layers, layers that contain transparency, shape layers, type layers, and selections.

To apply the Color Overlay effect :

1. Double-click a layer **A** on the Layers palette to open the Layer Style dialog box, or create a selection.

2. Click **Color Overlay.**

3. Do any of the following:

   Choose a **Blend Mode.**

   Click the **color** swatch, then choose a different color for the overlay.

   Adjust the **Opacity** of the overlay.

4. Click OK.**B**

To apply the Gradient Overlay effect:

1. Double-click a layer on the Layers palette to open the Layer Style dialog box.

2. Click **Gradient Overlay.C**

3. Do any of the following:

   Choose a **Blend Mode.**

   Adjust the **Opacity** of the overlay.

   Click the **Gradient** arrowhead, then choose a preset gradient from the Gradient Preset picker.

   Choose a **Style: Linear, Radial, Angle, Reflected,** or **Diamond.**

   Check **Reverse** to change the direction of the gradient.

   Check **Align with Layer** to align the gradient with visible pixels in the layer, or uncheck to align the gradient with the full canvas.

   Set the **Angle** of the gradient.

   Choose a **Scale** percentage for the placement of the midpoint of the gradient.

   Drag in the document window to **reposition** the gradient.

4. Click OK.**D** Read more about creating and editing gradients in Chapter 23.

A *The original image, with the Bevel and Emboss effect applied*

B *The **Color Overlay** effect applied*

C *We chose these options for the **Gradient Overlay** layer effect.*

D *After applying the **Gradient Overlay** effect to the original image (shown in **A**)*

The patterns you apply via the **Pattern Overlay** effect can range from ones with an obvious repeat, such as polka dots or stripes, to ones with an overall texture, resembling surfaces such as gritty sandpaper, woven fabric, or variegated stone.

To apply the Pattern Overlay effect:

1. Double-click a layer on the Layers palette to open the Layer Style dialog box.

2. Click **Pattern Overlay**.

3. Do any of the following:**B**

   Choose a **Blend Mode.**

   Adjust the **Opacity** of the overlay.

   Click the **Pattern** arrowhead, then choose a pattern preset in the picker. To load patterns from another library, choose from the picker menu.

   Click **Snap to Origin** to align the pattern with the upper left corner of the document. You can also drag in the document window to reposition the pattern.

   Choose a **Scale** percentage for the size of the pattern.

   Check **Link with Layer** to link the pattern to the layer so they'll move as a unit.

   If you've changed settings for the current pattern, click the **New Preset** button to add it as a new preset.

4. Click OK.**C**

   ➤ If you applied the Pattern Overlay effect but don't see it in the document, check to see if another effect is covering it, such as a Color Overlay.

A *The original type contains the Bevel and Emboss and Satin layer effects.*

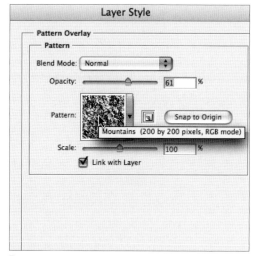

B *Choose options for the **Pattern Overlay** layer effect. We chose the Mountains pattern, which is in the Texture Fill library.*

C *With the **Pattern Overlay** layer effect added to the mix, now the type looks like polished granite.*

If you're partial to neon, you can achieve this illusion by using the **Stroke** effect.

To apply a Stroke effect:

1. Double-click a layer on the Layers palette to open the Layer Style dialog box.

2. Click **Stroke**.

3. Do any of the following:**A**

   Choose a **Size** (width) for the stroke.

   From the **Position** menu, choose whether you want the stroke to be on the **Outside**, **Inside**, or **Center** of the layer shapes.

   Choose a **Blend Mode.**

   Choose an **Opacity** percentage.

   Choose **Fill Type: Color, Gradient,** or **Pattern,** and choose options using the controls that become available. See the Color Overlay and Gradient Overlay information on page 315, or the Pattern Overlay information on the previous page.

4. Click OK.**B–C**

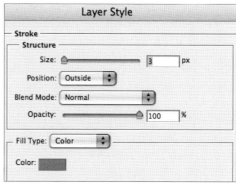

A *Options for the **Stroke** layer effect*

B *The Bevel and Emboss, Gradient Overlay, and **Stroke** effects are combined here. To achieve this result, apply the **Neutral Bevel** style in the Text Effects 2 style library (see page 319).*

PICK FROM THE PICKER

The thumbnails in the Contour Preset picker represent an assortment of **profiles.D** The gray areas in a profile represent opaque pixels; the white areas represent transparency. To close the picker, double-click a contour; or click the Contour arrowhead; or click somewhere outside the picker in the Layer Style dialog box.

C *The Bevel and Emboss, Gradient Overlay, and **Stroke** effects are used here too, with different presets, colors, and settings. (To achieve this look, apply the **Liquid Rainbow** style in the Text Effects style library.)*

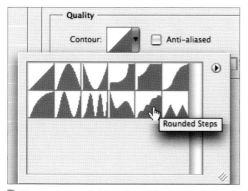

D *You can use tool tips to learn the names of the contours in the **Contour Preset** picker.*

Copying, moving, and removing layer effects

If you like how an effect looks on one layer, you can **copy it to another layer.**

To copy effects between layers:

Alt-drag/Option-drag any individual effect name from one layer to another.

You can also **move individual effects** (take them out of) one layer and move them to another layer without deleting any effects on the target layer.

To move an effect from one layer to another without replacing existing effects:

Drag any individual effect **name** from one layer to another.

And finally, you can also **move all the effects** from one layer to another, replacing any existing effects on the target layer and removing them from the source layer.

To move all the effects from one layer to another, replacing existing effects:

Drag the **Effects bar** from one layer to another.

Clicking (removing) the visibility icon for a layer effect or unchecking the box for an effect in the Layer Style dialog box doesn't remove the effect—it merely hides it from view. If you want to permanently **delete effects from a layer,** follow these instructions.

To remove layer effects:

Do either of the following:

Drag an individual effect **name** over the **Delete Layer** button at the bottom of the Layers palette.

To remove all effects from a layer, drag the **Effects bar** over the Delete Layer button.

➤ If you turn off an effect via the check box in the Layer Style dialog box and then turn it back on again the same way, or reapply an effect that was dragged individually to the Delete Layer button, the last-used options for that effect will redisplay.

Applying styles

You can conveniently store a collection of layer settings—such as layer effects, opacity, blending mode, fill opacity—collectively as a style on the **Styles** palette. Once stored, styles can be applied to any layer with a mere click of the mouse. To get acquainted with the Styles palette, apply one of the predefined styles.

To apply a style to a layer:

1. Show the **Styles** palette. You can choose a display mode for the palette from the palette menu: Text Only, Small Thumbnail (the default mode), Large Thumbnail Small List, Small List, or Large List.

2. Do one of the following:

   Click a layer (not the Background) on the **Layers** palette, then click a style on the **Styles** palette.**A-B**

   Drag a style name or thumbnail from the **Styles** palette over any selected or unselected layer on the **Layers** palette.

   Double-click a layer to open the Layer Style dialog box, click **Styles** at the top, click a style thumbnail, then click OK (**A**, next page).

➤ Normally, when you apply a style, it replaces any existing effects on the current layer. To add a style's effects to existing ones, Shift-click or Shift-drag the style. With Shift down or not, if two effects have the same name, effects in the new style replace existing effects in the layer.

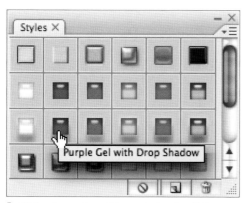

A *Click a* **layer,** *then click a style thumbnail (or name) on the* **Styles** *palette.*

B *These are a few of the* **styles** *that ship with Photoshop. Feel free to edit the effects from any predefined style—or create and save your own styles, as per the instructions on the following page.*

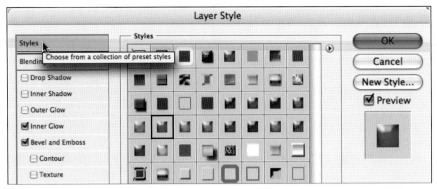

A *Styles can also be applied to a layer via our old friend the **Layer Style** dialog box. Click **Styles** at the top left side of the dialog box, then click a style thumbnail.*

When you **create a layer style**, you can decide whether the style will include the layer effects and/or Blending Options settings (such as layer opacity, blending mode, and fill opacity) that are currently applied to the selected layer.

To save a style to the Styles palette:

1. Do either of the following:

   On the **Layers** palette, click a layer,**B** then on the Styles palette, click the blank area **C** or click the **New Style** button.⊒

   On the **Layers** palette, double-click a layer to open the Layer Style dialog box, then click the **New Style** button.

2. Enter a **Name** for the new style, check whether you want to **Include Layer Effects** and/or **Include Layer Blending Options** in the style, then click OK. If the Layer Style dialog box is open, click OK. Your new style will appear as the last listing/thumbnail on the Styles palette.

➤ You can load other style libraries from the bottom of the Styles palette menu. To create a style library, see pages 394–397. The styles that are included with Photoshop are in Adobe Photoshop CS3/Presets/Styles.

➤ To remove a style from a layer (including reverting the blending mode and opacity to the default settings), right-click/Control-click a layer and choose Clear Layer Style.

➤ To copy a style from one layer to another, right-click/Control-click the layer that contains the style you want to copy and choose Copy Layer Style. Next, click another layer, then right-click/Control-click and choose Paste Layer Style.

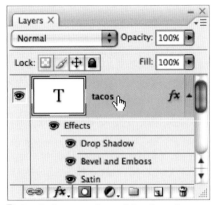

B *On the **Layers** palette, click a layer that contains the effects and/or other settings that you want to save as a style...*

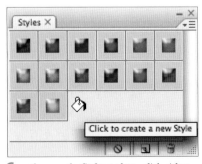

C *...then on the **Styles** palette, click either the blank area or the **New Style** button.*

You've probably already used a filter or two in an earlier chapter. In this chapter they're star players. Depending on which filters you apply and which settings you choose for them, the results can range from barely noticeable to total morph.**A** You can make an image look hand painted, silkscreened, or sketched; apply distortion or noise; create patterns or textures; make an image look like a mosaic or like it's being viewed through mottled glass—the creative possibilities are infinite. Once you start using the Filter Gallery, you'll see—time will fly by.

Using this chapter, you can learn techniques for applying filters, learn how to create and use Smart Filters, peruse an illustrated compendium of all the filters, combine filters to make a photo look hand drawn or painted (a quick exercise just to get you started), and create custom patterns.

FILTERS

21

Applying filters

You can apply filters to a whole layer or just to a selection on a layer. Most of the filters are applied either through the Filter Gallery or through an individual dialog box; a small handful of filters, such as Clouds and Blur, are applied in one step simply by choosing the filter name from the menu. If you apply a filter to a Smart Object layer, it becomes an editable, removable Smart Filter.

If you try applying a filter and find that it's not available, the cause is most likely the document color mode and/or bit depth. All the filters are available for RGB files; most filters are available for Grayscale and Lab Color files; even fewer are available for CMYK Color and 16 bits/channel files; still fewer are available for 32 bits/channel files; and none are available for Bitmap and Indexed Color files.

A *One tiger, three ways: The original image, the **Charcoal** filter applied, and the **Diffuse Glow** filter applied*

The **Filter Gallery** dialog box (**A**, next page) houses most of the Photoshop filters under one roof. Here you can preview dozens of filters and filter settings, show and hide each filter effect that you've previewed, and change the sequence in which you apply them.

To use the Filter Gallery:

1. Click an image layer or a Smart Object layer.

2. Choose Filter > **Filter Gallery.**

3. To change the zoom level for the preview, click the **Zoom Out** button ⊟ or **Zoom In** button ⊞ in the lower left corner of the dialog box or choose a zoom level from the menu. You can drag a magnified preview in the window or move it via the scroll bar(s) or arrows.

4. Do either of the following:

   In the middle pane of the dialog box, click an arrowhead to expand any of the six filter categories, then click a filter **thumbnail.**

   Once you've clicked one filter, you can then choose any other filter name from the **menu** below the Cancel button.

5. Choose settings for the filter on the right side. The filter you've chosen will be listed in the scroll list in the lower right.

6. Do any of the following optional steps:

   To apply an additional filter effect, click the **New Effect Layer** button, 🔳 click another filter thumbnail in any category, then choose settings.

   To **replace** one filter effect with another, select that filter effect name in the scroll list (don't click the New Effect Layer button),

then click a new thumbnail and choose settings. The most recently applied effect is listed first.

To **hide** a filter effect, select the effect name in the scroll list, then click the visibility icon 👁 (click again to redisplay the effect).

To change the **stacking order** of a filter effect to produce a different result in the image, drag the effect name upward or downward on the list.

To **remove** a filter effect from the list, select it, then click the Delete Effect Layer button. 🗑

7. When you're satisfied with the filter(s) and settings you've chosen, click OK.

➤ Alt-click/Option-click the visiblity icon to hide/show all the previews except the one you click on.

➤ If you choose an individual filter from the Filter menu that also happens to be in the Filter Gallery, the Filter Gallery opens automatically.

➤ If you get tired of using the same Photoshop filters, you can explore filter plug-ins from third-party suppliers.

REAPPLYING FILTERS

➤ To reapply the last-used filter using the same settings, choose Filter > **[last filter name]** (Ctrl-F/Cmd-F) .

➤ To reopen either the last-used filter dialog box or the Filter Gallery with the settings for the last-used filter displayed, press **Ctrl-Alt-F/ Cmd-Option-F.**

Click this button to hide the thumbnail pane and expand the preview window; click it again to redisplay the thumbnail pane.

*Once you've clicked one filter thumbnail, you can choose **other filters** from this menu.*

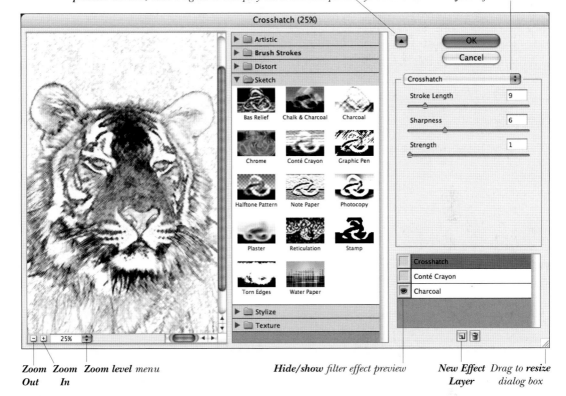

Zoom Out **Zoom In** **Zoom level** *menu*

Hide/show *filter effect preview*

New Effect Layer Drag to **resize** *dialog box*

A *The **Filter Gallery** dialog box has three sections: a preview on the left; filter categories with thumbnails in the middle; and on the right, filter settings and a list of the filter effects you've previewed so far.*

Preview window

Zoom Out and Zoom In buttons

B *Some filters are applied via a separate dialog box. Of those, some have a preview window and some don't.*

Using individual filter dialog boxes

➤ Some individual filter dialog boxes have a **preview** window.**B**

➤ Check **Preview** to preview the effect in both the dialog box and the document window.

➤ Click the + button to **zoom** in on the preview or click the – button to zoom out. We usually find we need to zoom out to gauge the effect. A line will blink on and off below the preview percentage while the preview is rendering. You can drag the image inside the preview window.

➤ In some filter dialog boxes, you can click with the square pointer in the document window and that area of the image will appear in the preview window.

Creating and using Smart Filters ★

Simply put, a Smart Filter is a filter that you apply to a Smart Object. Create the Smart Object layer first, then apply the filter to it and presto!—it's a Smart Filter. As with layer effects, you can edit or remove Smart Filters at any time, apply multiple filter effects to the same Smart Object layer, hide individual filter effects while keeping others visible, and move or copy filter effects from one Smart Object layer to another. In addition, you can edit the filter mask (which appears automatically), change the stacking order of the whole Smart Object layer, or drag and drop the layer to another file.

The file formats that support Photoshop layers —including PSD, PDF, and TIFF—also support Smart Filters. You can also apply updated third-party filters as Smart Filters.

To create a Smart Filter:

1. Click a Smart Object layer (see pages 302–304). *Optional:* Create a selection to restrict the filter effect. The selection shape will appear in the filter mask.

2. Apply a filter. The filter effects list will expand automatically to reveal the new filter name, and the Smart Filters listing will have a mask.**A**

➤ If you transform a Smart Object layer, any Smart Filters on that layer will be hidden temporarily until the transformation is completed.

The greatest advantage to using Smart Filters is that you can **edit** the **filter settings** at any time.

To edit the settings for a Smart Filter:

1. Do either of the following:

   Double-click next to the filter name on the Layers palette.

   Right-click/Control-click the filter name and choose **Edit Smart Filter** from the context menu.

2. If any Smart Filters are listed above the one you're editing, an alert will appear,**B** indicating that the filter effects will be hidden until you exit the Filter Gallery or individual filter dialog box. Click Don't Show Again to prevent the warning from appearing again, and click OK.

3. Make the desired changes in the filter dialog box, then click OK.

➤ To reapply a filter that is normally applied in one pass without a dialog box (such as Clouds), simply double-click the filter name.

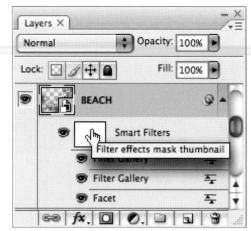

A *When you apply a filter to a Smart Object layer, the layer gains a **Smart Filters** listing and **filter mask**, with individual filters listed below. If you apply a filter by choosing Filter > Filter Gallery, the filter listing will be a generic Filter Gallery; if you choose an individual filter name, that filter name will be listed.*

B *This alert dialog box will appear if you try to **edit** a filter and there are other filters listed **above** it on the same Smart Object layer. Click OK.*

DISAPPEARING FILTER EFFECTS

When changing the document color mode or bit depth, if the document contains filters that aren't supported by the new color mode or depth, an alert dialog box will appear. If you click **Don't Rasterize** and then click **Don't Flatten,** this symbol ⬚ will display next to the filter names, indicating that the filter effect is currently inaccessible. If you convert the file to a mode or depth that does support the filter, the icon will disappear and the filter effect will become visible again. Note: The Extract, Liquify, Pattern Maker, and Vanishing Point filters can't be applied as Smart Filters, regardless of the document color mode or bit depth.

Each filter effect can have its own **blending mode** and **opacity**, separate from the blending options for the Smart Object layer. It's a lot to keep track of!

To apply blending options to a Smart Filter:

1. Right-click/Control-click a Smart Filter name and choose **Edit Smart Filter Blending Options** from the context menu. The Blending Options dialog box opens.**A**

2. Choose a blending **Mode** and **Opacity** (use the latter to fade the filter effect), then click OK. You can change these settings at any time.

To hide/show Smart Filter effects:

Do either of the following:

Click the **visibility** icon for the **Smart Filters** listing to hide all the Smart Filters on that layer.

Click the **visibility** icon for any individual Smart **Filter.** This may take longer to process than clicking the visibility icon for all the filters.

➤ You can restack any filter effect within the same Smart Object layer or move (drag) a Smart Filter or a whole stack of Smart Filters from one Smart Object layer to another (be patient while Photoshop processes the change).

To copy a filter effect from one Smart Object layer to another:

Expand the list of filter effects for the layer, then **Alt-drag/Option-drag** a filter effect into another Smart Object layer.

When you **delete a Smart Filter**, if there are any other filters on that layer, it may take a moment for Photoshop to update the display.

To delete a Smart Filter:

Do either of the following:

Right-click/Control-click a Smart Filter and choose **Delete Smart Filter.**

Drag the filter to the **Delete Layer** button.🗑

A Smart Object layer can have both a layer mask, which shows/hides pixels, and a **filter mask**, which shows/hides the filter effect.

To create a filter mask:

When you apply the first filter to a Smart Object layer, a filter mask appears automatically next to the Smart Filters listing. If you create a selection first, that selection shape will appear in the

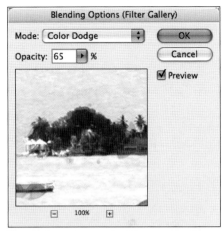

A *Each filter effect can have its own **Blending Options** (blending Mode and Opacity). If you think this can get confusing, you're right! And unfortunately, no indicator appears on the Layers palette to show when blending has been altered.*

USING THE FILTER MASK

You can do the same things to a **filter mask** as you can to a layer mask, including:

➤ Delete a filter mask by dragging it to the **Delete Layer** button.

➤ Click the filter mask thumbnail, then **paint** with black to hide the filter effect, with white to reveal hidden areas, or with a lower tool opacity (using black) to partially hide areas.

➤ **Alt-click/Option-click** the filter mask to display just the filter mask in the document window; repeat to redisplay the Smart Object layer.

➤ **Shift-click** the filter mask thumbnail to temporarily disable the mask (a red X will appear over the mask thumbnail); repeat to reenable it.

➤ As with standard layer masks, a filter mask appears as a listing on the **Channels** palette and can be loaded as a selection.

➤ A Smart Object layer can have both a **layer** mask and a **filter mask.**

---

mask. To create a filter mask if there is none (you deleted it), create a selection if desired, then right-click/Control-click the Smart Filters listing and choose **Add Filter Mask.**

Filter pro techniques

➤ Before applying a filter, create a **selection** on a layer; the filter will affect only pixels within the selection. If you create a selection before applying a Smart Filter, the selection shape will appear in the filter mask. For a soft transition between the filtered and nonfiltered areas, use **Refine Edge** to **feather** the selection before applying the filter.

➤ For greater flexibility, duplicate an image layer and apply filters to the duplicate—or even better, apply them as **Smart Filters** to a Smart Object layer. **A–B** You can edit, remove, mask, or change the opacity or blending mode of each Smart Filter effect individually at any time (see also the first task on the previous page). **C**

(The Edit > Fade command also lets you change the opacity or blending mode for the last edit, such as a filter, but it takes more steps, must be applied right after applying the filter, and doesn't apply to Smart Object layers.)

➤ All the Sketch filters except Chrome and Water Paper reduce the colors in a layer to just white and the current **Foreground color**, so remember to choose a Foreground color before opening the Filter Gallery.

➤ To make your filter results look less machine-made, uniform, or predictable, apply them in combination. This way, no single filter effect will stand out.

➤ To intensify the results of a filter, before applying it, pump up the brightness and contrast of the image via a **Levels** adjustment layer. Move the black Input Levels slider slightly to the right and the white Input Levels slider slightly to the left.

➤ If you apply a filter to a Smart Object layer, you can click the **filter mask**, then with the Brush tool, paint with black to mask the filter effect (lower the tool opacity for a partial mask) or with white to reveal the filter effect (**A–B**, next page). If you apply a filter to a duplicate layer, you can add and edit a layer mask the same way. The transition between the white and black areas on the mask can be soft, hard, or painterly, depending on your brush tip and settings.

A *The original image*

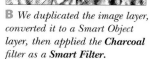

B *We duplicated the image layer, converted it to a Smart Object layer, then applied the **Charcoal** filter as a **Smart Filter**.*

C *We lowered the **opacity** of the **Smart Object** layer.*

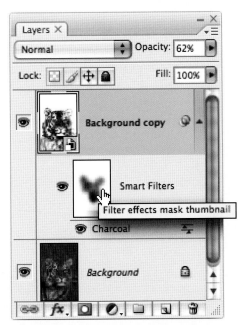

A *This is the **Layers** palette for figure **C** on the previous page. The Smart Objects layer has an **Opacity** of 62%. (We also could have lowered the Smart Filter layer opacity individually via Blending Options.)*

B *We clicked the filter mask, then used the **Brush** tool at 50% Opacity (Foreground color black) to partially restore the tiger's face to its original state.*

FILTERS IN OTHER CHAPTERS

To see if a specific filter is discussed in another chapter, look in the index for the filter name.

➤ If you get carried away and apply too many Smart Filters, you can simply drag them individually to the **trash.** To remove a non-Smart Filter, revert to an earlier document state or snapshot via the **History** palette. You can also save a successful combination of filter layers and opacities as a layer comp, which you can then revert back to if needed.

➤ If you've applied a filter to an image layer, you can selectively reduce its effect "by hand" with the **History Brush** tool. On the History palette, set the History Brush icon to a prefilter state, choose an opacity for the tool from the Options bar, then draw strokes on the image.

Continued on the following page

➤ To fade a filter effect gradually across the whole image, apply the **Black, White** gradient (linear or radial) to the filter mask on a Smart Object layer. The filter will apply fully to the image where the mask is white and fade to nil in areas where the mask is black.**A–C**

A We applied the **Charcoal filter** to a Smart Object layer (see **A** on page 326).

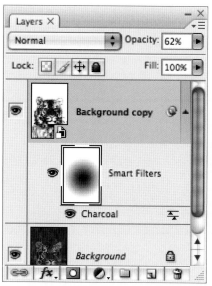

B We applied the Black, White **gradient** (radial type) to the **filter mask.**

C The gradient in the **filter mask** is diminishing the impact of the filter in the center of the image, thereby focusing our attention where we want it.

Illustrated directory of filters
Artistic filters

Original image

Colored Pencil

Cutout

Dry Brush

Film Grain

Fresco

Neon Glow (*choose a Foreground color first; choose a glow color in the Filter Gallery*)

Paint Daubs

Palette Knife

Artistic filters (continued)

Original image

Plastic Wrap

Poster Edges

Rough Pastels

Smudge Stick

Sponge

Underpainting

Watercolor

Blur filters

Blur, Blur More

Box Blur*

Gaussian Blur*

Lens Blur*

Motion Blur**

Radial Blur**

Shape Blur**

Smart Blur

Surface Blur

*Before applying this filter, we selected the water and background umbrellas.
**Before applying this filter, we selected the largest umbrellas, then chose Select > Inverse.

Brush Strokes filters

Original image

Accented Edges

Angled Strokes

Crosshatch

Dark Strokes

Ink Outlines

Spatter

Sprayed Strokes

Sumi-e

Distort filters

Diffuse Glow *(choose a Background color first)*

Displace

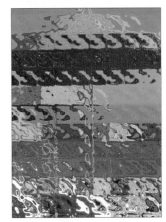

Glass

Lens Correction

Ocean Ripple

Pinch

Polar Coordinates

Ripple

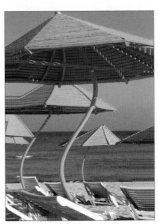

Shear

Distort filters (continued)

Original image

Spherize

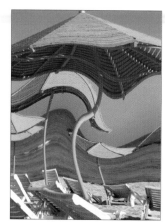

Twirl

Wave

Zigzag

Noise filters

Add Noise

Median

*(Not illustrated: Noise >
Despeckle, Dust & Scratches,
and Reduce Noise)*

Pixelate filters

Color Halftone

Crystallize

Facet

Fragment

Mezzotint

Mosaic

Pointillize *(choose a Background color first)*

Render filters

Original image

*Clouds**

*Difference Clouds**

*Fibers**

Lens Flare

*Choose Foreground and Background colors first.

Sharpen filters

Sharpen Edges

Smart Sharpen (see pages 264–266)

*For the **Unsharp Mask** filter, see pages 267–268.*

Sketch filters

Bas Relief*

Chalk & Charcoal*

Charcoal*

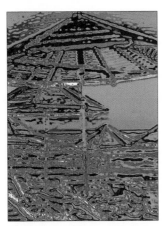

Chrome

Conté Crayon*

Graphic Pen*

Halftone Pattern*

Note Paper*

Photocopy*

*Choose Foreground and Background colors first.

Sketch filters (continued)

Original image

Plaster*

Reticulation

Stamp*

Torn Edges*

Water Paper

*Choose Foreground and Background colors first.

Stylize filters

Diffuse

Emboss

Extrude

Find Edges

Glowing Edges

Solarize

Tiles (choose a Foreground and/or Background color first)

Trace Contour

Wind

Texture filters

Original image

Craquelure

Grain (Soft)

Grain (Speckle)

Grain (Vertical)

Mosaic Tiles

Patchwork

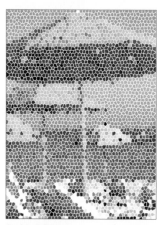

Stained Glass

Texturizer

Photos into drawings or paintings

In the instructions on this page and the next, you'll turn an image into a **drawing** or **watercolor**—in one case by reducing an image to lines and then painting on the filter mask, and in the other case by applying a series of filters. Hopefully, this exercise will inspire you to develop your own formulas.

To turn a photograph into a tinted drawing:

1. Duplicate an image layer, right-click/Control-click the duplicate and choose Convert to Smart Object, and keep the new Smart Object layer selected.**A**

2. Choose Filter > Stylize > **Find Edges.B**

3. Click the filter mask thumbnail on the Layers palette.

4. Choose the **Brush** tool, choose a large, soft brush tip, Normal mode, and an Opacity below 100% on the Options bar, press X to make the Foreground color black, then draw strokes on the image to reveal parts of the underlying layer.**C–D**

5. *Optional:* Lower the opacity of the Smart Object layer.

A *We converted an image layer into a **Smart Object** layer.*

B *We applied the **Find Edges** filter to the Smart Object layer.*

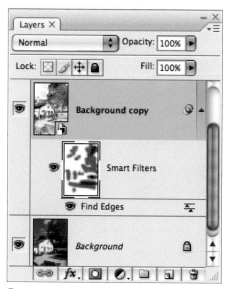

C *The **Layers** palette for the image shown at right*

D *We applied brush strokes to the **filter mask** to reveal some of the underlying image.*

There are so many ways to combine filters. In these instructions, you'll turn an image into a **watercolor** by applying the Median and Minimum filters. A medium- to light-toned image will work best for this exercise.

To create a watercolor:

1. Duplicate an image layer, right-click/Control-click the duplicate and choose Convert to Smart Object, and keep the new layer selected.**A**

2. Choose Filter > Noise > **Median.** The Median dialog box opens. Move the Radius slider to between 2 and 8, then click OK.

3. Choose Filter > Other > **Minimum.** The Minimum dialog box opens. Move the Radius slider to between 2 and 5, then click OK.

4. *Optional:* Choose Filter > Sharpen > Smart Sharpen, click Basic, try an Amount of 80–100%, adjust the Radius, then click OK.**B** Compare with the Photoshop Watercolor filter.**C**

A *The original image*

B *This **watercolor was** created by following the instructions above.*

C *The Photoshop **Watercolor** filter*

Applying the Pattern Maker filter

The **Pattern Maker** filter generates an endless assortment of randomized patterns from an area on the current layer or from imagery on the Clipboard. Instead of simply tiling the imagery as is, Photoshop jumbles the pixels to achieve more variations.**A**

You can use this filter to fill a layer with a pattern as a one-shot deal, or you can save your favorite pattern tiles as a preset to use with any tool or command that uses pattern presets, such as the Pattern Overlay effect in Layer Style, the Healing Brush or Pattern Stamp tool, or the Fill command.

Note: The Pattern Maker filter can be used only on 8-bit images in RGB Color, CMYK Color, Lab Color, and Grayscale modes.

To generate a pattern:

1. Duplicate a layer (not a Smart Object layer) to use for the pattern (Ctrl-J/Cmd-J) and keep the duplicate layer selected. The pattern you create will fill this layer.

2. Choose Filter > **Pattern Maker** (Ctrl-Alt-Shift-X/Cmd-Option-Shift-X). The Pattern Maker dialog box opens.

3. To generate a pattern in the current layer, choose the **Rectangular Marquee** tool 🔲 in the dialog box, then marquee an area to become a tile (you can marquee the whole image).

4. To specify the dimensions of the tile, do either of the following:

   Click **Use Image Size** to have the tile size match the current document dimensions.

   Choose specific **Width** and **Height** values.

5. From the **Offset** menu, choose whether you want the tiles to be offset (shifted) from one another (None, Horizontal, or Vertical). For either of the latter two options, choose an offset **Amount** (0–99%); the tiles will be offset from one another by that percentage of the tile dimension in the chosen direction.

6. Click **Generate** (Ctrl-G/Cmd-G). The tiled pattern will display in the preview area.

   ► A progress bar may appear while a tile is processing. You can press Esc to cancel it.

7. Click **Generate Again** to generate more pattern variations using the same options; change

Continued on the following page

ORIGINAL IMAGERY   PATTERNS

A *The **Pattern Maker** filter produces an infinite number of variations from any type of imagery.*

any of the options, such as the Width and/or Height, then click Generate Again.

➤ To use a different part of the image for the pattern, choose Show: Original in the Preview area, redraw the marquee, then click Generate Again.

8. In the **Tile History** area, do either of the following to navigate through the patterns that have been generated:

Click the **First Tile, Previous Tile, Next Tile,** or **Last Tile** button.**A**

Highlight the current tile number, type the **number** of the tile you want to view, then press Enter/Return.

9. Next, you'll delete any tiles that you don't want and save any of the tiles that you may want to use later. To delete a pattern tile, use the navigation buttons to locate the tile you want to delete, then click the **Delete Tile from History** button. When you delete a tile from the Tile History, its preview is discarded, too; this can't be undone.

10. To save a tile, navigate to the tile you want to save, click the **Save Preset Pattern** button, type a Name for the preset, then click OK.

Once a tile has been saved as a preset pattern, it becomes a swatch on the Pattern Preset picker and is available for any command or tool that uses that picker. Only the single tile will be saved, not the tiled pattern. To create and manage preset libraries, use the Preset Manager (see pages 394–395).

11. Click OK to exit the Pattern Maker dialog box.

➤ If transparent pixels are locked for the current layer, the pattern will replace only nontransparent pixels on that layer.

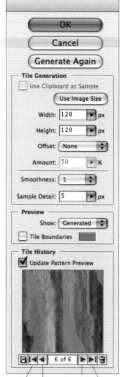

First   Previous Next Last
Tile   Tile   Tile   Tile

A *Use the* **Tile History** *buttons to* **view** *the tile variations the* **Pattern Maker** *filter has generated.*

PREVIEW OPTIONS IN THE PATTERN MAKER

➤ To magnify the preview, choose the **Zoom** tool (Z), then click the preview image; Alt-click/Option-click to zoom out. The current zoom level is listed in the lower left corner of the dialog box.

➤ You can drag the pattern in the preview window with the **Hand** tool (H) (or with the Spacebar held down if another tool is chosen in the dialog box).

➤ To see where the nonprinting tile boundaries are, check **Preview: Tile Boundaries.** To choose a different color for the boundaries (to contrast better with the imagery), click the color swatch, then choose a color from the Color Picker.

➤ To switch between the original image and the current pattern, choose **Show: Original** or **Generated.**

We've never heard the phrase "A word is worth a thousand pictures," but in Photoshop, where you can do such artful things with type, the line between pictures and words is blurred (sometimes literally!). In this chapter, you'll learn how to create and select editable type and apply a host of character and paragraph attributes. You'll also learn some fancy tricks, such as how to transform, warp, fade, and screen back type, and how to fill type with imagery.

Editable versus rasterized type

When you use the **Horizontal Type** tool or **Vertical Type** tool, a new layer appears and fully **editable** type appears instantly in the document window. You can easily change the attributes of editable type (such as the font, style, size, color, kerning, tracking, leading, alignment, and baseline shift), plus you can transform it, warp it, apply layer effects to it, change its blending mode, and change its opacity or fill percentage.

To apply other edits to type—such as filters, brush strokes, or the Fill command (to fill the type with a gradient or a pattern)—you have to **rasterize** the type layer first. And you can't have your cake and eat it, too: once type is rasterized, you can't edit its character attributes, such as the font, or edit its paragraph attributes, such as the alignment.

To apply typographic attributes, you'll use the **Character** palette, **A** the **Paragraph** palette, and the all-purpose **Options** bar (shown on the next page).

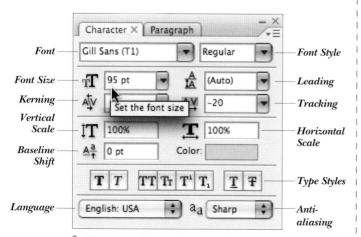

A **Character** *palette attributes can be applied to individual characters or to all the type on a layer.*

Creating editable type

Because **editable type** automatically appears on its own layer, it can be edited, moved, transformed, warped, restacked, or otherwise modified without affecting any other layers. You can be very casual about where you position editable type initially and about which typographic attributes you choose for it, because it's so easy to move and edit.

To create an editable type layer:

1. Choose the **Horizontal Type** tool or **Vertical Type** tool (T or Shift-T).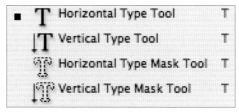A

2. Read the sidebar at right, then do either of the following:

   To create **point** type, click to define an insertion point.

   To create **paragraph** type, drag a marquee to define the bounding box for the text to fit into.

3. On the Options bar, do the following:

   Choose a **font family.**B A sample of each font displays on the menu.

   Choose a **font style.**

   Choose or enter a **font size** (you can use the scrubby slider).

   Choose an **anti-aliasing** method: Sharp (sharpest), Crisp (somewhat sharp), Strong (heavier), or Smooth (smoothest). Photoshop will smooth the edges of the type by introducing partially transparent pixels along the edges of the characters. With anti-aliasing off (None), the edges of the type will be jagged.**C–D**

> **POINT OR PARAGRAPH?**
>
> To create **point** type, click in the document window with the Horizontal Type tool or Vertical Type tool and then type some characters. The type will keep going, even disappearing off the edge of the canvas area, until you press Enter/Return. Use this method to create a few lines of text, and to control hyphenation and line breaks manually.
>
> To create **paragraph** type, which is more suitable for larger text blocks, draw a marquee in the document window with the Horizontal or Vertical Type tool to contain the type, then start typing. From the Paragraph palette menu, you can choose between two algorithms for paragraph type: Adobe Single-line Composer and Adobe Every-line Composer. The algorithms control the line wraps within the bounding box and the overall shape of the paragraph(s).

A To create **editable type**, choose the **Horizontal Type** tool or the **Vertical Type** tool. (The Type Mask tools create type-shaped selections.)

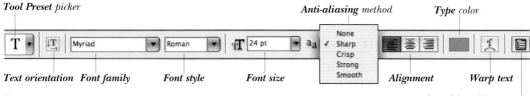

B The Options bar for the **Horizontal Type** tool

Tool Preset picker — Anti-aliasing method — Type color — Text orientation — Font family — Font style — Font size — Alignment — Warp text — Open/close **Character/Paragraph** palette group

C Anti-aliasing off

D Anti-aliasing on

Click an **alignment** button to align point type relative to your original insertion point, or to align paragraph type to the left edge, right edge, or center of the bounding box (see page 355).**A**

Click the **type color** swatch, then choose a color from the Color Picker, the Swatches palette, or the Color palette, or click a color in the document window.

4. Type the desired text in the document window. If you're creating point type, press Enter/Return where necessary, to create line breaks. For paragraph type, let the type wrap naturally to the edges of the bounding box.

5. To accept the new text, press Enter on the keypad or click the ✔ button on the Options bar. (To cancel it, press Esc or click the ⦸ button.) Each time you use the Horizontal or Vertical Type tool, Photoshop creates a new layer.**B** Later in this chapter, you'll use the Character and Paragraph palettes to change the attributes of your type.

➤ See page 82 for an explanation of the missing fonts alert icon.

➤ You can right-click/Control-click an editable type layer name and choose a different anti-aliasing method from the context menu.

➤ You can turn font menu previewing on/off and change the preview size for the Font menu in Preferences > Type: Font Preview Size. The preview speed is improved in CS3. ★

➤ Photoshop uses the vector outlines for a typeface when resizing editable type, when saving to the PDF and EPS formats, and when outputting to a PostScript printer. Editable type always outputs crisply at the printer resolution, not at the file resolution.

➤ If you create type in a Bitmap, Indexed Color, or Multichannel mode image, it will appear on the Background, not on a layer, and can't be edited.

A *The* ***Alignment*** *buttons control the position of paragraph type relative to its bounding box (or the position of point type relative to the insertion point). After typing each word shown above, we pressed Enter/Return to make each word into a separate paragraph, then aligned them* ***Center, Right,*** *and* ***Left,*** *respectively.*

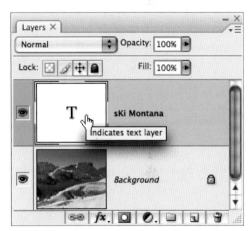

B *Editable type layers always have a* ***T*** *in the thumbnail and are named automatically by the first word or two of the type they contain.*

WORKING WITH TYPE LAYERS

If you place individual passages, words, or characters on separate layers, you'll be able to move them around or apply effects to them individually. If your type layers start to overpopulate, on the other hand, you can periodically delete any layers that you don't need and gather the ones you want to keep into layer groups.

Selecting type

Before you can change the character or paragraph attributes of your type or make copy changes, you have to select the characters you want to edit. You can either edit all the type on a layer, or edit just a few characters or words.

To select type for editing or style changes:

1. Do any of the following:

   To highlight type characters for editing, click a type layer, choose the **Horizontal Type** tool T or **Vertical Type** tool !T (T or Shift-T), click in the type to create an insertion point, then drag across **characters** or **words** to select them. **A** See also the sidebar at right.

   To select all the type on the layer, with any tool selected, double-click the **T** icon on the Layers palette. All the text on that layer will become selected and the appropriate type tool will become selected automatically.

   To change the attributes of all the type on the layer, such as the scale, tracking, leading, or style, or paragraph settings such as alignment or justification, just click the **layer.** (This doesn't select a type tool.)

2. After performing text edits or styling changes, to take the type tool out of edit mode and commit to your changes, do one of the following:

   Click the ✔ on the Options bar.

   Press Enter on the keypad.

   Click any other tool.

   Click a different layer.

   (To cancel your editing changes before committing to them, click the ⦸ on the Options bar or press Esc.)

➤ If you want to see the bounding box for a block of text, choose the Move tool (V), click the type layer on the Layers palette, and check Show Transform Controls on the Options bar. You can use the Move tool to move the type block in the document window.

A *Drag across the characters you want to **select**.*

SELECTING TYPE CHARACTERS

Choose the Horizontal Type or Vertical Type tool, then do any of the following:

Select consecutive **characters** or **words**	Drag across them. Or click at the beginning of a series of words, then Shift-click at the end.
Select a **word**	Double-click a word
Select **multiple words**	Double-click a word, then drag
Select a **line**	Triple-click a line
Select a **paragraph**	Quadruple-click a line
Select **all**	Double-click the T thumbnail on the Layers palette; or click in the text, then press Ctrl-A/Cmd-A

Converting type

To convert paragraph type to point type:

On the Layers palette, right-click/Control-click a type layer name and choose **Convert to Point Text.** A return will be added to the end of every line of type except the last. If the type object contains hidden (overflow) text, an alert dialog box will warn you that the hidden text will be deleted.

➤ We don't know of a command in Photoshop that reveals hidden characters (paragraph returns and the like).

To convert point type to paragraph type:

On the Layers palette, right-click/Control-click a type layer name and choose **Convert to Paragraph Text.** To reshape the resulting bounding box, see page 356. Be sure to delete any unwanted hyphens that Photoshop may have inserted.

Importing type from Adobe Illustrator as a Smart Object

If you create type in **Adobe Illustrator** and then import it into Photoshop by using either method outlined below, it becomes a **Smart Object** layer in Photoshop, which means its contents can be quickly edited at any time in Illustrator, and your edits will appear in Photoshop.

Note: If the type you want to import has stroke attributes or layer effects that you want to keep editable, follow Method 1 below. If you follow Method 2, a type layer containing those attributes or effects will be rasterized.

To create "smart" type from Adobe Illustrator:

Method 1 (AI format)

1. In Adobe Illustrator, make sure the type is on its own layer, then save the file in the **Illustrator Document** (.ai) format.

2. Open a file in Photoshop, then do either of the following:

   In Photoshop or Bridge, use File > **Place** to import the type file (see page 57).

Use **Copy** and **Paste** to paste a type object from Adobe Illustrator into the Photoshop file as a Smart Object.

A new Smart Object layer will appear on the Layers palette.

If you double-click the Smart Object layer thumbnail, an embedded file will open in Illustrator. If you edit it and then save and close the document, the type will update in the Photoshop document. Stroke attributes and layer effects will remain editable.

Method 2 (PSD format)

1. To create a Smart Object layer that can be edited as a separate Photoshop file, in Illustrator, choose File > **Export.** The Export dialog box opens.

2. Choose **Format: Photoshop (.psd),** then click Export. The Photoshop Export Options dialog box opens.

3. Click **Write Layers,** check **Preserve Text Editability, Maximum Editability,** check **Anti-alias,** then click OK.

4. Do either of the following:

   Open a Photoshop file, then in Photoshop or Bridge use File > **Place** to place the type file.

   Use File > **Open** to open the type file as a layered Photoshop file.

5. If you double-click the new Smart Object layer thumbnail, an embedded Photoshop file will appear onscreen, with the editable type in a layer group. If you edit the file and then save and close it, the type will update in the original Photoshop document.

   Note: If the Illustrator type contained layer effects, those elements will become separate rasterized image layers in the embedded Smart Object file and won't be editable via the Layer Style dialog box. The type will also be rasterized if it contained a stroke.

➤ To learn more about Smart Object layers, see pages 302–304.

Styling type

To assign the same **font size** (point size) to all currently selected characters, use the Options bar or the Character palette.

To scale type by choosing a value:

1. Do either of the following:

   On the Layers palette, double-click a T icon, then select the characters or words you want to scale.

   To scale all the characters on a layer, click the **layer**, but don't select anything.

2. Choose the **Horizontal Type** or **Vertical Type** tool; then, on the Options bar, use the **Font Size** icon as a scrubby slider (Alt-drag/Option-drag for finer increments),**A** or enter a value, or choose from the menu.**B** You can also change the font size via the Character palette.**C**

If the currently selected type characters are in more than one point size and you want to preserve their relative differences as you change their **scale**, use the **Move** tool.

To scale type using the Move tool:

1. On the Layers palette, click a type layer.

2. Choose the **Move** tool (V) and check **Show Transform Controls** on the Options bar to make the transform controls appear for the type layer.

3. Click any of the handles first, then do any of the following:

   To scale just the **height** or **width**, drag a side handle.

   To scale **both** the **height** and **width**, drag a corner handle.

   To preserve the **proportions** of the characters as you scale them, Shift-drag a corner handle.**D**

4. To commit to the scale change, click the ✔ button on the Options bar or double-click the text block. (To cancel the scale change before committing to it, click the ⊘ button on the Options bar or press Esc.)

▶ To change the Vertical Scale or Horizontal Scale via the Character palette, see the sidebar on page 354.

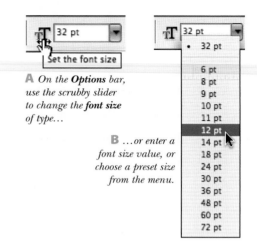

A *On the **Options** bar, use the scrubby slider to change the **font size** of type...*

B *...or enter a font size value, or choose a preset size from the menu.*

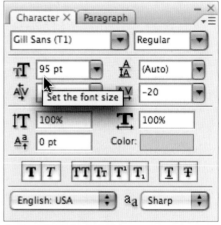

C *You can also change the font size via the **Font Size** scrubby slider, field, or menu on the **Character** palette.*

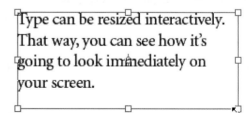

D *To preserve the proportions of type as you **resize** it interactively, **Shift-drag** a corner handle with the **Move** tool.*

Kerning affects the spacing between a pair of text characters.

To apply kerning:

Method 1

1. On the Layers palette, double-click a T icon.

2. Click to create an insertion point between any two characters.

3. Show the **Character** palette (see the sidebar), then do either of the following:

   From the **Kerning** menu, choose **Metrics** to apply the kerning value built into the current font or **Optical** to let Photoshop control the kerning.

   Use the **Kerning** icon ⁴Ꝟ as a scrubby slider; **A** or enter or choose a positive or negative kerning value. **B**

Method 2

   Choose a type tool, insert the cursor between two characters, then press **Alt/Option** plus the left or right **arrow** key. Add Ctrl/Cmd to the shortcut to apply kerning in a larger increment.

Tracking is like kerning, except that it affects multiple characters instead of a pair of characters.

To apply tracking:

1. On the Layers palette, do either of the following:

   To apply tracking to a whole layer, click the **layer.**

   To apply tracking to part of a layer, double-click a T icon, then select some characters or words.

2. Do either of the following:

   On the Character palette, use the **Tracking** icon ⁴Ꝟ as a scrubby slider **A** or enter or choose a positive or negative tracking value. **C**

   If type is selected, you can press **Alt/Option** and the left or right **arrow** key. Add Ctrl/Cmd to the shortcut to apply tracking in a larger increment.

➤ To reset the tracking value of selected characters to 0, press Ctrl-Shift-Q/Cmd-Control-Shift-Q.

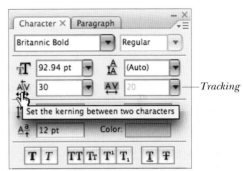

A *The Kerning and Tracking controls on the Character palette don't have equivalents on the Options bar. To change either value quickly, use the scrubby slider (or shortcut).*

B *Use a negative* ***kerning*** *value (we chose –100) to close the gap between two characters.*

C *On occasion, we might spread out a few words, as in the header in this illustration, but never a whole paragraph (horrors!)*

For paragraph type, you can choose a **Leading** value to control the space that separates each line of text from the line above it. Although each character can have its own leading value (the highest value in a line controls the line), it's simplest just to apply one leading value to either a whole line or a whole block of text.

To adjust leading in horizontal type:

1. Do either of the following:

   On the Layers palette, double-click the **T** icon for a type layer. *Optional:* Select a line or lines of text.

   Click a type **layer**.

   Note: Leading doesn't change the spacing above the first line in a paragraph.

2. Use the **Leading** icon 🅰 as a scrubby slider **A–C** (Alt-drag/Option-drag for finer increments), or enter a value in the field (.01 to 5000 pt.), or choose a preset value from the menu. The leading will change from Auto to a numerical value. If you're not sure what value to use, start with a number that's a couple of points larger than the current font size, then readjust if needed.

➤ The Auto setting for leading is calculated as a percentage of the font size. Choose Justification from the Paragraph palette menu, and note the Auto Leading percentage (the default value is 120%). At the default value, for example, the leading for 30-point type is 36 points.

➤ To adjust the vertical spacing between characters in vertical type, highlight the characters you want to adjust, then change the Tracking (not the leading) value on the Character palette.

CREATING PRESETS FOR YOUR TYPE TOOL

After styling your type, choose the Horizontal or Vertical Type tool, click the type layer, then click the **Tool Preset** picker thumbnail or arrowhead ⊤ on the far left side of the Options bar. Click the **New Tool Preset** button, 🖫 then click OK. You can now choose this tool preset from either the Tool Preset picker or the Tool Presets palette any time you create type. It's sort of like having a style sheet, because all your carefully chosen attributes are saved in the preset—but in this case you have to pick the preset before creating the type. Try creating different presets for your print and Web work.

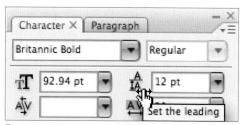

A *The* **Leading** *area on the* **Character** *palette*

B *90 pt. leading*

C *A* **leading** *value of 70 pt. brings the bottom line of type closer to the top line.*

To change the type style:

1. To modify a whole type layer, click the **layer;** or double-click a T icon, then select the type you want to style.

2. Click any **style** button on the **Character** palette **A** (you can use the tool tips to identify them).

➤ The Fractional Widths option on the Character palette menu allows Photoshop to use fractions of pixels for type spacing for optimal appearance (this applies to the entire layer). Be sure to keep this option checked unless you're setting small type for Web output.

➤ The Reset Character option on the Character palette menu resets the palette and any selected type to the factory-default Character palette settings.

Use the **baseline shift** feature to raise or lower type characters from the baseline or a path by one point at a time.

To shift characters from the normal baseline:

1. On the Layers palette, double-click a T icon, then select the characters or words you want to shift.

2. On the Character palette, use the **Baseline Shift** icon ▲ᵃ as a scrubby slider (Alt-drag/Option-drag for finer increments), or enter a baseline shift value.**B** A positive value raises characters upward from the normal baseline or path; a negative value moves them downward.**C–D**

➤ To shift whole lines of type, use leading—not baseline shift. To shift a whole layer, drag it with the Move tool.

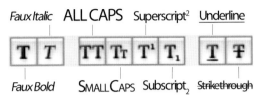

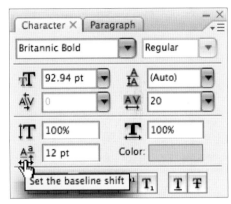

A *The **style** buttons on the Character palette*

B ***Baseline Shift*** *area, Character palette*

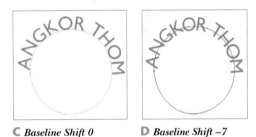

C *Baseline Shift 0*　　**D** *Baseline Shift –7*

DIFFERENT VALUES

You can enter values in any of these nondefault units on the Character and Paragraph palettes: **in** for inches, **pt** for points, **mm** for millimeters, **cm** for centimeters, **px** for pixels, or **pica** for picas. The value will be converted automatically to the current default unit, as specified in Preferences > Units & Rulers > Units: Type.

Changing type orientation

You can change the **orientation** of type from **horizontal to vertical**, or vice versa.

To change type orientation:

Do either of the following:

On the Layers palette, right-click/Control-click a type layer name and choose **Horizontal** or **Vertical** (the opposite of the current orientation).

On the Layers palette, double-click a type layer,**B** then, on the Options bar, click the **Change Text Orientation** button.🅃 **C**

Note: After changing the type orientation, you may need to reposition the type or adjust the tracking.

➤ To rotate vertical type a different way, double-click the type layer thumbnail (and highlight the characters you want to rotate if you don't want to rotate them all), then choose Standard Roman Vertical Alignment from the Character palette menu to uncheck the command.**D** This command isn't available for horizontal type.

MAKING TYPE NARROWER/WIDER

When we need narrow or wide characters, we use a condensed or extended typeface, which has balanced proportions built into its design. That said, you're welcome to play around with the scale features in Photoshop. First, click the type layer (or double-click the layer thumbnail then select some characters), then use the scrubby slider for **Vertical Scale** IT or **Horizontal Scale** T (0–1000%).**A**

stretch *Horizontal Scale 50%*

stretch *Horizontal Scale 100% (normal)*

stretch *Horizontal Scale 200%*

stretch *Vertical Scale 300%*

A *Type can be **scaled horizontally, vertically,** or* ***uniformly*** *(both — and best!).*

B *The original **vertical** type*

C *The same type after clicking the **Change Text Orientation** button on the **Options** bar*

D *The original vertical type after unchecking **Standard Roman Vertical Alignment** on the **Character** palette menu*

Applying paragraph settings

For paragraph type, Photoshop offers a range of formatting options. You forego the manual control you have with point text while gaining sophisticated layout tools. Using the **Paragraph** palette, you can choose basic settings for justification, alignment, indents, and paragraph spacing. Note: For a layout that includes large blocks of text, you may find it easier to create imagery in Photoshop and add the type in a layout or Web page creation program.

To set paragraph alignment and justification for horizontal type:

1. Do either of the following:

   On the Layers palette, double-click a T icon, then click in a paragraph or select a series of paragraphs.

   To modify all the type in a layer, click the **layer**, but don't select anything.

2. If the palette is open but collapsed to an icon, click the ¶ icon. If the Paragraph palette isn't open, click the ▤ button on the Options bar, then click the Paragraph tab.

3. Click an **alignment** and/or **justification** button at the top of the palette: **A**

   The buttons in the first group—**Left-Align Text, Center Text,** and **Right-Align Text**—align type to an edge or the center of the type bounding box. **B** (These options can also be used on point type.)

   The buttons in the second group—**Justify Last Left, Justify Last Centered,** and **Justify Last Right**—justify the type, forcing all but the last line to fill the space between the margins.

   The last button, **Justify All,** forces all the lines to fill the space, even the last line.

4. Check **Hyphenate** at the bottom of the palette to enable automatic hyphenation. We always check this option for justified text to help minimize gaps between words.

➤ To change the alignment and/or justification for vertical type, the procedure is the same as described above, except the buttons are labeled Top Align Text, Center Text, and Bottom Align Text.

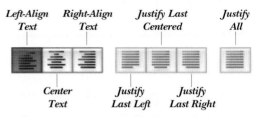

Left-Align Text   Right-Align Text   Justify Last Centered   Justify All

Center Text   Justify Last Left   Justify Last Right

A *The **alignment** and **justification** buttons at the top of the **Paragraph** palette, for horizontal type*

Left-Align Text

The reward for conformity was that everyone liked you except yourself.

Center Text

The reward for conformity was that everyone liked you except yourself.

Right-Align Text

The reward for conformity was that everyone liked you except yourself.

— *Rita Mae Brown*

B *Three **paragraph alignment** options*

COMPOSING AND RESETTING PARAGRAPHS

There are a couple of commands on the **Paragraph** palette menu that you should know about:

➤ Photoshop uses one of the two "Composer" options to evaluate potential word breaks, factoring in the current word and letter spacing values as specified in the Justification dialog box. **Adobe Single-Line Composer** does this line by line, whereas **Adobe Every-Line Composer** does it by evaluating the overall appearance of the paragraph. We prefer (love, actually) the latter method because it will adjust word breaks, when necessary, at the beginning of a paragraph in order to create more visually appealing breaks toward the end of the paragraph.

➤ **Reset Paragraph** resets all currently selected paragraphs to the factory default settings.

Transforming the bounding box

Follow these instructions to scale, rotate, or move the bounding box that holds paragraph type without scaling or distorting the characters inside it. The characters will reflow into the new shape.

To transform a type bounding box:

1. On the Layers palette, double-click the **T** icon for paragraph type.

2. Do one of the following:

   To **scale** the bounding box, position the cursor over a handle, pause, then drag.**A** (To preserve the proportions of the box, start dragging, then Shift-drag.) The type will reflow.**B**

   To **rotate** the box, position the cursor outside one of the corners of the box (you'll see a curved, double-arrow pointer), then drag.

   To **move** the whole type block, Ctrl-drag/Cmd-drag from inside the box (this is a temporary Move tool).

3. To accept the transformation, press Enter on the keypad or click the ✔ button on the Options bar. (To cancel it, press Esc or click the ⃠ button on the Options bar.)

➤ To align or distribute multiple type layers, see page 160.

A *Drag a handle to scale the* **bounding box***.*

B *When we made the bounding box wider, the type reflowed into the new shape.*

TRANSFORMING TYPE

The **transform** commands, such as Free Transform, will reshape both the bounding box and all the type inside it (see pages 298–301). You can move, scale, rotate, and skew both editable and rasterized type, and you can apply a distortion or perspective transformation to rasterized type. If you want to transform individual characters, put them on separate layers first. You can also transform point type with the **Move** tool (check Show Transform Controls on the Options bar to make the bounding box and handles appear).

Warping type

The **Warp Text** command, with its various style choices (arc, flag, arch, shell, wave, fish, etc.), transforms the bounding box that holds the type and distorts the type accordingly. Warped type remains fully editable!

To warp editable type:

1. Do either of the following:

   On the Layers palette, double-click a T icon, then click the **Warp Text** button 工 on the Options bar.

   Right-click/Control-click an editable type layer name and choose **Warp Text**.

2. The Warp Text dialog box opens.**A** Move the dialog box, if necessary, so you can still see the type in the document window.

3. From the **Style** menu, choose a preset warp style.

4. Click **Horizontal** or **Vertical** as the overall orientation for the distortion.

5. *Optional:* Move any of the sliders—Bend, Horizontal Distortion, or Vertical Distortion— noting the changes in the document window.

6. Click OK.**B–E** The **Warp Text** icon 工 will appear in the layer thumbnail. You can reopen the Warp Text dialog box at any time by

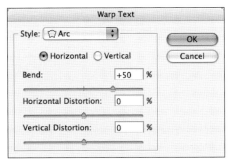

A *When using the **Warp Text** dialog box, you can either accept the default settings for a preset Style or move the sliders.*

repeating step 1 (above), and then choose a different style or adjust the sliders. To undo a warp, choose Style: None.

➤ Once you move the sliders in the Warp Text dialog box, those settings will be applied to any other Style you choose. To reset the sliders to the default settings, hold down Alt/Option and click Reset.

➤ To scale or reshape warped type to make it fit into a specific area of a composition, click the warped type layer, choose the Move tool (V), check Show Transform Controls on the Options bar, then reshape the bounding box.

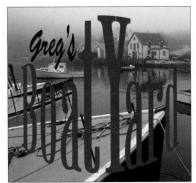

C *Style: **Shell Lower** for "Greg's," **Bulge** for "Boat Yard"*

D *Style: Flag*

B *Style: Arc*

E *Style: Rise*

Rasterizing type

To apply a filter or the Transform > Distort or Perspective command to type, or to draw strokes on type with a tool such as the Brush, you first have to convert it to pixels via the **Rasterize Type** command. Unfortunately, you can't change the typographic attributes of type once it's been rasterized.

To rasterize type into pixels:

1. *Optional:* To preserve the editable type layer, duplicate it (Ctrl-J/Cmd-J) and keep the duplicate layer selected.

2. Right-click/Control-click an editable type layer name and choose **Rasterize Type.** The layer thumbnail will update. Be creative! **B**

Filling type with imagery

Just to give you a few ideas, these are some of the ways that you can "fill" editable type with imagery:

➤ Use an editable type layer as the base layer in a **clipping mask** to clip the image layers above it. **A–B** You can edit (e.g., apply a filter) or reposition the image layers without affecting the type. To learn more about clipping masks, see page 296.

➤ Apply the **Pattern Overlay** effect to an editable type layer (see page 316). **C** You can scale or reposition the pattern within the type while the Layer Style dialog box is open. To create a custom pattern, with the Rectangular Marquee tool, select part of an image to use as a pattern tile, choose Edit > Define Pattern, click OK, then choose your new pattern in the Pattern Overlay pane of the Layer Style dialog box.

➤ Use a type selection in a **layer mask** (follow the instructions on the next page). **D**

A *In this image, the type is the base layer in a **clipping mask.***

B *This image was created in the same way as the previous one, except in this case we also **rasterized** the type layer, then softened the edges via the Gaussian Blur filter to make it look more "snowy."*

C *We applied the **Pattern Overlay** layer effect to the type layer—plus the Drop Shadow, Inner Shadow, Outer Glow, and Emboss effects! The image layer below the type layer contains a subtle pattern.*

D *In this image, a type selection that we converted to a **layer mask** is masking a group of image layers. Each image layer, in turn, contains a gradient in its own layer mask, which is softening the transitions between layers (see pages 150–151).*

To use type shapes as a layer mask:

1. Create an editable type layer.

2. Ctrl-click/Cmd-click the type layer thumb-nail.**A** A selection will display in the document window.

3. Hide the type layer (click the visibility icon).**B** The selection marquee will still be visible.

4. Click the image layer that you want to add the mask to. *Optional:* If necessary, choose a selection tool and move the type selection. (Don't use the Move tool for this, or you'll remove image pixels from the current layer.)

5. Do either of the following:

   To **reveal** layer pixels within the selection area, click the **Add Layer Mask** button ⬜ on the Layers palette.**C–E**

To **hide** layer pixels within the selection area, Alt-click/Option-click the **Add Layer Mask** button on the Layers palette.

The type will display as white or black areas in the layer mask thumbnail.

➤ To toggle the mask function between hide and reveal, click the layer mask thumbnail, then press Ctrl-I/Cmd-I.

➤ To reposition the type shape within the layer mask, unlink the layer mask from the layer first by clicking the link icon; then drag with the Move tool in the document window (relink the layer and mask when you're done).

A *Cmd-click the type layer thumbnail to create a* **selection** *from the type.*

B *Hide the type layer—but don't deselect!*

C *To reveal layer imagery within the selection, click the* **Add Layer Mask** *button (it's a "ski mask," ha-ha).*

D *To provide a solid backdrop for the type shapes, we added a layer below the image layer, which we filled with white.*

E *The* **Layers** *palette for the image shown at left*

Making type fade

In these instructions, you'll apply a gradient to a layer mask to make it seem as though the **type is fading** away.

To make type fade:

1. Click an editable or rasterized type layer.

2. Click the **Add Layer Mask** button ◻ at the bottom of the Layers palette. A layer mask thumbnail will appear next to the layer name. Keep the layer mask thumbnail selected.

3. Choose the **Gradient** tool (G or Shift-G).◻

4. On the Options bar:

   Click the **Gradient Preset** picker arrowhead, then click the **Foreground to Background** preset in the picker (the first swatch in the default gradient library).

   Click the **Linear** gradient button.

   Choose **Mode:** Normal, and an **Opacity** of 100%.

5. Make sure the layer mask thumbnail is still selected. In the document window, drag at least halfway across the type, from top to bottom or from left to right. The type layer mask will fill with a white-to-black gradient **A** and the type will be hidden where black is present in the layer mask.**B**

➤ To modify the type or the layer, click the type layer thumbnail; to modify the layer mask, click the layer mask thumbnail. For more about layer masks, see pages 292–295.

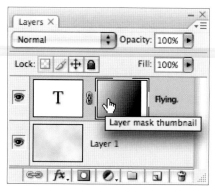

A A gradient in the **layer mask** is masking the type gradually.

B The type looks as if it's **fading** into thin air.

DON'T FORGET LAYER EFFECTS!

Layer effects **C** can be applied to both editable and rasterized type layers. To open the **Layer Style** dialog box, double-click next to a layer name. If you browse through Chapter 20, you'll see many examples of effects that we applied to type.

C We applied **layer effects** (Drop Shadow and Bevel) to the type shown in the previous figure to make it look three-dimensional.

Screening back type

In these instructions, you'll use a Levels adjustment layer to **screen back type** (we prefer this method to using the Type Mask tools). A lightened version of the image will be visible within the type shapes.

To screen back type:

1. Create a document that contains an image layer and an editable type layer (we recommend using a large point size in a bold or black style).

2. On the Layers palette, Ctrl-click/Cmd-click the T icon, then hide the type layer.

3. *Optional:* Reposition the selection by dragging it with a selection tool.

4. From the New Fill/Adjustment Layer menu, ⬤. choose **Levels.** The type will disappear from view temporarily.

5. In the Levels dialog box, **A** move the gray Input Levels (midtones) slider to the left to lighten the midtones in the type. You could also move the Input Levels highlights slider. Move the Output Levels shadows slider to the right to reduce the contrast in the type.

6. Click OK. **B–C**

➤ To swap the black and white areas in the mask (and lighten the image), click the adjustment layer mask thumbnail, then press Ctrl-I/Cmd-I.

➤ To reposition the mask on an adjustment layer, unlink it from the layer thumbnail, then drag it with the Move tool.

➤ You can apply layer effects to the adjustment layer (try it!).

➤ To screen back imagery behind type, see page 182.

A *The original document contains an image layer and an editable type layer.*

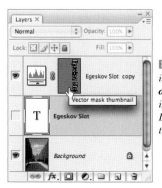

B *A vector mask in the Levels **adjustment layer** is restricting the Levels effect to just the type shapes.*

C *The type is **screened back.** Only pixels within the character shapes are affected by the **Levels** adjustment layer.*

Putting type in a spot color channel

To create type in a spot color channel:

1. Follow the instructions on page 407 to create a spot color channel.

2. Create editable type.

3. On the Layers palette, Ctrl-click/Cmd-click the **T** icon to select the type shapes.

4. Hide the type layer.

5. On the Channels palette, click the new **spot color** channel.

6. Choose Edit > **Fill,** choose Use: Black, Normal mode, choose an Opacity value that matches the tint (density) value of the spot color ink to be used on press, then click OK. The selection will fill with the color as specified in the spot color channel.

7. Deselect (Ctrl-D/Cmd-D).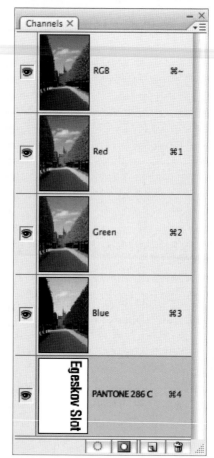

➤ Use the Move tool to reposition the type shapes in the spot color channel.

➤ You can't edit the text in a spot color channel —you have to start over. Fill the channel with White, 100% Opacity, edit the original type layer, then repeat the steps above.

A *Now that our type shapes are in a **spot color channel,** the type can be output to a separate printing plate by a commercial printer.*

A gradient is a soft blend between two or more opaque or semitransparent colors. Gradients can be used to enhance the background behind imagery or type or to add color to the "objects" themselves. In this chapter, you'll learn how to create gradients via the Gradient Editor and apply gradients via a Gradient Fill adjustment layer and the Gradient tool.

Creating a gradient fill layer

A gradient that you apply via a **gradient fill layer** appears in its own layer, complete with a layer mask that can be used to control how much of the gradient is visible. Like an adjustment layer, this type of gradient is editable, restackable, and removable—unlike a gradient that you apply directly to a layer. A good use for a gradient fill layer is to add color behind a silhouetted image or type.

To apply a gradient as a fill layer:

1. To have the gradient fill display behind a silhouetted image or type, click the layer directly below the image layer or type layer.

2. *Optional:* Select an area of the layer to confine the gradient to. With no selection present, the gradient will fill the entire layer.

3. From the New Fill/Adjustment Layer menu ⬤. on the Layers palette, choose **Gradient.** The Gradient Fill dialog box opens.

4. Click the gradient arrowhead at the top of the dialog box, click a gradient **preset** on the picker,**A** then click back in the dialog box. (To access other gradients, choose a library from the bottom of the picker menu; see also page 397.)

Continued on the following page

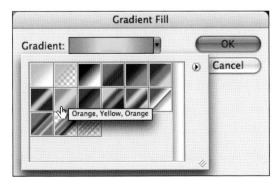

A *In the* **Gradient Fill** *dialog box, click the gradient arrowhead, then choose a gradient from the preset picker.*

5. Do all of the following:

Choose a gradient **Style: Linear, Radial, Angular, Reflected,** or **Diamond.A**

Choose an **Angle** by moving the dial or by entering a value.

Use the **Scale** slider to scale the gradient relative to the layer. The higher the scale, the more gradual the transition between colors in the gradient.

6. *Optional:* Drag in the document window (with the dialog box still open) to reposition the gradient. Cool!

7. Do any of the following optional steps:

Check/uncheck **Reverse** to swap the order of colors in the gradient.

Check **Dither** to minimize banding (stripes) in the gradient on print output.

If you created a selection (step 2), check **Align with Layer** to have the complete gradient fit within the selection; or uncheck this option to have the gradient stretch across the whole layer with only a portion of the gradient visible within the selection.

8. Click OK.**B–C**

➤ If the gradient fill layer is above the image layers, it will obscure the entire image. Lower the opacity of the gradient fill layer to reveal the underlying layer.

➤ Click the gradient fill layer, then change the layer blending mode.

➤ You can double-click the gradient fill layer thumbnail to reopen the Gradient Fill dialog box at any time and readjust the settings.

➤ To apply an editable Gradient Overlay effect, see page 315.

EDITING THE GRADIENT MASK

If you create a selection before creating a gradient fill layer, the selection will be represented as a white area within the **mask thumbnail** for the gradient fill layer on the Layers palette. To reshape the mask, click the layer mask thumbnail, then paint with white to enlarge the white area, black to enlarge the black area, or with the tool at a lower opacity to create a partial mask.

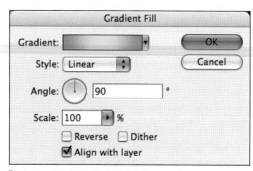

A *In the **Gradient Fill** dialog box, we chose a **preset** (Orange, Yellow, Orange) and chose **Style, Angle,** and **Scale** settings.*

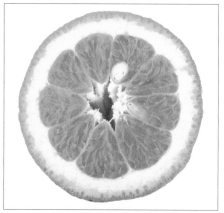

B *The original image contains a silhouetted image layer and a separate white Background.*

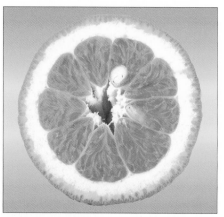

C *Below the silhouetted image layer, we added a **gradient fill layer**, which contains a linear gradient. The fill layer has an opacity of 65%.*

Using the Gradient tool

If you want to apply a gradient by dragging, use the **Gradient tool.** Each time you drag with the tool, an additional gradient is applied. Although you can't edit the results in the same way that you'd edit a gradient fill layer, by using the tool on a separate layer, at least you'll be able to change the layer blending mode and/or opacity.

To apply a gradient using the Gradient tool:

1. Create a new, blank layer for the gradient. *Optional:* To confine the gradient, create a selection.

2. Choose the **Gradient** tool (G or Shift-G).

3. On the Options bar: **A**

   Click the **Gradient Preset** picker arrowhead, then click a preset on the picker.

   Click a **gradient style** button: **Linear, Radial, Angle, Reflected,** or **Diamond.**

   Choose **Mode: Normal** and **Opacity** 100%.

4. Do any of the following optional steps:

   Check **Reverse** to swap the order of colors in the gradient.

   Check **Dither** to minimize banding (stripes) in the gradient on print output.

> **OTHER USES FOR THE GRADIENT TOOL**
>
> To create a gradual masking effect, you can use the **Gradient** tool on an image layer mask, adjustment layer mask, fill layer mask, or Smart Filter mask.

Check **Transparency** to enable any transparency that was edited into the gradient. With Transparency off, the gradient will be fully opaque.

5. For a Linear gradient, drag from one **side** or **corner** of the image or selection to the other. **B–C** For any other gradient style, drag from a **center** point outward. Shift-drag to constrain the gradient to a multiple of 45°. Drag a long distance to produce subtle transitions between colors or a short distance to produce abrupt transitions (this is equivalent to the Scale value in the Gradient Fill dialog box).

6. Change the gradient layer mode or opacity. **D**

➤ To delete a fill applied via the Gradient tool, click the prior state on the History palette.

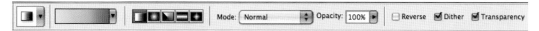

A *On the Options bar for the **Gradient** tool, we chose the **Yellow, Green, Blue** preset (it's in the Pastels library) and clicked the **Linear** style button.*

B *The original image*

C *We dragged with the **Gradient** tool diagonally from the middle of the image to the lower left on a new, blank layer (above the image layer).*

D *For the layer that contains the gradient, we changed the **Opacity** to 85% and the **blending mode** to **Overlay.***

Creating and editing gradient presets

You can **edit** any **gradient preset** in the picker or create new, **custom presets.** When you edit (or delete) a preset swatch, you don't change the original gradient in the current gradient library; instead, Photoshop ensures that you automatically edit or delete a copy of the preset.

To create or edit a gradient preset:

1. Do either of the following:

   Choose the **Gradient** tool (G or Shift-G), ▣ then click the Gradient thumbnail on the Options bar.**A**

   Double-click the thumbnail for an existing **Gradient Fill** layer, then click the gradient thumbnail at the top of the Gradient Fill dialog box.

2. The Gradient Editor opens.**B** Do either of the following:

   Click the preset swatch that you want to create a variation of. (As you start to edit the gradient, the Name will change to Custom; this shows that you're editing a copy of the gradient.)

   To create a gradient that uses the Foreground and Background colors that are in effect when

you apply the gradient, click the **Foreground to Background** preset (the first preset in the default gradient library).

3. For any gradient except Foreground to Background, click the starting (left) or ending (right) color stop under the gradient bar, then do either of the following:

   Click a color on the **Swatches** palette, or on the spectrum bar at the bottom of the Color palette, or in any open document window (the Eyedropper tool becomes selected automatically).

   Click the Color swatch at the bottom of the **Gradient Editor,** choose a color from the Color Picker or the Color Libraries dialog box, then click OK.

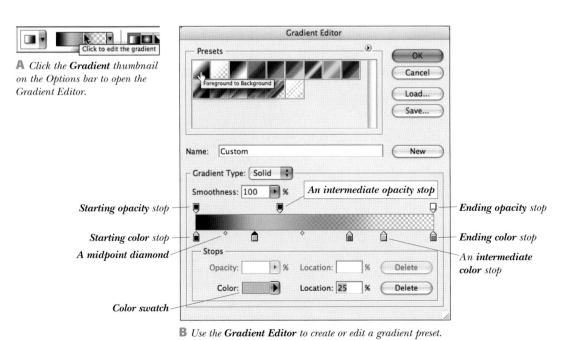

A Click the **Gradient** thumbnail on the Options bar to open the Gradient Editor.

B Use the **Gradient Editor** to create or edit a gradient preset.

Note: If you opened the Gradient Editor from the Options bar, a color stop that uses the Foreground color will have this checkerboard pattern: 🔳 and a stop that uses the Background color will look like this: 🔲.

4. Do any of these optional steps:

   To add an **intermediate** color to the gradient, click below the gradient bar to produce a new stop, then choose a color for the new stop, as per the previous step.**A–B**

   To add an **opacity stop,** click above the gradient bar, then use the scrubby slider to change the Opacity percentage (or click any existing opacity stop above the bar and change the Opacity percentage).

   Drag any color or opacity **stop** to change its location in the gradient.

   To control the **abruptness** of a color transition, click a color or opacity stop, then drag the **midpoint diamond** on either side of it. The diamond marks the point at which the two adjacent colors are 50% each.**C–E**

   To **delete** an opacity or color stop, drag it upward or downward off the bar.

   Use Ctrl-Z/Cmd-Z when you need to undo the previous edit (some edits can't be undone).

5. Don't click OK yet! To create a preset of your custom gradient, enter a name in the **Name** field, then click **New.**

6. Now you can click OK. Your new gradient is now available on the Gradient Preset picker (check the tool tip if you're skeptical).

➤ To save all the gradient presets currently on the picker as a library, see page 396.

➤ To load in other gradient preset libraries or to restore the default library, see page 397.

➤ To rename a gradient preset, double-click the swatch in the Gradient Editor (the Gradient Name dialog box opens), change the Name, then click OK.

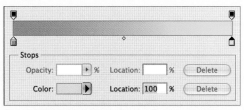

A *In the **Gradient Editor** dialog box, we created a two-color gradient.*

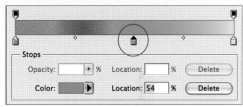

B *We clicked below the gradient bar to add an **intermediate** color.*

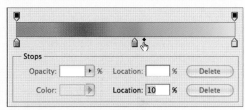

C *We moved the **midpoint diamond** to make the transition between the middle and ending color more abrupt.*

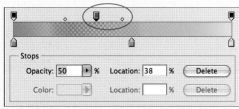

D *We clicked above the bar to **add** an intermediate **opacity** stop, lowered the opacity of the stop to 50%, and moved the right **midpoint diamond** closer to the new stop.*

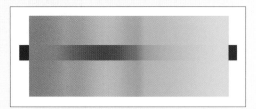

E *This is our **custom gradient,** applied to a layer above the Background. The opacity stop created a **semitransparent** area in the gradient.*

USING BLENDING MODES TO ENHANCE A GRADIENT

A *The* **radial gradient** *is on a separate layer below the silhouetted church tower. In the other illustrations, a* **blending mode** *is applied to the* **image** *(tower)* **layer.**

B *Multiply blending mode*

C *Color Burn blending mode*

D *Screen blending mode*

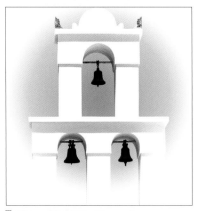

E *Linear Light blending mode*

F *Luminosity blending mode*

In this chapter, you'll learn various ways to finish and present your photos to clients, both in print and onscreen. You'll learn how to frame your subject matter as a vignette; create a hand-painted border; embed a watermark into an image; organize images into a contact sheet or picture package; create a PDF presentation; and create and present layer comps (multiple versions of a document), manually and via a PDF slide show.

Creating vignettes

Aside from the fact that **vignettes** look beautiful, they also have the effect of guiding the viewer's attention to a particular area of a photo (usually the center).

To create a vignette:

1. Do either of the following:

   Click an image layer and make sure Lock Transparent Pixels is off so the vignette can fade softly to transparency.

   Click the Background, then choose a Background color for the area around the vignette.

2. Choose the **Rectangular Marquee** tool, **Elliptical Marquee** tool (M or Shift-M), or **Lasso** tool (L or Shift-L), then select the part of the image that you want to keep.

3. Click **Refine Edge** on the Options bar, choose a **Feather** value, then click OK.

4. Right-click/Control-click in the document window and choose **Select Inverse.**

5. Press Backspace/Delete, then deselect.**A**

A *An oval, feathered edge adds just the right old-fashioned touch to this garden photo.*

Adding hand-painted borders

To make an image look more distinctive, you can create a **hand painted frame** or **paint the image** onto a white background.

To add a hand-painted border:

1. To expand the canvas area to accommodate a frame, choose Image > **Canvas Size** (Ctrl-Alt-C/Cmd-Option-C), choose Percent from the Width and Height menus, and enter 130 in both fields. Choose Canvas Extension Color: White, leave the white/gray Anchor square in the center of the grid, then click OK.

2. On the Layers palette, create a new, blank layer above an image layer, and keep it selected.

3. Choose the **Brush** tool (B or Shift-B).

4. On the Options bar:

   Click the **Brush Preset** picker thumbnail, then choose Large List from the picker menu to display the presets by name. Locate and click the Oil Pastel Large preset or another rough-looking brush tip, then move the **Master Diameter** slider to a setting that's appropriate for your document (we chose 300 px as our setting; our document is 3000 pixels wide).

   Choose **Mode:** Normal.

   Set the **Opacity** to 100% and the **Flow** to 60%.

5. Do either of the following:

   Press **D** to reset the Foreground and Background colors, then press **X** to reverse them.

   Choose the **Eyedropper** tool (I or Shift-I), then click a color in the image.

6. Drag across the outer edge of the image, covering some of the image. Shift-drag to draw straight strokes.

7. *Optional:* Change the layer blending mode for the layer that contains the brush strokes. **A-B**

To paint an image onto a white background:

1. Follow steps 1–5, above.

2. Choose Edit > **Fill**, choose **Use: White**, then click OK.

3. Click the **Add Layer Mask** button on the Layers palette, and keep the layer mask thumbnail selected.

4. Draw strokes in the document window with **black** to reveal the image. Release the mouse between strokes; Shift-drag for straight strokes. **C**

A *On a new, blank layer, we applied white brush strokes (**Oil Pastel Large** brush preset), and lowered the Opacity of the layer slightly to blend it with the image layer below.*

B *We picked up a color from the image with the **Eyedropper** tool, then painted strokes with the Brush tool (**Hard Pastel on Canvas** brush preset).*

C *We painted with black on a **layer mask** to reveal the underlying image. We also painted on the mask with white (low-opacity brush) to soften the edges.*

HAND-PAINTED FRAMES IN A MONTAGE

A *To create this montage, first we applied a hand-painted border to each image separately in its own file and merged each layer containing the brush strokes downward. Next, we dragged each image into a larger document that contains a textured background layer, and moved (and rotated one of) the layers to finish the composition.*

FAST FRAMES

Plug-ins that do the work of creating artistic frames for you are available from third-party suppliers, such as **Photo/Graphic Edges** from autofx.com and **PhotoFrame Pro** from ononesoftware.com.

Adding watermarks

If you're planning to display any of your images online, you can help protect them from unauthorized use by embedding a copyright or other **watermark** into them, like traditional watermarking on paper. In these instructions, you'll create a copyright shape with the **Custom Shape** tool, then save the shape as a tool preset for use in any document.

To embed a watermark into a file:

1. Choose the **Custom Shape** tool (U or Shift-U).

2. On the Options bar, do the following:

   Click the **Shape Layers** button.

   Click the **Shape** picker thumbnail, then click the copyright symbol © (it's in the default custom shape preset library) **A** or click a custom shape that you've created for this purpose (as per the instructions on the following page).

   Click the **Style** picker thumbnail, then click **Default Style (None)**.

   Click the **Color** swatch. In the Color Picker, choose white as the Foreground color, then click OK.

3. Shift-drag with the tool in the document window until the symbol is the desired size. A shape layer will appear on the Layers palette.

4. On the Layers palette, change the shape layer **Fill** value to 0%.

5. Double-click next to the layer name to open the Layer Style dialog box, then click **Bevel and Emboss** (don't check Contour). Choose Style: Inner Bevel, Technique: Smooth, Depth around 60–90%, Size 5–25, Soften 6–10, then click OK.**B**

6. You can use the **Move** tool to reposition the shape on the image. For a better view of the copyright symbol,**C** click another layer.

7. To save the shape style to the Styles palette, click the shape layer for the copyright mark on the Layers palette. On the Styles palette (Window > Styles), click the New Style button, type a name, then click OK.

   To save the shape style as a tool preset, see the second set of instructions on the next page.

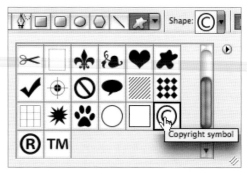

A *Click the Copyright symbol (or a custom shape) on the Custom Shape picker.*

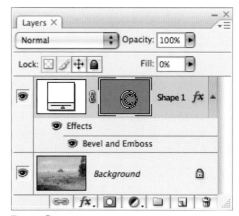

B *The © symbol appears in the mask for the shape layer on the Layers palette.*

C *The final watermark on the image*

You can also create a **custom watermark** by using the Type tool.

To create a custom watermark from text:

1. Choose the **Horizontal Type** tool, **T** create the desired text for the watermark, then scale and style it as desired. (To create the copyright symbol, we typed Alt+0169/Option-G.)

2. Choose Layer > Type > **Convert to Shape.**

3. Choose Edit > **Define Custom Shape,** enter a name, then click OK.

4. Delete the shape layer. Follow the steps on the previous page, except in step 2, choose your new custom shape from the Shape picker.**A**

If you save your custom watermark as a **Shape tool preset,** you'll be able to add it quickly to any image with the Custom Shape tool.

To save a watermark shape and style as a tool preset:

1. Follow steps 1–7 on the previous page.

2. Choose the **Custom Shape** tool.

3. On the Options bar, **B** make sure the copyright symbol or your custom shape is showing in the **Shape** thumbnail.

4. Click the **Style** thumbnail on the Options bar to open the Style picker, then click your custom style.

5. Click the **Tool Preset** picker thumbnail at the far left side of the Options bar, or display the **Tool Presets** palette.

6. On the picker or palette, click the **New Tool Preset** button, enter a name (leave Include Color unchecked), then click OK.**C**

7. To place the mark in any photo, with the Custom Shape tool selected, click your tool preset on the Tool Preset picker or the Tool Presets palette, then Shift-drag in the document window. Note: If Current Tool Only is checked on the picker or palette, you'll have to choose the Custom Shape tool to make the preset appear as a listing.

A *To create a custom watermark, we converted text into a **shape.***

B *Choose Shape, Style, and Color settings on the Options bar for the **Custom Shape** tool. We chose our custom watermark from the Shape picker and our custom style from the Style picker.*

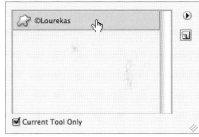

C *Our custom tool preset appears on the **Tool Preset** picker.*

Creating a contact sheet

You can use the three commands discussed next—Contact Sheet II, Picture Package, and PDF Presentation—to organize and display your images. Although they're accessible from Photoshop and Bridge, we prefer using Bridge, where we can select and organize our image thumbnails first.

In Photoshop, a **contact sheet** is an arrangement of image thumbnails in one document, like a contact sheet in traditional photography. The contact sheet can include optional captions.

To create a contact sheet:

1. Depending on which source option you're going to choose in step 3, you can either go to Bridge and select all the files that you want to include in the contact sheet or put all the files in one folder (but don't select the folder). The command can locate files in a folder, as well as in any nested subdirectories/subfolders in the same folder.

   Also make sure that all the files you want on the contact sheet are saved in a format that Photoshop can read (Raw files are readable).

2. In Bridge, choose Tools > Photoshop > **Contact Sheet II** (or in Photoshop, choose File > Automate > Contact Sheet II).

3. The Contact Sheet II dialog box opens (**A**, next page). For **Source Images**, choose **Use: Current Open Documents, Folder,** or **Selected Images from Bridge.** If you chose Folder, click **Browse/Choose**, click the folder that contains the files for the contact sheet, then click OK/Choose.

   Optional: We don't recommend checking Include All Subdirectories/Subfolders. If you do, the command is likely to produce a slew of contact sheets—a time-consuming process.

4. In the **Document** area:

   Choose a measurement unit from the Units menu, then enter overall **Width** and **Height** values for the sheet.

   Choose a **Resolution** for the contact sheet (approximately 200–240 ppi), and a **Mode** (for an inkjet printer, choose RGB).

CATALOG YOUR OWN PHOTOS

Remember the photos you downloaded and then burned onto CD-ROM disks? Generate a contact sheet of the photos on each disk, for easy reference.

Optional: Check Flatten All Layers to have all images (and optional captions) appear on a single layer, or uncheck this option to have each image and caption appear on a separate layer.

5. In the **Thumbnails** area:

   Choose a **Place** option for the direction in which the images are to be arranged.

   Enter the desired number of **Columns** and **Rows** for the contact sheet, based on how many images you're using and whether they're mostly in landscape or portrait format. The layout will preview on the right side of the dialog box, and the current page, number of images, and thumbnail size will also be listed.

   Check **Use Auto-Spacing** to have Photoshop calculate the spacing between thumbnails; or uncheck this option, then in the Vertical and Horizontal fields, enter the desired spacing between thumbnails.

   Optional: Check Rotate for Best Fit to let Photoshop reorient the thumbnails for a better fit on the sheet.

6. *Optional:* Check Use Filename as Caption to have a caption with the file name appear under each thumbnail. If you choose this option, also choose a Font and Font Size for the captions.

7. Click OK. Pause while the command creates a new file (**B**, next page). (To cancel the command while in progress, press Esc.) Save the file.

Contact Sheet II

Source Images

Use: Folder ⬍

Choose... He loves me:PEAR...TOS:Mexican food:

☐ Include All Subfolders

OK

Cancel

Document

Units: inches ⬍

Width: 10

Height: 8

Resolution: 300   pixels/inch ⬍

Mode: RGB Color ⬍

☑ Flatten All Layers

Page 1 of 1
12 of 12 Images
W: 2.5 in
H: 2.4 in

Press the
ESC key to
Cancel
processing
images

Thumbnails

Place: across fi... ⬍   ☑ Use Auto-Spacing

Columns: 4   Vertical: 0.014 in

Rows: 3   Horizontal: 0.014 in

☐ Rotate For Best Fit

☑ Use Filename As Caption

Font: Helvetica ⬍   Font Size: 12 pt ▾

A *In the **Contact Sheet II** dialog box, locate the images you want on the contact sheet and choose layout options that best suit the number and shape of those images.*

shutterstock_1195489...   shutterstock_1428313...   shutterstock_1444521...   shutterstock_1460507...

shutterstock_1719782...   shutterstock_1719783...   shutterstock_238198....   shutterstock_491754....

shutterstock_507818....   shutterstock_619936....   shutterstock_688569....   shutterstock_883673....

B *The final **contact sheet** file for a series of photos, with **filename captions***

Creating a picture package

The **Picture Package** command arranges an image in multiple sizes in one document, like a layout from a traditional portrait studio. You can use preset or custom sizes and configurations.

To create a picture package:

1. In Bridge, select the photo you're going to use, then choose Tools > Photoshop > **Picture Package.** The Picture Package dialog box opens (**A**, next page).

2. In the **Document** area, do the following:

   Choose a **Page Size** for the overall picture package.

   Choose a **Layout** option (in inches) for the page; note the preview in the Layout area.

   Choose a **Resolution** and a document color **Mode.**

   Optional: Check Flatten All Layers to have all images (and optional labels) appear on one layer, or uncheck this option to have each image/label appear on a separate layer.

3. In the **Label** area, do any of the following optional steps:

   To have labels appear under the images, choose a Content type. If you chose Custom Text, enter the desired label in the Custom Text field. Labels for other Content types will be extracted, if available, from the file's metadata.

   Choose a Font, Font Size, Color, and Opacity value for the text.

   Choose a Position for each label, relative to the image.

   Choose a Rotate option for the label or leave the menu on the default setting of None.

4. *Optional:* To customize the layout, click **Edit Layout** on the right side of the dialog box. The Picture Package Edit Layout dialog box opens (**B**, next page). Change the layout Name, then do any of the following:

   Choose a preset size from the Page Size menu or enter custom Width and Height settings in the current Units.

Click Add Zone to add a new thumbnail or placeholder box.

Click a thumbnail or placeholder box and drag a handle to resize it, or drag inside it to reposition it.

Click Delete Zone to delete the currently selected thumbnail or placeholder box.

To exit the dialog box, click Save, enter a file name, then click Save again. (To exit the Picture Package Edit Layout dialog box without accepting any changes, click Cancel, then click No.)

5. Click OK. Sit by idly while the command does its work (**C**, next page). (If you need to stop the command during processing, press Esc.)

6. Save the new picture package file in a format of your choice, such as PSD, TIFF, or PDF.

➤ To use more than one file in a picture package, in the Layout area, click a thumbnail. The Select an Image File dialog box opens. Locate a file, then click Open. The replacement image will display in the selected box. You can also drag pictures into an existing layout from Windows Explorer/Macintosh Finder or from Bridge.

➤ You can also get to the Picture Package command from Photoshop. Choose File > Automate > Picture Package, then for Source Images, choose Use: File, click Browse/ Choose, locate an image, then click Open; or choose Folder, click Browse/Choose, locate a folder, then click Choose to create a picture package for each image in that folder; or choose Frontmost Document to use the currently open, active document. See why we like using Bridge better?

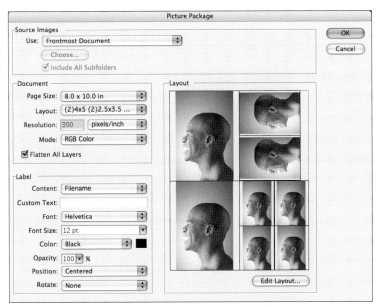

A *Choose Source Images, Document, and Label options in the **Picture Package** dialog box. This is the (2) 4 x 5 (2) 2.5 x 3.5 (4) 2 x 2.5 layout.*

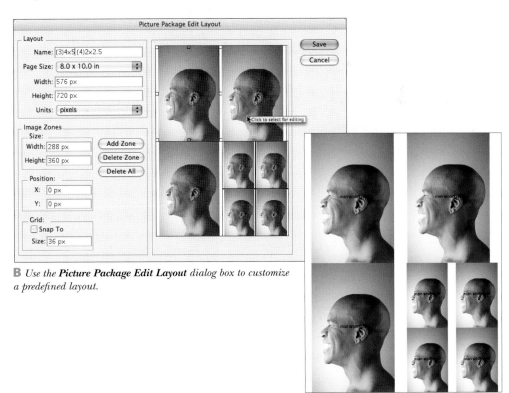

B *Use the **Picture Package Edit Layout** dialog box to customize a predefined layout.*

C *For this **picture package**, we chose Content: Filename, among other options.*

Creating a PDF presentation

Another way to package and send your files to a client is via a **PDF presentation.** If you choose the Presentation option, all the viewer has to do is double-click the slide show file to have it play onscreen. You can even make the finished presentation file size small enough to be included as an e-mail attachment.

To create a PDF presentation:

1. In Bridge, click the files to be included in the presentation, preferably no more than 10.

2. Choose Tools > Photoshop > **PDF Presentation.** The PDF Presentation dialog box opens (**A**, next page).

3. *Optional:* To include additional files in the presentation, you can click Add Open Files, which adds files that are currently open in Photoshop, or click Browse and locate the desired files. To delete the currently selected file name from the Source Files list, click Remove.

4. Under **Output Options:**

    Click **Save As: Multi-Page Document** to create one static multipage PDF file; or click **Presentation** to create a multipage PDF file plus a slide show, and choose Presentation Options for the show.

    From the **Background** menu, choose White, Black, or Gray for the area behind the images (the Background color determines the text color). ★

    Check to **Include** any of the following data to be listed under each image: Filename and Extension, Title, Description, Author Copyright, EXIF Info (f-stop and exposure time), or Annotations (note or audio annotations from the original file). ★

5. Click Save. A Save dialog box opens. Enter a file name, choose a location, uncheck Hide Extension, then click Save.

6. The Save Adobe PDF dialog box opens. In the **General** panel, choose Adobe PDF Preset: [Smallest File Size] and check View PDF After Saving. If the file will be opened from a Web server, also check Optimize for Fast Web Preview.

7. In the **Compression** panel, for Options, try using the Bicubic Downsampling To option with a value of 72 or 100 pixels/inch; leave Compression as JPEG; and set the Image Quality to Medium or Low. You'll need to experiment with these settings to achieve a small file size while preserving the image quality. Leave all other options at their default settings.

8. Click **Save PDF.** Pause while Photoshop creates a PDF file and launches Adobe Acrobat or Adobe Reader. If you chose the Presentation option, a slide show will commence; press Esc at any time to stop it. Note: To view the PDF, you or your client must have Adobe Reader installed.

➤ If you want all your PDF images to display at the same size, before using the PDF Presentation comand, copy each file to be included in the presentation, and using Image > Image Size, choose the same pixel dimensions for each copy.

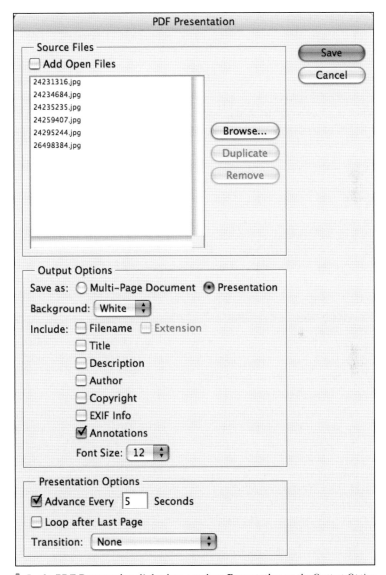

A *In the **PDF Presentation** dialog box, we chose **Presentation** as the Output Option.*

Creating and using layer comps

A **layer comp** (short for "composition") is a set of layer characteristics, including visibility, position, and any applied layer effects. Via the Layer Comps palette, you can store multiple comps in the same document, for easy presentation to clients.**A** To display a layer comp, you simply click the button for that comp on the palette.

To create a layer comp:

1. Create all the layers to be used in an image, including any fill or adjustment layers, masks, Smart Object layers, or type layers, and edit them to create a document version (apply filters, choose a layer blending mode, layer opacity, etc.).

2. Choose visibility (hide/show), position (location in the image), and appearance (layer effects) settings for each layer.

3. Show the Layer Comps palette, then click the **New Layer Comp** button 🔳 at the bottom of the palette. The New Layer Comp dialog box opens.**B**

4. Enter a **Name** for the comp, then check which layer settings you want saved in it: **Visibility**, **Position**, and/or **Appearance**.

5. *Optional:* Enter information in the Comment field to display on the palette when the list for that layer comp is expanded (such as explanatory notes for the client to read).**C**

6. Click OK. To create more layer comps, repeat steps 2–6.

➤ To bypass the Layer Comp Options dialog box as you create a comp, Alt-click/Option-click the New Layer Comp button.

➤ To change which layer characteristics a comp contains, double-click next to the comp name to open the Layer Comp Options dialog box, then check or uncheck any of the Apply to Layers options. To rename a comp, it's faster to simply double-click the comp name on the palette.

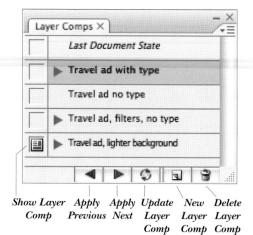

Show Layer Comp · Apply Previous · Apply Next · Update Layer Comp · New Layer Comp · Delete Layer Comp

A *Use the **Layer Comps** palette to create, store, apply, edit, update, and delete layer comps.*

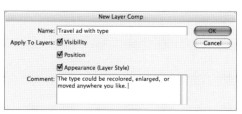

B *In the **New Layer Comp** dialog box, type a Name, decide which characteristics you want saved in the comp, and enter optional comments.*

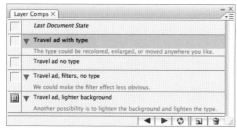

C *These comp lists are expanded to reveal **Comment** information.*

START FROM A DUPLICATE

If you don't want to create a new layer comp from scratch, start from a duplicate instead: Drag a layer comp name over the **New Layer Comp** button, 🔳 then follow the third set of instructions on the next page to edit and update the duplicate.

To display a layer comp:

Do either of the following:

On the **Layer Comps** palette, click in the left column to make the Layer Comp icon appear.

To cycle through the comps, click the **Apply Next Selected Layer Comp** or **Apply Previous Selected Layer Comp** button at the bottom of the palette.**A**

Let's say you edit your document, then display a few different layer comps. To get back to the **last working state** of the document, do as follows.

To restore the last document state:

On the Layer Comps palette, do either of the following:

Click in the left column next to the **Last Document State** listing.

Right-click/Control-click a layer comp and choose **Restore Last Document State.**

You can **update** any existing **layer comp** to incorporate new edits that you make to your document.

To update a layer comp:

1. On the Layer Comps palette, click the name of the layer comp that you want to update.

2. Edit or change the **visibility**, **position**, or **layer style** of any layers in the document.

3. Click the **Update Layer Comp** button at the bottom of the palette.

If you change the number of layers in a document that are recorded in a layer comp (e.g., delete or merge layers or change the document color mode), an **alert icon**, indicating that the Layer Comp Cannot Be Fully Restored, will appear next to the comp name(s). You can either ignore the alert icon, or you can clear it by doing the following.

To clear an alert icon:

Do one of the following:

Select the comp, click the alert icon, then click **Clear** in the alert dialog box.

Select the comp, then click the **Update Layer Comp** button.

Right-click/Control-click the alert icon and choose **Clear Layer Comp Warning** (or to clear all alert icons, choose **Clear All Layer Comp Warnings**).

A *A series of **layer comps**—all variations within the same image*

A PERMANENT SNAPSHOT

To preserve the original state of a document, create a **layer comp** when you first open your image (before making any edits). Yes, snapshots on the History palette serve a similar purpose, but they disappear when you close your document, whereas layer comps save and stay with the file.

When you **delete a layer comp,** it doesn't affect how your document looks or delete any layers.

To delete a layer comp:

1. On the Layer Comps palette, click the layer comp you want to delete.

2. Click the **Delete Layer Comp** button 🗑 at the bottom of the palette.

You can use an automate command to produce a multipage **PDF slide show** of your **layer comps.**

To create a PDF slide show of layer comps:

1. Open a Photoshop file that contains layer comps. *Optional:* To create the slide show from selected layer comps rather than all the comps on the palette, select those comps now (Ctrl-click/Cmd-click to select nonconsecutive comps).

2. Choose File > Scripts > **Layer Comps to PDF.** The Layer Comps to PDF dialog box opens.**A**

3. Click **Browse,** enter a file name, choose a location for the PDF file, then click Save.

4. If you selected layer comps in step 1, check **Selected Layer Comps Only.**

5. For **Slideshow Options,** check:

   Advance Every [ ] Seconds to have the comps display sequentially at the time interval you specify.

   Loop After Last Page to have the sequence of comps loop continuously (repeat from the beginning).

   If you don't enter an Advance value, the viewer will have to click the right or down arrow button to advance the show forward.

6. Click **Run.** The script will output the images to a PDF file. Click OK when the alert dialog box appears.

7. To view the slide show, open the file in Adobe Acrobat or Adobe Reader. (Press Esc at any time to end the presentation.)

➤ A related script for layer comps, File > Scripts > Layer Comps to Files, creates a flattened file for each comp.

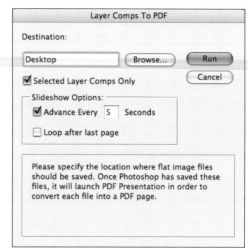

A *Use the **Layer Comps to PDF** dialog box to choose a location and options for your slideshow.*

Preferences are settings that apply to the application as a whole, such as which ruler units are used, or whether tool tips display onscreen. Most preference changes take effect immediately; a few take effect when you relaunch Photoshop or Bridge (exceptions are noted). In this chapter, in addition to learning about all the panes in the Preferences dialog box, you'll also learn how to save and load brush, tool, and other presets.

➤ To open the **Preferences** dialog box in Photoshop, press **Ctrl-K/Cmd-K** or choose Edit (Photoshop, in the Mac OS) > **Preferences** > **General** or one of the other choices on the submenu. In the Preferences dialog box, click one of the 10 pane names on the left side, **A** or click Prev or Next, or press Ctrl-1/Cmd-1 up through Ctrl-9/Cmd-9.

➤ To open the Preferences dialog box for Bridge, press **Ctrl-K/Cmd-K** or choose Edit (Bridge CS3, in the Mac OS) > **Preferences.**

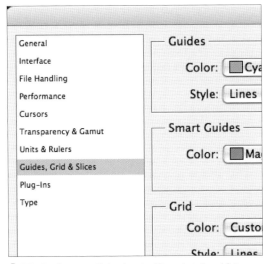

A *The **Preferences** dialog box in Photoshop has 10 panes.*

RESETTTING ALL PREFERENCES

To reset all the **Photoshop** or **Bridge** preferences to their default settings, hold down Ctrl-Alt-Shift/Cmd-Option-Shift as you launch the program. When the alert dialog box appears onscreen for Photoshop, click Yes to delete the Photoshop Settings file. When the Reset Setttings dialog box appears for Bridge, check Reset Preferences, then click OK.

Photoshop Preferences

General Preferences (**A**, next page)

As the default **Color Picker**, choose the Adobe (the default setting) or the system color picker.

Choose an **Image Interpolation** option for commands, such as scaling and resizing images, that involve resampling or transforming: Nearest Neighbor (preserve hard edges) is the fastest but least precise (use for hard-edged graphics); Bilinear is medium quality; Bicubic (best for smooth gradients) is higher quality but slower; Bicubic Smoother (best for enlargement); or Bicubic Sharper (best for reduction). The latter two options also produce high-quality results.

From the **UI Font Size** menu, choose Small (the default), Medium, or Large as the font size for the Photoshop user interface (menus, palettes, tool tips, Options bar, etc.). This takes effect upon relaunch.

Options

Check **Automatically Launch Bridge** to have Bridge launch in the background whenever you launch Photoshop.

Check **Auto-Update Open Documents** to have open Photoshop documents that you edit in other applications update automatically when you return to Photoshop.

Check **Beep When Done** to have a beep sound after each command is completed (useful for being notified when memory-intensive commands are done processing).

With **Dynamic Color Sliders** checked, colors above the sliders on the Color palette will update as you move the sliders.

Check **Export Clipboard** to keep the current Clipboard contents on the system's Clipboard when you switch between Photoshop and other applications.

With **Use Shift Key for Tool Switch** checked, to access a tool on a pop-out menu, you must press Shift plus the assigned letter (e.g., press Shift-R to cycle through the Blur, Sharpen, and Smudge tools). If you leave this option unchecked (as we do), you can press the letter without Shift.

Check **Resize Image During Paste/Place** to have pixel or vector images from other applications scale to fit the current canvas area automatically when imported using the Edit > Paste or File > Place command.

With **Zoom Resizes Windows** checked, the document window will resize when you change the view size via the Ctrl/Cmd- + (plus) or Ctrl/Cmd- - (minus) shortcut.

If your mouse has a scroll wheel and you check **Zoom with Scroll Wheel**, you can scroll the wheel to change the zoom level.

History Log

Check **History Log** to create a log of your Photoshop activity. For **Save Log Items To**, choose where the log will be saved: to the Metadata section of a file, to a separate Text File, or to Both (of the above). For the latter two options, click Choose and choose where you want the text file to be saved.

From the **Edit Log Items** menu, choose what you want saved in the log: Sessions Only to log when you launch or exit/quit Photoshop and which files were opened; Concise to log Sessions information plus a list of edits (as displayed on the History palette); or Detailed, which is like Concise, plus it also logs actions and the options and parameters used in each editing step.

Click **Reset All Warning Dialogs** to reenable any and all alert dialog boxes that you may have hidden by checking Don't Show Again.

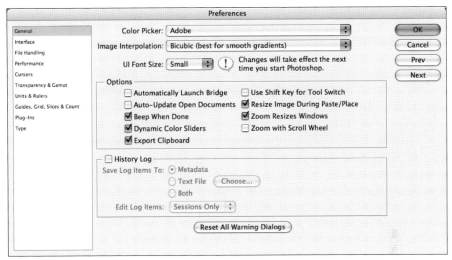

A *General Preferences*

Interface Preferences B ★

General

Check **Use Grayscale Toolbar Icon** ★ to have the icon at the top of the Tools palette [Ps] appear in grayscale (if you're creating a fully grayscale inter-face for Photoshop); uncheck for a color icon.[Ps]

Check **Show Channels in Color** to show RGB or CMYK channels in color on the Channels palette and in the document window when displayed individually. With this option off, channels display individually in grayscale (which is useful if you need to judge luminosity values).

Check **Show Menu Colors** to enable any back-ground colors assigned to menu commands via Edit > Menus and customized workspaces.

Check **Show Tool Tips** to permit the function and name of whichever tool, button, or palette feature the pointer is currently over (mouse button up) to appear briefly onscreen.

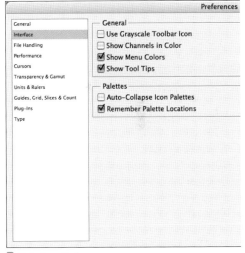

B *Interface Preferences*

Palettes

If **Auto-Collapse Icon Palettes** ★ is checked and you open a collapsed palette, it will collapse back to an icon when you click away from it. With this option unchecked, the palette will stay expanded.

With **Remember Palette Locations** checked, pal-ettes that are open when you exit/quit Photoshop will reopen in their last location upon relaunch, as opposed to the locations specified in the workspace last chosen under Window > Workspace.

File Handling Preferences A

File Saving Options

Choose **Image Previews:** Never Save to save files without a thumbnail preview for the desktop; or Always Save to have an updated preview save with your files each time they're saved; or Ask When Saving to decide which previews to include on a case-by-case basis via the Image Previews check boxes in the Save or Save As dialog box.

In the Mac OS, check Icon to have a thumbnail of an image display as its file icon on the Desktop and in the File > Open dialog box. Check Full Size to include a 72-ppi PICT preview for applications that require this option. Check Macintosh Thumbnail and/or Windows Thumbnail to have a thumbnail of an image display when selected in File > Open.

In the Mac OS, choose **Append File Extension:** Always or Ask When Saving to include a three-letter abbreviation of the file format (e.g., .tif) when saving files. This is helpful when converting files for Windows, and essential when saving files for the Web. Check Use Lower Case to have file extensions appear in lowercase characters instead of uppercase.

In Windows, choose **File Extension:** Use Lower Case or Use Upper Case.

File Compatibility

Check **Prefer Adobe Camera Raw for JPEG Files** ★ to have JPEG files that you open via File > Open open into Camera Raw by default (see page 228).

Check **Prefer Adobe Camera Raw for Supported Raw Files** ★ to have all Raw files that you open via

File > Open open into Camera Raw by default, as opposed to other software.

Check **Ignore EXIF profile tag** to have Photoshop ignore a camera's EXIF metadata color space information when opening files.

Check **Ask Before Saving Layered TIFF Files** to have an alert appear when a layered file is saved in the TIFF format, giving you the option to proceed with the save or not.

With **Maximize PSD and PSB File Compability:** Ask to force an alert to appear when you save a file, giving you the option to make your file compatible with previous versions of Photoshop and other applications; or choose **Always** (as we do) to maximize files automatically without an alert appearing. Including a flattened version adds to the file size but is necessary for exporting files to programs that don't read Photoshop layers.

Version Cue

Enable Version Cue Server File Management affects sharing and managing files among Adobe Creative Suite applications. When checked, you can click the Use Adobe Dialog button in the Open or Save dialog box in Photoshop to see a list of all the currently available Suite documents. For information about Version Cue, see Photoshop Help.

File list

In the **Recent file list contains [ ] files** field, enter the maximum number of files that can be listed at a time on the File > Open Recent submenu (0–30).

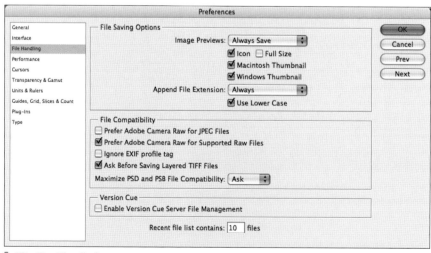

A *File Handling Preferences*

Performance Preferences A

Note: For changes made in this pane to take effect, you must relaunch Photoshop.

Use the Description window at the bottom of the dialog box to learn about the feature your pointer is currently over. ★

Memory Usage

Via the **Let Photoshop Use** field or slider, ★ specify the maximum percentage of your machine's RAM that Photoshop can use, or leave it at the default setting of 55% (Windows)/70% (Macintosh).

History & Cache ★

Enter the maximum number of **History States** to be listed on the History palette at a time (1–1000). Older states that exceed the maximum are deleted.

The image cache is designed to help speed up screen redraw when editing high-resolution files. Low-resolution versions of the file are saved in individual cache buffers and are used for updating the document onscreen. The higher the **Cache**

Levels value (1–8), the more buffers are used and the speedier the redraw but the more RAM is used. The Histogram palette also uses the current Cache Levels value to calculate pixel values based on cached data rather than actual data.

Scratch Disks ★

Check which hard drives you want to make available as **Scratch Disks** for Photoshop when available RAM is insufficient for processing or storing image data. To switch the order of the currently selected hard drive, click the up or down arrow.

➤ Hold down Ctrl-Alt/Cmd-Option when launching Photoshop to open the Scratch Disk Preferences dialog box.

GPU Settings ★

Lists which video cards, if any, are detected in your system. Most video cards enhance the rendering and display of 3D graphics.

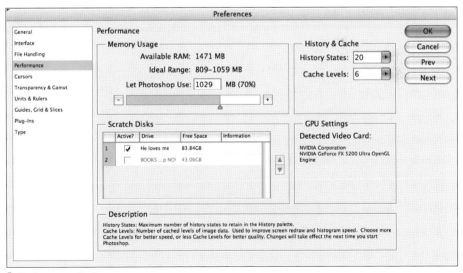

A *Performance Preferences*

Cursors Preferences A

Painting Cursors

For the **Painting Cursors** (Spot Healing Brush, Healing Brush, Brush, Pencil, Color Replacement, Clone Stamp, Pattern Stamp, History Brush, Art History Brush, Eraser, Background Eraser, Blur, Sharpen, Smudge, Dodge, Burn, and Sponge tools), click the type of cursor you want displayed onscreen as you use the tool: Standard for the tool icon; Precise for a crosshair; Normal Brush Tip for a half-size circle; or Full Size Brush Tip for a circle the full size of the current brush tip. For either of the latter two options, you can also check Show Crosshair in Brush Tip to have a crosshair appear in the center of the circle.

Other Cursors

For the **Other Cursors** (all those not listed under "Painting Cursors" above), click Standard to have the tool icon display onscreen as you use the tool, or click Precise to have a crosshair display onscreen instead.

➤ Press Caps Lock to turn nonprecise cursors into Precise cursors (crosshairs) or, if Precise is the current Preferences setting, to turn any Painting Cursor into a Full Size Brush Tip.

Transparency & Gamut Preferences B

Transparency Settings

Choose a **Grid Size** for the checkerboard that Photoshop uses to represent transparent areas on a layer. **C**

Change the **Grid Colors** for the transparency checkerboard by choosing Light, Medium, Dark, Red, Orange, Green, Blue, or Purple; or click each color swatch, then choose a color from the Color Picker.

Gamut Warning

To change the color that Photoshop uses for marking out-of-gamut colors when View > **Gamut Warning** is on, click the Color swatch, then choose a color from the Color Picker. You can also lower the Opacity of the Gamut Warning color to make it easier to see the image behind it.

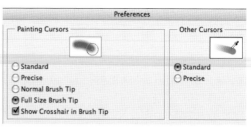

A *Cursors Preferences*

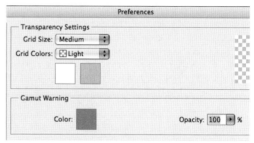

B *Transparency Preferences*

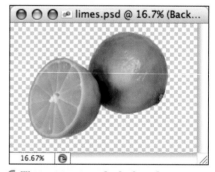

C *The transparency checkerboard*

Units & Rulers Preferences A

Units

Choose a unit of measure from the **Rulers** menu for the horizontal and vertical rulers that display in the document window. (Choose View > Rulers to show/hide the rulers.)

Choose a unit for **Type** (as shown on the Character palette and Options bar).

Note: If you change the measurement units via the Info palette, the ruler units will also change in this Preferences dialog box, and vice versa.

➤ To change ruler units quickly, right-click/Control-click either ruler in the document window and choose a unit from the context menu. Or to open the Preferences dialog box and get right to the Units & Rulers panel, double-click either ruler.

Column Size

Enter **Width** and **Gutter** values to allow the Image Size and Crop commands to fit images for a specific column width in a target layout program.

New Document Preset Resolutions

Enter **Print Resolution** and **Screen Resolution** values, which will display in the New dialog box when you choose a preset print or screen size, respectively. The default settings are 300 ppi for print output and 72 ppi for onscreen display.

Point/Pica Size

Click **PostScript** (the default setting) to have Photoshop use the PostScript value for calculating the points-to-inch ratio, or click **Traditional** to use the ancient, pre-desktop publishing value.

SYMBOLS TO USE IN ENTRY FIELDS	
Pixels	px
Inches	in or "
Centimeters	cm
Millimeters	mm
Points	pt
Picas	p
Percent	%

A *Units & Rulers* Preferences

Guides, Grid & Slices Preferences A

Note: Changes in this dialog box preview immediately in the document window.

Guides

Choose a **Color** for the removable ruler guides. Choose Lines or Dashed Lines for the guides **Style.B**

Smart Guides

Choose a **Color** for smart guides, the temporary lines that display onscreen as you move a layer or selection.

Grid

Choose a color for the nonprinting grid from the **Color** menu. For the grid **Style,** choose Lines, Dashed Lines, or Dots.

To have gridlines appear at specific intervals, choose the desired unit from the menu, then enter a **Gridline Every** value. If you choose Percent from the menu, gridlines will appear at those percentage intervals of the overall document, starting from the left edge. For the thinner gridlines between the main gridlines, enter a **Subdivisions** value.

➤ For the Guides, Smart Guides, and Grid color, you can choose Custom from the menu, then choose a color from the Color Picker or Color Libraries dialog box.

Slices

Choose a **Line Color** for the lines that mark slices. Check **Show Slice Numbers** to have a slice number display in the upper left corner of every slice.

Plug-ins Preferences C

Note: For changes made in this dialog box to take effect, you must relaunch Photoshop.

Plug-ins

In order to access third-party plug-ins that aren't in the Photoshop Plug-ins folder, you need to tell Photoshop where they're located. Check **Additional Plug-ins Folder,** locate the desired folder, then click Choose.

Some third-party plug-ins that were installed for earlier versions of Photoshop may require the previous Creative Suite version serial number in order to run properly. Enter that number in the **Legacy Photoshop Serial Number** field.

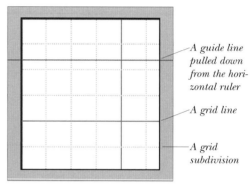

B *Guide and grid lines*

A guide line pulled down from the horizontal ruler

A grid line

A grid subdivision

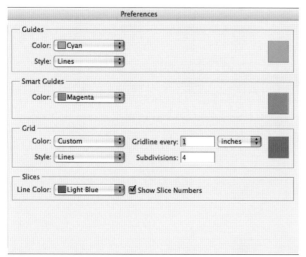

A **Guides, Grid & Slices** *Preferences*

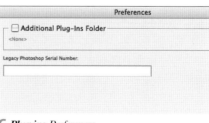

C **Plug-ins** *Preferences*

Type Preferences A

Type Options

Be sure to check **Use Smart Quotes** to have Photoshop insert typographically correct (curly) apostrophes and quotation marks automatically when you create type, instead of the incorrect foot and inch marks.

Check **Show Asian Text Options** to display options for Chinese, Japanese, and Korean type on the Character and Paragraph palettes.

Check **Enable Missing Glyph Protection** to ★ permit Photoshop to substitute Roman fonts for missing glyphs, such as Japanese or Chinese characters.

Check **Show Font Names in English** to have non-Roman font names on the Font menus display in English (e.g., "Adobe Ming Std").

Check **Font Preview Size** to display font previews on the Font menu on the Options bar and Character palette. For the preview size, choose Small, Medium, Large, Extra Large, or Huge. ★

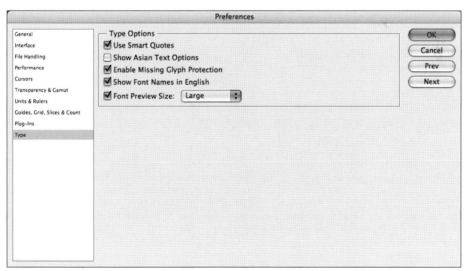

A *Type Preferences*

Bridge Preferences

General Preferences A ★

Appearance

Choose a value between Black and White for the overall **User Interface Brightness** (for the side panes) and for the **Image Backdrop** (the area behind the Content and Preview panels).

Choose an **Accent Color** for highlighted items.

Behavior

Check **When a Camera is Connected, Launch Adobe Photo Downloader** to make the Downloader the default system utility for acquiring photos (this option is Mac OS only).

Check **Double-click Edits Camera Raw Settings in Bridge** to have Raw files open into Camera Raw when double-clicked.

For **Number of Recent Items to Display**, enter the maximum number of folders (0–30) that can be listed at a time on the Look In menu at the top of the Bridge window.

Favorite Items

Check which items and folders you want listed in the **Favorites** panel automatically.

Thumbnails Preferences B ★

Performance and File Handling

Note: To implement Performance and File Handling changes, you must purge the folder cache (Tools > Cache submenu).

Check **Prefer Adobe Camera Raw for JPEG and TIFF Files** to have files in those formats open into Camera Raw when you select them and press Ctr-R/Cmd-R (see page 228).

For **When Creating Thumbnails Generate**, for the Preview panel, click whether you want Quick Thumbnails, High Quality Thumbnails, or Convert to High Quality [thumbnails] When Previewed.

For **Do Not Process Files Larger Than,** enter the maximum file size (the default is 200 MB) that you will permit Bridge to display as a thumbnail (large files process slowly).

Details

For **Additional Lines of Thumbnail Metadata,** check what file information you want listed below each image thumbnail in the Content panel.

Check **Show Tooltips** to allow tool tips to display when you rest the pointer on Bridge features, including information about image thumbnails.

A *General Preferences, in* **Bridge**

B *Thumbnails Preferences, in* **Bridge**

Metadata Preferences

Check which metadata categories you want displayed in the Metadata panel.

Labels Preferences

Check whether to **Require the Control/Command Key** [to be pressed] **to Apply Labels and Ratings** to selected file thumbnails. You can change the label names here, too, but not the colors.

File Type Associations Preferences

These settings tell Bridge which application to use when opening files of each type. Don't change these settings unless you know what you're doing!

Inspector Preferences ★

Select items for display in the Inspector panel in Version Cue, which displays information about Version Cue projects.

Startup Scripts Preferences ★

Depending on your usual workflow, check the scripts that you'll need to have running on a regular basis (to run automatically when you launch Bridge) and, to improve performance, uncheck the ones you won't need. (Read the description below the script name.) Startup Scripts Preferences changes take effect upon relaunch. If you're using the Adobe Creative Suite, keep the first 10 scripts checked.

Advanced Preferences A ★

Note: Most Advanced Preferences changes take effect upon relaunch.

Miscellaneous

Check **Enable Color Management in Bridge** to apply color management profiles to thumbnails displayed in the Preview panel.

Check **Use Software Rendering** to turn off hardware acceleration for the Preview panel (and for Slideshow, a feature that you can learn about in Photoshop Help).

International

Choose a **Language** for the Bridge interface and a language for the **Keyboard.**

Cache

Check **Automatically Export Caches to Folders When Possible** to have Bridge export the cache for image thumbnails to the folders the images are stored in.

Click **Choose** to specify a new location for the central database.

Click **Purge Cache** to purge all cached thumbnails from the central database to free up space on your hard disk or if you experience problems displaying thumbnails in Bridge.

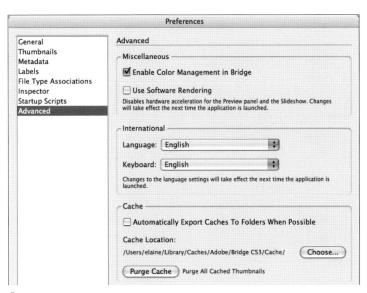

A *Advanced Preferences, in* **Bridge**

Using the Preset Manager

No doubt you've already become acquainted with many of the preset pickers in Photoshop, such as the Brush and Gradient Preset pickers. The Swatches and Brushes palette serve as preset pickers, too. Each item on a picker is called a **preset**, and each collection of presets that you can load onto a picker is called a **library**. You can use the **Preset Manager** to organize, append, replace, and reset which items load onto the preset pickers at startup, or you can make those changes in the individual preset pickers. Changes you make to an individual preset picker are reflected in the Preset Manager, and vice versa.

To use the Preset Manager:

1. Do either of the following:

   Choose Edit > **Preset Manager.**

   From the menu on any palette or picker that contains presets, such as the Brush Preset picker or Brushes palette, choose **Preset Manager.**

   The Preset Manager dialog box opens.**A**

2. Choose from the **Preset Type** menu (or use a shortcut, as shown in the figure below).

3. *Optional:* From the palette or picker menu, ◉ choose a view option for the Preset Manager (e.g., Text Only, Small Thumbnail, Large Thumbnail, Small List, or Large List). For

Brushes, you can choose Stroke Thumbnail to see a sample of the brush stroke alongside each brush thumbnail.

4. Do any of the following:

   From the bottom of the palette or picker menu, choose a library name. Click **Append** to add that library to the current library, or click **OK** to replace the current library with the new one.

   Click **Load**, locate a library that's not currently on the menu to append to the current presets, then click Load again.

   Respond to an alert prompt, if any, regarding saving changes to the current presets.

   Click a preset you want to delete (or Shift-click or Ctrl-click/Cmd-click multiple presets), then click **Delete.** The default presets can be deleted, and they can also be restored at any time (see the instructions on the next page and on page 383).

5. Click **Done.**

➤ Preset libraries can be shared among Photoshop users.

➤ Each type of preset library has its own file extension and default location (see the sidebar on page 397).

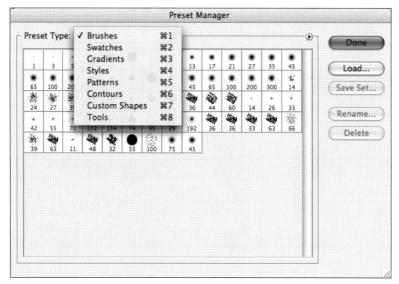

A *Choose a category from the **Preset Type** menu in the **Preset Manager** dialog box.*

Via the Preset Manager, you can **save** a **selection** of presets into a **library**, which Adobe also calls a "set." Once saved, you can load the library onto the appropriate picker at any time—or share it with other Photoshop users. (To save presets via an individual picker, follow the instructions on the next page.)

To save selected presets as a set:

1. Choose Edit > **Preset Manager** or choose **Preset Manager** from any picker or palette menu.

2. From the **Preset Type** menu, choose the category of presets that you want to create a set for.

3. Shift-click or Ctrl-click/Cmd-click the presets that you want to save as a set.**A**

4. Click **Save Set**, keep the default extension and location as is, then enter a name for the new library.

5. Click **Save**, then click Done to close the Preset Manager.

Via the Preset Manager, you can **reset** any category of presets to the factory defaults or you can **replace** the current presets with a library of your choice. (To reset presets via an individual picker, see the instructions on page 397.)

To reset or replace presets:

1. Choose Edit > **Preset Manager** or choose **Preset Manager** from any preset picker or palette menu.

2. From the **Preset Type** menu, choose the category of presets that you want to reset or replace.

3. *Optional:* Any unsaved presets on the list will be deleted in the next step, so we recommend saving the current library before proceeding (see the previous set of instructions).

4. From the **Preset Manager** menu, choose either of the following.**B**

   Reset [preset type] to restore the default library for the chosen type, then click Append to append the default presets to the current library, or click OK to replace the current library with the default presets (click Cancel if you change your mind).

   Replace [preset type], locate the library that you want to replace the current library with, then click Load.

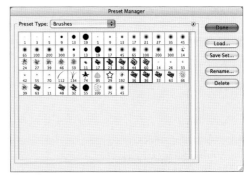

A *Shift-click the **presets** you want to save in a set.*

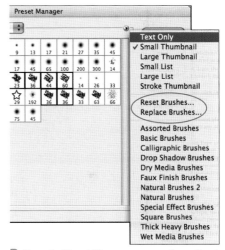

B *From the **Preset Manager** menu, choose **Reset** [preset type] or **Replace** [preset type].*

A PRESET BY ANY OTHER NAME

► To rename a preset when the Preset Manager is in a Thumbnail view, double-click the **thumbnail,** then change the name in the dialog box that opens.

► If the Preset Manager is in Text Only view or a List view, double-click the preset **name,** then change it right there.

► You can also select multiple presets and then click **Rename.** In this case, the naming dialog boxes will open one by one in succession.

Managing presets via pickers and palettes

A new preset will appear on the appropriate preset picker if you define a new pattern or custom shape via the Edit menu, add a new swatch to the Swatches palette, add a new style to the Styles palette, create a new gradient in the Gradient Editor dialog box, create a new contour in any Contour picker, or create a new brush or tool preset. The new preset will also display for that preset type in the Preset Manager.

New presets are saved in the Adobe Photoshop Preferences file temporarily and will display in the appropriate preset picker even after you relaunch Photoshop—that is, provided you don't replace the preset with another library, or reset that picker to the default library, or reset that preset type via the Preset Manager. If you do any of the above, your new presets will be discarded! Thankfully, there's a way to preserve all your hard work.

When you use the Preset Manager to create a library, or set (see the previous page), you can select the presets you want to include. When you save presets as a new library via an individual preset picker, all the presets on the picker are included; you can't pick and choose. To outsmart this limitation, before creating the library, just **delete** the **presets** you don't want.

Note: When you delete a preset from a picker or palette, no documents are altered and no presets are deleted from the library.

To delete a preset from a picker or palette:

Do either of the following:

On a preset picker or palette, Alt-click/Option-click a **preset** (scissors pointer).

Right-click/Control-click a preset and choose **Delete [preset name].** If an alert dialog box appears, click OK.

To save all the presets currently on a picker as a new library:

1. Make sure the preset picker or palette contains only the presets you want to save in a library (delete any unwanted presets as per the previous set of instructions).

2. From the palette or picker menu, choose **Save [preset type].**

3. Enter a name, leave the default extension and location as is, then click **Save.**

   Note: In order for your new library to appear on the palette/preset picker menu and the Preset Manager menu, **A** you must relaunch Photoshop.

➤ To create document presets, see page 56.

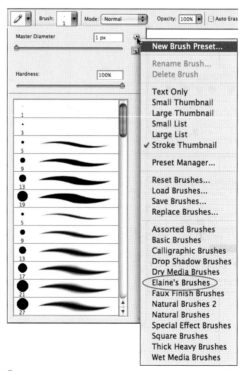

A *The new library (Elaine's Brushes) appears on the* **preset picker** *menu (and on the Preset Manager menu).*

In addition to the default presets and any **custom libraries** you've created, Photoshop supplies an assortment of **preset libraries** that you can **load** as needed. The libraries are available on the lower portion of the palette or picker menu when you select a tool that uses that palette or picker (for example, from the Brush Preset picker when you choose the Brush or Pencil tool).

To load a library of presets:

1. From the lower portion of the palette or the picker menu, choose the desired library name.

2. When the alert dialog box appears, click **Append** to add the additional presets to the palette/picker, or click **OK** to replace the current presets on the palette/picker with those in the library.

   Note: If you made changes to the current palette, another alert dialog box will appear. Click Save if you want to save your changes.

   ➤ To access a library that isn't listed on the menu (isn't in the default folder), choose Load [preset name] from the palette or picker menu, locate the desired library, then click Load.

Any presets that are on a picker or palette when you exit/quit Photoshop will appear again when you relaunch the application. You can **restore** the **factory default library** to any individual picker or palette.

To restore default presets:

1. Choose **Reset** [preset name] from the picker or palette menu.

2. When the alert dialog box appears, click **OK** to replace the existing presets on the palette/picker with the default presets.

   Note: If you made changes to the current palette, another alert dialog box will appear. Click Save if you want to save your changes.

HOW DO YOU CREATE A PRESET?

A **new preset** is created when you:

➤ Customize a brush via the Brushes palette or Brush Preset picker, then click the **New Preset** button on the palette or picker.

➤ Add a swatch to the **Swatches** palette.

➤ Create a gradient by clicking **New** in the **Gradient Editor.**

➤ Create a style by clicking the **New Style** button on the **Styles** palette or by clicking **New Style** in the **Layer Style** dialog box.

➤ Create a pattern via Edit > **Define Pattern** or Filter > **Pattern Maker.**

➤ Create a contour by choosing **New Contour** from the Contour preset picker in the **Layer Style** dialog box.

➤ Create a custom shape via Edit > **Define Custom Shape.**

➤ Create a tool preset (see the next page) by clicking the **New Tool Preset** button in the Tool Preset picker or on the Tool Presets palette.

LOCATIONS FOR SAVING A LIBRARY (SET)

The default location for storing presets that are **included** with Photoshop in Windows is [drive]:\ Program Files\Adobe\Adobe Photoshop CS3\ Presets\[preset category]. In the Mac OS, it's Applications/Adobe Photoshop CS3/Presets/[preset category]. Libraries saved in this location will display in the lower part of the appropriate picker menu upon relaunch.

The default location for **user-created** presets in Windows is [drive]:\Users\[user]\AppData\Roaming\ Adobe\Adobe Photoshop CS3\Presets\[preset category]. And in the Mac OS, it's [user name]/Library/ Application Support/Adobe/Adobe Photoshop CS3/ Presets/[preset category]. Libraries saved in this location display at the very bottom of the appropriate picker menu upon relaunch.

Creating tool presets

If you're looking for a worthwhile method for streamlining your workflow, **tool presets** fit the bill. For any tool, you can choose a preset (such as a brush or gradient), choose custom Options bar settings, and choose a Foreground color (if applicable), then save that collection of settings as a tool preset. Thereafter, when you use that tool, you can choose your tool preset from the **Tool Preset picker** on the Options bar or from the **Tool Presets palette.** Creating tool presets saves time in the long run and is worth the effort even for small variations.

If you check **Current Tool Only** on the Tool Presets palette or on the Tool Preset picker, only those tool presets that were created for the current tool will display on the palette and picker. If you uncheck Current Tool Only, the tool presets for all tools will display. (When you click a tool preset, the tool that uses that preset is selected automatically.)

To create a tool preset:

1. Choose and customize any tool. For example, you could customize the Brush tool via the Brush Preset picker and Options bar, and choose a Foreground color to save with the preset.

2. Do either of the following:

    On the Options bar, click the **Tool Preset** picker thumbnail or arrowhead.**A**

    Open the **Tool Presets** palette.**B** The palette icon looks like this.✕

3. Click the **New Tool Preset** button ▣ on the picker or palette. The New Tool Preset dialog box opens.

4. *Optional:* Change the tool preset name, if desired. And check Include Color, if available, to save the current Foreground color with the preset.

5. Click OK. The new tool preset will appear on, and can be chosen from, the Tool Preset picker and Tool Presets palette.

6. To preserve your tool presets for future use in any document, go the extra step and save them to a tool presets library by choosing **Save Tool Presets** from the picker or palette menu. You can also load any saved preset library via either menu.

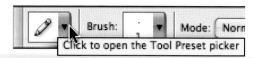

A *Click the thumbnail or arrowhead to open the Tool* **Preset** *picker.*

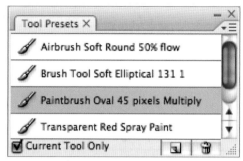

B *The* **Tool Presets** *palette has the same function as the Tool Preset picker.*

When your Photoshop image is done, you can output it on a laser printer, color printer (such as an inkjet), or imagesetter. In this chapter, you'll learn how to choose print options in Photoshop, print to an inkjet printer, create and print spot color channels, and prepare a file for commercial printing. (To export your file to another application or to optimize it for the Web, see the next chapter.)

To obtain a quality color print from an inkjet printer that matches your onscreen image, you can complete the color management setup that you started in Chapter 2 by following the steps on pages 400–405. We also recommend that you refer to Photoshop Help, which contains a wealth of specialized technical information and documentation for your specific printer model.

If you're preparing files for an output service provider, be sure to consult those experts about which specific settings and formats to choose. When you follow our basic instructions for printing from Photoshop, bear in mind that getting a good color print of an image requires a thorough understanding of the color management software that's built into your computer's operating system and the settings available on your printing device, which takes knowledge and experience.

Printing from Photoshop

Continuing the color management workflow that we started in Chapter 2, we'll show you how to print an image using a desktop inkjet color printer. The first step for any kind of print job is to tell Photoshop what type of printer and paper size you're using. Your printer driver and operating system determine which print options are available. The new **Print** dialog box in Photoshop CS3 includes a button that gives you one-click access to the **Page Setup** dialog box.

In Windows, the Page Setup command opens the confusingly named **[your printer] Properties** dialog box. Here you'll find many printer-specific options besides the basics of page size and paper type. In the Mac OS, you'll find equivalent options in the Print dialog box for your system, which opens when you

Continued on the following page

PRINT

26

click the Print button in the Print dialog box in Photoshop. Clear as mud?

To choose a paper size and orientation for an inkjet printer:

1. Choose File > **Print** (Ctrl-P/Cmd-P). The Print dialog box opens (**A**, next page).

2. From the **Printer** menu, choose the printer you want to use.

3. Click **Page Setup** to open the [Printer] Properties **A**/Page Setup dialog box.**B**

4. In Windows, from the **Source** menu, choose the tray that holds the media you want to print on. From the **Type** menu, choose the specific kind of media you want to use. The actual names of these menus may be different for your printer.

   In the Mac OS, from the **Format For** menu, choose your inkjet printer (yes, again!).

5. From the **Paper Size** menu, choose a paper size to print on. If your printer is capable of printing borderless pictures, choose a paper size that is listed as "(borderless)."

   Leave the Scale value at 100%. If you need to change the scale, it's better to do so in the Print dialog box, where you can preview the results.

6. Click OK. Now you're ready to choose other options in the Print dialog box (see the next page).

PRINT-RELATED SHORTCUTS

File > **Print**	Ctrl-P/Cmd-P	Choose printer options and print the file
File > **Print One Copy**	Ctrl-Alt-Shift-P/ Cmd-Option-Shift-P	Print a single copy based on current Print dialog box settings
Edit > **Color Settings**	Ctrl-Shift-K/ Cmd-Shift-K	Choose settings for the current working space and for RGB-to-CMYK conversion

A *The **Properties** dialog box for an Epson printer, in Windows*

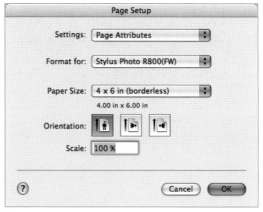

B *The **Page Setup** dialog box in the Mac OS*

The **Print** command in Photoshop CS3 presents you with a new dialog box that takes over many of the features of the old Print With Preview dialog box. It gives you a preview of the image on your chosen paper size, along with other options for adjusting the position, print size, color management, and output settings. In these instructions, you'll choose options for an inkjet printer.

To print to an inkjet printer: ★

1. Choose File > **Print** (Ctrl-P/Cmd-P). The Print dialog box opens, **A** complete with a preview.

2. Make sure the correct printer is chosen from the Printer menu.

3. If you haven't chosen page settings yet, click **Page Setup.** When you're done using the [Printer] Properties/Page Setup dialog, click OK to get back to the Print dialog.

4. Check **Center Image** to position the image in the center of the paper, or uncheck this option and enter new Top and Left values to change the position of the image on the paper. Your choice will be reflected in the preview.

INKJET PRINTERS

When printing to a desktop printer, leave your image in **RGB** Color mode. Although such printers print using CMYK inks (with some using six or more process ink colors), their drivers expect to receive RGB data and perform the conversion to printer ink colors internally. Use the installed profile that conforms to your printer model and paper.

---

5. Do either of the following optional steps to scale the print size:

   In the **Scaled Print Size** area, change the Scale percentage or enter specific Height and Width values (choose a Unit from the menu) to reduce or enlarge the image for printing purposes only. The Scale, Height, and Width options are interdependent; changing any one option will cause the other two to change.

   Check **Scale to Fit Media** to have the image fit automatically to the paper size you chose in Page Setup.

Continued on the following page

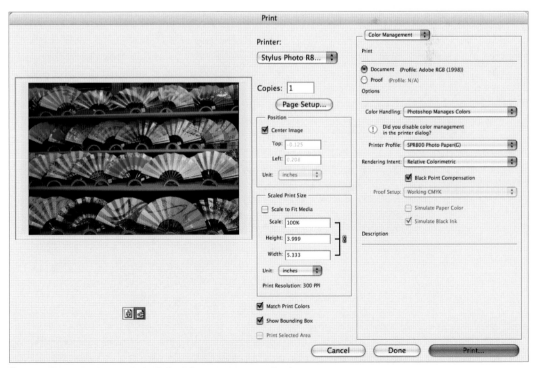

A *The **Print** dialog box, with the **Color Management** pane showing*

Note: Use the scaling features to scale your image in small amounts (i.e., fractions of an inch, or a few percentage points). For anything more than slight scaling, cancel out of the dialog box and use Image Size to scale your image (see pages 92–94).

Optional: Check **Show Bounding Box** to display the image boundary in the preview. Pull a handle or side of the box to scale your image slightly (for printing purposes only). If Center Image isn't checked, you can drag the whole bounding box to change the position of the image on the printed page.

6. From the menu in the top right corner of the dialog box, choose **Color Management** (**A**, next page). This is where you tell Photoshop to use the profile for your specific printer and paper.

7. In the Print area, click **Document** to use the current document color profile that's listed (if you're following our color management scenario, that profile should be Adobe RGB).

8. From the **Color Handling** menu in the Options area, choose **Photoshop Manages Colors** to let Photoshop handle color conversion (our preferred choice). Use this option when you have a profile for a specific printer, ink, and paper combination. Now choose your printer profile from the Printer Profile menu (this is the profile you downloaded in Chapter 2). You'll need to turn off color management in the printer driver (see pages 404–405).

9. From the **Rendering Intent** menu, choose the same intent you chose when you created

the soft-proof setting for your inkjet printer—most likely either Perceptual or Relative Colorimetric (see page 44).

10. Check **Black Point Compensation,** since you're printing the image in RGB mode. This option preserves shadow details by mapping the full color range of the document profile to the full range of the printer profile.

11. Check **Match Print Colors** to make the preview display the colors that the printer will produce. ★

12. When you're done choosing the above-mentioned options, do any of the following:

    Click **Print** to access the systemwide Print dialog box, then proceed with the steps on page 404.

    Press Alt/Option and click **Remember** to save your custom settings with the document. The Print dialog box will remain open. Now click **Print** and proceed with the steps on page 404. Note: If you click Reset, you'll lose all your custom settings—Ouch!

    Click **Done** to close the dialog box but preserve your settings. The settings will still be there the next time you open the dialog box, but they won't "stick" to the image that was open at the time they were chosen.

➤ The Proof option (under Color Management) enables your desktop printer to print a hard proof, which simulates what the image will look like if printed on a CMYK printer. From the Proof Setup menu, choose a profile for proofing. (Choices on this menu come from the View > Proof Setup submenu.) For more info, see pages 43–44 or Photoshop Help.

OTHER COLOR HANDLING CHOICES

Other options on the **Color Handling** menu in the Print dialog box (Color Management pane) include the following:

▶ Choose **Printer Manages Colors** to let the chosen printer handle color conversion. All of the file's color information will be sent to the printer along with the document profile, and the printer, not Photoshop, will manage the color conversion. This isn't a good choice if you use custom profiles or paper, since (depending on the features and quality of the printer driver) the printer may not be aware of your custom choices. Make sure to turn on color management options in the printer driver for the chosen printer.

▶ Choose **Separations** if your file is in CMYK mode and you want to print separations (see the sidebar on page 410).

▶ Choose **No Color Management** to prevent color values from being converted by Photoshop or the printer.

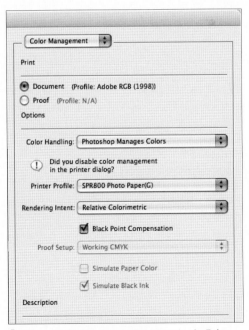

A *Choose Color Management settings in the Print dialog box in Photoshop.*

Configuring the printer

The next phase of printing is to use the system's **Print** dialog box to choose settings for your ink-jet printer and to turn off the color management option for your printer. The following instructions are written with the Epson Stylus and Canon Pixma printers in mind. If your printer is neither of those models, use these steps as guidelines and research the appropriate print quality for your printer, as well as the media and color management options.

In Windows, the dialog box that contains color management settings for printing is part of the printer driver software, not part of the system software. Therefore, the names and locations of the controls will vary from one manufacturer to another. In these instructions, we show you how to disable printer color management for the Epson printer driver.

To turn off color management for your printer in Windows:

1. Open the File > Print dialog box in Photoshop, then click **Print** to get to the Print dialog box for your system.

2. In the **Select Printer** area of the **General** tab, choose the name of your inkjet printer.**A**

3. Click **Preferences** to open the **Printing Preferences** dialog box for your printer (which is identical to the Properties dialog box that you used to choose the size and type of media).

4. In the **Main** tab of the Printing Preferences dialog box, click **Advanced**.**B** A different set of options appears, including controls for color management.

5. In the **Color Management** area, click **ICM**.**C** This switches color management from the Epson driver to the color management system that's built into Windows XP.

6. In the **ICC/ICM Profile** area, click **Off (No Color Adjustment)** to disable color management (**A**, next page).

7. Click **OK** to close the Printing Preferences dialog box and return to the Print dialog box. Now you're ready to click **Print**. Phew! You made it.

▶ To enable printer-based color management in Windows, follow steps 1–6 above, except choose Applied by Printer Software for step 5.

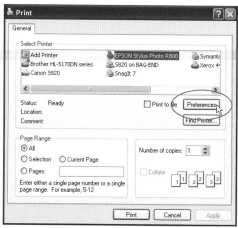

A The **Print** dialog box in Windows, with an Epson printer selected: Click **Preferences** to open the next dialog.

B In the Main tab of the **Printing Preferences** dialog box for an **Epson** printer, click **Advanced**.

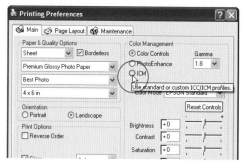

C Clicking the Advanced button reveals the **Color Management** options.

In the Mac OS, the dialog box that contains printer color management settings is part system software and part printer driver software. This means that although the locations of the controls are similar, the actual setting names will vary from one manufacturer to another.

To turn off color management for your printer in the Mac OS:

1. Open the File > Print dialog box in Photoshop, then click **Print** to get to the Print dialog box for your system.

2. From the **Printer** menu, choose the name of your inkjet printer.

3. From the third menu, choose **Quality & Media** (for Canon printers) **B** or **Print Settings** (for Epson printers).

4. Choose the **Media Type** (your chosen paper type) and the **Paper Source** (how the paper will feed into the printer).**C**

5. In the **Print Mode** area, click an option for the print quality.

6. Returning to the third menu from the top, choose **Color Options** (Canon) **D** or **Color Management** (Epson). A different set of options displays in the dialog box. Choose **None** from the **Color Correction** menu (Canon), or click **Off (No Color Adjustment)** (Epson).

7. Click **Print**. That was relatively painless.

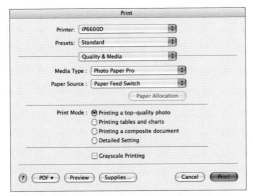

A Click **Off** in the **ICC/ICM Profile** area to turn off color management.

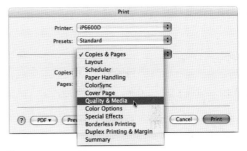

B The Canon Pixma **iP6600D** printer is chosen in the **Print** dialog box in the Mac OS. From the third menu, choose **Quality & Media.**

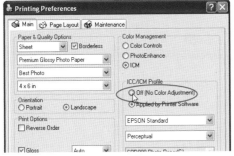

C For the **Quality & Media** settings, choose your paper type, paper source and print quality.

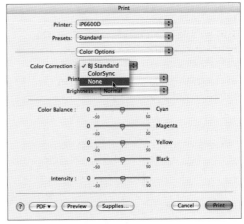

D From the third menu, choose **Color Options**, then choose **Color Correction: None.**

Choosing output options

This discussion of **output options** will be limited to the basic options we think you need to be aware of. For options not discussed here, see Photoshop Help.

To access options for printouts, from the menu in the upper right corner of the File > Print dialog box (in Photoshop), choose **Output.A** In the **Printing Marks** area, you'll find these options:

➤ **Calibration Bars** creates a grayscale and/or color calibration strip outside the image area.

➤ **Registration Marks** creates marks that a print shop uses to align color separations.

➤ **Corner Crop Marks** and **Center Crop Marks** create short little lines that a print shop uses as guidelines when trimming the printed pages.

➤ **Description** prints, outside the image area, whatever information is listed in the Description heading of File > File Info.

➤ **Labels** prints the file name, document color mode, and current channel name on each page (outside the image area).

The **Functions** area contains these options, among others:

➤ **Bleed** lets you specify a Width (distance) inward from the edge of the canvas area for the placement of crop marks (0–9.01 pt.).

➤ **Include Vector Data** causes the edges of any vector objects (such as type or shapes) to print at the printer resolution, not at the document resolution.

➤ When printing to a PostScript printer, choose an **Encoding** method. Binary is the default method. JPEG encoding (available only on PostScript Level 2 or higher printers) compresses image files and speeds up the transfer of data to the printer but produces a lower-quality image. If you run into problems with your print spooler or printer driver, choose ASCII85 encoding (a newer, more compact ASCII method). Both ASCII options double the size of the print files, and slow down printing accordingly.

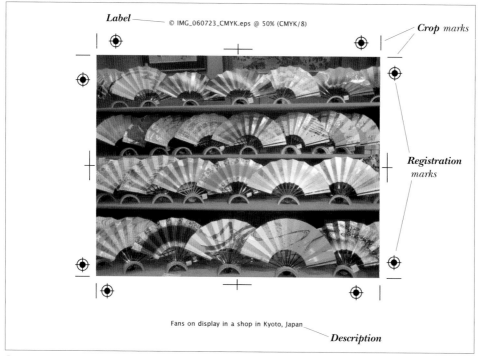

A *This printout shows some of the available **Output** options.*

Creating spot color channels

If you put a spot color in its own separate channel, when the image is color-separated, shapes on the **spot color channel** will appear on a separate plate.

To create a spot color channel:

1. Display the Channels palette, and drag it away from the Layers palette (via its tab) so you can see both palettes at once.

2. From the Channels palette menu, choose **New Spot Channel.**

3. Click the **Color** swatch,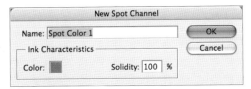A and, if necessary, click **Color Libraries** to get to the Color Libraries dialog box.

4. From the **Book** menu, choose a spot color matching system, such as a PANTONE system, click the desired color, then click OK.

5. *Optional:* To change the way color in the spot color channel is simulated onscreen, change the Solidity percentage under Ink Characteristics. At 100%, it will display as a solid color; at a lower percentage, it will look semitransparent.

6. Click OK. The new spot color channel will appear on the Channels palette, labeled with the name of your chosen color.B Any brush strokes that you apply or imagery that you create while the spot color channel is active will appear in that color. The spot color won't appear as a new layer on the Layers palette.

▶ To change the spot color that you've assigned to a channel, double-click the channel thumbnail, then follow steps 3–6, above, choosing the replacement color in step 4. The channel will be renamed automatically for the new color.

You can also create a spot color channel by **converting** an **alpha channel.**

To convert an alpha channel to a spot color channel:

1. Click an alpha channel on the Channels palette, then press Ctrl-I/Cmd-I to invert it.

2. Double-click the alpha channel thumbnail. The Channel Options dialog box opens.

3. Choose **Color Indicates: Spot Color.**

4. Click the **Color** swatch. If the Color Libraries dialog box doesn't open, click **Color Libraries.** Choose the desired spot color, then click OK.

5. Click OK. Now the black and/or gray areas in the channel represent the chosen spot color.

*A Click the **Color** swatch in the **New Spot Channel** dialog box.*

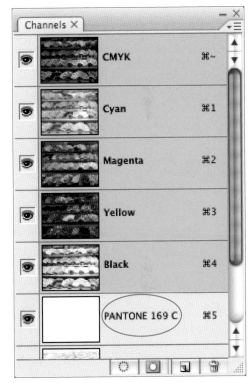

*B The **spot color channel** appears on the palette.*

COPYING TO A SPOT COLOR CHANNEL

▶ To copy an image **shape** to a spot color channel, make a selection on a layer first. With the selection active, create a new spot color channel using the Channels palette or click an existing spot color channel. Using Edit > FIll, fill the selection with black.

▶ To copy the **light and dark values** of an image to a spot color channel as shades of that spot color, create a selection, copy it to the Clipboard, create or click a spot color channel, then paste.

More about spot color channels

➤ To display a spot color channel along with all the core image channels, make sure a **visibility** (eye) icon is present for both the spot color channel and the topmost (composite) channel on the Channels palette. Or to display the spot color channel by itself, hide the composite channel by clicking its visibility icon.

➤ If you need to know the **opacity** percentage of an area on a spot color channel, click the spot color channel, then choose Actual Color mode for one of the color readouts on the Info palette. As you move the pointer over the image, note the K value on the Info palette.

➤ When a spot color channel is active on the Channels palette, only that channel can be edited—not any layers. To resume editing the most recently active layer, click the topmost (composite) channel.

➤ To add **type** to a spot color channel, see page 362.

➤ To **export** a document that contains spot color channels, save it in the Photoshop PDF or TIFF format. A file containing spot color channels that's saved in the PSD format will also color-separate correctly from InDesign.

LIGHTEN/DARKEN A SPOT COLOR TINT

Click a spot color channel on the Channels palette, then choose Image > Adjustments > **Levels.** To darken the tint, move the black **Input Levels** slider to the right; or to lighten the tint, move the black **Output Levels** slider to the right. Position the pointer over the image so you can get an opacity readout on the **Info** palette (choose Actual Color mode for one of the color readouts). Readjust either slider, if needed.

Printing spot color channels

Spot color channel colors **overprint** all other image colors, and the stacking order of spot color channels on the Channels palette controls the order in which spot colors overprint one another. If you need to prevent a spot color from overprinting, you must manually knock out (delete) any areas from other channels that fall beneath those spot color shapes (read more about this in Photoshop Help). Talk with your print shop before doing so, though, to see if this step is necessary.

The **Merge Spot Channel** command on the Channels palette menu merges any spot colors into the existing color channels and flattens all layers, allowing a composite (single-page) proof to be printed on a color printer. If you don't merge spot color channels, they'll print as separate pages. Merging a spot color channel into the other color channels changes the way colors look when printed, because CMYK inks can't exactly replicate spot color inks. When a spot color channel is merged into other color channels, its Solidity value determines the tint percentage of the merged spot color; the lower the Solidity, the more transparent the newly merged color.

➤ To produce an onscreen simulation of the ink opacity for the spot color plate, double-click a spot color channel. In the Spot Channel Options dialog box, choose a Solidity value. For an opaque ink, such as a metallic ink, enter a Solidity value of 90%; for a transparent, clear varnish, enter 0%. This value doesn't affect output unless you merge the spot color channels.

Custom colors that are applied to image or shape layers are converted to process colors on output. Only color areas on spot color channels will separate to spot color plates.

Here's a low-budget—but effective—way to add a **color tint** to a **grayscale print**. It will print as a monotone (from one plate).

To print a grayscale image using a spot color tint:

1. Open a file that's in Grayscale mode (or convert a copy of your file to Grayscale mode).

2. Choose Image > Mode > **Duotone.** The Duotone Options dialog box opens.

3. Choose Type: **Monotone.**

4. Click the **Ink 1** (black) color square, click Color Libraries, if necessary, choose a spot (nonprocess) color, such as a PANTONE color, then click OK.

5. In the Duotone Options dialog box, click the **Ink 1** curve (the square with the diagonal line).

6. In the **100%** field (for the darkest shadow value), enter the desired tint percentage value.**A** Leave the 0% field at 0 and all the other fields blank, then click OK.

7. Click OK to close the dialog box, then use File > Save As to save the file in the Photoshop PSD format for import into QuarkXPress 6.5 or later or InDesign CS or later. For an earlier version of either program, use the Photoshop EPS format. For import into InDesign CS, CS2, or CS3, you could also save the file as a PDF.

Preparing files for commercial printing

Computer monitors display additive colors by projecting red, green, and blue (RGB) light, whereas a commercial press prints subtractive colors using CMYK (cyan, magenta, yellow, and black) and/or spot color inks. Obtaining good CMYK color reproduction from a commercial press is an art.

Nowadays, with print shops creating their own profiles for their commercial presses, you don't need to concern yourself with creating a custom profile; you can leave this step to the pros. Do concern yourself with saving the custom profile from your print shop to the correct folder so it can be accessed from the Color Settings dialog box. The profile will control the CMYK conversion and can be used to create a soft proof. (In Chapter 2, we showed you where to save a custom profile and how to create a soft proof.)

When you're ready to convert your file for output to a commercial press, the first step is to set the current Working Spaces: CMYK menu in the Edit >

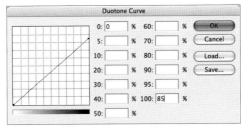

A *This is the **Duotone Curve** dialog box for a Monotone print. The 100% value has been lowered to the desired PANTONE tint percentage.*

QUESTIONS FOR YOUR PRINT SHOP

To set up your document correctly for four-color printing, be sure to ask your print shop these questions:

➤ What **lines-per-inch** setting is going to be used on the press for my job? Knowing this value will help you choose the appropriate scanning resolution.

➤ In which **file format** should the file be saved? Save the image in the requested format.

Continued on the following page

Color Settings dialog box in Photoshop to either the custom profile your print shop provided or to a predefined prepress profile. The CMYK profile will control the conversion of your images from RGB to CMYK mode.

To choose a predefined CMYK profile:

1. Choose Edit > **Color Settings** (Ctrl-Shift-K/ Cmd-Shift-K).

2. Do either of the following:

   From the **Settings** menu, choose the .csf profile you got from your commercial printer.

   From the **CMYK** menu in the Working Spaces area, choose a predefined prepress profile that matches your chosen press and paper type. If your print shop sent an .icc profile, choose it from this menu.**A**

The color correction workflow

Color correction is a complex process, and beyond the scope of this QuickStart Guide. Just as a brief introduction, though, these are the basic steps:

▶ **Calibrate** your monitor.

▶ Find out what type of press your image will be printed on and what **requirements** the print shop has, if any. Most Photoshop files aren't printed directly to a press, so ask whether you should import the Photoshop image into Adobe Illustrator, InDesign, or another program.

▶ Have the print shop send you their **printer profile** that describes the press, ink, and paper they'll use. Load this profile into the Color Settings dialog box (see page 40).

▶ Use the printer profile to create a **custom proof condition**, and **soft-proof** your image for that press (see page 44).

▶ Correct the overall color balance and the distribution of tonal values in the image.

▶ For an image that's going to be color-separated, Adobe recommends editing in **RGB Color mode** and then converting the document to **CMYK Color mode**. To control the conversion, use the printer profile that your print shop recommends. To output to a desktop printer, though, keep the image mode as RGB Color.

▶ **Sharpen** the image.

▶ Print a **CMYK color proof**, then analyze the proof. Readjust the Photoshop image, then print and analyze a second proof.

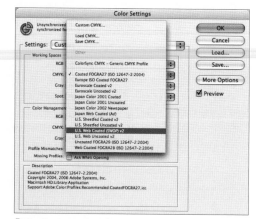

A In the **Color Settings** dialog box, choose a **CMYK** profile.

COLOR SEPARATIONS FROM PHOTOSHOP

You probably won't have occasion to print color separations directly from Photoshop, but if such a circumstance does arise, to print each channel as a separate page, do the following:

Convert the image to CMYK Color mode, then choose File > Print. Choose Color Management from the menu in the upper right corner of the Print dialog box. Under Print, click Document (the CMYK Working Space profile you've chosen in the Color Settings dialog box should be listed there). Under Options, choose Separations from the Color Handling menu. Next, choose Output from the menu in the upper right corner. Check any of the options in the Output panel, such as Calibration Bars, Registration Marks, Corner Crop Marks, Center Crop Marks, or Labels. Some of these options aren't available on non-PostScript printers. When you're done choosing settings in the Print dialog box, click Print, then click Print again.

When you're ready to export your Photoshop image, you need to save it in the proper format for the program you're going to import it into, whether it's a drawing, layout, multimedia, or Web page creation program. In this chapter, you'll learn how to save and prepare files for other programs for print output, and for viewing online.

Preparing files for other applications

Photoshop to QuarkXPress

To color-separate a Photoshop image in Quark-XPress, you can convert it to CMYK Color mode before importing it into QuarkXPress, or you can let QuarkXPress read the embedded profiles and convert your RGB TIFF into a CMYK TIFF. Ask your output service provider which program to use for the conversion. With the PSD Import XTension installed, QuarkXPress 6.5 and later can also import a PSD file, and the program lets you make simple modifications to imported layers, channels, and paths.

If you need to place only a portion of a Photoshop image into QuarkXpress 7, select an area of a layer, then create a new alpha channel. In QuarkXPress, choose File > Import Picture. Choose Item > Modify, click the Picture tab, then choose the new alpha channel from the Channel menu.

Photoshop to Adobe InDesign

InDesign can import PSD files directly, separate Photoshop PDFs (RGB or CMYK), and read ICC color profiles embedded in Photoshop files. In InDesign, you can turn Photoshop layer visibility on or off at any time and you can view layer comps. Alpha channels, layer masks, and transparency are preserved, eliminating the need for clipping masks. And being part of the Creative Suite, InDesign also lets you use Bridge for file and color management.

If you need to place only a portion of a Photoshop image into InDesign CS3, do either of the following:

➤ Select an area of a layer, then create a new alpha channel. In InDesign, choose File > Place. In the Image Import Options dialog box, choose the new **alpha channel.** The channel will mask parts of the image.

➤ Select an area of a layer, then create a layer mask. In InDesign, choose File > Place. In the Image Import Options dialog box, show the layer that contains the **layer mask** and hide any other layers. The mask will hide parts of the image.

EXPORT

27

Photoshop to Adobe Illustrator

Not surprisingly, files from Photoshop CS3 and Adobe Illustrator CS3 are compatible in many respects.

➤ If you **drag and drop** a Photoshop selection or layer into Illustrator, the imagery will appear on the Layers palette in Illustrator as a group containing both a generic clipping path layer and one or more image layers. Opacity settings are reset to 100%, the blending mode is reset to Normal, and layer and vector masks are applied to their respective layers.

➤ If you copy and **paste** a layer from Photoshop into Illustrator, layer masks are discarded.

➤ Via File > **Place**, you can place a whole Photoshop image or just a single layer comp into Illustrator. If you place a Photoshop image with the Link option checked, the image will appear on the Layers palette on a single image layer, and any masks will be applied. If you embed the Photoshop image as you place it (uncheck the Link option), you can also choose whether layers will be converted into objects or flattened into one layer. You'll also have the option to convert layers into objects or flatten them into one layer if you open a Photoshop image via File > **Open** in Illustrator.

If you decide to convert layers into objects, each layer will appear as an object on its own editable nested layer within a group; the Background (if any) will become a separate, opaque layer. All transparency values and blending modes will be preserved and will be listed as editable appearances in Illustrator; layer masks will become opacity masks. We prefer this approach because it preserves layer transparency.

➤ The presence of **adjustment layers** in a Photoshop image will prevent underlying Photoshop layers from becoming individual layers in Illustrator. To work around this limitation, merge any adjustment layers down before opening or placing the image in Illustrator.

➤ If you decide to **flatten** Photoshop layers into one layer, all transparency, blending modes, and layer mask effects will be preserved—visually—but they won't be editable in Illustrator.

➤ When you open or place a TIFF, EPS, or PSD file into Illustrator, the file resolution stays the same but the Photoshop image adopts the **color mode** of the Illustrator file. Illustrator raster filters, raster effects, and some vector effects can be applied to imported images.

Photoshop to CorelDRAW 12

➤ Save the file in the PSD (Photoshop) or PDF format, and in RGB Color or CMYK Color mode, then import it into a CorelDRAW file. CorelDRAW 12 can read a layered Photoshop image; each layer will become a separate object.

➤ You can also use the File > Export Paths to Illustrator command to export a Photoshop path to a file, and then open that file in CorelDRAW.

➤ Once imported into CorelDRAW, you can reposition the bitmap image, perform some bitmap edits on it, apply filters to it, convert it to a different color mode, change its color depth, and resample it by changing its image size and/or resolution.

Saving files in the TIFF format

TIFF is a versatile format that most applications, including QuarkXPress and Adobe InDesign, can import. This format recognizes color profiles and works with color management options. CMYK TIFFs can be color-separated by QuarkXPress and InDesign.

To save a file in the TIFF format:

1. *Optional:* If you intend to reproduce the image on a four-color printing press, convert it by choosing Image > Mode > **CMYK Color.**

2. Choose File > **Save As,** enter a name, choose Format: **TIFF,** and choose a location for the file.

3. You can check **Layers** to preserve any layers in your file, but note that few image or layout programs can work with a layered TIFF, and those that don't will flatten a TIFF upon import. You can also choose to save **Alpha Channels, Annotations,** or **Spot Colors.**

4. *Optional:* Check ICC Profile/Embed Color Profile to include the currently embedded color profile with the file. For more about color management, see pages 36–42.

5. Click **Save.** The TIFF Options dialog box opens.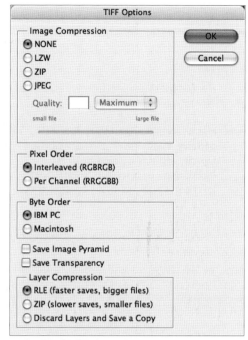

6. Choose an **Image Compression** method to reduce the storage size of the file. LZW is a non-lossy method; some programs can't open TIFFs that are saved with ZIP or JPEG compression. For files that are going to be color-separated, output service providers prefer noncompressed files (click None). For a layered TIFF, click a Layer Compression method at the bottom of the dialog box.

   Leave the **Pixel Order** on the default setting of **Interleaved (RGBRGB).**

7. Click **Byte Order: IBM PC** or **Macintosh,** depending on the platform the file will be used on.

8. *Optional:* Check **Save Image Pyramid** to create a file that contains multiple resolutions of the image. Photoshop doesn't currently offer options for opening image pyramids, but Adobe InDesign does.

   If your file contains transparency that you want to preserve, check **Save Transparency.** To access this option, the bottommost layer in the file must be a layer—not the Background.

9. Click OK.

A *The **TIFF Options** dialog box in the **Mac OS***

Saving files in the EPS format

For drawing and page layout programs that can't import Photoshop PSD or PDF files, the **Photoshop EPS** format is the next best option. When you save a file in the EPS format, layers are flattened and alpha channels and spot channels are discarded. The EPS format is available for files in any color mode except Multichannel, and only for 8-bits-per-channel images. To print an EPS file, you need a PostScript or PostScript-emulation printer.

To save a file in the EPS format:

1. *Optional:* If the image is going to be color-separated by another application, choose Image > Mode > **CMYK Color** to view how the mode conversion will affect the image, then choose Edit > Undo to undo the conversion.

2. Choose File > **Save As** (Ctrl-Shift-S/Cmd-Shift-S). The Save As dialog box opens.

3. Enter a file name, choose Format: **Photoshop EPS**, and choose a location in which to save the file.

   Optional: Check ICC Profile/Embed Color Profile to have Photoshop embed the document color profile or current working color space. For more about color management, see pages 36–42.

   Click Save. Note that any layers will be flattened. The EPS Options dialog box opens. **A–B**

4. From the **Preview** menu, choose TIFF (1 bit/pixel) to save the file with a black-and-white preview or TIFF (8 bits/pixel) to save the file with a grayscale or color preview. Mac users, choose one of the "Macintosh" previews only if you're sure you won't be opening the file on another platform.

5. In the Mac OS, choose **Encoding: Binary**, the default method used by PostScript printers. Binary-encoded files are smaller and process more quickly than ASCII files. In Windows, and for applications, PostScript printers, or printing utilities that can't handle binary files, you'll have to choose **ASCII or ASCII85**. JPEG is the fastest encoding method, but it causes some data loss. A JPEG file can print only on a PostScript Level 2 or higher printer.

6. If you changed the frequency, angle, or dot shape settings in the Halftone Screen dialog box in Photoshop, check **Include Halftone Screen.**

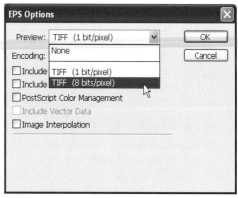

A *In the **EPS Options** dialog box in Windows, choose Preview and Encoding options.*

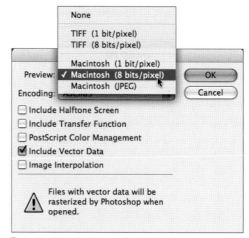

B *In the **EPS Options** dialog box in the Mac OS, choose Preview and Encoding options.*

(To get to the Halftone Screen dialog box, choose File > Print, choose Output from the menu in the upper right corner of the dialog box, then click Screen.)

7. The **PostScript Color Management Option** converts the file's color data to the printer's color space. Don't choose this option if you're going to import the file into another color-managed application (such as InDesign), as unpredictable color shifts may result.

8. If your page contains vector elements, such as shapes or type, check **Include Vector Data.** Although saved vector data in EPS files is available to other applications, as an alert will tell you when you reopen the file in Photoshop, the vector data will be rasterized.

9. Checking **Image Interpolation** allows other applications to resample pixels to reduce jagged edges on low-resolution printouts.

10. Click OK.

MAKING FILES COMPATIBLE

If you want to open a Photoshop (PSD) file in another application, find out if the target application requires you to choose **Always** from the File Compatibility: **Maximize PSD and PSB File Compatibility** menu in Preferences > File Handling. This option saves a composite preview with the layered version for applications that don't support layers and saves a rasterized copy of any vector art for those applications that don't support vector data. This option produces larger files that take longer to save, but it's an acceptable trade-off for compatibility.

BIG SQUEEZE

➤ To reduce the storage size of an image, use a compression program such as **WinZip** or **PKZip** in Windows or **Stuffit** in the Mac OS. (Macintosh users can also Control-click a file name in the Finder and choose Create Archive from [file name] to create a ZIP file.) This kind of compression is non-lossy, meaning it doesn't cause data loss.

➤ If you don't have compression software, choose File > Save As, and choose TIFF from the Format menu. If you want to save the file without alpha channels, also uncheck Alpha Channels. Click Save. When the TIFF Options dialog box opens, check LZW or ZIP under Image Compression. Note: LZW and ZIP compression are non-lossy, but not all programs can import files in these formats, and some programs will import an LZW or ZIP TIFF only if it doesn't contain alpha channels. The JPEG option compresses files more compactly than LZW or ZIP but causes additional image data loss with each compression. The data loss may not be noticeable onscreen but will be very noticeable in high-resolution print output, making this format more suitable for Web output than for print output.

Saving files in the PDF format

PDF (Portable Document Format) files can be opened in many Windows and Mac applications, and in Adobe Reader and Acrobat Standard or Professional. 8-bit and 16-bit images in any color mode except Multichannel can be saved as a PDF (but not 32-bit files). Photoshop can create two kinds of PDF files, depending on which preset you choose in the Save Adobe PDF dialog box.

The default PDF format, Photoshop PDF, preserves image, font, layer, and vector data, but it can contain only one image per file. To create a Photoshop PDF file, make sure Preserve Photoshop Editing Capabilities is checked in the Save Adobe PDF dialog box.

Photoshop can also create generic PDF files, which are similar in format to PDFs from graphics and page layout applications, and unlike Photoshop PDF, they can contain multiple images or pages. To save a Photoshop image as a generic PDF file, uncheck Preserve Photoshop Editing Capabilities in the Save Adobe PDF dialog box. This flattens and rasterizes the image, so your ability to reedit the image in Photoshop will be very limited.

To save a file in the PDF format:

1. Choose File > **Save As**, type a name in the File Name/Save As field, choose a location in which to save the file, choose Format: **Photoshop PDF**, then click Save. If an alert dialog box appears, click OK. The Save Adobe PDF Options dialog box opens.**A**

2. From the **Adobe PDF Preset** menu, choose one of the predefined settings, depending on

how the file will be used (press, Internet, etc.). The first two presets mentioned below embed all fonts automatically, compress your files using JPEG at Maximum quality, and create large Photoshop PDF files that are compatible with Adobe Acrobat 5 and later. The above-mentioned Preserve Photoshop Editing Capabilities option is selected for both:

High Quality Print (the default preset) creates PDF files for desktop printers and color proofing devices. Color conversion is handled by the printer driver.

Press Quality is for high-quality prepress output. Colors are converted to CMYK.

For these presets, Preserve Photoshop Editing Capabilities is not checked, so they produce generic PDF files:

PDF/X-1a, PDF/X-3, and PDF/X-4 ★ create PDF files that will be checked for compliance with specific printing standards, thus helping to eliminate printing problems. The resulting file will be compatible with Acrobat 4 and later or, in the case of PDF/X-4, compatible with Acrobat 5 and later.

Smallest File Size uses high levels of JPEG compression to produce very compact PDF files for output to the Web, e-mail, etc.

➤ Read about the currently selected preset in the Description field.

3. Click **Save PDF**, then click Yes in the alert box.

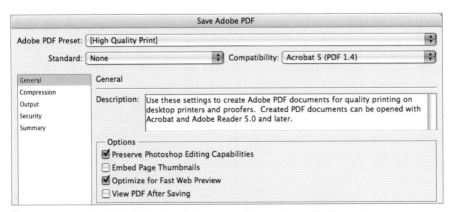

A *In the **Save Adobe PDF** dialog box, choose a preset from the **Adobe PDF Preset** menu.*

Saving files for the Web

Issues of file size and transmission of data come into play when preparing graphics for viewing online, as opposed to print. When you optimize your files for online viewing (resave your files within format, storage size, and color parameters), your goal will be to compress your images enough that they download quickly on the Web while preserving their quality as much as possible. The two main issues you need to address when optimizing files are the image size and the file format (GIF or JPEG).

Image size

The length of time it takes for an image to load into a Web page is related directly to its **file size.** The file size, in turn, is governed by the dimensions of the image in pixels and the amount and kind of compression you apply to the file.

When choosing dimensions for your image, keep in mind that most people view the Web in a browser window that's about 800 x 600 pixels, so that provides you with an upper limit. Remember also that Web browsers always display images at 100% magnification, so use the Image > Image Size command to set the image's resolution to 72 ppi, and make sure to choose View > Actual Pixels to help you judge the image size when choosing final dimensions for your image.

Although the GIF and JPEG formats cause a small reduction in image quality as they compress files, the resulting smaller file sizes download more quickly on the Web, so it's worth it. Note that some images are more compressible than others. For example, a document with a solid background color and a few solid-color shapes will compress a great deal, whereas a large document with many color areas, textures, or patterns won't compress nearly as much. Your choice of file format will also affect how much the image is compressed.

File format

GIF and **JPEG,** the two file formats most commonly used for Web graphics, are appropriate for different types of images:

➤ **GIF** is an 8-bit format, meaning it can include up to 256 colors. It's a good choice for images that contain flat-color areas or shapes with well-defined edges (such as type), for which color fidelity is important. As these kinds of images contain fewer colors to begin with than continuous-tone (photographic) images, the color restriction won't have a negative impact. And if your image contains transparency, GIF is your only choice, as it supports transparency (JPEG does not).

You don't have to use the full complement of 256 colors when saving a file in the GIF format. If you lower the color depth of a GIF file, you reduce the size of the file and the number of colors it contains, so the file will download more quickly (the set of colors in a GIF is called the color table). Color reduction may produce dithered (grainy) edges and duller colors, but you'll achieve the desired reduction in file size.

➤ Because it retains the full 24-bit color depth, the **JPEG** format does a better job of preserving color fidelity for continuous-tone images (such as photographs) than GIF. Another advantage of JPEG is its compression power; it can shrink an image significantly without lowering its quality. When saving an image in JPEG format, you can choose a quality setting. It won't surprise you to learn that higher-quality settings produce larger files and lower settings produce smaller files. Unlike the GIF format, JPEG doesn't preserve transparency.

Each time an image is optimized in the JPEG format, some image data is lost; the greater the compression, the greater the loss, To prevent data loss, edit and save your image, then optimize a copy of the file for Web output using the JPEG format.

Don't panic! You'll learn the steps for optimization later in this chapter.

Previewing optimized files

In the **Save for Web & Devices** dialog box, you'll find everything you need to optimize graphics for the Web. Here, multiple previews let you test the effects of different optimization settings.

For a more definitive test, click the **Preview in [default browser]** button at the bottom of the dialog box to open your optimized image in the default Web browser application that's installed on your computer. Or to choose another browser that's installed in your system, from the menu next to the button, choose a browser name or choose Other and locate a browser application.

To use the Save for Web & Devices previews:

1. Choose File > **Save for Web & Devices**. The dialog box opens.**A**

2. Click the **4-Up** tab to see the original image and three previews simultaneously. Photoshop will use the current optimization options to generate the first preview (to the right of the original), then automatically generate the two other previews as variations on the current optimization settings. You can click any preview and change the optimization settings for just that preview.

Preview tabs   *Optimization options*

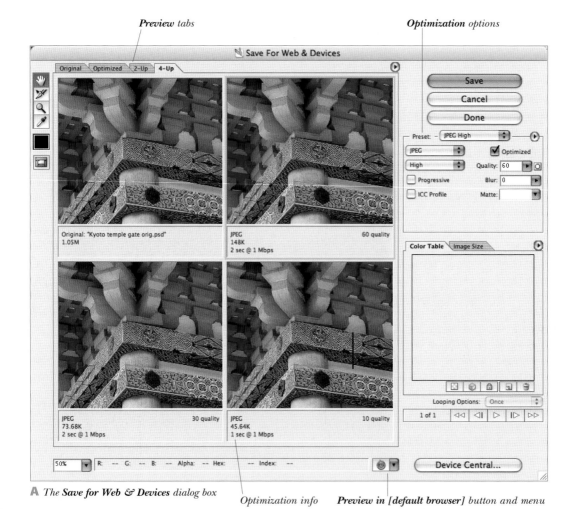

A *The **Save for Web & Devices** dialog box*   *Optimization info*   *Preview in [default browser] button and menu*

Optimizing files for the Web

Before optimizing a file as a JPEG or GIF, it's best to change its resolution to 72 ppi (screen resolution) and resize it to the desired dimensions.

To optimize a file in the GIF format:

1. Save your file.

2. Choose File > **Save for Web & Devices** (Ctrl-Alt-Shift-S/Cmd-Opt-Shift-S) to open the Save for Web & Devices dialog box.

3. Click the **2-Up** tab at the top of the dialog box to display both the original and optimized previews of the image.

4. Do either of the following:

   From the **Preset** menu, choose one of the GIF options. Leave the preset settings as is, then click Save. The Save Optimized As dialog box opens. Leave the name as is, choose a location, then click Save.

   Follow the remaining steps to choose **custom** optimization settings.

5. From the **Optimized File Format** menu, choose GIF.**A**

6. From the **Color Reduction Algorithm** menu, choose a method for reducing the number of colors in the image (see the sidebar at right) (**A**, next page).

7. Choose the maximum number of **Colors** to be generated in the color table by choosing a pre-set from the menu or by entering an exact number in the field. Lowering the number of colors reduces the file size.

8. Choose a dither method from the **Dither Algorithm** menu. Dithering is a procsss by which Photoshop mixes dots of a few different colors to simulate a greater color range. Although the Diffusion option produces a larger file size, it also yields the best compromise between quality and file size. With no dither option chosen (choose None), gradients may exhibit banding.

   Also choose a **Dither** percentage. A high dither value will produce more color simulation and a larger file size (**B**, next page).

9. Check **Transparency** to preserve fully transparent pixels in the image. The Transparency

Continued on the following page

Color Reduction Algorithm menu

Optimized File Format menu   Optimize menu

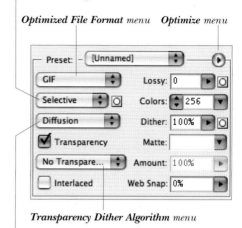

Transparency Dither Algorithm menu

Dither Algorithm menu

A *Choose* **optimization** *options for the* **GIF** *file format in the* **Save for Web & Devices** *dialog box.*

COLOR REDUCTION ALGORITHMS

▶ **Restrictive (Web)** generates a color table by changing the image colors to those that are available on the standard Web-safe palette. (This palette contains only the 216 colors that the Windows and Macintosh browser palettes have in common.) This choice produces the least number of colors and the smallest file size but not necessarily the best image quality.

▶ **Perceptual** generates a color table based on the colors currently in the document, with a bias toward how people actually perceive colors.

▶ **Selective,** the default option, generates a color table based on the colors currently in the image, with a bias toward preserving flat colors, Web-safe colors, and overall color integrity.

▶ **Adaptive** generates a color table based on the part of the color spectrum that represents the most colors in the document. This choice produces a slightly larger optimized file.

option allows for the creation of nonrectangular image borders. With Transparency unchecked, transparent pixels will be filled with the current color chosen on the Matte menu. Regardless of the Transparency setting, the GIF format doesn't preserve semitransparent pixels.

10. To control how semitransparent pixels along the edge of an image blend with the background of a Web page (such as on the edges of anti-aliased elements), choose a **Matte** option.**C** Set the Matte color to the color of the Web page background—if you happen to know what that color is. Any soft-edged effect (such as a Drop Shadow) on top of transparent areas will fill with the current Matte color. If the background color is unknown, set Matte to None; this will create a hard, jagged edge.**D**

Another option is to choose **Matte: None,** then check Transparency and choose one of three options from the **Transparency Dither Algorithm** menu. These effects will look the same on any background. **Diffusion** applies a random pattern to semitransparent pixels and diffuses it across adjacent pixels. This method usually produces the most subtle results and allows you to set the dithering amount. **Pattern** applies a halftone pattern to the semitransparent pixels. **Noise** applies a pattern similar to Diffusion without affecting neighboring pixels.

11. *Optional:* You can adjust the **Lossy** value to further reduce the file size of the optimized image. As the name "Lossy" implies, this option discards some image data, but the savings in file size may justify the slight reduction in image quality.

12. Click Save. The Save Optimized As dialog box opens. Leave the name as is, choose a location, then click Save.

➤ To save a current (Unnamed) set of palette options, choose Save Settings from the Optimize menu.⊙ Enter a name (in Windows, include the .irs extension), locate and open the Adobe Photoshop CS3 > Presets > Optimized Settings folder, then click Save. Your saved set will now be available on the Preset menu in the Save for Web & Devices dialog box for any document.

A *An image optimized as a GIF with **32** colors using the **Selective** algorithm but **no dither***

B *The same image, but optimized with **100%** dither*

C *An image optimized as a **GIF** with **Transparency** checked and **Matte** set to **black** (resulting in a thin line of that color along the edge of each shape)*

D *An image optimized as a **GIF** with **Transparency** checked and **Matte** set to **None** (resulting in a hard edge along each shape)*

JPEG is the format of choice for optimizing continuous-tone imagery (photographs, paintings, gradients, and blends). If you optimize to this format, the file's 24-bit color will be preserved and its colors will be seen and enjoyed by any viewer whose display is set to thousands or millions of colors. Two drawbacks to JPEG are that its compression method eliminates image data and that it doesn't preserve transparency.

To optimize an image in the JPEG format:

1. Save your file.

2. Choose File > **Save for Web & Devices** (Ctrl-Alt-Shift-S/Cmd-Opt-Shift-S) to open the Save for Web & Devices dialog box (**A**, page 418).

3. Click the **2-Up** tab at the top of the dialog box to display both the original and optimized previews of the image.

4. Do either of the following:

   From the **Preset** menu,**A** choose one of the JPEG options. Leave the preset settings as is, then click Save. The Save Optimized As dialog box opens. Leave the name as is, choose a location, then click Save.

   Follow the remaining steps to choose **custom** optimization settings.

5. From the **Optimized File Format** menu, choose JPEG.

6. Do either of the following:

   From the **Compression Quality** menu, choose a quality level for the optimized image **B–C** (and **A**, next page).

   Move the **Quality** slider to the desired compression level.

   ▶ The higher the compression quality, the higher the image quality—and the larger the file size.

7. Increase the **Blur** value to lessen the visibility of JPEG artifacts that arise from the JPEG compression method, and to reduce the file size. Be careful not to overblur the image, though, or the details will be softened too much. The Blur setting can be lowered later to reclaim some of the diminished sharpness.

8. Choose a **Matte** color to be substituted for areas of transparency in the original image. If you

Continued on the following page

Compression Quality menu

Optimized File Format menu   *Optimize menu*

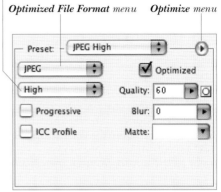

A *Choose **optimization** options for a **JPEG** file in the **Save for Web & Devices** dialog box.*

B *A **JPEG** optimized with **High Quality***

C *A **JPEG** optimized with **Medium Quality***

choose None, transparent areas will appear as white.

Note: The JPEG format doesn't support transparency. To have the Matte color simulate transparency, make it the same solid color as the background of the Web page (if that color is known).

9. Leave the Progressive and ICC Profile options unchecked.

10. *Optional:* Check Optimized to produce the smallest file size.

11. Click **Save.** The Save Optimized As dialog box opens. Leave the name as is, choose a location, then click Save.

➤ To save a current (Unnamed) set of palette options, choose Save Settings from the Optimize menu. Enter a name (in Windows, include the .irs extension), locate and open the Adobe Photoshop CS3 > Presets > Optimized Settings folder, then click Save. Your saved set will now be available on the Preset menu in the Save for Web & Devices dialog box for any document.

D *A **JPEG** optimized with **Low Quality***

INDEX

Photography credits

ShutterStock.com
Photographs on the following pages © ShutterStock.com

pp. 1, 153, 159, 180, 181, 238–240, 370, 371, Styve Reineck

pp. 27, 119, 329–340, Magdalena Bujak

pp. 62, Ariusz Nawrocki

pp. 63, 223, Rohit Seth

pp. 68, 235, Robert Kyllo

p. 72, Mark Yuill

pp. 83–85, 97–100, Jason Stitt

pp. 91, 96, 101, Ajt

p. 103, Elke Dennis

pp. 118, 129, 199, Galina Barskaya

p. 119, Elke Dennis

pp. 120, 121, 127, Karin Lau

pp. 122, 123, 132, Robert Sarosiek

pp. 124, 125, 132, Steve Maehl

pp. 128, 131, 133, 135, 292–294, Dhoxax

pp. 130, 303, 368, Radovan

pp. 137, 138, 259, Lario Tus

p. 139, Taolmor

pp. 141, 150–153, Faberfoto

p. 142, Bobby Deal/RealDealPhoto

pp. 142, 272, 273, Miranda Zeegers

pp. 143–145, 152, 153, 157, 158, 198, 371, Vera Bogaerts

pp. 146, 147, Lois M. Kosch

p. 148, Kristian Peetz

pp. 150, 151, 156, Jarno Gonzalez Zarraonandia

pp. 150, 371, Kheng Guan Toh

p. 150, Zdorov Kirill Vladimirovich

pp. 150, 151, 156, Alexander Gitlits

p. 150, Doug Stacey

p. 174, Dario Diament

pp. 185, 192–196, 202, 205, 260, 261, Liv Friis-larsen

pp.191, 383, Andrew F. Kazmierski

pp. 203, 204, Laura Frenkel

p. 222, Afaizal

pp. 247, 250, Keith Levit

pp. 253, 254, 288, Brian Stewart-Coxon

pp. 255–257, Maria Weidner

pp. 264–266, 276, 285, Zina Seletskaya

pp. 269, 277, Nick Stubbs

pp. 280, 281, 284, Franck Camhi

p. 282, Photobank.ch

p. 289, Linda Bucklin

pp. 289, 291, Gina Smith

pp. 301, 363, 388, Nicole Waring

pp. 308, 309, Timothy Large

p. 343, Wiz Data, Inc.

p. 348, Connors Bros.

pp. 352, 354, Beat Glauser

p. 364, Gilmanshin

p. 365, Alfio Ferlito

Photos.com
Photographs on the following pages © 2007 JupiterImages.com

pp. 45, 57

p. 93

pp. 95, 274, 275

pp. 149, 321, 323, 326–328

pp. 161, 168–170, 224

p. 177

pp. 197, 200, 201, 279

pp. 206, 207, 270

p. 232

p. 252

pp. 267, 268, 343

p. 270

pp. 298, 300

pp. 356, 357

p. 377

PhotoDisc (Getty Images) Gettyimages.com
Photographs on the following pages © PhotoDisc

p. 50, PhotoDisc

pp. 269, 283, PhotoDisc

p. 343, PhotoDisc.

Others

pp. 401, 418, 420 © Victor Gavenda

All other photographs © Elaine Weinmann and Peter Lourekas

p. 341 © Elaine Weinmann, access to garden courtesy firstbornmultimedia.com